The Interpreting Handbook
Part 1

by
Brian Cerney, Ph.D.

By Brian Cerney, Ph.D.

First Edition

The Interpreting Handbook, Part 1

ISBN: 0-9762742-1-3

Hand & Mind Publishing
Colorado Springs, CO

Preview

This book examines the complex process of interpreting and how people can improve their ability to work within and between languages. Many people who work as interpreters or transliterators have never explored linguistics; they may even feel overwhelmed by the idea of learning about linguistics. This book is designed to be a friendly tour of how languages work and how we can improve our work with languages. It is intended to be a guidebook, something you will keep next to your dictionary and use over and over again as you and your co-workers continue to improve your skills.

Working interpreters and students alike face the challenge of self-analysis and improvement within and outside of training programs. This book was designed to clearly identify the components of successful interpreting and to provide the essential tools needed for self-analysis and professional development. Many working interpreters are uncertain about the requirements of various certification processes and what kinds of performances result in successfully attaining certification. This book addresses these questions and lets working interpreters know how to self-diagnose problems in their interpreting and find solutions. This book is intended to help interpreters do more than achieve certification by continuing to improve their professional skills. The field of professional interpreting is always advancing and this book provides guidance for advancing professional interpreters.

Students of interpreting are rarely ready to attempt certification until they have completed several years of practical interpreting work after graduation; but they also need to have an understanding of the skills required to become professional and certified interpreters. This text provides a plan for continued professional development for students of interpreting: both as students and as graduates.

Dedication

To my wife, Janet, and our children, Tasha, Anna and Alosha; and to the memory of my Gallaudet classmate, June Zimmer, who passed away at the end of 1993 in Manchester, New Hampshire.

The Graph and the River
by Brian Cerney
{Inspired by Theresa B. Smith (1983)}

I read this article the other day
Researched by more than a few
The local river they had defined
Reporting a depth of fifty-two

But what unit of measure had they used?
Was it hands or feet or miles?
Was only a single measurement made?
Or a numerous series of trials?

Another group, too, had studied hard
Proposing a model "complete"
The river was measured from A to B:
A width of eighty-eight feet

A monograph found the river to be
As thick as split pea soup
The author lambasted the careless techniques
Of both the above-mentioned groups

I decided to look for the answer myself
To settle it once and for all
I'd measure the river's depth and width
During a three-week span in the Fall.

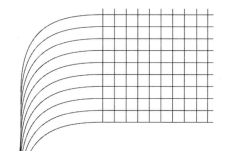

But what would the depth be when it rained?
(When the sky more river would lend)
Where did the plane of the surface begin?
And where did the raindrop end?

"This river is yet but a river"
Such concepts I had failed to catch
While the river defined itself perfectly well
My graphs offered only a scratch

I now realized that we all were right
And all just as equally wrong.
For a river is more than the sum of its parts
And a bird is more than its song

With our grand attempts to describe a thing
No matter abstract or concrete
We must keep in mind one important thing:
Our description never will be complete.

Let us all remember to gain the value we can
Of the work by those from before;
But never stop asking questions and learning
From the new finds just outside our door.

Table of Contents

Bibliography and Appendices

List of Figures

Table of Contents

The Interpreting Handbook
Part 1

by
Brian Cerney, Ph.D.

Hand & Mind Publishing
Colorado Springs, CO

Chapter 0
The Metachapter

"Meta-Dialogue"

Phaedrus and Timoth entered the grand hallway. Phaedrus gazed at Timoth with admiration. "Well, Timoth, you have graduated from our training and now through Zeno's generosity you will enjoy quite a productive residency through the guidance of Rasmus."

Timoth smiled as they approached the doorway, "I hope I live up to everyone's expectations."

Inside, Rasmus and Zeno were looking toward the doorway. Zeno smiled as Timoth and Phaedrus entered the room. "Good afternoon Phaedrus. Good afternoon Timoth. It's good to see the two of you again." Zeno gestured for Timoth and Rasmus to step toward each other, "Rasmus, this is your new Apprentice, Timoth. Timoth, your assigned Mentor, Rasmus."

Timoth and Rasmus shook hands and exchanged greetings.

Rasmus placed a hand on Timoth's shoulder, "You will do well. Just trust yourself and always seek to learn a new thing each day. You have already taught yourself well through Phaedrus' training, now you will continue to teach yourself through your own experiences."

Timoth's eyebrows furrowed, "What do you mean that I taught myself well through Phaedrus' training?"

Phaedrus stepped forward, "Rasmus refers to the eternal truth of education: No mind can force another to learn... true learning can only come from within the mind that learns. We present the information, the challenges, the guidance; but you, Timoth, you and your classmates are the ones who must choose to learn from these things."

Zeno addressed Timoth directly, "And here we recognize that a transitional time is needed to bring the graduate into full capability as a Server. We look forward to your time with us, Timoth. When you have completed your time here as an Apprentice, we will review your progress and personal goals. Many of our Apprentices continue on with us as Independent Servers and some become Mentors themselves."

Timoth glanced down, "Well, it's going to be a long time before that ever happens to me."

Rasmus laughed while reaching toward a nearby table and picked up the book lying there. "Timoth, here is your handbook. I think you will find it very helpful as you spend time with us here."

Timoth glanced at the cover, "The Interpreting Handbook," then opened it, flipped through several pages, returned to the table of contents and then flipped through more pages. "Hmm... I see the author uses dialogues at the beginning of each chapter. Why is that?"

Rasmus nodded, "It is based on the ancient principles of Socrates and Plato, which have been implemented by numerous authors since that time. The author uses dialogues to introduce concepts to the reader in a more casual way before exploring them in depth during the rest of each chapter."

Timoth pointed a finger at a page in the book, "But this one character seems always to be asking questions. Doesn't that character know anything?"

"Of course, but the inquisitive character needs some guidance to understand that the answers to the questions are already in the character's mind."

"Well, that makes sense. Of course! A person has to have some knowledge of the topic to ask the question in the first place. That sort of pins down which pieces are understood and which need more thought... hmm!"

Rasmus smiled. "And so I see we have already established a good beginning. I will see you tomorrow morning in my office."

Timoth and Rasmus shook hands. Rasmus departed as Phaedrus and Timoth exited Zeno's office. Timoth smiled while looking at Phaedrus "Thanks for getting me here. I'll do my best."

"Doing your best is what got you here in the first place."

Chapter 0 - The Metachapter
"The Key to Education is to Trick People into Teaching Themselves." - 1998 BC

0.0 The Overview
OK, so you've never heard of a "Chapter 0" before and you've never seen anything called a "metachapter" either. But if you know enough about language and how English words combine to create new meaning, you can predict that this chapter is a chapter about chapters. Indeed, it is exactly that. Most books call it a preface, but as linguists, we know about languages, and we can use pieces of words to make new words with the hope that they stimulate a little interest in the reader. If you are a working interpreter, or an advancing student of interpreting, then you *are* a linguist. You might not feel comfortable with that label yet, but I hope that once you have read through this book, completed the suggested activities at the end of each chapter, and used the ideas here to improve your own interpreting then you will feel perfectly comfortable calling yourself a *linguist*.

The key to self-improvement is having self-motivation. This means that you should have a sense of *what* you need to learn and some ideas about *how* you will learn it. *You* are always the one guiding your own education. Even if this book is required reading for a course you are taking, *you* still determine how much of it you are exposed to. If you aren't interested in reading any more about how the book is organized, then you can go ahead and skip to Chapter One... it's OK, you don't even need my permission. You are the reader, therefore you can read the book any way you want to. Read the summaries first, or read the book randomly, just open to a page and start reading anywhere; you're in charge! Of course, you might have a quiz or an exam on specific parts of the book, so following your teacher's (or independent study coordinator's) syllabus might be to your advantage, too.

So this metachapter is where I get to tell you what I was thinking when I wrote this book. Many times I have been reading a book or article and wondered to myself "What on Earth was this guy thinking?!!" ... so here is my explanation of my vision for this book. It begins with who I am and how I got here. Interpreting is that way too. Success as an interpreter very much depends on WHO you are and WHAT life experiences lead you to becoming an interpreter.

0.1 The Author
My name is Brian Cerney. I came to the profession of interpreting through the side door. What I mean is that I wasn't exactly born into the Deaf community (my entire family is hearing). Most deaf people I know were not born into the Deaf community either. But I am not deaf... well, not completely. I sometimes refer to myself as Left Deaf. In audiological terms I am monaurally deaf, which (for me) means I am deaf in my left ear: 100%. No one could really measure it accurately because when the audiologists cranked up the volume (on the left side of the headset) toward 100 dB, my skull would transmit the sound vibrations to my right ear and I could "hear".

In societal terms being left-deaf means people never even suspect this audiological fact about me unless they are within three feet of my left ear and attempt to converse with me through spoken language. If you have a sharp eye for details, you'll notice that the right side of my mouth (the side closest to my "good" ear) is a little more flexible than the left side of my mouth. Growing up left-deaf gave me a permanent curiosity about the

Deaf community. I had deaf classmates in high school and in college, but I never learned sign language (my high school classmate was "oral") until my sophomore year at the University of Rochester. Of course, Rochester, NY has a very active Deaf community, and I happened to be in a pretty good place to begin exploring my "left" side.

I understood before I began learning ASL that I was not culturally Deaf. I had seen the stage play "Children of a Lesser God" twice before I began my excursion into ASL and the Deaf community. At each performance I was in the balcony and below me was a sea of moving hands. I knew I would some day get involved with this community, but I also knew that I needed to be invited in, I didn't have a full birthright to it.

I have met many other monaurally deaf people, some left-deaf, some right-deaf. Most of them don't care to talk about their "condition." Perhaps they see themselves as impaired in some way. I always drew strength from the fact that I was different from nearly everyone else. Before my family knew that my deafness was centered in the cochlea of my left inner ear, they expected that I would have middle-ear surgery to correct my condition. At the Center of Science and Industry (COSI) in Columbus, Ohio, there was a permanent exhibit on the ear. Part of this exhibit showed a videotape of middle-ear bone-replacement surgery. Many times we would get to that floor of the museum and see that exhibit and my mother would remind me that I would be having that surgery when I got older. I am sure many other kids might have been thrilled at the prospect of fixing a problem... but I just saw the surgery as a way to change who I was... I did not look forward to having it.

Finally the time came to see if I was a candidate for the surgery. My examination results indicated that surgery would not correct my condition – I was relieved and pleased with these results. I didn't feel any need for correction, and finally I knew I would be allowed to stay the same person I had always known myself to be. When I later learned that most members of the Deaf community don't want to have surgery to change themselves, I understood completely. The change isn't really for your benefit; it's for the benefit of other people who get frustrated with your "differentness."

After graduating high school I left Ohio and its two-dozen colleges and headed out of state to Rochester, New York to study chemical engineering. My dad was a physician and my sister and two brothers had all gone to college with the intention of entering the field of professional medicine. My sister is the one who got closest to it: she's a mental health therapist. My oldest brother pursued chemistry as his pre-med focus. He's now an investment analyst. My other brother pursued biology. He's now a songwriter in Nashville. So I pursued chemical engineering because I figured I could always focus on engineering, chemistry, or go on to med school. The one big problem with that grand scheme was that I really didn't like chemistry and beyond that, I really had no particular interest in any kind of engineering.

What I actually did enjoy was taking English courses: Shakespeare, Chaucer, and a few other authors. I also enjoyed psychology, computer science, education, and related explorations into the human experience (or simulations of the human experience through artificial intelligence: computers). I was all set to pursue a degree in cognitive science when I discovered American Sign Language. At first I had merely learned some vocabulary in a YMCA non-credit course taught by some NTID interpreters: no course syllabus, just a group of students who asked the interpreters how to sign English words.

When we were done, we all thought we knew how to sign; but I hadn't even talked with a Deaf person yet!

One of my fraternity brothers, majoring in Electrical Engineering, was taking "Sign Communication I" as an elective which was "totally unrelated to Electrical Engineering," and asked if I wanted to come along. He was one of a handful of people who was aware that I was left-deaf (not a fact that I advertised very much at the time) and for over a decade he was the only person I knew on this planet who would move to position himself so as to be on my right side before I could begin to make those maneuvers myself. I went to his "Sign Communication" class with him, found that a Deaf person was teaching the class, and that auditing the class would not be permitted. I was interested in learning more and so I dropped a film class in order to make room for "Sign Communication I."

Dorothy Wilkins ended up teaching all three of my sign courses at the University of Rochester. They were offered through the Medical Center and had originally been intended for hospital staff to improve their communication skills. When I took the courses, they had been "discovered" by the River Campus students and I never had a hospital employee as a classmate after "Sign Communication I" was finished. It was during "Sign Communication II" that I began to learn about ASL structure. Finally in "American Sign Language I" we explored grammatical structures in ASL, having already achieved pretty good fluency in making sign vocabulary.

Somewhere during these courses I learned about Gallaudet College[1] and decided that I wanted to attend the linguistics program there after I graduated from the University of Rochester. I also applied for the Basic Interpreter Training Program (BITP) at the National Technical Institute for the Deaf and was admitted into one of the last classes of that intensive summer training program. By today's standards it seems bizarre (and perhaps in reality it truly was bizarre) but thirty people came into that program in June of 1985 and only eight weeks later, thirty people had graduated with certificates in Interpreting. By September of 1985, I had moved my worldly possessions to Washington, DC, and was beginning my graduate studies in Linguistics, living with Deaf people as roommates and throughout the dorm, learning to live without a phone, and learning more about the Deaf community than any course or library of videos and books can ever reveal.

While I was at Gallaudet I attempted to find work as an interpreter. After all, I had just graduated from the BITP and even though my instructors had told me (as they had told all of my classmates) that we needed to gradually improve our skills, I believed that I knew better. I marched right over to Gallaudet Interpreting Services (GIS) and requested an interview for employment. William Isham was kind enough to allow the interview to take place. It began with a demonstration of my skills: interpret two out of the three deaf people on the videotape from ASL to English. I looked at the first segment for a few moments and then, without having even attempted to interpret any of it, I asked to see the next segment. After a few moments I realized I would not be working for GIS any time soon, but I asked if I could see the third segment, just out of curiosity. Like the previous two segments, I had not the slightest idea what the Deaf people were saying; therefore I couldn't even begin the process of interpreting. Bill gave me a copy of one of his articles and some encouraging words on how to develop my skills and I left the GIS offices determined to keep working so that some day I could come back, try again, and succeed.

---

[1] Now known as Gallaudet University.

I find it interesting in retrospect that while I kept telling myself over and over that I did not intend to become a professional interpreter, things kept happening which pushed me in that direction. I had applied to the BITP only because I had completed all of the University of Rochester's available credited courses in sign language and knew that I needed to get better before I went to Gallaudet. I applied to GIS because I needed money while I was at school. I applied to the Dorm Communication Center (DCC) for the same reasons. At the DCC we took messages for students (phone service was very restricted in those days, only a few ground-floor students had their own phones), lent TTYs to students who didn't have their own, and interpreted phone calls (local or long distance) because the concept of telephone relay services was not yet widespread or well funded. At the DCC I was finally earning money, at least in part, as an interpreter.

In many ways, telephone interpreting is an ideal way for a developing interpreter to enter the profession. Consecutive by nature, telephone interpreting allows clarification of each source text before presenting the target text. It allows for significant pre-conferencing prior to placing the call (an essential element for successful pizza orders) and it reveals the different levels of patience and cooperation between people who know the deaf person (such as friends and family members) and people who don't (such as taxi dispatchers and auto mechanics). It was through a coworker, after we had both graduated, that I actually entered the world of simultaneous interpreting in 1987. Rhonda Jacobs asked me to help interpret a rather fast-paced graduate-level course and I agreed to help out as best as I could.

In those days, team interpreting meant "you read your book while I interpret, then I'll read mine while you interpret." I got a surprising amount of reading done while being paid to interpret. As I worked with many different interpreters at the University of Maryland I saw that we all understood the same principles: work in half hour shifts, don't pay too much attention to the working interpreter during your "break" and don't talk about the work too much when you're done.

A few years later, Richelle Hammett, the new coordinator of interpreting at the University of Maryland, was scheduled as my interpreting team member. I expected that she would probably start with a review and assessment of my skills. On the first night of our work together I volunteered to interpret the first "shift" and she had her notepad out and wrote throughout that first half hour. Each time she put the pen to paper I wondered what I had just done wrong. I really tried to do my best, my most complete and accurate, interpreting. She just kept writing. Then after the first thirty minutes were done we switched, but she had left her notepad sitting on the desk. I tried not to look at it and then I noticed that at the top it said "Hi Brian!" I kept reading and the first page or so was just a nice note to me about how she was glad to be working with me and "isn't this an interesting class?" and so on. The rest of her notes were more of a loose outline of the topics discussed, occasionally with questions about the meaning of a technical term, but with very little feedback about how to improve my interpreting and no indication that I had done anything wrong. When I was done reading, I realized that I needed to keep up the same kind of notetaking; I wasn't going to be reading the book that I had brought with me!

Soon after this introduction to true team interpreting I had a different assignment with another "enlightened" interpreter. Eric Deemer helped me understand some of the finer points of team interpreting. I came to understand that perhaps instead of working for strict time periods, we should instead work until we *needed* to switch. This meant that we had to pay attention to each other's work: we had to monitor whether the interpretation was accurate and whether the message was still being produced with clarity. We might go forty minutes each, at the beginning of a three-hour class, and be switching at fifteen minute increments near the end. When the class session was over, we would sit and discuss the work we had just completed – sometimes for forty-five minutes or more. These were revolutionary ideas to me at the time; and they also represented my first steps into true professionalism.

Around this time I took and passed the RID certification exams for interpreting (CI) and "transliteration" (CT). I continued to work as I had for several years at Gallaudet: teaching English to undergraduates and working as a Research Associate with the Gallaudet Research Institute. I eventually stopped the teaching part during the last year of the GRI research project. Then the research project ended and I was among eight research associates looking for new research projects. I didn't find one; and so in October of 1990, after all of those years of trying not to be a professional interpreter, I had actually come to the point in my life that that's exactly what I had become because all my other labels of professional status (teacher, researcher) had disappeared.

From 1990 until 1994 my primary profession was interpreting. During those years my wife, who had graduated from Gallaudet with a masters in Deaf Education, and I adopted three deaf children. I continued my studies and completed a variety of coursework at the University of Maryland, Georgetown University, and more courses at Gallaudet. I taught remedial English to international students at the Northern Virginia Community College. In 1993 I completed my second masters degree (in Education and Human Development from the University of Maryland) and started looking for other opportunities to serve the interpreting profession. By August of 1994 I had moved my family to Pittsburgh, PA to begin coordinating and teaching at the Interpreter Training Program at the Community College of Allegheny County (CCAC).

0.2 The Book

Shortly after I began teaching interpreting at CCAC, I found that I needed to develop a significant amount of my own material for my students; there were no existing books that accurately described linguistic principles in an appropriate way for undergraduate students studying the interpreting process. After many years of working on committees with RID, I had come to understand many of the principles of RID's national certification exams and worked toward clear descriptions of the process. The definitions of interpreting versus "transliteration" in particular required intensive comparisons of the expectations for each exam.

Prior to 1995, RID certification candidates for the CT exam were told to refer to Frishberg's *Interpreting: An Introduction* for a definition of the process of "transliteration." Frishberg's definitions included the use of Manual English Codes, signed English, and English-like signing:

> "Sign language interpreters have used the term 'transliteration' to refer to the process of changing an English text into Manually Coded English (or vice versa). An interpreter who transliterates, also called a 'transliterator,' gives the viewer English in a visually accessible form." (Frishberg, 1990:19).

"Certificate of Transliteration (CT): ability to transliterate between signed English and spoken English in both sign-to-voice and voice-to-sign." (Frishberg, 1990:96).

"Transliteration Certificate (TC): ability to transliterate between English and an English-like signing." (Frishberg, 1990:97).

In 1995 a pool of RID performance examination raters were asked to generate a definition of interpreting and "transliteration" based on the performances of passing and failing candidates for both performance exams. The results of their work was finalized in December of 1995 and published in the February, 1996 RID Views:

What is "Transliteration"?
Many candidates for the RID Certificate of Transliteration (CT) examination have requested guidance in an effort to understand the goal of the English-to-sign portion of the exam. Raters have reviewed the minimum standard in addition to various performances of passing and failing candidates, and have agreed upon the following description of rating criteria for the current performance evaluation for the Certificate of Transliteration.

The three broad categories of variables that Raters evaluate for the English-to-sign portion have been described: Grammar and Vocabulary, Processing, and Mouth Movement Patterns.

Grammar and Vocabulary
• Use of space for role taking (characterization)
• Use of space for subject-object agreement and verb inflections
• Conceptually correct sign choices (based on meaning rather than form)
• Some amount of "initialization" but only to the extent that initialization is used by deaf adults (not to the extent of Manual English Codes).

Processing
• Lexical to Phrasal level[s] of processing, e.g. ranges from "word meaning for word meaning" to "more than words, less than sentences"
• Some restructuring or paraphrasing for clearer conveyance of meaning
• Some additions of ASL signs which enhance the clarity of the visual message (modals, [such as CAN, WILL, and MUST placed at the end of sentences], classifier constructions, indexing, and listing structures)
• Detailed English morphology (e.g. manual English coding of "ing," "ed," and the copula) which is conveyed on the mouth but not with manual signs.

Mouth Movement Patterns
• Cohesive English sentences are visibly presented on the lips, either as exact words from the original text or as English paraphrasing of the original text.

Finally, overriding all of these details is the requirement that the target message resulting from the transliteration process remains true and accurate with regard to the source text. There should be no substitutions (missing a concept from the original and replacing it with a different concept) and no significant omissions (all of the main points and nearly all of the supporting details of the source text should be reflected in the target text).

In order to gain further guidance, the RID Raters recommend that candidates for testing read Elizabeth Winston's article, "Transliteration: What's the Message?" [Winston, E. 1989. In The Sociolinguistics of the Deaf Community, Ceil Lucas, Ed. San Diego, CA: Academic Press] The description of transliteration in this article is determined to be an accurate description of the performance of a successful candidate for the Certificate of Transliteration performance examination. (RID Views, February, 1996:24)

It takes a long time to write a book. I've revisited every chapter many times. Every Unit in the book has expanded and shrunk multiple times as I juggled ideas within and between chapters, sometimes pulling information out into two chapters, then reconsidering and putting the two pieces back into one. In the end I decided that four units, each with six chapters would provide some sort of balance which would allow a fairly comprehensive overview of the profession of interpreting while allowing teachers the flexibility to figure out which parts of the book would usefully apply to their courses.

Units three and four are published as a separate text and they cover self-improvement techniques and working in specialized settings. The first twelve chapters are presented in this text. The first unit, containing six chapters, provides the essential elements of linguistics for successful interpreting. The second unit (chapters seven through twelve) reviews the essentials for interpreting and related work. I hope these first twelve chapters present an organized and uncomplicated explanation of linguistic principles and interpreting. If you don't think it does, please let me know... I consider this work as perpetually "in progress."

0.3 The Summary

This text was made possible by encouragement from the RID home office, particularly Clay Nettles, Deb Stebbins, and Stuart S. Nealy. Thanks go also to my parents, Charles and Phyllis Cerney, for their support in so many ways; and to my wife, Janet Cerney, and our children, Tasha, Anna, and Alosha, who allowed me the time to do revisions at home and at work. I also appreciate the comments of my students, the first guinea pigs of this effort, who helped me to clarify and improve the text as I handed out chapters to them one by one and then handed out quizzes which tested them on each chapter as part of their course grade (please accept my apologies). To you, the reader: no book can ever completely encompass any topic... please take advantage of the suggested activities at the end of each chapter and check out the readings in the bibliography to more fully explore the topics raised within these pages.

M.C. Escher's *Hand with Reflecting Sphere* (1935)

Chapter 1
Communication

"Communication"

Rasmus took a step back from the artwork hanging on the wall. "What does this say to you?"

Timoth glanced up from the theory book. "What does what say to me?"

"This print by M.C. Escher. I just bought it at the store. I love the way Escher draws us into his world. See how the globe reflects the hand that is holding it? But we also see the image of the person attached to the hand as he looks at the globe and we also see the room he's in: the object, the person, and the physical surroundings. And here we are observing all of it, understanding it on our own terms, within our own physical surroundings. In fact, the print itself is part of our physical surroundings now."

"What are you talking about? It's just a piece of artwork. Sure, it's interesting, but it doesn't 'say' anything to me."

"Ah, Timoth. You see the world but you do not understand it. Here is an opportunity to reflect on your chosen field of work as an interpreter; but you refuse to learn from it. You see the object and yet you ignore it. How will you make your own progress if you do not incorporate the progress made by others before you?"

Timoth placed a marker in the book and closed it. "Now wait a minute. I thought we were talking about your new piece of artwork. How does a piece of art help me to become a better interpreter? Are you trying to tell me that Escher was an interpreter?"

"In a sense, yes. He understood the world around him and documented his perspectives in his art with the understanding that others would then interact with his work."

"Interact? It's just a print: it's ink and paper. How can I interact with a document?"

"What's that thing in your hands right there?"

"This? This is my book, 'The Interpreting Handbook'. What does this have to do with art?"

"Does the book speak to you in any way? Does it communicate anything to you?"

"Well, it's not exactly an audio book, if that's what you mean. But it's giving me information about the profession of interpreting... so, yes, I guess it communicates useful information."

"So a book can communicate to you. But who is doing the communication?"

"Who is doing the communication? Um.... well, I'm the one reading it."

"Yes, and I hope you keep on reading; but still, communication requires two. Who is communicating with you?"

"You mean the author?"

"Sure... the author. But the author is not in this room, is he?"

"Well, no, of course not. But his work – this book – is in the room."

"And that work 'speaks' to you in some way?"

"Sometimes it does... sometimes I'm not quite sure what he's getting at. What are *you* getting at?"

"My point is that we communicate in different ways. What we do, how we do it, how we arrange our physical settings, the books we read, the art we look at, the things we create. Everything about us communicates something to everyone we encounter. Even if they encounter the things we have created years later, we continue to communicate even to people we will never meet."

"So, in other words, everything communicates something to us, even if we don't know the creator?"

"Well put. Now, keep on reading."

Chapter 1 - Communication

"Make Sure You Know The Rules Before You Play Someone's Game." - 1997 BC

1.0 Overview

This section provides basic definitions for *communication* and *language*. The value of defining these terms is to understand the essential components of the work of interpreters, translators and transliterators. Many people who perform interpreting work have never actually studied communication and language, and may even feel overwhelmed by the idea of having to learn about linguistics. These first several chapters are designed to be a friendly tour of how communication and languages work. Once interpreters understand the main ideas, they can further explore those elements that interest them the most on their own. We will begin by defining the difference between communication and language. We will then identify several significant factors that contribute to successful communication. In *Chapter Two* we will explore seven interactive levels of language. Subsequent chapters will explore language variation, various ways to encode languages, and how languages mix, merge, and emerge.

1.1 Communication and Language

Before we can begin talking about working between two languages we must investigate the definition of *communication*, the definition of *language*, and the difference between communication and language. Most animals (if not all) have the ability to communicate – and some forms of communication are more complex than others. *Communication Systems* are the use of symbols to convey information between members of a community. The symbols may be sounds, grunts, spoken words, or bird songs; the symbols may be posturing, such as placing hands on hips, signed words, or the dance of honeybees.

What does it mean to communicate? ***Communication is one mind's perception of a message that another mind has expressed.*** (STOP. Read that again, slowly this time). Communication can be *immediate* such as seeing someone smile or saying hello. It can be *delayed* such as seeing an arrow painted on a tree or an old sign that describes an historical landmark. Communication takes place between living things, but it is not limited to humans. Animals can indicate (communicate) that they are angry or injured. They can stake out territory, seek and find mates, issue warnings, and indicate submission. Some forms of communication are more complex than others: Many mammals are able to growl and bare their teeth to communicate a threat or warning to a potential foe. Bees can indicate sources of pollen through complex dances. Whales are said to produce every year a new complex song, which is shared throughout their species. Humans from different countries, who share no common language, can still bargain and negotiate trades with each other. *Communication simply requires at least two minds and the means of expressing and perceiving information.*

Communication is a broad category that includes all possibilities of language; but communication includes much, much more than only language. Animals have the ability to communicate at least within their species and generally between species. Humans, being a specific kind of animal, share some of these communication abilities; but humans are able to move beyond mere communication when they use language. Figure 1.1 shows the relationships between animal communication, human communication, and language.

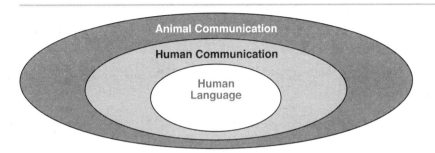

Figure 1.1 – Animal & Human Communication and Language

We will further explore the differences between communication and language in Chapter Two. For now, however, we will continue to explore the more general category of communication: *one mind's perception of a message that another mind has expressed.*

Communication begins with the *intention* to communicate. This requires intelligence and therefore a brain, or mind, capable of thought and knowledge. The mind's intention, or meaning, may be either *Conscious* or *Unconscious*. Conscious intentions, where the mind is aware of its own intentions to communicate, are the most easily recognized. Requesting assistance, issuing a warning, or expressing affection are all possible conscious intentions for communication, especially when words are used such as "give me a hand, please", "back off!", or "you're so sweet!"

Unconscious intentions, where the mind is not directly aware of its own intentions to communicate, are less obvious. A request for assistance may be expressed as simply as a glance toward a nearby person. A warning can consist of a fierce stare. An expression of affection may be communicated by the dilation of the eyes' pupils when a certain person comes into view. Unconscious intentions may also be expressed in the vocal inflections or facial expressions that accompany a message composed of words. People who are lying often find it difficult to make direct eye contact with the people they are lying to. A liar is usually not aware of the fact that his body is warning us not to believe what he is saying. In many cultures a nodding head is an indicator of truthfulness. Shaking one's head side to side while strongly affirming a statement (such as we commonly see in advertising, e.g. "I use it every day!") may be a result of the person's subconscious directing part of the expression of communication. Their words say "I use this product every day" but their body subconsciously says, "I am not telling you the truth." A child may state that she is "not scared" but her vocal inflection and facial expression may reveal that she is actually quite frightened. Our unconscious mind is almost always expressing our *emotional* state. Our conscious mind provides the ability to communicate things *beyond* emotion.

Four components are always present in any act of communication: 1) Background Knowledge of Participants, 2) Expressive Modalities of Communication, 3) Perceptive Modalities of Communication, and 4) Physical Context. An understanding of each of these components will make us more aware of the additional communication that can simultaneously co-occur with language and help us understand the truthfulness or emotion surrounding a message.

Background Knowledge can help us to understand the topic of discussion, to make predictions about how it might be organized, and to know which kinds of communication may be inappropriate for the situation at hand. A deeper understanding of *Expressive Modalities of Communication* may help us determine the goals of the communication. A person may gesture to indicate that an unseen person is able to overhear the communication in a room (such as one's boss) while the conversation is conducted with the intention that the unseen person will "overhear" it. A person's facial expression and body posture may indicate extreme anger while their words are produced with amazing calm. Knowing about *Perceptive Modalities* helps us to analyze physical settings and eliminate potential sources of noise or disruption to the communication. It also helps us to understand potential misperceptions of information. *Physical Contexts* shape all of our communication not only because of potential *noise* in our environment, but because certain settings are restricted to certain kinds of communication such as sermons in a church or cheers at a basketball court. The next segments of this chapter further explore these four primary components of communication.

1.2 Background Knowledge
Success in communicating the mind's intention will depend on the person's *Background Knowledge*, which includes the following four kinds of knowledge:
1) Knowledge of *how* to communicate,
2) Knowledge of *what* can be communicated,
3) Knowledge of *others* who are able to understand the communication, and
4) Knowledge of how the *physical environment* will impact the communication.

Figure 1.2 below provides our initial graphic representation of the mind and lists the variables influencing communication, which are all contained within the mind: its two levels of self-awareness (conscious and unconscious), and the four kinds of knowledge which influence communication. An interpreter keenly aware of these factors will be equipped to perform the best possible interpretation for the topic, setting, and participants.

Knowledge about Communication
Knowledge about Topics & Facts
Knowledge about Other People
Knowledge about Physical Setting

Conscious Intent of Communication
Unconcsious Intent of Communication

Figure 1.2 – The Mind and Communication

A mind that does not yet know these things can still communicate; but communication is more successful if that mind is aware of all four kinds of knowledge. A newborn child instinctively cries when hungry or uncomfortable. The child has no significant knowledge in any of these four areas and yet succeeds in communicating general distress. It is important to note, however, that the caretaker must be able to perceive the newborn's cries and also must have enough background knowledge about communication to recognize the child's cries as meaningful: it is still up to the caretaker to understand the communication correctly. Within a month a newborn infant will have much more knowledge about communication and can express much more specific requests (still without words) which a caretaker can more efficiently understand. Every communication experience in life builds on our knowledge of *how* we can communicate.

Background knowledge may also be shared. If two participants in communication share significant background knowledge, then they will require less new information in order to effectively communicate. This is best exemplified by "in-jokes" and situations where one "just had to be there to understand." If I mention that an actor's words told me one thing in a commercial but her body movement told me another, then I expect that you will understand what I mean if you already read section 1.1; and if you didn't read that section, you might be very confused.

Background Knowledge and *Culture* overlap significantly. The culturally appropriate behaviors known to a community of people are a part of their *Background Knowledge*; but *Background Knowledge* extends beyond *Culture*. *Culture* is the set of shared knowledge and values within a community, but *Background Knowledge* is the set of knowledge and experience that any *individual* has. *Background Knowledge* includes all the knowledge of one's culture; but it also includes information known about other cultures, and indeed every piece of information, both substantial and trivial, known to each communication participant. Not all of that information is equally active all of the time. We make assumptions about what a message likely means based on recent topics of communication, past experiences with the person generating the message, our estimate of the other person's background knowledge, and, of course, the physical context.

Without the common background knowledge of what a phone flasher is, we might not even see any relationship between a flashing light and the actions of a deaf person who suddenly stops all other activity and begins typing on a TTY. Likewise, the use of the word TTY in the previous sentence also assumes a shared background knowledge between the reader and the author. People of distant cultures may have little overlap in their background knowledge. Some people living in equatorial climates may have no understanding of the concept of snow. Many people living in particularly oppressive non-democratic countries may have no understanding of the concept of "rights".

1.3 Semiotics - The Nuts and Bolts of Communication

Before we can begin to communicate we must have a means of doing it. *Semiotics* is the study of all possible signaling systems. For the purposes of this book we will generalize this to mean the study of all possible forms of communication. Semiotics includes the study of language, but also includes so much more. Gesture, body posture, proximity, odor, taste, and sound may all communicate things not only among humans but animals as well. Any possible means of communication – a raised eyebrow, a handshake, the clearing of one's throat – can be analyzed and understood; but each may take on distinct appropriate uses. One culture may use an upward palm gesture to call another person closer, while other cultures may do nearly the same gesture for the same reason, except that they produce the gesture with the palm facing down. Producing the same gesture but with only the index finger moving may be appropriate to call children closer, but an adult in some cultures may understand the same gesture as an insult.

1.3.1 Expressive Modalities of Communication
    We use the term "modality" to refer to any medium of communication. There are five basic expressive modalities of communication: *image, odor, sound, taste,* and *texture.* All avenues of expressing communication require muscle movement and typically include things such as lungs, vocal chords, facial muscles, and limbs. The cries of newborns are expressed through movement of the diaphragm, which moves air out of the lungs, through vibrating vocal chords and through an open mouth. In addition, crying newborns are likely to have contorted facial expressions and may also wildly flail their arms and legs. In this way crying newborns are multimedia presentations, simultaneously expressing communication in numerous ways including sound and image (and sometimes odor).
    Muscle movement requires nerve connections to the brain. Various diseases and medical conditions can disrupt the nerve connections (such as Cerebral Palsy or Parkinson's Disease) or deteriorate the muscle's ability to move effectively (such as Muscular Dystrophy). Such conditions, therefore, can disrupt not only people's ability to move comfortably but also their ability to express communication. These kinds of medical conditions, which impede communication ability, are often misperceived as a mental deficiency. This perception means that many people will not have enough patience to allow the time for effective communication. If you find yourself interpreting in a situation where a consumer has physical difficulties expressing communication it may serve you well to ask the participants to have patience because it may require additional time for you to do your work effectively and accurately.

1.3.2 Perceptive Modalities of Communication
    As you might suspect, there is a one-to-one correspondence of *expressive* modalities to *perceptive* modalities. All are related to the five senses: *hearing, sight, smell, taste,* and *touch.* All senses require nerve connections to the brain. Sight also requires muscular control (not only to direct the eyes to the source of communication, but also to bring it into focus). The multimedia presentation of the crying newborn will likely be perceived first by hearing, then by sight (and perhaps smell!), and finally by touch. The newborn may perceive that you are providing food by using all five senses: seeing a bottle, smelling and tasting the formula, feeling the texture of the nipple, and hearing the sounds made as liquid is drawn into the mouth.
    Various diseases and medical conditions (such as rubella or a sustained high fever) can disrupt the nerve connections of sensation or deteriorate the organ's ability to activate the nerves effectively: Retinitis Pigmentosa, Macular Degeneration and cataracts are conditions which damage the eye; ossified bones in the middle ear, a damaged cochlea or the absence of fluid within the inner ear will disrupt hearing. Such conditions, therefore, can disrupt a person's ability to perceive communication. A blind person would perceive the newborn's cry through the sense of hearing, a deaf person would perceive it through sight, and a DeafBlind person would perceive it through touch if they were in contact

with any object vibrating as a result of the child's cry or movement. As long as just *one* of the newborn's senses remained functional it would likely still understand when it was being fed.

Disruptions to a person's perceptive abilities, like disruptions to expressive abilities, are often misperceived as a mental deficiency. Many people will try to help a person who is disabled, but the person should always be consulted as to whether they wish to have any help at all. No matter how many perceptive modalities are disrupted, the mind perceiving the communication must still be respected.

There are additional challenges for interpreters working with consumers who cannot perceive all of the modalities in which communication is expressed. Not only does the interpreter have to work on communicating the linguistic information, but also the non-linguistic, semiotic elements of the physical setting. Deaf consumers need to be informed of auditory environmental stimulus. Blind consumers need to be informed of visual environmental stimulus. DeafBlind consumers need to be informed of both kinds of information.

1.3.3 Production and Perception of Non-linguistic Communication

Images and sight allow for visual communication. Non-linguistic visual communication includes eye contact, facial expressions, body postures, gestures, pictures or drawings, and written or printed symbols. The physical environment is largely perceived through sight as well. Communication about the physical environment to another person can be accomplished as simply as making eye contact with a person and then looking at an immediate danger to that person (such as an oncoming car).

Visual information should be conveyed to blind people as part of interpretations. The body posture and facial expression of people can provide significant input to understanding a message. When English words such as "this" and "that" are used, they are often accompanied by gestures that identify the referent of each word. These referents will need to be fully identified for the blind consumer to understand the message correctly. Knowing that a person has just raised her hand will help explain why a lecture comes to a sudden halt and the teacher says, "Do you have a question?"

Odors and Smell allow for olfactory communication. Olfactory communication is generally non-linguistic[2] and includes perfumes and colognes, body odors, and aromas from cooking or offering food. All physical environments will have some odor (or perhaps a lack of odor) associated with them. Our attention to the odor may be minimal. Odor is more likely to play a role in communication through perfumes and food aromas. The smell of a fresh apple pie, for example, may be perceived as an invitation to enter the kitchen.

Sound and hearing allow for auditory communication. Non-linguistic auditory communication includes grunts, squeals, sighs, hiccups, humming, music, footsteps, rustling paper, banging doors, and kicking furniture. Sounds permeate almost every physical environment. Even very quiet rooms often have some hum or hiss such as from electrical lights, furnaces, or just the wind against the windowpane. A sigh may be an indication of frustration. Footsteps may indicate that someone is about to knock at the

---

[2] There actually have been attempts to manipulate odors for linguistic communication, but these experiments have not yielded success for effective communication.

door. Rustling papers may indicate nervousness. Banging doors and kicking furniture may indicate frustration or anger. If an interpreter is working with a deaf consumer and does not provide access to these sounds, then the consumer is not receiving the same communication as hearing people who are in the room. These auditory environmental stimuli may seem trivial, but there have been many instances where a door being slammed shut was the impetus for an angry lecture about a person's attitude.

Think about the auditory information that is taken for granted. If someone knocks at a door, it is perfectly logical for someone inside the room to approach the door, ask who is there, and perhaps open the door. If you didn't hear the knock, it would seem bizarre that someone in the room arbitrarily decided to walk to the door, talk to it, and suddenly cause a person to appear at the moment that the door was opened. Knowing that there is a knock at the door clearly helps explain why a person is standing there when another person decides to open it.

Similarly, a person who is continuously coughing in the back of the room communicates several things with every cough: 1) the person is not completely healthy, 2) the person may be contagious to others in the room, 3) the person is still in the room and has not yet left. If the person decides to leave, you would understand that they might wish to get a drink of water and that they are not being deliberately rude. If at some point you are expected to meet and shake hands with each person in the room you may understand why the person does not offer to shake hands with you (or you may understand that you might wish to wash your hands if the person does shake hands with you). If at some point another person asks the cougher to leave the room and get a drink of water, you would understand such a request to be fairly normal.

Taste allows for gustatory communication. Gustatory communication is limited to tasting or consuming foods, beverages, and non-food items. Tasting spoiled food may communicate that one's host has either been careless or perhaps even rude.

Touch and *Texture* allow for tactile communication. Non-linguistic tactile communication includes such things as holding hands, giving a hug, pats on the back, tickling, massaging, punching, and scratching. Certain aspects of physical environments are perceived tactually including the temperature of the room. A warm room in the winter may indicate that one's host is concerned for her guests and wishes to ensure they are comfortable. A warm room in the summer may indicate opposite information, or perhaps indicate that the host is unable to afford air conditioning.

Image, *Sound*, and *Texture* are the three most easily manipulated modalities for expressing communication. Figure 1.3 overlays the abilities to *express* and *perceive* communication with our previous representation of the mind.

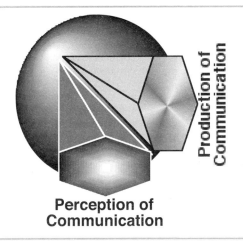

Figure 1.3 – The Communicating Mind

1.4 Physical Context

The *Physical Context* is the setting for the communication and surrounds the expression and perception of communication. *Physical Contexts* will always affect the clarity of the communication and also influence how each mind within a physical context will understand the communication. The *Physical Context* absorbs and reflects the communication. Sound waves will echo in large empty spaces or be obscured by the whirring of a film projector or an electric fan. Light waves remain bright in empty lightly colored rooms. Low light makes visual perception of an image difficult but bright, glaring light can be equally disruptive. Backlighting provides such a strong contrast of high and low light that can cause headaches from straining the eye muscles.

All communication expressed by a person becomes part of the *Physical Context*. Each communicator must be able to perceive some form of the *Physical Context* along with the communication expressed by another person. In addition to perceiving the physical context and the communication expressed by another person, both communicators are generally able to perceive (monitor) their own expression of communication. In other words, hearing people using speech to communicate, will perceive their own speech at the same time that they produce it. It is actually through this self-monitoring that infants modify their own speech production when babbling. It is in part due to *an inability* to self-monitor that deaf children generally have difficulty matching their speech patterns to the hearing people around them.

The perception of communication may use different senses, especially between deaf and hearing people: Deaf people communicating through speech sounds may perceive their own expression of communication primarily through the sense of touch (feeling the vibrations of their own throat and head as they make spoken sounds) while the hearing people will not likely *feel* the deaf person's sounds so much as *hear* it. Hearing people will most readily monitor their own communication as they speak (they might also notice the vibrations in their own bodies but are likely to ignore this information) while the deaf people will mostly depend on vision to understand the physical movements of the hearing person's face, rather than depending upon the sounds themselves. This mismatch of expression and perception of communication leads to significant difficulties and frustration. Communication will be most natural and successful if both the sender and receiver perceive all of their communication through the same senses. Figure 1.4 below shows the communication links between two minds within a *Physical Context*.

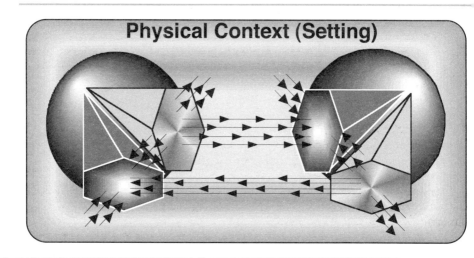

Physical Context (Setting)

Figure 1.4 –Communicating Minds Within a Shared Physical Setting

Physical Context, or the setting for the communication, is the most important variable to understand for any issue of communication. Every act of communication occurs within a physical setting. Generally, both participants of the communication will share the same setting, but through such modern advances as satellite communications, computers, telephones, and books it is now possible for two participants to communicate without sharing the same physical setting. Communication through recorded media (such as writing, and more recently through audio, video, and data recordings) allows each perceiver of the communication to be in a distinct setting; and also allows the communication to reach across great expanses of distance and time. Even so, each participant will be at least aware of her own physical environment and *may* also be aware of each other participant's environment as well.

For the remaining, more mundane situations of normal, everyday communication the physical context may carry great significance as part of the overall communication. The fact that humans put a great amount of effort into creating distinct physical environments certainly contributes to the impact these environments have upon communication. We build offices, homes, cars, public buses, religious centers, hospitals, funeral homes, warehouses, retail centers, bedrooms, and bathrooms. We generally acknowledge that certain kinds of communication are more or less appropriate for each of these settings.

Beyond just the structure of the physical surroundings is the activity that is taking place within the setting. Religious centers are generally associated with ceremonies but may also house social gatherings and bingo games. Lecture halls may host prestigious international guests, weekly chemistry lessons, or weekend film screenings.

Within the *Physical Context* of a lecture being presented in a lecture hall, or of a ceremony being performed within a chapel, we would generally expect that side conversations should be whispered. We would also expect that there might be questions from the audience at the end of the lecture but that there usually are no questions from the audience during, or after, a religious ceremony. These expected behaviors overlap with the first primary factor of communication: *Background Knowledge*.

So each of the primary factors (*Background Knowledge, Expressive Modalities, Perceptive Modalities,* and *Physical Context*) combines and overlaps with the others to make up communication. But what of the *intentions* behind the expression of communication and the *meanings* derived upon perceiving communication? These elements fall in the realm of *Pragmatics*.

1.5 Pragmatics - Doing Things Through Communication

Not all communication seems to serve a purpose, but in general terms, *communication accomplishes goals*. The goal may be as simple as having another mind pay attention to your own (such as a cat repeatedly brushing up against your leg and purring until you pick up the cat). The goal of the cat is to be picked up. The semiotics of the cat's communication include brushing up against your leg and purring. One possible result of this communication is that you pick up the cat.

The goal may be as significant as a declaration of war. The goal of the members of a governing body might be to initiate a process to approve the funding and implementation of war. The semiotics would include the writing of a document directly declaring war upon another government or group. The result would be that a state of war would have been initiated. While *Semiotics* is the study of all possible communication systems, *Pragmatics* is the study of the *goals* and *results* of communication. The *goals* are basically the action desired by the mind expressing communication. The *results* are the action of the mind(s) perceiving the communication. The *desired action* can also be understood as *meaning*.

1.5.1 Meaning Versus Communication

Meaning is independent of communication. This may seem an odd statement, but it is not necessarily obvious. A gust of cold wind may mean that a cold front is on its way; but the gust of wind could only be considered communication if your religion or philosophy provides for the mind of a Higher Power to have been the one using the wind to communicate to you. The mind may find many meaningful aspects of the physical context, but only those manipulated by another mind can be considered as *communication*. Likewise, many efforts at communication may exist within a physical context (such as a signpost obscured by overgrown weeds) that will still fail to communicate if another mind fails to perceive it. Even when perceived, an attempt at communication may not be understood fully if the perceiver does not know who the expresser is (such as carved initials on a tree trunk) or if the perceiver does not know the intention of the communication (such as a child's picture on a refrigerator). The perceiver's mind may use the physical context and background knowledge to try to determine the meaning of the attempt at communication.

Communication is the understanding (by one mind) of a message, which another mind has expressed; but *what one mind intends need not coincide with the other mind's understanding.* (STOP. Read that last sentence again, slowly). A gesture pointing toward a hornet nest may be intended as a warning. One perceiver may understand it as a warning, while another perceiver may understand it as a request to move toward the nest. Each perceiver has perceived the message; but each has determined it's meaning differently. In other words, the two perceivers' minds have engaged in communication with the initiator's mind, but each perceiver's mind has understood a different meaning.

Communication merely describes a kind of link between minds; meanings exist separately within each mind. The meaning of the initiator's mind might have no similarities at all to the meaning understood by the perceiver's mind; and therefore, *meaning is independent of communication.* This suggests that interpreters are responsible only for their own understanding of the message. It is impossible to fully know what another person understands through communication. If you are asked whether a consumer understands another consumer 's meaning, the only honest response is to verify your own understanding of the meaning and describe your attempt to express that meaning to the other consumer.

1.5.2 Expression and Perception Versus Meaning

Expression and perception of communication are likewise distinct from meaning. One person may say "It's hot in here" and wish the other to do something about it (such as turn on a fan or open a window or turn off the heat, etc.) Another person in the room may perceive the communication and yet not understand the first person's intention. This other person may merely agree with the first person but take no action. Communication has taken place, clearly influenced by a shared physical context; but not everyone understood the same intention (or meaning) of the communication. This demonstrates that the words that are used in communication don't actually contain any meaning at all: *it is the perceiver's mind that determines a meaning.* Meaning is in the mind and communication reaches between minds; but each mind is always free to determine its own meaning or even *if* there is any meaning at all. Two people can look at the same line of clouds in the sky and one may understand that it means a cold front is coming while the other merely sees clouds. Both minds have perceived the clouds, but only one has attached any meaning to their perception.

1.6 Variation in Communication

We have already identified communication as one mind's perception of a message, which another mind has expressed; but there are many ways that such communication can take place. Most often we intend to communicate with a specific person or a specific group of people; but it is often the case that other people are also able to perceive our expression of communication. In restaurants it is common to overhear the conversation at the next table. Professional spies (and amateurs too) *intentionally* eavesdrop or spy upon the communication of others. The communication that occurs between any two minds may be *intentional* or *unintentional.*

Both the means of expressing and the means of perceiving communication can function simultaneously in face-to-face communication; but other forms of communication (exchanged letters or E-Mail, telephone calls via TTY or relay operators) may limit the ability to simultaneously express and perceive communication. These forms of communication become consecutive: one party must complete a portion of communication before the other party can reciprocate. The timing of communication may be *immediate* or *delayed*.

Some forms of communication are only one-way, such as most television broadcasts, street signs, billboards, and the writings from deceased authors. One-way communication, like consecutive communication, also prohibits the simultaneous expression and perception of communication between two minds. In fact, it restricts one mind to only perceiving the communication of another mind. In this way, it is possible for communication to be *interactive* or *only one-way*.

We will now further investigate these three variables: *Intention*, *Immediacy*, and *Interactivity*. Each of these three variables has three general levels that we can categorize as being positive [+], negative [-], or mixed [+/-].

1.6.1 Intention Versus Incidence

Intention is the expression of communication toward specific perceivers. Was the communication intended to be sent to all the people who received it? A private conversation would be intentional [+ Intention] between two people engaged in it, but might be incidentally overheard [- Intention] by a third party. This happens often in restaurants where people sitting back to back in a series of booths may be able to overhear the conversation going on just behind them. The people expressing their communication intend it for the other people sitting in the same booth, but not for the person in the next booth. Some communication fits somewhere between being intentional and incidental: A public performance of a play or lecture may not be intended for any one specific audience member, yet it is intended to communicate with the entire audience [+/- Intention].

Interpreters face this variable every time they interpret. On one hand, they are incidental over-hearers of the message because the communication is intended for the interpreter's consumers, but not necessarily for the interpreter. But of course, the interpreter is physically present, cannot be ignored, and plays a very active role in the room. When the communication shifts to be intentional to the interpreter and only incidental to the consumers, this creates a serious disruption. Interpreter's are often asked personal questions or for advice by either consumer, often in the midst of interpreting. Ignoring intentional communication creates the impression of rudeness and may foment an uncooperative attitude among the consumers. Participating in a lengthy exchange with a single consumer will alienate the other consumer and provide an adversarial atmosphere. The interpreter's challenge is to acknowledge the intentional communication and return the communication to an exchange between the consumers as soon as possible.

1.6.2 Immediate Versus Delayed Access

Immediacy is the perception of communication at the time it is expressed. Is the communication received at the same time it is created, or is there a delay? Face-to-face interaction is the most immediate form of communication [+ Immediacy]. Written communication can be significantly delayed, especially if you are reading a book written hundreds of years ago [- Immediacy]. Likewise, audio and video recordings provide a delay between the creation of the communication and its comprehension. Attending an interpreted lecture may be both immediate and delayed: the events of the lecture (presenter's body posture, use of visual aids, etc.) can be seen immediately while the linguistic information may be delayed by several seconds for simultaneous interpreting and even longer for consecutive interpreting [+/- Immediacy].

Interpreters who have immediate access to both sets of consumers may have the option to ask for clarification, but immediate communication also creates an expectation among the consumers that the interpreter will not further delay the communication process. Interpreted communication will *always* be delayed, at least in comparison to non-interpreted communication. A short delay in access may be relatively unimportant for lectures but can become extremely detrimental for a brainstorming session or for counting votes in a business meeting. The level of need for immediacy may influence the approaches taken in providing the interpretation: either to attempt to shorten the processing time of the interpreting or sometimes to deliberately lengthen the time to process the consumers' communication. Processing time of the interpretation may be shortened so that the resulting interpretation is less grammatical, yet understandable. Processing time of the consumers' communication may be lengthened by requesting participants take turns (eg. raising hands to be recognized before speaking) or requesting that a consecutive interpreting process be used rather than attempting simultaneous interpreting.

1.6.3 Amount of Interactivity

Interactivity is the ability of the perceiver to reply to the initiator. Is the communication one-way (monologic), mostly one-way, or two-way (dialogic)? Most conversations will be two-way, especially if people are asking and answering questions [+ Interactivity]. Watching information on television is generally a one-way (to the viewer) communication event [- Interactivity]. A lecture may be mostly one-way, but how the audience reacts to a joke (or fails to react to it) can make a significant impact on how the presenter proceeds [+/- Interactivity]. Other terminology that has been used to describe this difference in communication is *Monologue* (monologic discourse) versus *Dialogue* (dialogic discourse).

The concept of dialogue [+ Interactivity] can include more than two people; but the amount of interactivity may be different for multiple receivers of the same communication. A restaurant conversation will be interactive [+ Interactivity] for the people at one booth, but be mostly non-interactive [+/- Interactivity] for the person seated at the next booth (who *could* turn around and say something). The same conversation would be non-interactive [- Interactivity] to anyone listening to a recording of it.

The level of interactivity of the communication clearly has an impact upon the work of interpreting. Interpreters working in highly interactive settings (such as group discussions) may find it hard to provide access to overlapping communication. Non-interactive communication (such as interpreting a videotaped message) prevents the possibility of interrupting the communication for clarification.

1.6.4 Simultaneous Occurrence of Variables in Communication

Each of the three communication variables (*Intention*, *Immediacy*, and *Interactivity*) plays a role in every communication situation. Interactive communication tends to co-occur with immediate communication, (such as in a face-to-face conversation); but it is still possible to have interactive communication which is not immediate (such as the exchange of letters between two friends). It is also possible to have immediate communication that is not interactive (such as watching a live satellite broadcast on television). Figure 1.5 below provides some examples of the application of these variables.

Intentional	Immediate	Interactive	Examples
+	+	+	Talking with someone, face-to-face or by phone
+	+	+ / −	Attending a lecture; Watching a play or other performance
+	+	−	Hearing your name over an airport's Public Address system; Seeing / hearing someone say hello to you on a live broadcast
+	−	+	Exchanging E-Mail with a friend; writing letters back and forth
+	−	−	Seeing / hearing someone say hello to you on a recorded broadcast; Reading of a Last Will and Testament
+ / −	+	−	Watching a live satellite-broadcast lecture or television show (along with a thousand other people)
+ / −	−	−	Hearing / watching a recorded lecture or performance; Reading a book; Watching a recorded television broadcast
−	+	+ / −	Hearing / watching other people converse face-to-face or by phone
−	+	−	Hearing another person's name over an airport's P.A. system; Seeing someone say hello to someone else on a live broadcast
−	−	−	Reading two other people's E-mail or letters to each other

KEY: "+" means the condition is present, "-" means the condition is absent, "+/-" means the condition may or may not be present.

Figure 1.5 - Intentional, Immediate, & Interactive Aspects of Communication

An understanding of these three communication variables will help to identify different applications of *Transcommunication* in Unit Two. The next chapter will further define language. The rest of this chapter reviews what we have learned so far.

1.7 Summary

This chapter has defined *Communication* as one mind's perception of a message, which another mind has expressed. We identified language as a subset of *human communication*, which itself is a subset of *animal communication*. All communication requires at least two minds, each of which will have certain *Background Knowledge*. *Background Knowledge* consists of four things: 1) knowledge of *how* to communicate, 2) knowledge of *what* can be communicated, 3) knowledge of *others* who might be able to understand the communication, and 4) knowledge of how the *physical environment* will permit the communication to take place. *Culture* (the set of shared knowledge and values within a community) is part of *Background Knowledge*. The intent of communication additionally may be either *conscious* or *unconscious*.

All communication takes place within *Physical Contexts*, which can directly influence both the *Expression* and *Perception* of communication. Communication is expressed and perceived through matched sets of *expressive modalities* (which require muscle movement, controlled by nerves) and *sensory perception* (which generally require only nerve connections). The five sets are *Image-Vision*, *Sound-Hearing*, *Texture-Touch*, *Odor-Smell*, and *Taste-Taste*[3]. These matched sets of expression and perception are a significant part of *Semiotics*, which is the study of all possible communication systems.

While semiotics provides the means of communication, *Pragmatics* is the study of the *goals* and *results* of communication. Each mind is free to determine its own meaning. Therefore, meaning is *independent* of the expression and perception of communication.

Three additional variables significantly influence how communication takes place: 1) *Intention* – the expression of communication toward specific perceivers, 2) *Immediacy* – the perception of communication at the same time that it is expressed, and 3) *Interactivity* – the ability of the perceiver to reply to the initiator.

---

[3] If you have a better label for the "taste-taste" pair, please share it with me. Remember that taste is not limited to food items.

1.7.1 Review Questions
1. What is the definition of communication?
2. What is the definition of Semiotics?
3. What is the definition of Pragmatics?
4. What is the difference between *conscious* and *unconscious* intention?
5. List several examples of unconscious intention in communication.
6. What are the four components present in any form of communication?
7. What four factors combine as *Background Knowledge*?
8. How are *Culture* and *Background Knowledge* related?
9. What five variables constitute *Expressive Modalities of Communication*?
10. What five variables constitute *Perceptive Modalities of Communication*?
11. Which three matched sets of *Expressive* and *Perceptive Modalities* are the most easily manipulated for communication?
12. In what ways can the *Physical Context* impact upon communication?
13. What is meant by the following phrase: "Meaning is independent of communication"?
14. Which three factors (beginning with the letter "I") have additional impact upon communication.
15. Identify the +, -, or +/- features for the following scenario: Reading questions written in a textbook.

1.7.2 Suggested Activities
1. Describe five different facial expressions that can be meaningful in your native culture and identify the possible meanings for each. Are there any circumstances where the same facial expression may have a different meaning?
2. List ten different gestures or body postures that can be meaningful in your native culture and identify the possible meanings for each. Are there any situations where these gestures or postures may have a different meaning?
3. List ten different meaningful sounds in your native culture that are not actually words and identify the correct use of each (ex. "Shhh" is a common sound made to indicate that people should be quiet).
4. Observe the natural body postures of people talking to each other. What different kinds of postures can you find? What might these postures indicate about the communication that is taking place?
5. Identify twenty different things that are in your current physical context. Out of the things you have identified, how many are the result of another mind's expression? How many of the twenty items do you perceive as *meaningful*?

Chapter 2
Language

"Language"

Timoth entered the room and blurted out "Isn't it just a matter of formality?"

Rasmus looked up from the dictionary on the reading stand. "Isn't *what* just a matter of formality?"

"This 'register' business everyone gets so worked up about. Wouldn't it be easier to just say whether something was formal or informal?"

"Of course it would be easier; but it would also be terribly inaccurate." Rasmus reached for a book on the top shelf. "Here, see this book? It lists hundreds of professional fields and identifies the requirements of each." Rasmus placed the book on the desk, opened it, and continued, "Here near the beginning is 'Architecture', near the middle is 'Medicine', and at the end is 'Zoology'."

Timoth sat down at the desk across from Rasmus. "I'll bet there's a point to all of this somewhere... I can just feel it."

"Yes, there is. Think of your average informal conversation on the street. Now, how would people in the fields I just mentioned communicate differently with their fellow peers on the job?"

"Well, they would likely use some specific vocabulary like 'I-beam,' or 'scalpel', or 'invertebrate'... stuff like that."

"Yes, they are all likely to have different special vocabularies, although the medicine folks are likely to overlap a bit with the zoology folks. But suppose a group of zoologists went out for lunch at a restaurant. Would they talk to each other in the same way as they did at work?"

Timoth gazed out the window, hoping to see if any zoologists were outside. "I don't know."

"Well, you were the one who brought up the 'formal' versus 'informal' dichotomy. Wouldn't you consider the work place more formal and the restaurant less formal?"

"I suppose it depends on which restaurant they go to," said Timoth, with a laugh.

"Aha! So the physical environment might actually make a difference in how they communicate? Suppose two zoologists are talking at work and their supervisor comes in. Would their manner of communication change at all?"

Timoth desperately wanted a zoologist or two to slip into the room at this moment. "Well, I suppose it might depend on what they were talking about before the supervisor came in and whether the supervisor was going to join that conversation or tell them to get back to their zoology." Timoth decided a smile might be better than a laugh this time.

"Well, done!" said Rasmus. "You've backed into the third variable: Topic. What the conversation is about might influence how it is discussed."

"Third variable? What were the other two?"

Rasmus held out three fingers and pointed to each in turn: "First you have the physical setting, second you have the participants themselves along with their relative status, and third you have the topic of their discussion."

Timoth extended the same three fingers and pointed silently to each. "So just three variables? Is it really that easy?"

Rasmus smiled. "I'm glad you are starting to consider these things easy. Yes, three primary variables; but also how the communication took place: writing, signing, speaking, shouting, etc. That's the fourth and final variable to what we call 'Register'."

"So formality can't exist without all four of these factors. Formality is only the tip of the iceberg. It's not that register is a matter of formality, but that formality is a matter of register!"

"By George, I think you've got it!"

Chapter 2 - Language

2.0 Overview

This chapter investigates language and its place as a subdivision of human communication. The technical term for using language to talk about language is *Metalinguistics*. The words "noun", "verb" and "adjective" are excellent examples of metalinguistics because they are words (pieces of language) that describe pieces of language. Any book on interpreting or translation is a metalinguistic work. You have a metalinguistic discussion any time you talk with peers or consumers about language. One of the advantages of metalinguistic ability is that it helps children (and adults) to learn second languages (O'Malley & Chamot, 1990). Another advantage is it allows us to analyze interpretations and the process of interpreting.

This chapter will provide a systematic explanation of language structure that will help organize our understanding of what language is and how it relates to interpreting and transliteration. We will review different ways of expressing and perceiving language and will then explore "*The Linguistic Pyramid*" which organizes seven interactive levels of language. *Chapter Three* will explore language use. Subsequent chapters will explore language variation and other aspects of language.

2.1 What is Language?

Any animal may use symbols (such as sounds or body movements) to convey information between members of a community, but the word *language* can only describe certain types of communication systems. The previous chapter defined communication as follows: one mind's perception of a message, which another mind has expressed. *Language* is a specific kind of communication that meets all four of the following additional requirements:

1) The communication must be *systematic*: it must have rules that apply to the production and organization of the symbols (i.e. grammatical rules).

2) The communication system must allow for an *infinite* number of ways to encode any given message.

3) The communication system must pass between at least *two generations* of active users.

4) The communication system must be flexible enough to accept *change over time* and between users.

In sum, **language is the systematic use of symbols to express and perceive information between members of a community, in which the system is rule-governed, has infinite production possibilities, is intergenerational, and changes over time.** Humans are the only species on Earth that have the ability to communicate via language.

Prior to 1960, the definition of language specifically *excluded* gestural communication systems because another part of the definition of language was that it be spoken. In 1960, William Stokoe became the first person to systematically study a signed language. He began by exploring the first part of the definition: Stokoe analyzed the rules for the formation and organization of the symbols. In the landmark work he published that year, *Sign Language Structure*, he identified three basic parts which come together to form signs: handshape, location, and movement. In 1970, Robbin Battison (among others) identified a fourth characteristic: palm orientation. The importance of facial movements was eventually recognized (for example, Liddell, 1977).

Stokoe later expressed all of these various aspects of signed languages as an even simpler notion of two things: *actor* and *action*. In other words, something *acts* (a hand at the side of the head, the muscles in the cheek to one side of the nose) and an *action* takes place (the tip of the hand taps the side of the forehead, the cheek muscle contracts and "wrinkles" one side of the nose). Other researchers identified the rules for ordering the signs (grammar), the ability to follow the rules while encoding the same message in an infinite number of ways (productivity), the fact that the language has been handed down through multiple generations of users (intergenerational transmission), and the ability for the language to adapt and change over time (chronological change).

With all of these requirements met, the old requirement that language must also be spoken has since been eliminated. Linguists around the world now acknowledge rule-governed signed communication systems as languages. William Stokoe was the person who gave the name "American Sign Language" to the signed language used in the United States of America and most of Canada. Other signed languages have different symbols, and different rules than ASL. These signed languages generally reflect the names of the countries or provinces in which they are used such as British Sign Language, Australian Sign Language, French Sign Language, Italian Sign Language, Quebec Sign Language, etc. So far there have been no signed languages that have been shown to follow exactly the same rules for any spoken language. In other words, French Sign Language (LSF) is not based upon spoken French; and Italian Sign Language (LSI) is not based upon spoken Italian. These titles simply indicate that the people who use LSF generally reside in France and the people who use LSI generally reside in Italy. Likewise the title ASL identifies that the users of the language generally reside in (North) America (the United States and Canada).

2.2 Channels and Modes

Now that we understand language as a subset of communication, we can further explore a few more ideas about language. To begin, let's consider the three possible language channels. *Language Channels* are the three basic ways of expressing language: signed, spoken, and written. English can be expressed in two channels (written English and spoken English) while American Sign Language is most commonly expressed in one channel (signed ASL) but may also be expressed in one of several writing systems proposed for ASL (although none are widely used at this time). *Channels* are distinct from *Modes*.

In the previous section we explored the five primary *modes* of expressing communication: image, odor, sound, taste, and texture. Only three expressive modalities are used to express language: image, sound, and texture. These three expressive modalities again match to our senses, which detect the elements of language. Languages are generally perceived and understood through the senses of sight, hearing, or touch. While it is clearly possible to *communicate* through food or perfume, we will exclude the senses of taste and smell from our discussion of modalities related to *language*.

Channels and *Modes* are related, but not as a one-to-one match. Generally, a spoken language is encoded through sound; written and signed languages are encoded through images. But spoken languages can be written in phonetic alphabets or encoded visually with manual cues. Written symbols can be spelled out or transferred into Morse code tones. Texture is a common language-encoding mechanism for blind and DeafBlind people and can likewise encode signed, spoken, or written languages.

Expressive Modalities are not limited to language use. We saw in the previous chapter that they are available for all forms of communication: music uses sound; paintings use images (and some paintings of Elvis also use texture – velvet). It is quite possible, even common, to use an encoding modality *without* using language. For example, an infant's random gestures, babbling, and occasional physical contact with a caregiver would be examples of using all three encoding modalities (images, sounds, and textures) but expressing no language at all through any of them. The child may certainly communicate, but the requirements that define language (such as being rule-governed and shared by a community) have not been met – at least, not yet.

In order to communicate, however, we must "express and perceive information between members of a community." This means that whatever has been expressed must be perceived for the communication to take place. *Perceptive Modalities* are the means by which a message is perceived such as hearing, seeing or touching. Specifically we will identify these as *visual perception* (seeing images), *auditory perception* (hearing sounds), and *tactile perception* (feeling textures).

The three channels of written language, signed language, and spoken language can be expressed through image, sound, or texture. Within the channel of writing we might first think of printing versus cursive writing. It is also possible to express written languages through dots and dashes for Morse code (or raised dots on a flat surface for Braille). Morse code and Braille are not languages – they are *Language Encoding Systems*. **Language Encoding Systems are finite and closed sets of symbols which express the basic structural components of a language.** If those symbols (letters of the alphabet, dots and dashes) are embossed so that they can be detected by touch alone, they still encode a written channel but the expressive modality is texture and the perceptive modality is tactile. Figure 2.1, below, categorizes the most common *Language Encoding Systems* by *Language Channel*, and by *Expressive / Perceptive Modality*.

Language Channels	Expressive / Perceptive Modalities		
	Image / Visual	**Sound / Auditory**	**Texture / Tactile**
Written Languages	• Written Symbols • Typed Symbols • Fingerspelling • Morse Code Symbols • Semaphore	• Morse Code Tones • Spelling Aloud	• Brailled Symbols • Raised Letters • Palm Printing • Tactile Fingerspelling
Signed Languages	• Signed Symbols		• Tactile Signing
Spoken Languages	• Phonetic Alphabets • Manual Cues • Mouth Movements	• Spoken Symbols	• Tadoma • Tactile Manual Cues

Figure 2.1 – Language Encoding Systems

You may have noticed that one space in the middle of the grid has no examples. Signed languages are not expressed through sound nor are they perceived through auditory perception. While it is possible to make sounds while producing a signed language, these sounds do not effectively represent the basic structural components of signed languages. It is possible to use a spoken language to describe how to produce elements of a signed language. It is even possible to rearrange the order of words in a spoken language to match the word order of a signed language; however, neither of these examples can be considered a *language encoding system* for signed languages.

2.3 The Linguistic Pyramid

Now that we have a working definition of what language is we can explore the elements at work *within* language. One part of the definition for language is that the system is rule-governed. We will use an organizing strategy called the *Linguistic Pyramid* to identify the larger parts of the system of language. The idea of a pyramid reveals very plainly that the bottom-most layers support the weight of the layers above and so on. This provides a useful way to think of language because even the most complex use of language still requires the most basic elements to be produced. Let's have a look before defining each part of the *Linguistic Pyramid*.

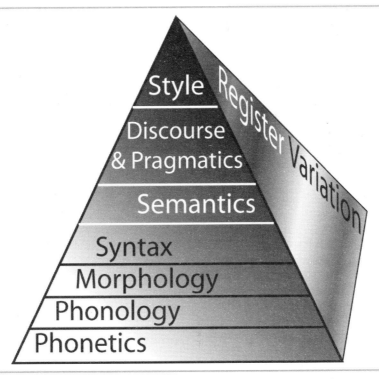

Figure 2.2 - The Linguistic Pyramid

2.3.1 Phonetics

Language can be thought of as a series of different skills and rules that overlap and build one upon another. At the bottom, most basic level we have *phonetics*, which consists of the foundational support of language. In spoken languages we have airflow, points of articulation within the mouth, vocal chord vibrations, and other changes in the mouth, pharynx and larynx. When all of these pieces are put together we can produce *consonants* and *vowels* and suddenly we're making the sounds of spoken languages. In signed languages we have finger, thumb and limb extensions, rotations, and contractions, which allow us to establish handshapes, orientations, and movements between locations. Without the foundation of *phonetics*, we can't get very far linguistically.

Phonetics is the study of how elements of language are *physically produced*. This means that muscles have to move and body parts must contact each other (or nearly contact each other). Phonetics focuses on the physical elements of producing a language. These physical elements are the result of *muscle movement* and are the most observable elements of language production. Phonetics attempts to explain the behavior that produces the building blocks of language.

In the previous chapter we investigated the expression of communication as *semiotics*. *Phonetics*, being the use of muscles to express language, is a subset of semiotics. It is still possible to express communication beyond language and some of this is called paralinguistics. *Paralinguistics*, a separate subset of semiotics, includes non-linguistic vocal inflection (such as changes in pitch and volume) or facial expression (such as mouth and eyebrow movements) for *affect* and emphasis. It is important to note that vocal inflection and facial expression also have linguistic uses, specifically as a part of grammar (vocal inflections and facial expressions may be the only indicator that a sentence is a question versus a statement). Beyond *Paralinguistics* is the remainder of semiotics, which includes vocal signals, eye gaze, visual gestures, and body postures. Figure 2.3, below, shows the relationships of *Paralinguistics* and *Phonetics* as separate subsets of *Semiotics*:

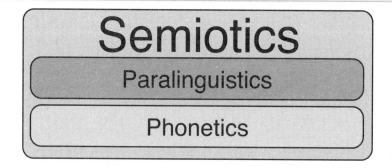

Figure 2.3 - Semiotics, Paralinguistics & Phonetics

2.3.2 Phonology

It isn't good enough just to have building blocks. We need some rules to guide how the building blocks are assembled and this is the realm of *phonology*. Some languages let you put groups of consonants together at the beginnings or ends of words. In English we have problems pronouncing things like "tlzis" or "gbrang" because we don't like these particular consonant clusters at the beginnings of our words. American Sign Language doesn't like having too many two-handed signs where each hand has a different hand shape. Those two-handed signs in which the hands do not use the same handshapes are generally limited: the non-dominant hand can only use a few specific handshapes (Battison, 1978).

We use slash marks (//) to indicate speech *sounds* rather than letters. What you are reading right now is composed of letters (the written channel). If you read aloud, you produce sounds (the spoken channel). Often a letter is not pronounced they way it is spelled. Some simple examples include the letters "gh" in the word "enough", where the last sound is pronounced /f/; and the letter "c" may be pronounced as /s/ as in the word "pencil" (/pensil/) or as a /k/ as in the word "cap" (/kap/). More subtle examples include the words "caps" and "cabs" where the letter "s" sounds like /s/ in the word "caps" (/kaps/) but sounds like /z/ in the word "cabs" (/kabz/).

Phonology is the study of how language elements are *combined*. One way to do this is to inventory the words used in a language and find patterns. One pattern in English is that we can place up to *three consonants* in a row at the beginning of our words; but to do so, the first of these must be the sound /s/, the second sound must either be /k/, /p/ or /t/ and the third sound must be either /l/ or /r/. These combinations can be found in words like "sclerosis", "scream", "split", "spray", and "street".

Phonological analysis will always make use of the level below it: *phonetics*. Each group of sounds (in the above examples) shares certain phonetic principles. The first of these sounds, /s/, is a *sibilant*. Sibilants are produced by restricting the flow of air so that a hissing sound is generated. As it happens, /s/ is a *voiceless* sibilant, meaning that the vocals chords are not vibrating when the sound is produced. The second group of sounds, /k/, /p/ or /t/, are all *stops*. Stops are produced when the airflow is interrupted by a closure of the mouth. The sound /k/ closes the middle of the tongue against the roof of the mouth, the sound /p/ closes the lips together, while the sound /t/ places the tip of the tongue against the base of the upper teeth. All three of these sounds are *voiceless consonants*.

The third group of sounds /l/ or /r/ are both *liquids*. Liquids restrict the airflow through a partial closing of the mouth. The sound /l/ is produced almost the same way that /t/ is produced, except that the tongue is not widened to close the airflow of the mouth, therefore air travels around the sides of the tongue. The sound /r/ is often produced, in American English at least, by a rounding of the lips. Both /l/ and /r/ are *voiced*, meaning that the vocal chords are moving when these sounds are produced.

Knowing how each sound is produced (phonetics) can lead to an explanation of which sounds are allowed to combine and which are not (phonology). The fact that the first two of these sounds are voiceless helps us understand a point of similarity between them. Knowing this similarity helps us predict that mixing of voiced with voiceless consonants (such as /zk/, /zt/, /zp/, /sg/, /sb/, or /sd/) are unlikely combinations at the beginnings of English words. The fact that both the /t/ and /l/ sounds are made with nearly identical tongue placement also helps us predict that the sequence /stl/ is *not* included in the possible combinations of three consonants at the beginning of English words.

All of this is indeed very technical, but the point is to demonstrate not only that there are rules at work here, but that there is already an overlap between the levels of the

Linguistic Pyramid: the rules governing combinations of speech sounds in English (phonology) are related to how those speech sounds are produced (phonetics). In other words, we can't do too much work on the second level of the pyramid without building upward from the first level of the pyramid. Each step upward depends on the levels beneath.

One example of phonetics influencing the phonology of ASL is the comfort in producing certain handshapes. ASL makes use of three different handshapes that extend only one finger (or the thumb). Extending the ring finger alone is uncomfortable, and is not used in ASL. Likewise, extending the middle finger alone is also uncomfortable (and a culturally taboo handshape, as well). Pinky extension occurs in isolation, but also combines with index-finger extension and/or thumb extension. The only times that ASL uses an extended ring finger is when at least two other fingers are also extended[4]. In this way the phonetic limits of comfortable handshapes directly influences the handshapes that are used in ASL

2.3.3 Morphology

Equipped with the building blocks (phonetics) and special rules that govern the kinds of combinations that are allowed (phonology), we can now start building something meaningful. The whole point of language is to tell people what we mean; and the smallest unit of meaning, linguistically, is the morpheme. **Morphology is the study of how bits of meaning (morphemes) combine with other bits of meaning (other morphemes) to form words.** The individual sounds /h/, /o/, /r/, and /s/ have no significant meaning by themselves but when put together in the order above they form the English word "horse" which brings to mind rather large, four-legged animals which may be useful to cowboys, rodeo stars, and polo players: that is one basic meaning of the word "horse".

As it happens the word "horse" contains the letters "o" and "r" which, when combined, create the English word "or"; but the concepts related to the word "or" have rather little to do with a horse. These two words, "horse" and "or", happen to have some *phonological* similarities, but they are separate and unrelated *morphemes*. *Phonology* indicates that these are all English sounds and that these sounds are combined in ways that English allows. *Morphology* lets us understand that there are different basic meanings attached. The combination of "horse" is a four-legged animal. The combination of "or" is a conjunction which is used to join more than one noun, verb, or clause. Both of these words are *free morphemes*, which can stand alone and still have meaning. In contrast is the category of *bound morphemes*, which only have meaning when they are attached to free morphemes.

One of the most obvious combinations of *free* and *bound* morphemes in English is our very predictable use of the written letter "s" being combined with nouns to mean "more than one" of the noun. When we bind the right bits together we can talk about "more than one horse" with the word "horses" because the "s" bit, which in this case conveys a

---

[4] Note that BSL *does* have a handshape using an extended ring finger along with an extended pinky finger and that this combination is *not* an ASL handshape. Likewise BSL historically made use of the extended middle finger in BSL signs without any taboo meanings associated to it. Cultural influences, such as through American films, have begun to cause some BSL signers to modify their handshape inventory and eliminate the extended middle finger as a BSL handshape.

meaning of plurality[5], gets bound to the "horse" bit. So the word "horses" contains exactly *two* morphemes.

Some people confuse the idea of a *morpheme* with that of a *syllable*. These two things (morphemes and syllables) may often overlap, but they are not the same. An example of the difference between syllables and morphemes is the English word "artichoke", which has three syllables but contains only one meaning. The letters "art" form part of the word "artichoke" but they don't reveal any meanings of the word "art". In other words, the concepts of music, literature, paintings, or sculpture are not a meaningful part of the word "artichoke". Likewise the letters "choke" form part of the word "artichoke" but, similarly, do not indicate the concept of restricted breathing as part of the word "artichoke". So syllables and morphemes are different things: syllables are groups of *phonemes* surrounding a single vowel sound, morphemes are pieces of *meaning*.

Lets review the example of the morpheme "horse" and the morpheme "s" combining together to make the word "horses" (which is a single word with two morphemes in it). The "horse" part is a *free morpheme*, meaning that it can stand alone as a word all by itself. The "s" part is a *bound morpheme*, meaning that it cannot stand alone, but rather it must combine with a free morpheme to be meaningful. *Every word in this sentence is a free morpheme.* (Hey, wake up! Did you check that last sentence? Check it out before you keep reading).

Bound morphemes include many different pieces of meaning, including (for example) the letter "s" (which was attached to the word "morpheme" at the beginning of this sentence) and the letters "ed" which were attached (twice, now) to the word "attach" in this sentence. Those were quick examples so you might want to read the previous sentence again and find the examples. No, *really*, read it again, the examples are *imbedded* in the sentence.

Both *free* and *bound* morphemes contain phonemes (just when you thought you understood the difference between the two, now you are forced to make a connection!). Let's return to some earlier examples: "caps" (/kaps/) and "cabs" (/kabz/). Notice that in the *spellings* of the words I used the letter "s" in both of them and that it changed the meaning to "more than one cap" and "more than one cab". The same morpheme – a bound morpheme of plurality – was attached to each of the free morphemes "cap" and "cab"; but notice the *sounds* made for the letter "s" are different. When the plural morpheme comes after a voiceless consonant (such as /p/) then it takes the *voiceless* form /s/. When the plural morpheme comes after a voiced consonant (such as /b/) then it takes the *voiced* form /z/. When added to the word "horse" (/hors/), which already ends in the sound /s/, the plural morpheme adds a vowel and sounds like /iz/ (horsiz). The amazing thing is that we hear three different combinations of sounds (/s/, /z/, and /iz/) and still understand them to mean the same thing: more-than-one of something. This is how phonetics, phonology, and morphology overlap. We understand that this one piece of plural meaning (morphology) has three different English sounds (phonology) whose use can be predicted based on how the sounds are made (phonetics).

---

[5] English also uses the same phonological piece "s" for possessives and to mark third-person singular subject agreement in verbs. Thus the letter "s" actually has three distinct English morphemes associated with it.

American Sign Language and British Sign Language are both morphologically rich languages in comparison to English. While English depends largely on the sequential combination of affixes (prefixes and suffixes in this case), ASL and BSL manage to use space in a very efficient way morphologically: various bits of meaning can be combined with others *at the same time*. A simple example is the use of *numeral incorporation*. The handshape component alone may represent the numerical part of a sign's meaning. But it is not possible to generate a sign with *only* a handshape. The remaining components (location, movement, and palm orientation) may represent the meaning of "weeks," for example. Both ASL and BSL use the same handshape for the number two. This handshape could then be combined with specific palm orientation, location and movement. The resulting combination would have the specific combined meaning of "two-weeks", and would be understood in both BSL and ASL to have that combined meaning.

While BSL and ASL share the same handshape for the number two, they have distinct handshapes for some other numbers. The ASL handshape for the number six is identical to one of the BSL variants for the number three (Cerney, 1987) and therefore the same physical sign production for the ASL concept of "six weeks" would be mistaken in England to mean "three weeks". While ASL and BSL do share some similarities in vocabulary (such as having identical production and meaning for the sign UNDERSTAND) they have significant differences including different sets of possible handshapes for each language (Cerney, 1987). It has been estimated that ASL and BSL share only about 30% of their respective vocabularies (James Kyle, personal communication).

2.3.4 Syntax

We can take this idea one step further by arranging our bits of meaning in a line. If I have two brown horses I probably want to use a word order like "two brown horses" to talk about them in English. But if I'm not using English, I might mix up that order and talk about my "brown horses two" or even my "horses two brown." But if I know the rules of word order, or syntax, in my language, then I am likely to keep my words right order in the... I mean... in the right order. **Syntax is the study of word orders and the rules governing word orders in a language.**

One approach to syntax is that there are *basic* word orders to which rules may apply to generate more *complex* word orders. A basic word order in English is *Subject-Verb-Object*, noted simply as "SVO". If we have an object, however, that often means the verb can *act* on the object. These kinds of verbs are called "transitive". Verbs that do not act on objects are called "intransitive". The basic word order for English sentences with intransitive verbs would be SV – Subject-Verb. A verb's ability to act on an object is part of its *morphology*. So once again we see an overlap between different levels of the linguistic pyramid.

ASL shares the same *underlying* word order (SV or SVO) of English (Liddell, 1980). But this doesn't mean that every ASL sentence (or even that a majority of them) will follow the typical patterns of English. The underlying word order is only a *starting* point and many syntactic rules, such as *topicalization*, allow for changes in the word order. In ASL this might mean that my topic is the two horses and my comment is that they are *brown*; or perhaps my topic is the brown horses and my comment is that there are *two* of them.

Many people who learn about the *Linguistic Pyramid* are curious to know where "grammar" sits within the pyramid. *Grammar* is the combination of *morphology* and *syntax* and therefore it is within those two levels that "grammar" can be found. Grammar includes the correct use of *free* and *bound* morphemes to indicate plurality as well as the correct word order as in the following sentence: "Grammar has two components." In this example sentence the word "Grammar" serves as a noun (morphology) and also as the subject of the sentence (syntax); the word "has" is the third-person, present-tense form of a transitive verb; the phrase "two components" consists first of an adjective "two" and a noun "components" which itself was constructed of the free morpheme "component" and the bound morpheme "s".

Now, you may be sitting there, thinking to yourself, "gosh this sure is complex... how could I ever learn this stuff?" But the fact is that you already know how to use language. You probably had never encountered the sentence "Grammar has two components" before, but you were able to understand it. If language had no rules you wouldn't be able to read and understand *anything*. We know and follow the rules of a language that we know, even if we can't define or explain the rules. What the *Linguistic Pyramid* helps us to do is to organize and explain the rules that we are already following. Once we have them organized, we can use them to our advantage. But first, we need to climb a few more steps in the pyramid.

2.3.5 Semantics

Well all of this is fine, you say, but where does interpreting fit into all of this? It doesn't yet. You see, we need all of the building blocks and rules to use language, but we need to have a message before language is worth much. Noam Chomsky proposed one famous example of a meaningless sentence: "Colorless green ideas sleep furiously." Grammatically this is a legitimate English sentence, but it has no meaning. In fact, it has contradictory meaning (how can something that is colorless also be green?) There is no reasonable context in which this sentence makes any sense.

Semantics is the study of meaning in words, phrases and sentences (in contrast with morphology, which is the study of pieces of meaning and how the pieces combine). *Lexical Semantics* focuses on words; *Structural Semantics* focuses on the meanings built between groups of words (phrases and sentences). A common example of structural semantics is the English word "run" meaning a physical activity for joggers ("I run every morning") but in other contexts the same word may mean an unraveling in clothing ("there is a run in my stocking"). Semantics includes the idea of *conceptual accuracy* (using the right word for the right concept). It is context that provides the ability to determine that accuracy. *Context* means more than just the surrounding words in a sentence. Let's take an example sentence of "It will run." Without any context we would assume the word run is being used in its *Primary Sense*: using legs to propel a person or animal forward at a quick pace. But additional context can help us understand the meaning of "it" and "run" more accurately.

Referent of "It"	Ambiguity	Clarifying Context
Colored fabric fading:	"It will run	if you wash it in warm water"
A stage performance:	"It will run	for two more weeks on Broadway"
An automobile motor:	"It will run	once you replace the spark plugs"
Fabric unraveling:	"It will run	if you snag it on something sharp"

Figure 2.4 – Meaning In Context

Semantics also includes the notion that there are various relationships of meaning between words such as *opposites* like "old" and "young" where one could say "not young" instead of saying "old". Other examples include *hierarchies* where we understand that a large general category such as "food" has many sub-categories such as "fruits" and "meats". "Fruits" contains things such as "Apples" and "Pears". "Apples" contains varieties such as "Golden Delicious" and "Granny Smith".

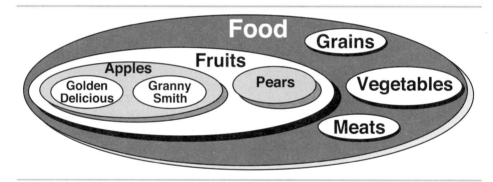

Figure 2.5 – Semantic Hierarchies

But the words "Granny Smith" might also refer to someone's elderly relative and "Apple" might also refer to a kind of computer. The context surrounding the use of the word will generally make it clear what the meaning is, but sometimes will still leave ambiguities such as in the sentence "Visiting relatives can be annoying", which may describe the task of visiting other relatives as an unpleasant one or refer to the irritation which might be caused by relatives visiting you.

Semantics began as a vague field, and, quite honestly, is still rather vague, because we cannot *see* meaning; we can only agree to what the meaning is. So when we say, "what does DOG mean in English?" we can turn to the dictionary or we can argue that it may mean certain prototypical bits and pieces of dogs (such as four legs, a snout with teeth inside, ears, fur, a tail, and so on). When the word DOG is used in context, however, it may really mean my dog, or the first dog I ever met, or that really nasty animal down the street, or for that matter, Snoopy, Lassie, Marmaduke, or Toto. So when you have all these possibilities just for the word "DOG," imagine the complications that can come up for a whole language full of words used in a whole world full of contexts.

So here we are with semantics. Surely that's good enough for interpreting, right? I mean, all we have to do is understand what the words mean in the source language, find the words that mean the same thing in the target language, and say those words in complete sentences with accurate grammar and clear enunciation. Isn't it *exactly* as simple as that? Well that's fine if we want to turn a comedy routine into a dry and pointless lecture; but we might not get hired again in our lifetimes (and that's not good because we need the work!)

2.3.6 Discourse and Pragmatics

While semantics focuses on what a word or an utterance means, given its context, we still need a higher level to investigate how people use language with each other. *Discourse* is how we use language beyond the sentence level. ***Pragmatics* is how social and environmental factors influence the meanings of the speaker** and is a co-partner to discourse. *Discourse Analysis* is the study of how people organize and use language to do things. When we ask, "Could you pass the pepper, please?" we aren't really looking for a "yes" or "no" answer. We really *do* want the pepper and we want it before our food gets *cold*. The pragmatics of this situation is that we actually want the pepper, but we also need to be polite. The *discourse feature* used to accomplish this goal is the use of a yes/no question, which is culturally recognized as a polite way of making a request.

When we ask, "Could I ask a question?" we tend to ignore the fact that we just did. And when friends start lambasting a particularly nasty co-worker who, by chance, has just entered the room, you can quickly change the discussion to how odd the weather has been lately which (if your friends are paying attention) will let them know that it is time to stop the lambasting.

Let's take an example sentence and several possible responses to it. Example: "I want the red one." Response A: "Certainly. Is there anything else I can get for you today?" Response B: "Well, maybe, if you're good, we can come back and get it." Response C: "What we *want* and what we *get* don't always match up, do they?" Response D: "Mr. Smith already purchased it." Response E: "Oh, I didn't know you were such a connoisseur!"

The example sentence appears to be a request, but it may simply be a statement without any intention of accomplishing a transaction. *What situations* are likely to surround each response? Probably each could be spoken in a store, but they might be uttered as people look through a catalogue, peer through a window, or survey the landscape. We simply don't know what "one" refers to. But we would understand that whatever it *does* refer to, there is probably *only* one that is red, and very likely to be others, which have colors *other* than red.

Which responses mean "yes" and which mean "no"? Response A implies "yes" even though that word is never stated. Likewise responses C and D imply a "no" without directly saying so. Response B implies "maybe" but might actually end up meaning "no". Response E does not seem to indicate any affirmative or negative, but rather appears to be a comment about the requester.

Who are the people making these utterances? Responses A and D are likely to come from a sales clerk. Responses B and C are likely to come from a parent (or at least a person with authority for making purchases). Response E might well come from a peer. *What is the effect* of each response? Responses A and D appear to be polite interaction. Response B may be a request for postponing while also an indication that it is time to leave. Response C may be an indication that no further requests should be made (and perhaps no further utterances at all). Response E may be a joke or at least a jovial response to indicate camaraderie.

Our use of emphasis, pauses, and repetition also influence the way we use words to communicate. Let's revisit the example from above with a few modifications: "I want the red one (pause) the red one." This might be uttered as a store clerk begins to get the pink one. Gestures, eye gaze, body posture all can influence how we understand people's intentions. Let's take the same example, but trimmed a bit: "I want that one" and combine it with a pointing gesture with eye gaze directly at the desired object and the body leaning forward. All of these additional physical behaviors are called *paralinguistic* features. Paralinguistic features are things, which are not by themselves language, but can occur simultaneously with language. They support the linguistic message and could well be investigated as part of *discourse analysis*.

Knowing *how to build* words and sentences is certainly an essential part of using language, but knowing the *way we use* words and sentences is nearly as important as what those words and sentences are. We need to know how our consumers are using the words they say in a source text; but then we also need to know the appropriate ways to say those things in the target language. This is real work, and it is also real interpreting.

2.3.7 Style and Idiolect

Where do we go from here? Well, there is one more upward level toward completing the *Linguistic Pyramid*: Style. When we understand the message well enough to adequately predict where it is going; and we also understand the person creating the message well enough to know her purpose, her tendencies, her idiosyncrasies of language use; then we have entered a *stylistic* understanding of the source text. *Style* **is how a single person organizes and uses language.**

One aspect of *literary criticism* is the investigation of the stylistics of writers; and stylistics is the capstone of this investigation into linguistics. If we look at discourse as the way a community uses language, then style is the way a single member of a community uses and organizes language. Bakhtin states that "Any utterance ... is individual and therefore can reflect the individuality of the speaker (or writer); that is, it possesses individual style." (Bakhtin, 1986: 63). When cousin Bob always mispronounces certain words, uses other words in unique ways, or, in general, has his peculiar ways with language, then we are talking about his individual linguistic style.

Style includes the predictable linguistic use of certain words or phrases and topics of discussion. It also includes predictable paralinguistic features such as pitch, quality of voice, gestures, and facial expressions. Paralinguistic features are most noticeable at the discourse and style levels of the *Linguistic Pyramid*. Those features that identify people's attitudes, beliefs, and emotions about their messages can be considered as stylistic.

Style is what impressionists and impersonators depend on for entertainment. Imitations of John Wayne, Ed Sullivan, Rod Serling, and US presidents abound in the field of entertainment. The most entertaining are often those who most completely match the style and idiosyncrasies of the person being imitated. More specifically, a successful impressionist uses elements of a person's *Idiolect*. *Idiolect*, a subset of *Style*, is the way that an individual uses language, which includes the regular occurrence of certain behaviors that are not considered the norm for the larger language community. *Idiolect* includes regular mispronunciations, word usage, and gestural behaviors.

Beyond *Idiolect*, stylistics also includes the *organization* of a message, such as whether it starts off with the main point and then builds the arguments or, alternatively, slowly works toward a point but never directly mentions it. If a person's message is endlessly going off in different tangents then their style is very different from someone who identifies the main points and is quickly finished. The *Organizational Style* is different from *Idiolect*, because many people with very different idiolects can share very similar organizational styles.

Understanding the organization of a text is an essential aspect of being able to regenerate that text in another language. If an interpreter has access to the outline of a presentation (and if the presenter will actually follow that outline) then the interpreter will have significant ability to predict the message, understand its organization, and maintain its main point and supporting details accurately. Understanding the organizational style of a message allows the interpreter to know which elements are to be compared or contrasted. The interpreter who does not have prior access to an outline may still be able to succeed at making these kinds of predictions if presenters follow an expected organizational style or announce their intentions when they start a presentation.

A stylistic understanding of a source text can be helpful, if not essential, in the interpreting process. Understanding the organizational style helps make predictions about the source text and its creator. If we are also able to generate some form of equivalence of the presenter's individual linguistic tendencies[6] in the target language, then we are being about as accurate and true to the source as possible.

2.3.8 Register and Register Variation

Now that we have all the building blocks in place and have built the *Linguistic Pyramid* from the base of *phonetics* to the capstone of *style*, we can turn the whole thing sideways and look at one way that language gets modified. Touching on all of the levels of the *Linguistic Pyramid* is what has come to be called *Register Variation*.

Gregory and Carroll (1978) defined *register* as being composed of four elements contained in three categories: the *field* (a combination of subject matter and location or setting), the *mode* (language form or signal), and the *tenor* (relation of speakers). Register is here defined as being composed of all four of the variables identified in their three categories: *setting*, *signal*, *speakers*, and *subject*.

Settings could be conference rooms, lecture halls, park benches, religious sanctuaries, auto repair shops, or bedrooms. The *signal* is simply the language channel, mode, and *language encoding system* used to communicate, such as conversing in signed ASL or making a public presentation in spoken English. The *speakers* may be strangers or may know each other well. They may only interact at work or may also know each other

---

[6] This is not to say that we should imitate our source speakers to the point of making fun of them; neither should we attempt to match extreme emotions, except in dramatic presentations.

socially. *Subjects* of discussion could be work, politics, the weather, sports, shared experiences, or learning something new. **Register Variation is the change in language based on *where* the communication is happening, *how* the communication is taking place, *who* is talking to whom, and about *what* topic: Who, What, Where, and How.** *Register Variation* affects every level of the *Linguistic Pyramid*. The most obvious changes are in the vocabulary we use, such as "choo choo" to a child, "train" in general terms, and "the express" to people who know about trains. Another obvious area is in syntax such as "Hello there!", "It's nice to meet you", and "I am so pleased to make your acquaintance." *Register Variation* includes the different ways that we pronounce our words as in the differences between "Wha cha doin?" and "What are you doing?"

Some people prefer to think of *Register* as meaning a certain level of formality; but register is much more than just a measure of formality. Martin Joos (1961, 1968) proposed a theoretical division of the ways people talk: *intimate, casual, consultative, formal, frozen.* Many people trying to understand register variation have borrowed his five-way division, but these simple categories don't capture the subtleties of *Register Variation* and Joos did not even use that label. His label for this five-way division of language variation was the "five clocks" (Joos, 1961, 1968). Some people have latched on to his writings as an explanation of *Register Variation*, in part because it proposes a nice small number of divisions – five (just the right number to count on your hand). While Joos' "five clocks" and the concept of register variation are related, it is important to understand that studies of register variation do not limit themselves to only five divisions, nor are there only five kinds of register being dealt with by the consumers of interpreting services.

While the level of formality can certainly impact upon register, formality level does not equal register. Charles Ferguson (1977) gave this explanation of register:

> One of the central facts about human language is the way it varies in structure depending on the use to which it is put. Every speech community and every individual user of language exhibits this kind of variation in language behavior. It is not only the semantic content which varies according to the use but also phonological and syntactic patterns, choice of vocabulary and forms of discourse. In some societies this variation can be illustrated dramatically by turning the dial of a radio to find a particular program. It often takes less than a sentence of speech to decide whether we are hearing a news broadcast, commercial message, 'soap opera', campaign speech, or sermon. (Ferguson, 1977: 210).

Hatim & Mason (1990) identified a helpful difference between "Language Users" and "Language Use". Variation for *Language Users* may be based on region, social class, gender, ethnicity, and generational differences. *Language Use* is directly tied to register variation: 1) where they are talking (settings), 2) how people talk (signals), 3) who they are talking to (speakers), and 4) what they are talking about (subjects).

Significant variation may be demonstrated in the choices a person makes when they are talking to their boss or talking to their child. To the Boss - clear pronunciation of technical words and jargon with some routine phrases that are only understood in the work environment. To the child - some pronunciations of words (such as "choo choo") that the child understands (but would not be appropriate for use with adults), simpler sentences, and occasionally incorrect morphology in an attempt to reduce the difficulty for the child to understand.

Of course we are always modifying how we communicate, even with the same people, depending on where we are and what we are talking about. We even see differences between people in the same situation talking about the same thing: Let's suppose that we wish to apologize to our boss for messing up the "Jones account." We are likely to say (rather meekly) things like "Um, boss, I'm really sorry that I messed up the Jones account and I'll never do it again." whereas our boss is likely to say (with significant force) things like "Johnson, this is the last time this company can afford to absorb your mistakes. The next time you'll be fired!"

Now let's suppose that on a different occasion you've actually impressed the boss: "Johnson, I want to tell you how pleased I am with the work you put into the Smith account. Thanks to you, this company can afford to purchase a company car for your division." To which you might reply "Thank you, sir!" or even "Gee, thanks, boss!" Each person in each exchange is speaking in very different ways, yet these would all fit in the realm of Joos' "consultative clock." So understand that register variation is a grand, all encompassing idea, not just five little divisions of communicative behavior.

As we learn a language, we continue to develop our variation in register over time. As we encounter new topics, new people, and new places we observe and adopt new ways of modifying our communication. Register development is tied to the continual expansion of our language skills. Each successive development includes every level of the *Linguistic Pyramid* as we adapt our phonology, morphology, syntax, semantics, etc to our new experiences. Figure 2.6 represents the expansion of our register development over time.

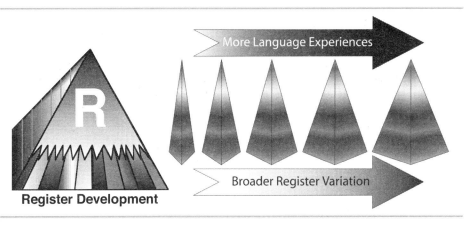

Figure 2.6 – Emerging Register Variations

2.4 Language Comprehension, Expression and Development

Now that we have defined the seven levels of the *Linguistic Pyramid* we should recognize that there is a difference between language *comprehension* and language *expression*. Generally our language skills are *greater in comprehension* than in production (we understand more than we can comfortably express). We may understand a vast amount of vocabulary but only feel comfortable using a smaller part of that vocabulary. We might be able to figure out the general meaning of a sentence with words that we don't fully understand, such as "He obfuscated for so long that they eventually just gave up." The word "obfuscate" obviously means something non-cooperative, but without a dictionary, we may be very hesitant to try to use the word in our own sentence. We also can understand significant variations of our language including dialect, sociolect, individual stylistics, and register variation; however we are not likely to *produce* more than a small portion of the varieties that we can *comprehend*. Thus the *Linguistic Pyramid* must represent both *Language Comprehension* and *Language Expression*. (Well, have you looked up the word *obfuscated* yet? I'm not going to tell you what it means, look it up yourself!)

As we have discussed previously, each language user also has the ability to vary their language production based on *where* they are, *who* they are talking with, *what* they are talking about, and *how* the communication is being expressed and perceived. These four variables constitute *Register Variation*; but our various registers are developed over time. *Register Development* depends upon multiple language experiences, such as how language is used in a church, on a soccer field, in a classroom, and so on. Each experience broadens the entire *Linguistic Pyramid* as new pronunciations, words, word orders, and meanings are understood and incorporated into one's overall knowledge of a language.

There are actually four faces of the Linguistic Pyramid: 1) the bottom represents the phonetics of perceptive and productive language. The three ascending sides represent 2) Language Comprehension, 3) Language Expression, and 4) Register Variation (represented as a collection of thin slivers, each expanding the pyramid further across its base). Figure 2.7, below, identifies each of the four faces of the Linguistic Pyramid and the names of each adjoining face. Think of it as a spatial relation test. It might actually help if you photocopy Figure 2.7, cut along the lines and tape the pieces together into a pyramid.

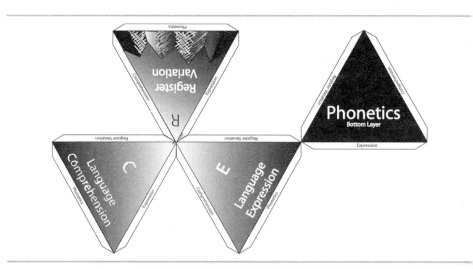

Figure 2.7 - Four Sides of the Linguistic Pyramid

We will revisit the *Linguistic Pyramid* throughout the rest of this text. It is the basis for scientifically understanding any language and we will eventually use it to systematically analyze the work of interpreting.

2.5 Language as a Subset of Communication

With all of the layers of the *Linguistic Pyramid* in place we should also recognize that language, as a specific subset of communication, includes both *production* (which begins with the phonetics of language expression) and *perception* (which is essential for language comprehension). Phonetics (the most basic layer of the *Linguistic Pyramid*) is the production of all language elements. Every other layer of the Linguistic Pyramid is built on that base for both production of language and the perception of language. The production of a message depends upon muscles moving anatomy. If these movements (or they're resulting evidence, such as writing) are perceived, then the perceiving mind begins with only the results of another person's muscle movement. The perceiving mind can attempt to reconstruct the message by applying successive layers of the *Linguistic Pyramid* to the incoming pieces. The reconstruction will be guided by the perceiver's mind, background knowledge, linguistics skills, etc. Because each perceiver's mind is unique, it is possible for multiple perceivers of the same message to generate their own nuances in meaning, or even to completely misunderstand (or outright *miss*) portions of the producer's message.

We must also recognize that additional elements of communication will generally accompany the use of language. In other words, language rarely occurs in isolation from other simultaneous paralinguistic and semiotic aspects of communication such as gestures, intonation patterns, facial expressions, etc. Therefore most attempts to communicate through language will include additional communication *outside* of language. The graphic below places the *Linguistic Pyramid* within the previous representation of communication.

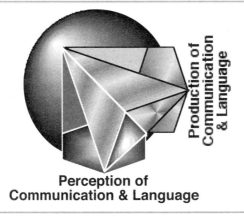

**Perception of
Communication & Language**

Figure 2.8 - The Mind's Linguistic Perception & Production

Before we go much further it might be useful to review the elements of this graphic that were previously introduced. The sphere represents the *Mind* and its knowledge about communication, about people, about facts and topics, and about the physical setting. It also includes the *conscious* and/or *unconscious* intentions to communicate. The dark-shaded hexagon-cone represents *perception* and *comprehension* of communication. The light-shaded hexagon-cone represents production and expression of communication. The addition comes in the form of the *Linguistic Pyramid,* which rests between these last two elements, half representing language comprehension as a portion of overall communication comprehension, the other half representing language production as a portion of overall communication production. The capstone of the *Linguistic Pyramid* is closest to the mind of the individual, while the phonetic base of the pyramid is included in the semiotic production and perception of the communication.

But as we discovered in the first chapter, another mind is required to establish communication. Likewise two minds are required to establish *linguistic* communication, which is represented in the following graphic.

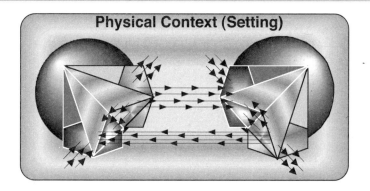

Figure 2.9 - Linguistic Communication Within a Physical Setting

This image is similar to the one presented in Figure 1.4 of chapter one, but this graphic has the addition of the *Linguistic Pyramid* overlaid upon each person's perception and production of communication. Figure 2.9 recognizes the previously mentioned elements of linguistic communication and places them in a physical setting, which provides part of the context for understanding the message. The physical setting also influences the clarity of the communication, as both participants perceive information from the environment that may have relevance to communication; or may cause interference by means of visual or auditory noise. Likewise both participants potentially generate movement, which may be part of communication or may add to the visual or auditory noise in the environment. In the midst of all of this perception is the participants' ability to monitor their own production of communication, language, and noise.

Finally, it is important to recognize that all the elements of *Register Variation* are represented in this model: 1) *Topic* (intention of communication within the mind) 2) *Language Use* (as part of the overall communication), 3) *Participants* (at least two minds engaged in communication), and 4) *Physical Setting* (providing context and also influencing message clarity).

2.6 Summary

This section has presented a number of important components of language. We began by investigating the differences between *communication* and *language*. Then we identified three distinct *channels* of language (signed, spoken, and written) along with a wide variety of *Language Encoding Systems*. Next the concept of the *Linguistic Pyramid* was introduced which identified seven interactive levels (phonetics, phonology, morphology, syntax, semantics, discourse, and stylistics) and the concept of *Register Variation*, which crosses all of these levels. Finally we placed the Linguistic Pyramid into the previous models of communication, including *productive* and *perceptive* aspects of linguistic communication.

2.6.1 Review Questions

1. How is *language* different than *communication*?
2. What researcher first brought attention to signed languages as legitimate languages?
3. How many language channels are there?
4. Which senses are used to detect language?
5. What is the difference between *Language Channels* and *Modes of Perception*?
6. How many levels are there in the *Linguistic Pyramid*?
7. What is the most basic, lowest level of the *Linguistic Pyramid*?
8. What is the difference between *phonology* and *phonetics*?
9. Which two levels of the *Linguistic Pyramid* relate to grammar?
10. What is the difference between *morphology* and *semantics*?
11. What is the difference between *discourse* and *stylistics*?
12. What four variables contribute to the concept of *register*?
13. Aside from *Phonetics*, at the base of the *Linguistic Pyramid*, what do each of the three remaining faces of the pyramid represent?

2.6.2 Suggested Activities

1. Think of three complete sentences (in either a signed or spoken language) that are each composed of only one word. What kinds of sentences are possible?
2. Watch or listen to a story (in either a signed or spoken language). Identify all the nouns in the first minute of the story. How many of the nouns were repeated within the first minute? How many of the nouns were replaced by pronouns during the first minute? How many of the nouns are conceptually related to one another? Now try retelling that same first minute of the story without using any of the nouns more than one time and without using any pronouns at all. How different does it seem from the original? Does it still make sense? Now try telling the same first minute of the story without any nouns and only using the appropriate pronouns. How interesting is the story without nouns?

Chapter 3
Language Use

"Language Use"

Timoth flipped through several pages in the book. "Pragmatics and Discourse... I don't get it."

Rasmus put several papers in a drawer and closed it, then turned toward Timoth and said "Happy Birthday!"

Timoth stared at Rasmus for a moment and finally said, "My birthday is two months away. Why are you wishing me 'happy birthday' today?"

"Wishing? I'm not wishing anything. I just said two words: 'happy' and 'birthday'. Why would you infer that I meant anything more than a list of two vocabulary items?"

Timoth's jaw dropped about an inch. Closing the book and fixing eye-gaze to Rasmus, Timoth said, "You can't be serious... a list of vocabulary items? What's the point of that?"

Rasmus smiled and leaned further back in the chair, waiting for Timoth to calm down.

Timoth stood, "You make me work too hard!" and then began to pace back and forth in front of Rasmus' desk. "OK... So I hear the words 'happy birthday' and I assume you are wishing me a happy birthday; but you say you are only listing two words."

"Keep going."

Timoth stopped pacing, and glaring at Rasmus said, "Meaning... meaning is something that each person's mind determines, so I determined the meaning of a "wish" while you CLAIM to be only intending to "list."

"So far, so good..."

Timoth walked to the chair and sat down. "The book says that pragmatics deals with people's communication goals and intentions, but also with the effects and results that are achieved by the communication."

Rasmus smiled.

"I don't understand. People saying 'happy birthday' are generally *wishing* that to the people they say it to. But you say it was only a list of two words. I can't figure it out." Timoth's head sank into cupped hands.

Rasmus leaned forward. "And you believed me when I said I was making a list?"

Timoth looked up at Rasmus. "You were lying?"

Rasmus leaned back. "Did I *say* I was lying?"

Timoth sighed and leaned back in the chair, gazing at the ceiling. "Why do you do this to me? OK. Hmm. You said you were making a list but your *intention* was for me to think about my problem – pragmatics. Saying 'happy birthday' is a culturally accepted way to wish someone a happy birthday. It is very unlikely that you would simply rattle off a list of two words for no reason, so your goal or intention was clearly to make me think about intention and goals."

"Almost there!"

"Almost?! I thought I was done!"

"You asked me if I was lying. I *never said* that I had lied", said Rasmus, with a grin.

"No. But through pragmatics I understood that you *had* lied because I knew that you really were not just making a list but saying 'happy birthday' to force me to think about pragmatics. And then you asked me a question in return... 'Did I say I was lying?' I understood that to be a denial. But you didn't *directly* deny that you lied. So pragmatics allows us to read between the lines and understand a person's true intentions?"

"Congratulations!"

Timoth smiled. "I guess that means that I got it right!"

Chapter 3 – Language Use

3.0 Overview

This chapter explores language use, including pragmatics, discourse, and language fluency. The discussion of *pragmatics* will provide a brief overview of *Grice's Maxims*, *Direct Speech Acts*, *Indirect Speech Acts*, and *Conversational Implicature*. The overview of *discourse* introduces basic concepts for the analysis of *narratives* and *conversations*. The section on *language fluency* introduces the basic concepts known as *BICS* and *CALP* as well as how the labels of A, B, and C languages interact with BICS and CALP to define language fluency. These concepts are essential aspects for effective interpreting because it is a matter of how language is used that determines the effect it has on the participants in communication. Interpreters generate target texts that affect the target consumer. It is very valuable for an interpreter to be able to recognize the intended (and unintended) effects of a source text in order to be able to work toward generating a target text that produces similar effects.

3.1 Pragmatics Revisited

Connected to the *Linguistic Pyramid* is the mind's *intent* for communication. We discussed this concept in a previous section and it can be referred to as *Pragmatics*: the study of the goals and results of communication. When we ask, "Could you pass the salt please?" we aren't really looking for a "yes" or "no" answer. We really want the salt and we want it before our food gets cold. When we ask, "Can I ask a question?" we tend to ignore the fact that we just did. And when friends start lambasting a particularly nasty co-worker who, by chance, has just entered the room, you can quickly change the discussion to who won the game last night, which (if your friends are paying attention) will let them know that it is time to stop the lambasting. If those examples seem somewhat familiar already (or maybe even *really* familiar), then you have been doing a good job reading, understanding, and *remembering* this text, which is part of my goal in creating this textbook.

Pragmatics in the mind of the person *expressing* the communication encompasses the *goals* of the communication. One of the intentions mentioned in the examples above includes getting a container of salt, but an accompanying goal is to obtain the salt without being rude or insulting anyone. The following sentences might just as quickly move the saltshaker your way:

1) "Give me the salt."
2) "This food is very bland."

Sentence one might be seen as being less polite than "Could you pass the pepper please?" while sentence two is more likely to insult the chef. Pragmatics includes *all* of the goals as well as all of the effects of the communication, not just the most obvious result. I once heard a linguistics professor ask his students about the possibilities of answering the question "Do you take this man to be your lawfully wedded husband?" The generally acceptable answers are either "Yes" or "I do". It is theoretically possible to answer "No" or "I do not"; but I have never seen these responses or even heard about real situations where either response was uttered. There are still other ways of saying "yes," such as "uh-huh," "You're darn tootin'," or even by asking questions such as "Are you suggesting that I wouldn't?" or "Is the Pope Catholic?" The pragmatics of the situation restrict the likelihood of using these alternate ways of saying "yes". They are recognized as being *unacceptable* choices.

Pragmatics, in the mind of the *perceiver* of the communication, encompasses the *results or effects* of the communication. The perceiver's results are frequently different than the producer's goals. Even the polite request "Could you pass the salt, please?" can be understood by the chef as an insult. Responding to the question "Do you take this man to be your lawfully wedded husband?" with the words "Is the Pope Catholic?" might still be understood as an acceptable response by some of the people who have the authority to perform marriages. Which responses are acceptable will depend greatly upon the people involved in the communication.

Deborah Tannen (1990) has done extensive work investigating the communication differences between men and women. Much of her research falls within the area of pragmatics and the different goals that men and women appear to have for communication. Tannen has demonstrated that women are likely to mention problems as a way of initiating conversation and look for other participants to build rapport by relating their experiences with similar problems. Men, however, are likely to perceive the mentioning of a problem as a request for help in finding a solution and are likely to work as quickly as they can toward resolution rather then expanding the topic into a conversation. Tannen's research also indicates that men tend to be very conscious of hierarchical relationships and work to avoid being seen as one-down in relation to another person. Men often joke with each other using "put-downs" about each other, which, even jokingly, has the effect of raising the one *issuing* the put-down above the person *being* put-down. Women tend to issue compliments to each other, rather than issuing put-downs. The goals behind the communication are better understood within each gender group and are more likely to be misunderstood *between* the gender groups. These general pragmatic differences between men and women can introduce additional challenges when *interpreting* between men and women.

3.1.1 Grice's Maxims

A philosopher named H.P. Grice (1975) came up with what he called a *Cooperative Principle*, which he suggested people use every time they engage in mutual communication. The Cooperative Principle includes four *maxims* related to 1) quality, 2) quantity, 3) relevance and 4) manner.

The *maxim of quality* suggests that we should only say those things we think are true and that we have evidence for. The *maxim of quantity* suggests that what we say shouldn't be so brief as to leave everyone confused about what we mean. Neither should we say so much that our audience gets bored. The *maxim of relevance* is simply that we stay on topic. The *maxim of manner* suggests that we present our information in an orderly and timely fashion and not be ambiguous.

In English or in ASL we can break these maxims by telling lies or making up information. That would break the maxim of *quality*. If a computer manual for beginners says that to solve a problem you have to reboot the computer, but nowhere does it say what you have to do to reboot (or what reboot means) then the manual is violating the maxim of *quantity* (and is likely to be thrown at the computer by a frustrated office worker). If someone is asking directions and the person being asked starts to give the history of one of the landmarks, they are not being *relevant* to the task of giving directions. If the same person mixes up the directions and puts things out of order, then that person is breaking the maxim of *manner*. So basically *Grice's maxims* ask us all to do four things in normal daily conversation: be *accurate*, give the *right amount* of information necessary, be *relevant* and provide information *clearly and concisely*.

All of these maxims tie in to the codes of ethics that govern what we do as interpreters. The maxim of *quality* says that we should give information that we believe to be true. When we interpret, the *source consumer* has already made the decision of "what is true". It is up to us to make sure that the information produced by each consumer is regenerated in the interpretation with the same convictions as each consumer.

The maxim of *quantity* says that we should give as much information as necessary. When we interpret, the *source consumer* has already made the decision of "what is necessary". It is up to us to make sure that all of that information is included in the interpretation. If it is not physically possible to provide all of the information (such as may occur during simultaneous interpreting) then we must ensure that all of the main points are preserved and as many of the supporting details as possible.

The maxim of *relevance* says that what we say should be related to the conversation. This maxim helps us to make predictions about what is being said. When a person breaks this maxim, we often have to search to find a reason for the change in topic. Sometimes we realize that it is all related if we are patient enough for the speaker to return to the main point. Regardless, we must work to maintain the same amount of relevance as the source text.

The maxim of *manner* says that we should not be incoherent in what we say. If the source message really is incoherent, however, then we are responsible for keeping it just as incoherent, especially in mental health therapy sessions. If the message is clear, we have to work to keep it just as clear in the interpretation.

3.1.2 Direct Speech Acts

When we use language, we generally are using it for a specific purpose: to get someone to do something in response. The response may be to perform an action or to understand an argument. We can work toward these responses in very obvious ways with what are called *direct speech acts*.

Direct speech acts can identify within them the act that they are making. Such acts could be commands, requests, promises, warnings, advice, and even bets. Here are some example sentences:

- "I *command* you to take that hill!"
- "I *request* a meeting with you."
- "I *promise* to be back by midnight"
- "I'm *warning* you, don't do it again!"
- "I would *advise* you to try a different one."
- "I *bet* you five bucks that my team wins."

It is also possible to perform direct speech acts without overtly identifying what the act is. Generally we can perform the same kinds of direct speech acts in the same ways with both English and ASL. Here are the same example sentences without the *performative verbs*[7] in them:

- "Take that hill!"
- "Can I meet with you?"
- "I'll be back by midnight"
- "Don't do it again!"
- "Try a different one."
- "Five bucks says that my team wins."

In English we might wish to ask for directions. We could say, "I ask you to please tell me where the nearest metro is." Or we could (more naturally) say, "Where is the nearest metro?" While the first version is more awkward, both of these examples are requests for information. Although we don't often specify what we are doing in English, ASL does seem to make more use of performative verbs, such as ASK or QUESTION, in order to clarify requests from commands.

Often when we make a promise, however, we are likely to use the word promise, but we can still make promises without the word promise: "I promise I will pay you back tomorrow," vs. "I will pay you back tomorrow."

In these examples we are actually doing something with the words we say. We can use our words to do many things. Juries can *find* people guilty of crimes. Judges can *sentence* people to years of prison time. Congress can *declare* war. Pastors can *pronounce* people husbands and wives. These are all actions that take place simply in the *saying* that they are so. To a smaller degree, we do the same things every day.

The most common things we do with words are attempts to direct some kind of action. We call these speech acts "directives." When we say, "Go to the store and get a loaf of bread." we are using a directive. We can modify directives so that they are less offensive, such as "If you don't mind, could you please go to the store and get a loaf of bread." In different power relationships we are more or less likely to use modifications to our directives. A military sergeant is *less likely* to modify a directive to new recruits ("*If you don't mind,* maggot, give me twenty!"). A freshman in high school might use more modifications when talking to a senior ("*Um, excuse me,* can I get through here?"). So basically the notion that we can do things with words is what *direct speech acts* are all about. By *saying* something we also are *doing* something.

Whenever we interpret, we need to be aware of what the speaker of the source text is trying *to do* with their words. Are they trying to *convince* people of something? Are they *asking* for information? Are they *demanding* something? We must ensure that our interpretations carry the same kinds of speech acts in them.

For example, suppose a hearing consumer says, "What is your name?" This question is a request for information. If we do not convey it as a question, the deaf person may feel he has just been renamed "What." ("Ladies and gentlemen, allow me to introduce… Miss What!") If we convey the *request* in English as a *request* in ASL, with proper word order and facial grammar, then the deaf consumer is likely to respond in a way that the hearing consumer expected.

---

[7] Performative Verbs are verbs that directly state, or identify, the direct speech act being accomplished, such as *command, request, promise, advise, warn,* or *bet.*

3.1.3 Indirect Speech Acts

While direct speech acts are *obvious* attempts at getting someone to do something, there are also less obvious ways, which on the surface seem to be doing something other than what we really want. These are called *indirect speech acts*. Indirect speech acts occur when the form of the utterance does not overtly reveal what the real action is. A warning might be disguised as a promise, a command disguised as a request, advice disguised as a statement. Again there are similarities in how these are done between ASL and English, but there are cultural differences in how often indirect speech acts are used. Here are some of the same example sentences[8] changed to indirect speech acts:

- "Do you think you could take that hill soon?"
- "We ought to meet sometime soon."
- "I promise you will be in pain if you do that again."
- "If a guy were smart he'd try a different one."

In English we might wish to have an action done but we might also not want to sound bossy. Instead of using a direct command such as "Close the window." We could ask, "Could you close the window." We could even be less direct and say "Gosh it's cold in here." These last two are examples of indirect speech acts. They are still *directives*, but they are disguised in forms other than a direct request. The first one, "Could you close the window," does specify the action we want, but instead of framing it within a *command* structure, it makes use of a *request* form. The latter example, "Gosh it's cold in here," is a hint, which is even less direct than the first example because it does not even specify the action desired. It doesn't even specify that anyone should do anything at all, yet it can still function as a command if the speaker is in a position of authority.

If the speaker were not in a position of authority, then the same statements would be understood as requests, which *could* be refused. In this case the first example is now a direct speech act because it really is a request, one that could receive an answer of "no." The last example about being cold is still an indirect request so long as the person really did want someone to do something.

So basically the use of *direct* and *indirect* speech acts is happening all the time. Every time we say something we are at least telling other people to listen to us and perhaps agree with us. Beyond listening and agreeing we might even want people to do other things or we might wish to indicate that we will do certain things. We can present a case for *everything that has ever been said* to be a speech act or even a set of speech acts with the purpose of accomplishing some goal.

Whenever we interpret, we must keep in mind what the *goals of the speaker* are. Is the speaker trying to *convince* us, *inspire* us, *encourage* us, *warn* us, *promise* things to us, *ask* things of us? Is the speaker being clear, through *direct speech acts*, that they want this kind of action; or are they using *indirect speech acts* to accomplish their goals? We can sometimes match the use of direct speech acts in one language to direct speech acts in another; and likewise we can sometimes match indirect speech acts in one language to indirect speech acts in another; but ASL tends to be *more direct* while English is *less direct*. This means we must be able to regenerate some *direct* speech acts in ASL as

---

[8] The direct speech acts of *promises* and *bets* are not easily accomplished as *indirect speech acts*, and therefore are not included in the examples.

indirect speech acts in English, and we must also have the ability to regenerate some *indirect* speech acts in English as *direct* speech acts in ASL. If the hearing consumer gives a hint as a form of a directive, such as "There's a pencil on the table." we might wish to regenerate the directive in ASL as "PENCIL THERE, GIVE-ME, PLEASE." Likewise, a direct request in ASL like "TELL ME YOUR PHONE-NUMBER" might be regenerated as "Could I have your phone number (please)?"

3.1.4 Conversational Implicature

"Eat your waffle. You will become strong." These two sentences suggest a cause and effect relationship between them. Such connections between ideas are called *Conversational Implicature*. In reality these are two separate sentences. Eating a waffle may have no effect on one's strength; but the juxtaposition of these two sentences would leave you believing that you had just been told that waffles make you strong.

Advertisers depend upon implicatures so that consumers will make connections between ideas that have not been overtly connected. For example, the phrase "New and Improved" does not state what the "Old and Unimproved" were. Each time a corn flake is made, it is newer than those made the day before; and if there was ever an improvement made, even a hundred years ago, then today's cornflake is improved as compared to the corn flakes made a hundred-and-one years ago. What the consumer understands is that today's corn flake is different and better than yesterday's corn flake, but the advertisement didn't directly make that claim. It is actually very likely that today's corn flake is exactly identical to yesterday's corn flake; the only thing different is the advertising on the box.

I once read a spaghetti sauce label that made the claim that the contents of the can had "More than five times the amount of meat" contained in a rival's product. When I looked at the rival's product, I noticed that the rival's sauce contained *no meat whatsoever*. The advertising made two implications at once: 1) it implied that the rival product actually contained *some amount* of meat and 2) it implied that there was an *incredibly larger quantity* of meat contained in the advertised product. Notice that the advertised product was said to have "more" than five times the amount of meat. It did not claim to have *exactly* five times the amount of meat – if it was *exactly equal* to five times the amount of meat then it would also have had *no meat at all* (five times zero still equals zero). Given that the rival product contained no meat, the advertised product merely needed one single scrap of meat in order to live up to its claim. It could even have accurately claimed that it had more than *ten million* times the meat of the other product!

Conversational implicatures provide a particular area of concern for interpreters. Often the implicature is indeed intended, and is actually essential for creating a target text that will result in the target consumer understanding the source consumer's intentions. The interpreter *might* choose to directly generate the implicature and restate the example sentences as "Eat your waffle because it will make you strong." The potential risk is that the source consumer can claim, "I didn't say that" and be technically accurate. If this happens, then it may cause consumers to doubt an interpreter's abilities. When in doubt about the source consumer's intentions, the interpreter should strive to maintain the separate pieces of information: "Eat your waffle. You will become strong." This allows the target consumers to make their own conversational implicatures.

3.2 Discourse Analysis

A significant part of communicating intentions and goals is *how* they are communicated. *Discourse Analysis* offers an exploration into how people organize their ideas. Traditionally discourse analysis has focused on two distinct forms of communication: *Narratives* and *Conversations*. Narratives are primarily *monologic* communication where one person is telling a story; although listeners to the story may contribute some elements of the narrative, such as questions or reactions. Conversations are typically *dialogic* and require negotiations between two (or more) people to exchange turns and advance various topics in the conversation. Understanding how discourse is organized is extremely beneficial to the work of professional interpreters. Not all languages organize their discourse in parallel ways. Understanding the similarities and differences between each language's organization patterns can ease the process of interpreting.

3.2.1 Discourse Analysis of Narratives

Narrative structures in English tend to follow similar patterns, beginning with an ABSTRACT, then ORIENTATION clauses, followed by the introduction of COMPLICATING ACTION, EVALUATION statements, some form of RESULT or RESOLUTION, and finally the CODA.

The ABSTRACT announces that a story is about to begin. It can be overt - "Let me tell you the story about ..." or subtle - "That's when I met Bob." It may even be given by another person "John, tell us about how you met Ellen."

ORIENTATION clauses provide set-up and will generally occur after the abstract and before the complicating action, but they can also occur in the midst of other parts of the narrative. They tend to be past progressive tense in English such as "I was going to the store on New Year's Day..."

COMPLICATING ACTION involves utterances that describe events in the same order as the chronological order of the events. "I went into the room. I saw an earring on the floor and I bent down to pick it up. Suddenly this woman came into the room."

EVALUATION utterances are asides to the story. They may reveal the thoughts of the narrator or other characters, such as "I was really nervous". They may be comments from the listeners "I bet you were nervous."

RESULT or RESOLUTION utterances convey the *highlight* of the narrative: "And then she kissed me!"

CODA is the conclusion and exit from the narrative mode. "And three months later we were married!"

This same pattern (*abstract, orientation, complicating action, evaluation, resolution, and coda*) is generally true in both English and ASL narratives. Other structures of organization may come into play for either language. One common structure for ASL is the use of *constructed dialogues*, which is less commonly used in English. Constructed dialogues (in either language) may be attempts to report an actual dialogue, or they may be hypothetical conversations. Constructed dialogues in ASL make use of various nonmanual signals and signing space to establish a representation of conversation, but told by a single person.

Cynthia Roy's research (1989) indicated that constructed dialogues within an ASL academic lecture provided a challenge for interpreters generating an English target text. The direct audience of the ASL lecture (understanding the lecture in ASL, not through an interpretation) agreed that they had seen an appropriate academic lecture. Roy used this lecture as a source text for several interpreters to generate English interpretations, which were then evaluated by hearing people who had not seen the original ASL lecture. Some of the English interpretations maintained the use of constructed dialogues, but the evaluators perceived the interpretation as being a *children's story* rather than an *academic lecture*.

3.2.2 Discourse Analysis of Conversations

Conversational structures in English tend to occur in dyads. That is, even when three or more people are participating in a conversation, there are generally two people engaged in the conversation at any point and additional people participate to lesser extents. This does not mean that the entire conversation will be primarily between two people, but in general the level of participation between three or more people in a conversation will not be balanced equally all of the time. If more than three people have a balance of participation all of the time then it is likely that there are actually *multiple conversations* taking place rather than a single conversation with multiple participants.

Successful conversations require clear signals of when turns end and that another participant is about to take a turn. These signals identify the boundaries of *Conversational Exchanges*. We tend to signal the end of our turn with 1) *discourse markers* such as "so..." or "anyway...", 2) *direct signaling* such as "So what do you think?" or "Do you agree?", 3) *vocal paralinguistic features*, such as modifying the pitch, volume, or speed of the last few words of our turn, or 4) *gestural paralinguistic features*, such as using body movements or eye gaze which signals our willingness to let another person take a turn.

In ASL one person may offer a turn to the other conversation partner by making eye contact or by asking a question. Turns can be taken by moving the hands into signing space to wave/signal or to just start signing, thus taking a conversational turn.

We don't always end our turns with signals but are sometimes cut off by someone who had opted to take a turn. It is possible to self-select to take a turn, to select the next speaker, or to self-select to take a second turn when no one else has opted to take a turn after your turn has ended.

Another term for conversational exchanges is ADJACENCY PAIRS. These generally consist of INITIATING utterances (I), RESPONSE utterances (R), and FEEDBACK utterances (F). The following exchange is an example of these kinds of utterances:

> A: Did you finish the project? (I)
> B: Yup! I finished at midnight (R)
> A: Great! (F) I bet you're tired. (I)
> B: A little. (R) What time did you start today? (I)
> A: Six-thirty. (R)

Other general ways that we organize our conversations are with 1) OPENINGS such as "How's it going?" or "Excuse me...", 2) FEEDBACK REQUESTS from the speaker such as "you with me so far?" or "right?...", 3) CLARIFICATION REQUESTS from the listener such as "you mean..." or "come again?", 4) TOPIC CHANGES such as "Oh! that reminds me..." or "before I forget...", and 5) CLOSINGS such as "Well, gotta go" or "Thanks for stopping by."

Cynthia Roy (1989b) investigated the interpreter's role in turn exchanges. She analyzed videotape of an interpreted conversation between a deaf student and a hearing teacher for a college course. Her conclusions were that *interpreters* actually determine the turn exchanges between the two conversation partners. In effect, each is having a conversation with the interpreter and neither consumer is easily able to take a turn without the consent of the interpreter. Understanding this dynamic helps interpreters to understand the need to be responsive to various signals that both hearing and deaf consumers are generating regarding turn taking.

Part of the problem with turn taking in interpreted conversations is the fact that the participants are not attending to the same signaling devices for turn taking. Only the interpreter is aware of both languages' ways of indicating the ends of conversational turns. Another part of the problem is the inherent time-delay due to interpreting. Signals for turn taking in conversations tend to be fairly spontaneous and very immediate. Because of the time delay through interpreting it may be necessary for the interpreter to interrupt the conversation flow in order to allow for one consumer or the other to take a turn.

3.3 Language Fluency

A very significant factor to consider is the fluency of the people communicating with each other. Children achieve basic fluency at the point that their ability meets the definition of language. So what was that definition of language again? *Language is the systematic use of symbols to express and perceive information between members of a community, in which the system is rule-governed, has infinite production possibilities, is intergenerational, and changes over time.*

Children begin their road to fluency by learning how to make the *words* of the language (*systematic use of symbols*). This requires that they use these words to *express* and *perceive* information with other people. If the children are acquiring the language of adults then their acquisition is *intergenerational*. Children finally achieve fluency when they start to apply *rules* to the language they are learning so that they create new sentences that they have never heard before. All of this normally happens by the time a child is four years old. This doesn't mean that the child is *finished* learning that language, but we can now say that the child is *fluent* in her first language(s). This process in children is called *language acquisition*, rather than *language learning*, because the child is not usually taught the rules; instead, the child figures them out all on her own. In fact, efforts to *directly teach* the rules to young children are usually rejected or misunderstood by the child.

Adults pursuing *second language fluency* generally begin from the knowledge they already have about their native language(s). There is significant research indicating that after puberty, when a child becomes an adult, the ability to *acquire* a language is significantly diminished. This means that adults generally have to learn at least part of their second language through direct instruction about vocabulary and rules. As a general rule, the *younger* a person is when they start to learn a second language, the *easier* it will be to attain fluency.

So what is fluency? If a child achieves fluency by the age of four, how long does it take an adult to achieve it? Of course the answer is "it depends" but the same test applies to both child fluency and adult fluency. If the adult is *systematically using symbols* to *express* and *perceive* information with other people (a skill usually achieved halfway through an introductory class) then the road to fluency has begun. The rest of the battle is that the use is *rule-governed*, using the rules of the language being learned, not the rules of the native language(s) already known to the adult learner. Once the adult can *intuitively* express new and grammatical sentences (not just memorized patterns) then that adult has achieved basic fluency. We generally should expect that level of skill before completion of intermediate-level classes. As mentioned before, four-year-old children, like new learners of a second language, can be fluent, yet still have much to learn about their language.

It is important to remember two sides of the *Linguistic Pyramid*: *Language Comprehension* and *Language Production*. Generally we have greater ability to understand a message than to produce it. Comprehension is where true fluency begins. Second-language learners generally begin with a reversal of this normal pattern. They initially exhibit a greater ability to *produce* the elements of language, while struggling to *comprehend* spontaneous information. In other words, second-language learners start out with an ability to easily make themselves understood, but frequently need repetition or very slow presentations of the second language in order to comprehend accurately. People are not *fluent* in a language until their ability to comprehend *at least matches* their ability to produce the language. The next section will help to differentiate different kinds of fluency.

3.3.1 BICS and CALP

J. Cummins (1984) proposed two distinct kinds of language fluency. One is the ability to exchange greetings, make purchases, issue complaints and just generally *interact* with other people. This is known as *Basic Interpersonal Communication Skills* (BICS). A higher level of fluency is the ability to use more complex grammatical structures of the language in order to understand and create academic lectures, understand legal procedures, and participate in technical discussions. This is known as *Cognitive Academic Language Proficiency* (CALP). With these two labels it is possible to better define the kind of fluency a person has.

During an internationally publicized California trial in the 1990s there was much confusion about why one particular witness needed an interpreter when she could speak perfectly intelligible English sentences. Rosa Lopez was an immigrant from El Salvador. Her native language was Spanish and the court interpreter was providing interpretations of the attorney's questions from English into Spanish, but she would respond directly in clear English. So why did Rosa need an interpreter?

If we understand the difference between BICS and CALP, we can understand the need for the interpreter. The language of a courtroom is very formal, even painfully technical in the precision used to ask questions. Sometimes this precise use of questions can then be used against a witness who may have misunderstood the intent of different questions and appear to be changing their testimony. Rosa Lopez had dropped out of school at the age of nine to help her family harvest crops. The value of having an interpreter in the courtroom was to ensure that she clearly understood the questions, which required *Cognitive Academic Language Proficiency* in English. The responses (often as simple as "yes" or "no") rarely required more than *Basic Interpersonal*

Communication Skills and therefore could be expressed directly rather than through the services of the interpreter.

BICS provides basic conversational fluency and can mislead people to believe that a person is completely fluent in a language. CALP typically begins when a person learns to read and begins to explore academic and technical uses of a language. BICS fluency is more easily achieved but may depend on memorized routine phrases more than true ability to generate original grammatical sentences. CALP fluency requires BICS fluency first. CALP fluency in both languages is required for a person to function as a professional interpreter.

3.3.2 A, B, and C Languages

Now that we have a working understanding of *fluency*, we can explore another set of labels that help us define the linguistic skills of interpreters. These labels are "A", "B", and "C" Languages. These labels help us to quickly identify the strong, middle, and weak language abilities of an interpreter. An "A" language is one in which the interpreter not only has *Cognitive Academic Language Proficiency*, but is also considered natively fluent (or near-native). Interpreters who were raised past puberty in bilingual environments will usually have two "A" languages. A person who begins by using one language, but then learns others later in life will probably have only one "A" language. If that person has managed to eliminate any hint of an accent and can pass as a native user of a language then she has become "near-native" and can count that language as an "A" language.

The next category is the "B" language. "B" languages are those languages that are controlled into CALP, but not to the level of native fluency. In my own experience, I grew up using English as my native language and have English as my "A" language. Although my fluency in ASL is sufficient to attain RID Certification as an interpreter, subtle aspects of my language use will reveal to a careful observer that I am not a native user of the language. Therefore ASL is my "B" language.

"A" languages are not always one's native language. A friend of mine, Vut, grew up in Thailand and then moved to the US when he was seven. Vut completed a Bachelors degree in Engineering and worked with the US Navy. He clearly has both BICS and CALP skills in English, but it is still noticeable that English is not his native language. English is Vut's "B" language. Although he still knows Thai and uses it regularly with his family, he only knows how to speak Thai at a BICS level of fluency – he never received any significant formal education in Thai. When he visited Thailand as an adult, he found that he could not read the newspaper, advertisements, or even street signs. He felt like a child when asking for directions because although he could communicate and understand the responses, he could not read for himself to know when he had arrived at the correct street. Although it is his native language (and he still *sounds* like a native to other Thai users), Thai functions as a "C" language for Vut.

"C" languages are languages that are not known beyond BICS fluency. They may be useful for basic communication as long as both parties to the communication are willing to negotiate meaning. If Vut were to relocate to Thailand, he might eventually achieve CALP in Thai, which combined with his native pronunciation and BICS abilities would allow Thai – currently his "C" language – to become an "A" language.

As a general rule, interpretations are most likely to be idiomatic (natural) and culturally complete when the target language is one of the interpreter's "A" languages.

The range of interpretations into a "B" language are likely to be either literal (word-for-word) or a mixture of literal and idiomatic, but not likely to be wholly idiomatic, or natural. Therefore there is a general preference for interpreters to work into one of their "A" languages rather than their "B" languages. It is unacceptable for an interpreter to attempt professional work involving any of their "C" languages.

3.3.3 Multilingual, Monolingual, and Semilingual Language Abilities

No human being is *guaranteed* to attain language fluency. Fluency requires social interactions with other community members who share the same language. Even if there are *multiple* languages within the community (or multiple communities with different languages) children will still naturally acquire *every* language that they are regularly and interactively exposed to. Interactive exposure to language requires *access* to the modality of expression for the language channels being used. This means that a deaf child does not have natural, interactive exposure to spoken English expressed through sound. Likewise a blind child does not have natural interactive exposure to written English expressed through images. Modifications that transfer sound to image for a deaf child (such as manual cues), or image to texture for a blind child (such as Braille) can provide access. Language access can only become true language exposure if the child regularly encounters the language in an accessible form. Thus the use of manual cues may provide access, but deaf children must be *regularly exposed* to this visual encoding of spoken languages if they are to gain fluency via manual cues. Likewise the blind child must have regular exposure to written language via Braille in order to gain fluency through the encoding system of Braille.

So there are two key variables: *access* and *interactive exposure*. I know a family where the children's grandmother is monolingual in Cantonese. For one year she lived with her daughter and son-in-law and she had regular daily interaction with her grandchildren. The children understood her and were beginning to develop BICS skills in Cantonese. Once the grandmother relocated to another city the children no longer had regular, interactive exposure to Cantonese. The children now have no significant ability to speak or understand anything in Cantonese.

A child who does not yet have BICS fluency in any language is considered to be *Alingual* (without language). This may occur where the child does not have either *access* or *regular exposure* to any language. The child may know some basic vocabulary items but will not consistently demonstrate grammatical sentences in the language. If the child has this kind of partial knowledge of more than one language then the child is considered to be *Semilingual*. One of the greatest dangers is that an *Alingual* or *Semilingual* child will fail to gain fluency in a language before puberty. Research suggests that once the physical changes of puberty have taken place, the human mind is no longer capable of attaining native fluency in a first language.

Most children easily attain at least *monolingual fluency* in a language, meaning that they have at least BICS skill in one language; but research also indicates that a child who has attained monolingual fluency prior to puberty will retain some ability to gain fluency in any number of *additional* languages.

If a person gains fluency in two languages then the person is *bilingual*. The challenge for a child to become bilingual is to have access and regular exposure to *both* languages with predictable patterns for the use of each language. This means that the child will know when each language is the right one to use. One example of predictable patterns of language use includes having some people who only use one language while other people only use another (such as a mother who speaks French and a father who speaks German). Predictable patterns of language use can also include the use of one language only in certain settings (such as special community events) or the use of one language only for specific purposes (such as in religious services).

As children receive more accessible interactive exposure to a language, they will gain greater fluency in that language. If a child is only exposed to Hebrew during attendance of large-group religious services and otherwise only exposed to English then the child is not likely to gain even BICS skills in Hebrew. If that same child has weekly *interactive* religious instruction in Hebrew, then the child's language fluency is much more likely to develop into BICS and perhaps even into CALP. A deaf child who is consistently exposed to spoken English through manual cues at home, and to American Sign Language at school, is very likely to attain *balanced bilingualism*. Balanced bilingualism occurs when a person has achieved equal levels of fluency in both languages (such as having BICS and CALP in both languages).

If a person gains at least BICS fluency in three or more languages then the person is *multilingual*. Generally multilingual skills require that the language of the home is different than the language of the majority community surrounding the home and that there be yet another language used regularly either in the home or in the surrounding community. While multilingualism is possible, it is less common than bilingualism. The primary reason for this is that multilingualism requires regular exposure to three or more languages in three or more language communities. There are very few *stable* multilingual communities. The conditions that lead to multilingualism are unlikely except in the cases of people moving to a new language community, marrying into a new language community, or both.

3.4 Summary

This section has presented a number of important components of language. We began by investigating several different aspects of *Pragmatics*, such as the four maxims of Grice's *Cooperative Principle*, direct speech acts, indirect speech acts, and conversational implicature. We then explored two different aspects of discourse analysis: narratives and conversations.

We explored different kinds of fluency starting with *Basic Interpersonal Communication Skills* (BICS) and *Cognitive Academic Language Proficiency* (CALP). We identified the differences between "A", "B", and "C" languages and how language fluency in one language can affect the process of learning a second language. Next we explored the labels of *Alingual, Semilingual, Monolingual, Bilingual,* and *Multilingual* language abilities.

All of these topics have direct impact upon the interpreting process. The best way to master these topics is to continually strive for greater language fluency in every language that you use in your interpreting work. This includes observing the language use of other people but also thinking reflectively about your own language use and how language is used to accomplish things, often without directly stating the intended goals of the communication. Another form of analysis that can be helpful is to compare the different ways that each language accomplishes things. Is one language more direct than the other? Try to think of several different, yet appropriate, ways to accomplish the same thing in each language. Verify your approaches with native users of each language.

3.4.1 Review Questions

1. What are the four maxims of Grice's *Cooperative Principle*?
2. How are Grice's four maxims relevant to interpreting?
3. Provide two examples each of *Indirect Speech Acts* and *Direct Speech Acts.*
4. Provide your own example of conversational implicature.
5. What are the primary components of most narratives?
6. What kinds of turn-signaling devices are used in ASL and English conversations?
7. What do the acronyms BICS and CALP represent?
8. What kinds of fluency are identified by the labels "A", "B", and "C" languages?
9. What is the difference between *Alingual* and *Semilingual* language ability?
10. What two important variables must be present for a person to attain *monolingual fluency* in a language?
11. What does *balanced bilingualism* mean?
12. What kinds of conditions would lead to a person becoming *multilingual*?

3.4.2 Suggested Activities

1. Generate six sentences that are *direct speech acts* that use performative verbs to identify the speech act being generated. Now convert each sentence into a direct speech act that does *not* directly identify the speech act being accomplished. Example: "I *order* you to give me that briefcase." might become "Give me that brief case."
2. Generate six *indirect speech acts* for each of the sentences you generated in the task above. Example: "Could you give me that brief case?"
3. Watch or Listen to a lecture (in either a signed or spoken language). What discourse markers (organizing words) are used to organize the lecture? What parts of the lecture help you predict parts that are coming up later? What parts review previous information? What does the presenter do to let you know that a piece of information is particularly important?
4. Watch a videotaped recording of an interpretation of a conversation (one-to-one interpreting)[9]. Identify the different ways that each consumer of interpreting services signaled turn exchanges. Identify how the interpreter signaled these turn exchanges.

---

[9] Various samples of one-to-one interpreting can be purchased from Sign Enhancers, Inc.

Chapter 4
Language Variation

"Language Variation"

Rasmus looked closely at Timoth and said, "You're serious?"

Timoth repeated, "Yes, he was signing English."

"Surely you mean fingerspelling!?"

"No. *Signing* English."

"There is no such thing as signing English! You can write it or speak it. You can encode the writing with Braille, fingerspelling, semaphore, Morse, typed text, or squiggly lines on paper. You can encode the speaking with cues or various combinations of the larynx, tongue, and oral cavity. But there is no way to *sign* any *spoken* language."

"I saw him doing it."

"Tell me *exactly* what you saw."

Timoth went into the best detail possible. Signs and sign pieces that could be matched to English syntax. Mouth movement patterns that matched English words.

Rasmus looked Timoth in the eye again. "So what makes you think all of that was English?"

Timoth answered, "Because I could hear English in my head. It made sense to me and it didn't look like the signing we see here in the community."

"Did it ever occur to you that you know English?"

"What do you mean? Of course I know English. What has that to do with anything?"

Rasmus smiled. "You, Timoth, have used your native-language knowledge to process another person's communication output. You saw some similarities in syntax and you came to the conclusion that his communication output was the same as one of your native languages."

"You mean it wasn't English?"

"He has no more ability to *sign* English than you or I are able to *speak* OSL!"

"Well if it wasn't English, then what was it?"

"Timoth, you have much to learn about variety in languages. You recognized the signs, yes?"

"Of course. If I hadn't understood the signs, how could I have communicated with him?"

"And what language do the signs come from, Our Sign Language or English?"

Timoth fingerspelled "O-S-L"

"Communication is easy, Timoth. Language is hard. An ape can communicate, but the only primates to ever acquire or learn a language are called humans. That doesn't mean that we *always* use language to communicate, but it does give us the edge."

Timoth stared at the ground for a moment, then looked at Rasmus, "You mean that he wasn't using any language at all?"

Rasmus laughed. "How am I supposed to know? You met one person. Are there others who share his communication system? Is it orderly and rule-governed? What is its history? Until we know the answers to these questions it is not possible to determine whether you saw language or merely communication."

Timoth smiled and looked at Rasmus. "So you don't know all the answers!"

"No, Timoth. But I do know many of the questions."

Chapter 4 – Language Variation

"May You Live in Interesting Times." - Ancient Chinese Curse

4.0 Overview

In any language community there will be some amount of variety in how the language is used between different people. There are many factors that influence these varieties of language use. Every person has their own idiosyncrasies in how they use their language including different ways of talking with different kinds of people. As the previous chapter mentioned, *Register Variation* can account for the changes in the way we pronounce our words, which words we use, what we mean by our words, and even what kind of word orders we use.

When we communicate with children or foreigners, we tend to use the most basic patterns of our language with them because we assume that they will not understand the more complicated patterns of our language. In English we may take a passive construction such as "John was delivered the summons last night" and convey it very differently to a non-native user of English: "The police gave John a paper last night. The paper says that John must go to a court of law." Every language on earth has basic sentence patterns and rules that allow transformations from those basic patterns to more complex sentences.

This chapter begins with a brief discussion of three basic factors influencing communication and then provides an introduction to language variation. The primary focus of this chapter is the history of research regarding variation in American Sign Language. A secondary goal is to present a revised model of language contact between ASL and English which can be generally applied to describe all language contact between signed and spoken languages world-wide.

4.1 Language Variation

There are five primary kinds of variation in language: *Register Variation*, *Variation in Language Fluency*, *Dialect*, *Sociolect*, and *Language Contact*. We have already investigated *Register Variation* as part of the *Linguistic Pyramid*: every language user is likely to vary how they use their language based on register (how they are communicating, who is talking to whom, about what topic, and in what setting). *Language Fluency* is of concern primarily when a person has not had full access to a language during childhood. *Register* and *Fluency* can explain language variation within a single person.

The remaining labels (*Dialect*, *Sociolect*, and *Language Contact*) identify variation between users of language. *Dialect* (also known as *Regional Dialect*) refers to variation in language based on geography, such as differences in spoken English between folks from Sydney, London, Toronto, and Dallas. *Sociolect* (also known as *Social Dialect*) refers to variation in language based on any of four sub variables: 1) social class (such as differences between the aristocracy and East Enders in London), 2) gender (differences between men and women), 3) ethnicity (differences between distinct cultures which share the same language), and 4) generation membership (chronological differences between younger and older users of the language). *Language Contact* refers to variation in language based on the interaction of two or more languages.

4.1.1 Dialect Variation

Dialects *are variations of a language that are used in differing geographical regions.* Generally this regional variation of a language is intelligible to regional neighbors who speak other dialects of the same language. The labels of *language* and *dialect* may be employed for political purposes, however. Swedish and Norwegian are reported to be mutually intelligible and ought to be considered dialects of the same language. But since each region has a different government, politics dictates that they be identified as distinct languages: Norway wouldn't want to suggest that their national language is a dialect of Swedish; and neither would Sweden want to acknowledge that their national language is a dialect of Norwegian. So Sweden and Norway have mutually intelligible languages that really ought to be considered dialects of the same language.

China offers the opposite dilemma. China is a vast country with over one billion inhabitants. Written Chinese is used throughout the country, but written Chinese is not a phonetic system: its symbols don't identify any aspect of pronunciation. Written Chinese is built out of ideographs which represent meaning independent of sound. Native users of this written system need not share the same spoken language at all. In fact, at the extreme corners of the country, Chinese people speak in ways that are not mutually intelligible at all. Officially, the Chinese government considers each of these different languages as dialects of one national language: Chinese. Although many of the "dialects" of Chinese are not mutually intelligible, they are called dialects rather than languages in order to provide the appearance of cohesion within the country.

The variations of English between Australia, Canada, Great Britain, and the United States are all correctly identified as *Dialects*. They each have variations in vocabulary and in usage of the language, but remain, for the most part, mutually intelligible. The Signed Languages of each location, however, are less mutually intelligible. American Sign Language is used in both the United States and Canada, but parts of Canada also use Quebec Sign Language (LSQ). British Sign Language (BSL) and Australian Sign Language (Auslan) are historically related to each other but only distantly related to American Sign Language. ASL, Auslan, BSL, and LSQ all have historical relations to French Sign Language, but all are now distinct languages, not dialects of any one single language.

Regional Dialect in signed languages appears to be significantly tied to variation between residential schools for deaf children. Vocabulary choices for some common concepts (for example: garbage, candy, hospital, laundry) may have completely unrelated signs at one or another residential school. Other lexical items, such as "birthday" or "picnic" in ASL, are notoriously different nationwide. ASL users can often easily generate lengthy listings of multiple signs which have been seen from various ASL users from different locations in the US and Canada.

4.1.2 Sociolect Variation

Sociolects *are differences in language production and language use that are based on* *social differences.* These social groups may be based on class, gender, ethnicity, or generational differences. Eric Shapiro (1993) performed interviews with deaf adult women of different socio-economic status. His results indicated some differences in the use of nonmanual elements of ASL and also in the length of utterance with the higher class status linked to reduced nonmanuals and increased utterance lengths.

Several attempts at discerning differences in the use of ASL between men and women have been attempted (Mansfield, 1993; McMurtie, 1993; Bridges, 1992; and Nowell, 1989). Nowell (1989) attempted to find differences in turn-taking strategies and length of turn between a man and woman during an interview, but was unable to identify any statistically significant difference except between on-task versus off-task communication where the woman demonstrated a larger portion of communication between interview segments when the researcher would leave the room but the videocamera continued to collect data[10]. McMurtie (1993) investigated devices for providing feedback during ASL conversations between four deaf adults, two male and two female. Her results indicate no significant differences between the men and women, who all used four different feedback markers (head nods, smiles, the sign CORRECT, and the sign YES). Malloy and Doner (1995) investigated elements of cohesion in an ASL conversation between a man and woman and determined only a slight difference in the use of reiteration (used more by the man).

Bridges (1992) investigated and identified a variety of lexical differences in the use of sexual signs between men and women. Mansfield (1993) demonstrated lexical differences between men and women when discussing items used for feminine hygiene and other objects generally associated with either men or women. Therefore the research has shown the most significant variation in ASL between men and women to be a difference in familiarity and use of some lexical items.

Lexical difference was also the most significant variation found in research of ethnic variation in ASL (Woodward, 1976; Aramburo, 1989; Guggenheim, 1992). Bruce (1993) identified only a slight difference in the production of head nods for feedback during interviews conducted between black and white versus black and black Deaf people.

Studies in generational variation in ASL include Gartner and Watts (1996), who identified lexical variation, and Blattberg, et. al (1995) who determined not only that older signers make more frequent use of fingerspelling, but also use it in a distinctly different, cohesive way. They found that older deaf signers would spell items in various spatial locations to associate the fingerspelled item to previous portions of their discourse. Kelly (1995) identified a pattern of alternating fingerspelling and production of related lexical items among Deaf senior citizens.

Across all four possible influences upon sociolect (social class, gender, ethnicity, and generation) the most significant impact noted within ASL to date has been upon lexical choice – the words. Less significant differences have been noted for the amount of nonmanual features and the use of feedback, and cohesion (except for the use of fingerspelling as an element for cohesion among older signers, which *does* appear to be a significant difference). This research indicates that the most common element of variation for both *regional dialect* and *sociolect* variation is lexical variation (vocabulary). Thus the greatest impact upon the interpreting process will be either recognizing or being able to produce the correct ASL vocabulary given the region, gender, ethnicity, and generation of the consumers.

---

[10] This is a common research technique used to capture "natural" language use without the influence of the researcher in the room.

4.1.3 Register Variation

Register Variation was previously discussed in detail in Chapter Two as part of the *Linguistic Pyramid*. Register variation can account for differences in phonology, morphology, syntax and discourse strategies. In short, *Register Variation* is simply the influence of four variables upon communication: participants, topic, physical context, and expressive modality. In even simpler terms these boil down to *Who*, *What*, *Where*, and *How*. For a more complete explanation, please review section 2.3.8.

4.1.4 Idiomatic Language Use

We can expand the concept of *Register Variation* to an important concept for interpreting: *Idiomatic use* of language. Idiomatic use of language occurs when a message is produced in such a way that it appears to be completely normal and natural. It is very likely that a native speaker of a language will have little difficulty demonstrating idiomatic language use. In fact, we depend on idiomatic language use as one means of determining that a person is a native language user. If a person uses grammatical, yet "odd" sentences then the language use is not idiomatic. One example is a sign posted in a restaurant which said "English speeched goodly here" which was obviously not written by a native user of the language. Idiomatic language use means that the grammatical structure is not only correct but also appropriate and that the words are commonly used for the intended meaning.

4.1.5 Language Contact

Language Contact occurs when bilinguals interact and switch between elements of their shared languages. They may begin conversing in one language, momentarily borrow a word or phrase from another language, and then return to using the first language. This is known as *Code Switching*. Another form of language contact involves a more continuous mixing of language elements, such as using the vocabulary of one language and the syntax of another. This is known as *Code Mixing*. Variation in ASL due to *Language Contact* has been researched much more than ASL variation related to *Dialect* or *Sociolect*. The next two sections of this chapter are devoted to exploring language contact.

4.2 The History of ASL Language Contact Research

In the late 1950's William Stokoe began collecting evidence that American Sign Language was indeed a language. Since that time there has been a growing understanding of the complexity of ASL, the general rules for producing words, ordering words, and the shades of meaning that those words convey. This does not mean that ASL had no rules prior to Stokoe's research. In 1913, the National Association of the Deaf began to document and preserve American Sign Language on film. These historic films document the rule-governed use of ASL long before the language was ever subjected to linguistic analysis. Clearly, the language was flourishing long before 1913. There are records of the existence of signed languages used among deaf people prior to 1817. That was the year that United States of America witnessed the opening of its first permanent school for deaf children. Hartford, Connecticut was where deaf students from across New England interacted with their teacher, Laurent Clerc, a deaf man from France. Clerc was tri-lingual (at least) knowing French Sign Language (LSF), French, and English. He would become influential in the future of American Sign Language as his native sign language (LSF) and his students' different kinds of signing all merged into post-1817 American Sign Language.

As the understanding of ASL as a language developed, a separate movement was also taking place, which sought to expand the use of ASL as a tool for teaching English. This movement began in the 1960's and initially sought to borrow ASL words in an attempt to combine them with English syntax. This resulted in several manual English codes. The development of these codes and the continued exploration of American Sign Language created a need to distinguish between signing styles which reflected the language of American Sign Language and signing styles which did not reflect a natural signed language but rather reflected the use of ASL signs to encode elements of English.

In the midst of this attempt to delineate language from code came an observation of language variety first noted by William Stokoe and then expanded upon by James Woodward. Stokoe had noticed that his students would structure their sign production one way when they talked with him, but they structured their sign production another way when they communicated with each other. Woodward studied this variation in language use and gave it the title "Pidgin Sign English" which lead to the commonly used acronym "PSE". The use of the word "Pidgin", however, is not an accurate label for what we now understand as a normal form of *language contact*.

4.2.1 Stokoe's Research on ASL Variation

William Stokoe (1960) first introduced the idea of a single line, or continuum, representing "possible communication behavior of American deaf persons" which would have "... at one end a completely normal American English exchange, the 'listener' with perfect lip reading ability receiving all that the speaker with perfect articulation is saying. At the opposite end would be a completely visual exchange, the 'speaker' and the 'hearer' using only a system of gesture, facial expression, and manual configurations as symbols. Of course, neither end is reached in actuality." (p 31) This line is represented below in figure 4.1.

Figure 4.1 - Traditional ASL-English Continuum

But as soon as Stokoe proposes this representation of communication in the deaf community, he immediately dismisses it: "... the actually observed communication is a combination in all degrees of these two, with or without vocal, whispered, or silent articulation as supplement or accompaniment." (p 32). Thus Stokoe proposes a two-dimensional line and then indicates that much more than two dimensions are present.

Stokoe first noted variety in ASL in his 1960 monograph and suggested that the level of bilingualism in the signer may influence their language use: "Presumably their language habits will be more or less affected by the extent to which English is their second language...but two languages that can be used simultaneously (at least at a word level) may be more strongly drawn into syntactical conformity" (p 80, parenthesis in original).

Stokoe explored other researchers' descriptions of variation in language and encountered Charles Ferguson's use of the word *Diglossia*, which is the use of one language for formal (high) situations and another language for informal (low) situations. Stokoe (1969) formally proposed that Ferguson's description of diglossia be applied to the language variation in the deaf community. English structures appeared to influence the ordering of ASL signs in formal, or "high" situations. Less English structures appeared in informal, or "low" situations.

4.2.2 Woodward's Research on ASL Variation

James Woodward mentioned diglossia in 1972 and suggested ways of studying it. In the same paper he mentions what he called "pidgin sign English" as the resulting communication of signing and speaking at the same time. Thus from Woodward's initial review, "pidgin sign English" referred only to the mixture of language which occurred from simultaneously combining two communication modes to express a single message, while *diglossia* referred to the choices of language based on setting, topic and activity. He suggested that ASL and American English occupy different ends of a single "diglossic scale".

Within one year, Woodward had formally coined the acronym "PSE" and published a preliminary description of it. Woodward (1973) was no longer identifying "PSE" as the simultaneous communication of two languages in two different modalities (speaking and signing at the same time). Woodward was now defining "PSE" as a *third* variety of language, distinct from ASL, but yet mixing ASL and English features. Within his 1973 paper Woodward acknowledged that research on, and definitions of, Pidgin and Creole languages were still in development. Woodward described "PSE" as having the following characteristics: 1) *Articles* (not a feature of ASL) may or may not be used, if used typically they were spellings of the English words "A" and "T-H-E". 2) *Plurality* by reduplication (an ASL feature) may or may not be used. Marking the plurality separately (an English feature) was not generally used. 3) Use of the copula[11] (not a feature of ASL) was generally represented by a single ASL sign commonly glossed as TRUE. 4) Progressive aspect (an ASL feature) was sometimes maintained through verb reduplication. 5) Perfective aspect (an ASL feature) was also sometimes maintained through the use of the sign commonly glossed as FINISH (Woodward noted that PSE users tended to use a specific variety of this sign (FINISH) which is more restricted in general ASL usage, but did not fully describe these differences). It is interesting to note that every method used to represent all five of these characteristics of "PSE" already exists in ASL. In other words, Woodward identified no new components that were either unique to English or unique to "PSE".

---

[11] In English the copula is represented by words such as *is, am, are, was, were*, etc.

In the 1973 paper, Woodward refers to the diglossic scale of his 1972 work as "a continuum of language varieties between ASL and Manual English". In truth, the 1972 work did not indicate that this continuum moved between two manually represented forms. This marks a shift in Woodward's discussion of the representations of English used by the Deaf community and may reflect rapid developments and changes of thought in signed language research in the early 1970s. Of concern is the notion that these representations of language varieties do not overlap. While both suggest that the language of ASL occupy one end of the continuum, the other end is either occupied by a language - American English, or by a manual representation of the language - Manual English. The first (1972) continuum moves between languages but across modality (signed verses spoken/written). The second (1973) continuum maintains a single modality (signing) but moves between language and an encoding of language. In the first model, PSE represents the use of two modalities at the same time - simultaneous communication (Woodward's initial proposal of 1972). In the second, PSE represents signing with influences of both Manual English (which is not clearly defined) and ASL, but makes no predictions about simultaneous productions in spoken English.

Woodward's initial descriptions do not coincide completely, but rather indicate a shifting of focus, beginning with signing and speaking at the same time and changing to a focus on different kinds of signing, regardless of accompanying speech. The point of this analysis is that Woodward's introduction of the term "Pidgin Sign English" always identified natural variation in ASL signing which was either influenced by simultaneous speech or by the recent inventions of manual English codes.[12]   In other words, Woodward's own research actually supports the notion that "PSE" is not a separate language. Instead "PSE" is simply natural variation of Deaf ASL users interacting with hearing English users.

4.2.3 Other Research on ASL Variation

Reilly and McIntire (1980) noted that "PSE" utilized many English structures for creating complex sentences, which is atypical of pidgin languages in general. Hoffmeister and Shettle (1983) identified three variables affecting the variation of deaf, adult use of ASL with different audiences: 1) ASL fluency, 2) Non-vocal expressiveness ("body language"), and 3) ASL-associated traits (reduced mouthing of English words and repetition, or restatement, of facts). Each of these factors was generated at *maximal* levels among deaf adult audiences, but at *minimal* levels among hearing adult audiences, and somewhere in between the two from an 11-year old deaf child.

Dennis Cokely (1983, 1984) reassessed the issue of "PSE" by first reviewing what have become more complete definitions of both pidgins and the process of pidginization. Cokely concludes that the phenomenon described by Woodward does not legitimately constitute a pidgin, even though some of the elements of pidginization are evident. Specifically Cokely proposes that these varieties of ASL constitute attempts to communicate by hearing learners of ASL (which may include errors, over generalizations of ASL and influences of English). The attempts are then assessed by deaf people as "learner's grammar." The deaf people then respond by using a reduced form of ASL or "foreigner register" which is used to assist communication with people not yet fluent in the target language. Cokely's explanation may not include all instances of "PSE", but it

---

[12] Note that manual English codes were also derived from ASL.

does place the *language use* clearly as part of ASL, not a separate entity lost somewhere between two languages, and definitely not a *pidgin*.

Although he did not specifically research the mix of ASL and English, Lou Fant (1990) cautioned us to understand that ASL has within it the possibility of significant variation:

> There is no such thing as "pure" ASL any more than there is such a thing as "pure" English. There is good ASL, fair ASL, and poor ASL, grammatically speaking, but there is no "pure" ASL. When someone talks about "pure" or "real" ASL, they generally mean that which is used by deaf people in relaxed, social settings, or the sort of ASL used for telling stories and jokes. A moment's reflection should reveal that to depict ASL as grammatically correct and good only when it is used in those circumstances demeans the language. (Fant, 1990: 30)

Lucas and Valli (1992) extensively researched this area and found significant variety in what they call "Contact Signing". They not only found instances of *Contact Signing* between most (although not all) interactions of deaf and hearing people, but they also found instances of *Contact Signing* in some interactions of deaf people with other deaf people. Their analysis indicates that *Contact Signing* consists of the use of grammatically simple ASL word orders while generally avoiding the use of many complex ASL elements (such as nonmanual negation, aspectual inflection, conditionals, rhetorical questions, and topicalization) yet including some basic elements of English (such as mouthing of English words, use of uniquely English word order, signs for English morphological inflections, and prepositions). Lucas and Valli emphasized that these results came from contact between the two languages of English and ASL and did not constitute an otherwise natural variety of ASL.

4.2.4 Summary of ASL Variation Research

It is interesting to note that nearly all of the documented elements attributed to English were produced using manual and non-manual components already present within ASL, such as fingerspelling and mouth movement patterns. The single exception is the use of word orders that are unique to English. While the result is clearly influenced by English, only certain parts of syntax seem inherently limited to English. In other words, all the elements composing the signs themselves exist within the confines of American Sign Language (either they are ASL signs or are modified ASL signs). It is only certain word orders that seem to be uniquely influenced by English.

The various labels of *Diglossia*, *Pidgin*, and *Foreigner Talk* already have specific meanings and cannot be appropriately used to describe English-influenced ASL variation. *Contact Signing* appears to be the only accurate label. It is important to note that in order to identify the difference between ASL and Contact Signing we must observe elements which are unique to English, not merely in overlap between ASL and English. In other words we must see 1) the mouthing of English words, 2) the use of uniquely English word order, 3) signs for English morphological inflections, and 4) prepositions. Only by identifying these four features can we clearly determine that any given utterance demonstrated *Contact Signing*. We have already noted the potential variation within ASL for dialect and sociolect above. *Register Variation* also allows for significant personal differences in ASL production. The main point is this: there is no such thing as "signed English," "Pidgin Sign English," or even "English-based signing." If the signs are from ASL then the result must be a variety of ASL (grammatical or ungrammatical). If the signs are from BSL (British Sign Language) or from Auslan (Australian Sign Language), then it is a variety of those languages. If the signs are invented, or gibberish, then the signing isn't any language at all. Regardless of the combinations, signing is never English.

4.3 A Revised Model of Language Contact in ASL

Previous models of language contact between ASL and English (Stokoe, 1960; Woodward, 1972 & 1973) have attempted to use a single line, or continuum. An inherent flaw with such an approach is that it ignores the reality that the two different languages (ASL and English) do not share the same language channel (signed versus spoken/written).

As we discussed in Chapter Two, there are three language channels: signed, spoken, and written. To place a signed and a spoken language on the same continuum implies that there is some point between the two that is both signed and spoken. At first glance this may seem to be possible, but in fact the co-occurrence of speech and signs still reflect two different channels rather than some new merger between the two. Just as it is possible to gesture and grunt at the same time, each piece of communication is expressed in a different mode and requires different senses to perceive it. A deaf person will most readily notice the gesture while a blind person will most readily notice the grunt.

An accurate model of the interaction between ASL and English must maintain two distinct continua: one representing the signed channel (expressed through image and perceived through sight) and another representing the spoken channel (expressed through sound and perceived through hearing).

Previous models indicated that each end of the single-line continuum represented grammatical use of each language (ASL at one end and English at the other end). Although each language channel may be influenced by the other language, the variety will ultimately range from grammatical use of each language to ungrammatical use. As a result of these explorations of variety in ASL and influences of English upon some of these varieties, the following graphic representation of language interaction between ASL and English is proposed.

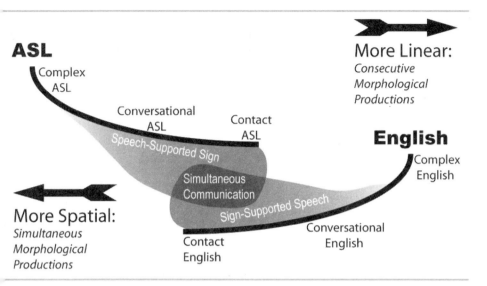

Figure 4.2 - Language Continua: ASL and English

This model recognizes not only that two different *languages* are in contact but also two different *channels* (a signed language and a spoken language). The main components of the model are two distinct lines: one for spoken information, the other for signed information. Grammatical ASL occupies slightly more than one half of the signing line (including complex and conversational ASL), while grammatical English represents slightly more than one half of the speaking line (including complex and conversational English). The remainder of the signing line is labeled as contact signing while the remainder of the speaking line is labeled as contact speaking. Each line represents more complex grammatical structures at their high ends, simpler or basic grammatical structures toward the middle, and ungrammatical, non-standard structures at the lower ends.

In the space between these lines is the realm of possibilities for co-occurring signing and speaking, also known as *Simultaneous Communication*. In the middle, between the lower portions of each channel, are the most basic structures of ASL and English, which for both languages are simple Subject-Verb or Subject-Verb-Object sentences (Liddell, 1980). Since both sentence patterns appear in both languages, it is physically *possible* to utter complete sentences in both languages at the same time. Examples would be "I'm tired / 1PP TIRED" (SV sentence) and "I want my book / 1PP WANT 1PP-POSS BOOK".

Some people may argue that mouth movement patterns reflecting complete English words are an indication that the rules of ASL are not being followed. It is true that certain aspects of ASL require specific mouth movement patterns which are not related to English speech patterns, however, much of ASL does not require specific mouth movement patterns. Likewise, during normal productions of spoken English it is possible to either keep one's hands immobile or, at the other extreme, to gesture wildly. Hand movement does not indicate whether English is being used or not, but certainly some hand movements can play a significant role in the clarity of the message (a classic example is the use of hand gestures to clarify the use of phrases such as "that one" or "this item"). Whether the hands produce ASL signs or simple gestures does not determine that an accompanying spoken message is (or is not) English. Likewise the movement of the lips alone cannot determine that an accompanying signed message is (or is not) ASL.

It is physically *possible* to simultaneously produce a signed message that follows the rules of ASL while also producing a spoken message that follows the rules of English (as in the two examples "I'm tired" and "I want my book", above); however there is no expectation that this happens very often. It is only possible to follow the rules of both languages simultaneously when the most *basic* structures in each language are used – most likely resulting in two-word or three-word sentences. It is also entirely possible to simultaneously utter *nonsense* in both modalities at the same time, regardless of "sentence" length. The production of true *Simultaneous Communication* is very limited and also is likely to shift into sentence structures of basic contact signing and contact speaking (or simply to exit legitimate language structures altogether and become either signed nonsense or spoken nonsense, or both). If any word orders more lengthy than SV or SVO are attempted, true simultaneous language production is nearly impossible.

Moving along the extreme lower end of the *Contact ASL* portion of the signing line means that ASL signs are being used in sentence patterns that are unique to English and therefore require a shared knowledge of ASL and English by both the presenter and the receiver in order to be effective for communication. If grammatical speech occurs simultaneously with ungrammatical sign productions, then this is considered Sign-Supported Speech (Johnson, Liddell & Erting, 1989) because the mode that contains the more linguistically complete message is the spoken modality and the signs, at best, support the spoken message. An example of Sign-Supported Speech would be as follows: "The ball was hit by the boy / BALL HIT B-Y BOY". In this example, the English sentence is a standard passive construction and is perfectly grammatical. The ASL sentence is not grammatical but can be understood correctly if the person receiving the message knows about the structure for English passive constructions. So the signed channel presents ASL *Contact Signing* while the spoken channel presents standard English.

In contrast to Sign-Supported Speech is Speech-Supported Sign, which may appear when a grammatical ASL message co-occurs with ungrammatical elements of spoken English. Spoken English ordered along the lines of ASL grammar has yet to be intensively studied but its existence has been noted as "CODA speak" (Jacobs, 1992; S Neumann-Solow, personal communication; B. Schick, personal communication) in which hearing children of deaf adults (CODAs) use their knowledge of two languages to produce spoken utterances of English words, often with non-standard pronunciations which represent the manners in which their deaf parents may have pronounced the English words. An example of Speech Supported Sign would be as follows: "My teacher mad, now have cha homework / 1PP-POSS TEACHER ANGRY, NOW HAVE LARGE HOMEWORK". In this example the ASL sentence applies a standard *Pronoun Drop* in the second clause. Fluent users of ASL would understand that the student has the homework and not the teacher. The English version is ungrammatical and will depend entirely on context to reach the same meaning. It also requires the person receiving it to know enough about ASL to understand the lexical substitution of "cha" for "a lot of" or "gobs of", etc. "Cha" is not a word in ASL, but it is a likely vocal expression for the mouth movement that can accompany some ASL signs describing dimensions.

4.4 Register Variation in ASL

While *Contact Signing* appears to be a common phenomenon within the American Deaf community (and likely within any Deaf community with regular interaction with hearing, non-native signers) it does not explain all variation within ASL. Flanagan et. al. (1995) reviewed the data tapes from Lucas and Valli's study of *Contact Signing*. They investigated two of the participants who had not incorporated features of contact signing. It was found that these two participants had still modified their ASL production. The researchers identified this modification as *Foreigner Talk*. *Foreigner Talk* was identified by Charles Ferguson (1977) and includes simplifications such as a slower pace, larger volume, basic forms without contractions or complex morphology, and repetitions.

These simplification may also be a part of *Contact Signing* and so Flanagan et. al. had to determine that these elements were occurring while the four English-based elements of *Contact Signing* were *not* occurring. By making this distinction they demonstrated that *Foreigner Talk* is distinct from contact signing in that *Foreigner Talk* is a simplified register of a language while contact signing includes elements outside of the language. They also determined that the use of *Foreigner Talk* was determined not by hearing status, but rather by *fluency* in ASL.

Other research of register variation in ASL has included the influence of topic and setting rather than only the participants. Zimmer (1989b) investigated the variation of a native signer in three distinct topic/settings: an informal discussion of being a househusband, a television interview, and a formal presentation. Her research indicated differences within the lower portion of the linguistic pyramid: phonology, and morphology/vocabulary.

Metzger (1993) also investigated the influence of participant status upon register. Within identical settings and topics of discussion, two discussions were videotaped: the first between the deaf subject and his deaf friend, the second between the same deaf subject and a prominent member of the Deaf community. The focus of this research was on the production of pronouns, which have informal, standard, and formal variations. Metzger's research indicated more use of informal variants with the friend and more use of standard pronouns with the prominent Deaf community member. Metzger also discovered that the use of constructed dialogue (also known as role shifting) was repeatedly evident within the informal conversation and completely absent in the more formal conversation.

4.5 Summary

This chapter has explored variation due to *dialect, sociolect, register variation,* and *language contact. Regional Dialect* is the difference in language use due to variation by general regions.   Larger differences typically occur between locations of greater difference while minor differences are more likely to take place in locations closer to each other.   As an example, British natives are generally able to distinguish the variations in speech between people from Bristol and Brighton, Liverpool and London, Cardiff and Caerphilly, Edinburgh and Glasgow.   Americans and Australians may not be able to so cleanly distinguish those differences, but certainly recognize differences from American dialects and Australian dialects. *Sociolect* variation is based on social status including the sub variables of ethnicity, gender, age and social-economic standing.

The research on *register variation* in ASL has indicated that there is a slightly broader range of variation than *sociolect* or *dialect* research has shown.   Dialect and sociolect research has indicated that the primary area of variation is in *Lexical choice* (vocabulary). Register variation, however, includes variables beyond lexical choice, such as the use of constructed dialogue.

Variation due to *Language Contact* provides the greatest amount of variation in ASL. This is due to the many possibilities for interaction between ASL and English.   It is also influenced by the nearly infinite number of combinations of Deaf and hearing participants in conversations, each having different levels of language fluency in ASL and in English. *Language Contact* variation depends on the interaction between languages.   The research on *Language Contact* variation in American Sign Language indicates that while there may be some relationship between English syntax and the grammatical structures of ASL production among bilinguals, the resulting language production is correctly identified as *Contact ASL* and not as a dialect or a language separate from ASL.   Just like all other languages, ASL can exhibit lexical differences based on dialect, sociolect, or register variation.

4.5.1 Review Questions

1. What four variables influence the development of sociolects?
2. What is the difference between sociolects and dialects?
3. What year did William Stokoe first identify variation in ASL?
4. Which level of the linguistic pyramid was the focus of the first study of American Sign Language?
5. Identify the three phrases other than "Contact Signing" which have been used to describe language contact between ASL and English.
6. What label did Woodward develop and why is that label now understood to be inaccurate?
7. What was the primary flaw with attempting to represent language contact between ASL and English with a single continuum line?
8. Where are complex grammatical structures of ASL and English located on the revised ASL/English continua?
9. What are the three descriptors used to define the space between ASL and English within the revised ASL/English continua?
10. Flanagan et. al. (1995) identified the occurrence of true *Foreigner Talk* within ASL. How is *Foreigner Talk* different than *Contact Signing*?

4.5.2 Suggested Activities

1. Think of a common children's story, such as "Goldilocks and the Three Bears," and tell it (in either a signed or spoken language) as though you were from another part of the country using a different dialect of the same language. Try telling the story again using different sociolects of the same language (class, gender, ethnicity, generation). Tell the story in different registers, as though it were a news report, a play-by-play sports broadcast, a suspense-filled mystery, or an academic lecture.
2. Observe three different examples of communication in very different settings (such as a church, a grocery store, and a classroom). Identify at least ten ways that each kind of communication is different from the other kinds (including gestures, postures, pronunciation differences, vocabulary choices, and complexity of grammar).

Chapter 5
Language Encoding Systems

"Language Encoding Systems"

Timoth's eyes looked up from the book and toward Rasmus "Encoding systems... does that mean secret codes?"
Happily Rasmus replied, "Maybe you don't realize that the question you just asked used an encoding system."
In disbelief, Timoth asked, "All communication uses encoding systems?" Timoth's eyes closed as Rasmus waited.
Some moments later Timoth continued, "Give me an example."

Moving toward the desk, Rasmus asked, "Let's start with this. What would you say this is?"
Easily, Timoth answered, "A desk!"
Smiling, Rasmus continued, "Now, what is the French word for this same object?"
Slowly this time, Timoth responded, "Rasmus... it has been years since I studied French... but the word 'bureau' comes to mind."
Again, Rasmus smiled, "Exactly, but what comes to your mind when you hear that word 'bureau' in an English conversation?"
Gazing at the ceiling, Timoth answered, "The Government."
Emptying a pack of playing cards onto the desk, Rasmus continued, "Every language uses encoding systems which are known to the people who make up the culture surrounding that language. Within one language and culture you instantly know a word to have one primary meaning but the same word can have a different, unrelated meaning to another language and culture." Rasmus began sorting the cards on the desk. "I can use just about anything as an encoding system, signs, speech, written symbols. If we share the same system, I can even use these playing cards to encode a message."

n less than three minutes, Rasmus had rearranged the playing cards into a stack and handed them to Timoth. "Now, how many letters are there in English? How could the number of playing cards represent that number of letters? Go through these in order and write down your observations."

lowly Timoth looked through the cards. "A pack of playing cards has fifty-two cards, which is the same as twenty-six times two. So playing cards could give you two of every letter in the alphabet... but I'd have to use one group of cards for the first thirteen letters and one group for the second thirteen letters. I could use Black cards for 'A' through 'M' and use Red cards for 'N' through 'Z'."

nching along the edge of the desk, Timoth placed each card in order "Spades... 9 of spades, 7 of hearts, 6 of diamonds, 7 of diamonds, 9 of clubs, King of clubs, 5 of spades, 6 of spades, 2 of hearts, 5 of hearts, Queen of clubs, 8 of diamonds, 3 of spades, 8 of clubs, joker." Timoth stopped. "What do I do with a joker?"

odding, Rasmus reached for the remaining cards, "It seems that you already know... you stop."

arefully, Timoth read the message: "Encoded message seems to be 'Its time for lunch', right?"

pening the desk drawer, Rasmus placed the cards inside and replied, "Fun, isn't it?"

oorknob in hand, Timoth asked, "Is there any limit to how we can encode messages?"

xiting the room, Rasmus declared "Limits? There are many ways to encode a message, but you have to look for them. You never know what hidden messages you'll find!"

Chapter 5 – Language Encoding Systems
"Life is an Eternal Game." - 1998 BC

5.0 Overview

All expression of language is done through encoding systems. Speech sounds may encode spoken language, hand gestures may encode signed language, and dots of ink may encode written language. These encoding systems represent the phonemes of a language (otherwise represented by the phonology level of the linguistic pyramid) and are the result of muscle movements (phonetics... the bottom level of the linguistic pyramid, just below phonology). But not all encoding systems actually encode language. This chapter begins with a review of the building blocks of languages (phonology) in order to lay the foundation required for Chapter Six, where we will explore why *Manual English Codes* do not encode English.

5.1 Signs and Signed Phonemes

Signed languages rely upon the movement of fingers, hands and arms to generate the majority of phonemes which in turn build morphemes and a vocabulary. William Stokoe (1965) identified three parameters for the phonemes of American Sign Language: Handshape, Location, and Movement. Soon after this work was published, Robbin Battison (1970) was among others who identified a fourth parameter: palm orientation. Researcher's have since proposed a "fifth parameter" of non-manual *mouth movements* but this appears to be a more active parameter for British Sign Language (Woll, personal communication) and signed languages other than ASL. So signed languages in general appear to be built out of five parameters, of which ASL only *actively* uses four for the construction of vocabulary items.

5.1.1 Handshape

Every signed language depends on the hands and a variety of possible handshapes as part of its phonology. One of the difficulties in transcribing all the possible handshapes is deciding an economical approach. This was effectively accomplished by Scott Liddell and Robert Johnson (1985, 1990) when they separated handshape transcription[13] into two primary variables: finger extension and thumb position.

Fingers can be extended in a variety of ways. The extended fingers can be spread or kept together. The total number of possible basic finger configurations (extended/unextended, plus spread/unspread) is twenty-six (and this does not count any bending of the fingers or spreading of some but not all fingers); but there appears to be a systematic restriction on the number of combinations which are used within any given sign language. Liddell and Johnson (1985, 1990) determined that the most basic approach to transcribing all of the possible configurations would begin by identifying the five possible sets of finger extensions (0,1,2,3,or 4) and then establish symbols for the particular combinations of finger extensions that are observed in natural sign use. The chart below identifies the primary finger configurations used in signed languages.

---

[13] Liddell and Johnson's transcription is not the only system for transcribing handshapes of signs. In fact, the L&J transcription system has continued to change since its first inception, but this simplified version is offered here because it has a solid history of use among signed language linguists.

0 fingers extended	
A	Four fingers closed
T	All fingers closed, thumb under index
N	All fingers closed, thumb under middle
M	All fingers closed, thumb under ring
1 finger extended	
1	All but index closed
D	Index open, all three other fingers partly open
!	All but middle closed
I	All but pinky closed
Y	All but pinky, pinky spread
2 fingers extended	
=	All but pinky and index closed, unspread
>	All but pinky and index closed, both spread*
2	All but pinky and ring closed, both spread*
H	All but index and middle closed, unspread
V	All but index and middle closed, spread
K	Ring & pinky closed, index open, middle pt. open
R	Ring and pinky closed, index and middle crossed
3 fingers extended	
W	All but pinky open and unspread
6	All but pinky open and spread
7	All but ring open and spread
8	All but middle open and spread
F	All but index open and unspread
9	All but index open and spread
4 fingers extended	
B	All four fingers open and unspread
4	All four fingers open and spread

Figure 5.1 - Liddell & Johnson Finger Notations
(*additions by Cerney)

Transcription of handshapes begins with these symbols for finger extensions followed by additional information that indicates how straight the fingers are. These are known as diacritical markings and consist of four possible options: 1) no significant bending of the fingers (absence of a diacritical marking), 2) slight bending at all the knuckles of the extended fingers (lax position), 3) significant bending of the most distal two knuckles (hooked position), and 4) bending only at the base knuckle (flattened position). The markings for each possible option are listed below:

	no bending of the handshape (straight fingers)
~	slight bending of all knuckles (lax)
"	significant bending of the two distal knuckles (hooked)
ʌ	bending of the base knuckle, next to the palm (flattened)

Figure 5.2 – Finger Diacritical Markings

Thumb position is noted separately from the symbols that identify finger extensions. Thumb configuration is reduced to two primary possibilities: either the thumb is moved forward so that the pad of the thumb faces the palm of the hand (opposed) or it is in line with the fingers (unopposed). It is also significant whether the thumb contacts the fingers and if so, how. The notations for these possible thumb positions are as follows:

o	opposed (facing the palm, opposing fingers)
u	unopposed (in line with fingers)
-	thumb is closed over (contacts) the palm or closest finger
p	thumb makes pad-to-pad contact with the closest finger
c	thumb makes other contact[14] with the closest finger

Figure 5.3 – Thumb Diacritical Markings

The result of the combination of finger notation with thumb notation is a string of between two and four characters as the examples below demonstrate:

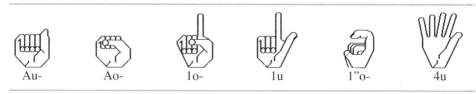

| Au- | Ao- | 1o- | 1u | 1"o- | 4u |

Figure 5.4 - Handshape Transcription Examples

---

[14] NOTE: This is a simplification of the Liddell & Johnson transcription system, which actually provides some more detailed options for thumb contact.

ASL uses different handshapes to differentiate the sign THINK from the sign KNOW. These two signs use identical locations, movements, and palm orientations, leaving handshape as the only parameter that distinguishes them.

The handshape for THINK consists of the extended index finger while all other fingers are closed down to the palm. The thumb is moved to oppose the palm of the hand and is closed over the unextended fingers. In Liddell & Johnson notation, this is noted as "1o-". "1" represents the finger configuration, "o" represents the fact that the thumb is opposed to the palm, and "-" represents the closure of the thumb against the unextended fingers[15]. Figure 5.5 illustrates this handshape.

Figure 5.5 - Handshape for ASL sign THINK (1o-)

The handshape for KNOW consists of the extension of all four fingers, but unspread. The thumb is aligned with the palm of the hand but is not closed against the palm. In Liddell & Johnson notation, this is noted as "Ba". "B" represents the finger configuration, and "a" represents the fact that the thumb is aligned with the palm. Figure 5.6 illustrates this handshape.

Figure 5.6 - Handshape for ASL sign KNOW (Ba)

These two handshapes (1o- and Ba) are very common handshapes in ASL and are very likely to appear in every signed language because of their simplicity and their ease of production. Infants are generally able to produce the 1o- handshape by the time they are twelve months of age. Soon afterward, they are also able to produce the Bo- handshape. More complex handshapes such as 2o- and 7o- (illustrated below) are less likely to occur in every signed language.

---

[15] NOTE: The notation "1o-" is stated as "one oh closed" in English.

Figure 5.7 - Handshape 2o-

In fact, 2o- is not an ASL handshape; it is, however, a handshape found in BSL (British Sign Language) and in Auslan (Australian Sign Language). In particular, these signed languages use the 2o- handshape in their signs for "seven" and "seventeen." ASL uses the 7o- handshape in these signs.

Figure 5.8 - Handshape 7o-

While handshape will be an essential feature for any signed language, the collection of handshapes that are part of one signed language will not overlap completely with the handshapes used in most other signed languages.

5.1.2 Location
There are a multitude of locations in ASL, as there will be for any signed language. A great majority of these locations are on the face. Part of the ability for the face to have so many distinct locations is that there are many more distinct features per square inch on the face as compared to the rest of the upper body. The top of the head, the side of the forehead, the space above the eyes, to the side of the eyes, on the nose, to one side of it, beside the ear, at the jaw, the corner of the mouth, and the chin – all of these provide distinct landmarks to differentiate locations within a very compact physical space. Larger, less distinct areas include the chest, shoulder, upper arm, forearm, wrist, and non dominant hand. Figure 5.9 identifies many of the locations used in ASL and other signed languages.

One of the most common examples of the significance of signing space is the comparison of the ASL signs ONION, APPLE, and KEY. All three of these signs use the same handshape (1"o-) on the dominant hand with the same palm orientations and movements. The single factor that distinguishes these signs is the locations at which each is produced. ONION is produced at the of the three locations: the side of the eye (EY). APPLE is produced at a slightly lower location on the face, the side of the mouth (MO). KEY is produced within the palm of the Non Dominant hand (ND).

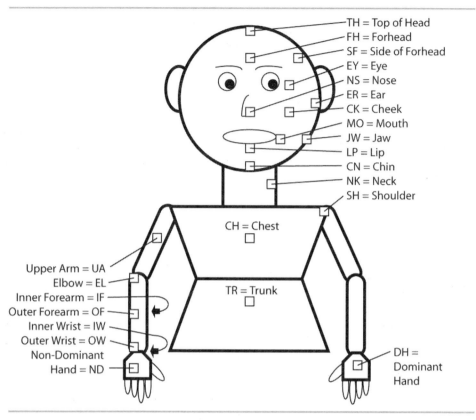

TH = Top of Head
FH = Forhead
SF = Side of Forhead
EY = Eye
NS = Nose
ER = Ear
CK = Cheek
MO = Mouth
JW = Jaw
LP = Lip
CN = Chin
NK = Neck
SH = Shoulder

CH = Chest

Upper Arm = UA
Elbow = EL
Inner Forearm = IF
Outer Forearm = OF
Inner Wrist = IW
Outer Wrist = OW
Non-Dominant
Hand = ND

TR = Trunk

DH =
Dominant
Hand

Figure 5.9 - Liddell & Johnson Location Transcription

5.1.3 Movement

Movement patterns in ASL, for example, are significant enough to distinguish some nouns from their related verbs. The most famous example was initially described by Ted Supalla in his landmark work "How Many Seats in a Chair?" (1978). Supalla identified a pattern in ASL whereby some nouns are marked by short, repeated movements while their corresponding verbs are produced with singular movements. SIT and CHAIR is one such example where SIT is produced with a single downward movement of the H~o-handshape[16] toward the non-dominant hand (also in the H~o- handshape). The exact same handshapes, locations, and palm orientations are used in the noun form, CHAIR, which is distinguished only in the movement pattern: down, then up (just above the ND hand), then back down again.

---

[16] NOTE: for the example sited, both palms are oriented downward. A different palm orientation would generate a different sign, such as NAME. Palm orientation is addressed in the next section of this chapter.

5.1.4 Palm Orientation

Palm orientation was the fourth parameter of signed languages to be identified (by Robbin Battison, among others). It differentiates such signs as DO-DO and TWENTY. DO-DO is a question form in ASL (meaning roughly, "what is there to do?" or "what shall we do?") which is produced by moving the 1o handshape to a 1^op handshape and back again, repeatedly. All of this is done in neutral space, ahead of the shoulder, with the palm facing upward. TWENTY repeats the same handshapes, the same movements between them, and the same location, but is distinct in that the palm faces outward, rather than upward.

5.1.5 Mouth Movements

Valli and Lucas (1992) proposed mouth movements as a fifth parameter of ASL signs. While it appears that mouth movements may be a parameter of other signed languages (such as British Sign Language), they do not appear to function as a *phonemic* parameter in ASL. In other words, mouth movements do not appear to mark distinct ASL word meanings when all the other four parameters (handshape, location, movement, palm orientation) are identical. The example often cited is a contrast between the ASL signs LATE and NOT-YET where the Bu handshape is held to the side of the TRunk, and repeatedly moves between the palm facing downward and the fingertips facing downward. The LATE version is done with no specific mouth movement while the NOT-YET version is done with the tongue protruding between the teeth.

The use of tongue protrusion between teeth has been previously documented in ASL to coincide with ASL verb production to express the concept of carelessness (Cokely and Baker, 1980). Because it provides *additional* information to the base meaning of the signed verb, this particular mouth movement functions as *adverbial* information. Its combination with the sign LATE merely indicates a *careless lateness* rather than a distinct difference of meaning such as that as found between the ASL signs ONION, APPLE and KEY (noted in section 5.1.2 above).

In British Sign Language, however, mouth movement does appear to function as a parameter and may distinguish lexical meaning between the BSL signs HUSBAND and WIFE. These signs are produced identically with only mouth movements identifying the gender of the spouse (Bencie Woll, personal communication). Likewise the BSL numbers for FOUR and NINE, when produced on one hand, are identical and yet are clearly distinguished by mouth movements, just as the numbers FOURTEEN and NINETEEN, and FORTY and NINETY are also distinguished from one another by mouth movements (Cerney, 1987). In all of these cases, the mouth movement patterns can be related to the mouth movements required to utter the English words, but may not completely replicate the movements necessary for standard pronunciation of each English word. In other words, the mouth movement patterns are a shortened or reduced version of the movements required for speech with only the most visible aspects remaining (such as both lips coming together for HUSBAND and the lower lip touching the teeth for WIFE).

5.2 Speech and Spoken Phonemes

Spoken languages rely upon the movement of the diaphragm, tongue, jaw, and vocal cords to generate the majority of phonemes, which in turn build morphemes and a vocabulary. Speech sounds are frequently divided first into consonants and vowels, each group can be further subdivided into places of articulation (usually determined by tongue placement) while consonants are additionally differentiated by the activity of the vocal cords.

5.2.1 Consonants

In the most basic terms, consonants are created by obstructing the airflow that moves from the lungs through the mouth. Some of this obstruction is complete, some is partial, and some is barely distinguished from the relative non-obstruction found in vowels. Some of the consonant sounds include sound made by vibrating the vocal cords; other consonant sounds are almost silent. The chart below identifies the *phonetic* properties of English consonants. Each speech sound in figure 5.10 is represented by regular alphabetic letters rather than using a phonetic alphabet such as the *International Phonetic Alphabet* (IPA). The use of standard alphabetic letters requires that some letters be combined to represent what is in fact a single sound.

Consonant Category	Point of Articulation	Voiced Consonants	Voiceless Consonants
Stops	Bilabial	b	p
	Alveolar	d	t
	Velar	g	k
Fricatives	Labiodental	v	f
	Interdental	Th	th
	Alveolar	z	s
	Palatal	zh	sh
	Glottal		h
Affricates	Alveolar-Palatal	j (d + zh)	ch (t + sh)
Nasals	Bilabial	m	
	Alveolar	n	
	Velar	ng	
Liquids	Lateral	l	
	Retroflex	r	
Glides	Bilabial	w	hw
	Palatal	y	

Figure 5.10 - Spoken English Consonants Chart

There are many ways to obstruct the flow of air during the production of speech sounds. *Stops* completely block the flow of air. *Fricatives* partially block the flow of air. *Affricates* combine a brief stop with a fricative. *Nasals* force the airflow through the nose. *Liquids* force the air around the tongue. *Glides* barely restrict the airflow and are almost vowels.

Likewise, there are many points of articulation within the mouth that add to the variety of possible speech sounds. *Bilabials* are formed when the lips come together. *Labiodentals* are formed when the lower lip touches the upper teeth. *Interdentals* are formed when the tongue protrudes between the teeth. *Alveolars* are formed behind the upper teeth. *Palatals* are formed at the middle of the roof of the mouth. *Velars* are formed at the back of the roof of the mouth. *Glottals* are formed in the top of the throat. *Laterals* place the tip of the tongue against the roof of the mouth but leave open space on either side of the tongue. *Retroflex* means that the tip of the tongue is curled back toward the roof of the mouth.

5.2.2 Vowels

Vowels are formed by reshaping the oral cavity (known to most people as "the mouth") in order to affect the relative sound made while air flows out of the lungs and across vibrating vocal cords. Tongue height and the forward/rearward placement of the tongue combine with mouth shape to generate all of the vowels of English. The following chart identifies the phonetic properties of English vowels. Each speech sound in figure 5.11 is represented by regular alphabetic letters rather than using a phonetic alphabet such as the IPA. This requires some letters to be combined to represent what is in fact a single sound.

Height	Tension	Front	Central	Back
High	*Tense*	ee (meet)		ue (Tuesday)
	Lax	i (mitt)		oo (took)
Mid	*Tense*		ur (burn)	oe (toe)
	Lax	e (met)	uh (bun)	aw (bawl)
Low	*Lax*	a (mat)		ah (bah!)

Figure 5.11 - Spoken English Vowels Chart

When sequences of two vowels are combined they are called diphthongs. English has four diphthongs: A, Oy, I, and Ow.

Diphthong		Initial Vowel		Final Vowel	Example
A	=	e	+	i	"Fail"
Oy	=	aw	+	i	"Foil"
I	=	ah	+	i	"File"
Ow	=	ah	+	oo	"Foul"

Figure 5.12 - Spoken English Diphthongs Chart

5.3 Writing and Orthography

English and romance languages[17] share the same basic writing system, although variations are used as needed, such as the enya (ñ) in Spanish. Russian uses the Cyrillic alphabet (named after Saint Cyril who traveled to Russia from the Mediterranean), which incorporates many aspects of the Greek alphabet. We will explore Cyrillic writing a little more when we discuss transliteration in chapter 7.

Writing systems need not be alphabetic. Some languages use *syllabic* writing systems – called syllabaries – which require significantly more symbols to identify all the possible combinations of consonants and vowels. An example (using English sounds) would be to establish a separate symbol for each of the following syllables: ba = ♋ , be = ℔ , bi = ⊁ , bo = ☐ , and bu = ◆ (and so on for each possible vowel and consonant combination). Once each possible combination is identified, however, it requires significantly fewer characters to encode words as compared to alphabetic systems. Thus the overall inventory of symbols is much greater than a standard alphabet, but the number of written characters needed to represent syllables is cut in half.

The remaining writing system is the use of *logographs*, also known as ideographs, to represent concepts. This approach is independent of any representation of the speech sounds made in the spoken channel of the language. Chinese is written using this approach and requires very complex equipment or computer software to correctly generate the multiple thousands of characters, which constitute this logographic writing system (it is estimated that knowledge of a minimum of 5000 different characters are necessary just to read an average newspaper in Chinese).

5.4 Specialty Encoding Systems

Spoken and signed languages *generally* occur with participants sharing the same physical space. Written languages, however, provide the ability for participants to communicate between different physical locations and even across significant gaps in time. All written languages began as specialty encoding systems, used initially to record fiscal transactions, then used by the elite, but now widespread so that it has become a full channel of language in its own right. Over the years people have developed a multitude of specialty encoding systems for a variety of reasons. Some of the specialty encoding systems, which were created for specific populations or specific purposes, include *Manual Cues, Braille, Fingerspelling, Morse Code, Semaphore,* and *Secret Codes.*

5.4.1 Manual Cues

Manual Cues are fairly unique among the specialty encoding systems because they were developed to visually encode the *spoken* channel; all of the remaining encoding systems discussed in this portion of chapter five are used to encode the *written* channel. Orin Cornet, Ph.D. developed *Manual Cues* in 1966 specifically for use with deaf people because lipreading is not visually complete enough to distinguish all of the different sounds of spoken language. Dr. Cornett learned of the difficulties that deaf children had with reading when he read a government report that found most deaf high school students were reading at only a third-grade level.

---

[17] *Romance languages* include languages with Latin roots such as French, Spanish, Italian, and Romanian.

Cornett began searching for ways that would expose deaf children to the sounds of spoken language without the ambiguity of lipreading. After investigating fingerspelling and the Dutch "Mouth/Hand" system, he devised what he called *Cued Speech*. Eight handshapes and four locations combine with the normal lip movements of spoken language to reveal the speech sounds being made without ambiguity. In this way, deaf children can access the sounds of spoken language and become native users of the same language that their parents use.

As a quick example, the sounds /m/, /b/, and /p/ are all formed, in part, by closing the lips together. This means that the following words would all look identical on the lips: mom, mob, mop, bomb, bob, and pop. Cornett's encoding system disambiguates normal lip and tongue movements by simultaneously adding distinct hand configurations. By using a different handshape for the three consonant sounds /m/, /b/, and /p/, each of the words in the example above would be produced in visually distinct ways such that a deaf person who knows manual cues and spoken English will be able to accurately identify each word. Manual cues provide sufficient clarity to distinguish all of the twenty-five consonant sounds and all of the fifteen vowel sounds (including the four diphthongs) of spoken American English.

The system has been expanded to provide accurate visual cues for at least thirty other spoken languages including French, Spanish, Swahili, and Mandarin Chinese. Additionally, the system is sufficiently accurate such that it can represent dialectical differences within a language. For example, it is possible to encode the dialectical differences of English spoken in New England, the Southern American states, Ireland, Great Britain, India, and South Africa. Spoken French is cued with an additional, fifth location to provide for nasalized vowels. Mandarin Chinese cues may vary the palm orientation through additional movements in order to provide access to the tonal differences of vowels.

Originally, Cornet labeled his manual cues as "cued speech" but this has turned out to be a misnomer in that actual speech is not a requirement in the use of the encoding system, nor does the system provide access to how speech sounds are produced. What manual cues do provide access to is the unambiguous identification of each speech sound. In this way it removes all the guesswork of lipreading so that deaf people may visually acquire a spoken language as one of their native languages.

Manual English cues for standard American English include eight handshapes, four locations, and four movement patterns, along with normally occurring mouth configurations. The only phonetic variable of signed languages that is not varied in manual cues for spoken English is palm orientation: all manual cues for spoken English are produced with the palm of the hand facing the cuer. The following charts place illustrations of the eight handshapes of manual cues within the chart of *English Consonants*, which was presented in section 5.2, above.

Consonant Category	Point of Articulation	Voiced Consonants	Voiceless Consonants
Stops	*Bilabial*	b 	p 
	Alveolar	d 	t 
	Velar	g 	k 
Fricatives	*Labiodental*	v 	f 
	Interdental	Th 	th 
	Alveolar	z 	s 
	Palatal	zh 	Sh 
	Glottal		h 
Affricates	*Alveolar-Palatal*	j 	ch 

Figure 5.13 - Cued English Consonants Chart (part 1)

Consonant Category	Point of Articulation	Voiced Consonants	Voiceless Consonants
Nasals	*Bilabial*	 m	
	Alveolar	 n	
	Velar	 ng	
Liquids	*Lateral*	 l	
	Retroflex	 r	
Glides	*Bilabial*	 w	 hw
	Palatal	 y	

Figure 5.14 - Cued English Consonants Chart (part 2)

The next chart (Figure 5.15) places illustrations of the four locations of manual cues within the chart of *English Vowels*, which was also presented in section 5.2, above.

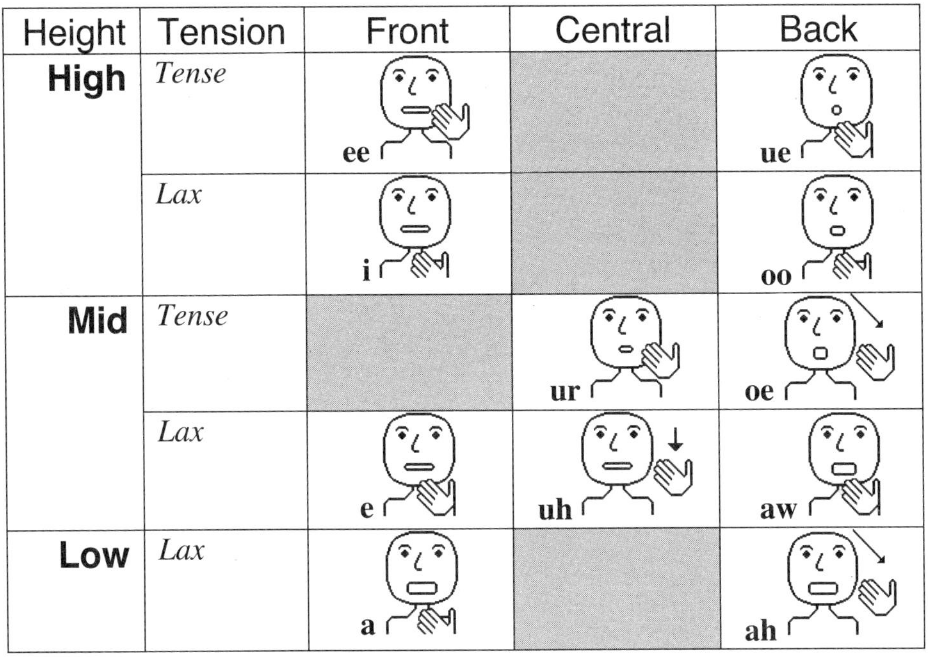

Height	Tension	Front	Central	Back
High	*Tense*	ee		ue
	Lax	i		oo
Mid	*Tense*		ur	oe
	Lax	e	uh	aw
Low	*Lax*	a		ah

Figure 5.15 - Cued English Vowels Chart

Figure 5.16 identifies the combinations of cued vowels that result in the four diphthongs of English.

Diphthong		Initial Vowel		Final Vowel	Example
A	=	e	+	i	"Fail"
Oy	=	aw	+	i	"Foil"
I	=	ah	+	i	"File"
Ow	=	ah	+	oo	"Foul"

Figure 5.16 - Cued English Diphthongs Chart

Cues are presented as Consonant-Vowel syllables. This combination allows for cues to simultaneously represent both a consonant and a vowel and therefore requires less complexity than fingerspelling. Cueing can demonstrate rhyme schemes in poetry even when the words do not visually match, such as the words "bake" and "break". It is even possible to reveal puns without having to explain them. Fingerspelling conveys written language information, but cueing conveys the phonic information so that children who are learning to read can use the same techniques as hearing children to "sound things out". The following are some examples of how cueing is used to visually represent English speech sounds:

Single syllable

The word "chew" or "choo" would be produced as a single combination of handshape 8 at the chin location while saying the sounds /chue/.

Repeated Syllable

The word "choo-choo" would be produced as a repeated combination of handshape 8 at the chin location while saying the sounds /chue/ /chue/.

Initial Vowel Syllable

The word "achoo!" (the English word for the sound a sneeze makes) would be produced in two parts. The first part would place the 5 handshape at the throat location while saying the sound /uh/. The second part would be the combination of handshape 8 at the chin location while saying the sounds /chue/.

Final Consonant Syllable

The word "choose" would be produced in two parts. The first part would be the combination of handshape 8 at the chin location while saying the sounds /chue/. The second part would produce handshape 2 at the side location while saying the sound /z/.

Research indicates that deaf children who regularly use manual cues have comparable skills to non-deaf children in reading and writing (Alegria, Dejean, Capouillez & Leybaert, 1990; Alegria, Lechat & Leybaert, 1990; LaSasso, Crain & Leybaert, 2003; Lechat & Leybaert, 2001; Leybaert & Charlierr, 1996; Wandel, 1989). With cued language input, a deaf child has access to the speech sounds of any spoken language on a par with hearing children. The use of cues allows a deaf child to establish an intuitive understanding of spoken language, which can then be used in the process of reading.

The advantage for interpreters to know how to use cues is that it provides an additional visual encoding tool, which is faster than fingerspelling and does not require the interpreter to know how the word is spelled. Cueing can readily be used for spelling tests (because it does not reveal the spelling, only the sound), and foreign language instruction (such as Spanish or French class). Cueing is one of many visual language-encoding tools, such as fingerspelling. The system can be quickly learned, although it takes practice to develop fluency in cueing at normal speech rates.

5.4.2 Braille

Braille is a tactile encoding system for written languages that was invented in the 1800's by Louis Braille, a French musician and educator. It makes use of raised dots within a 2 x 3 cell (a total of six possible dots). Each letter of the Roman alphabet is assigned a unique configuration of between one and five dots. The numbers 1 through 9 are represented by the letters A through I respectively; J is used to represent a zero. As Figure 5.17 illustrates, it is also possible to represent the dots via image, rather than texture, but Braille was developed with the intention of being a textural/tactile encoding system specifically for blind people.

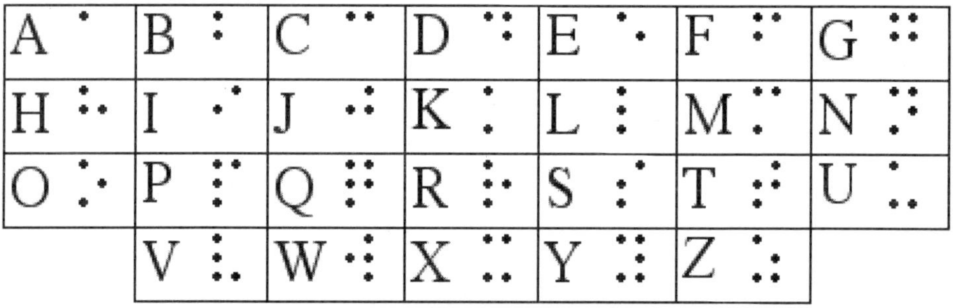

A ⠁	B ⠃	C ⠉	D ⠙	E ⠑	F ⠋	G ⠛
H ⠓	I ⠊	J ⠚	K ⠅	L ⠇	M ⠍	N ⠝
O ⠕	P ⠏	Q ⠟	R ⠗	S ⠎	T ⠞	U ⠥
V ⠧	W ⠺	X ⠭	Y ⠽	Z ⠵		

Figure 5.17 - Brailled Alphabet

5.4.3 Fingerspelling

One-handed fingerspelling was illustrated in print in the late 1500's when a book written by a Franciscan monk, Fray Melchor de Yebra, was finally published (seven years after his 1586 death). Popular folklore indicates that the one-handed alphabet had been developed to allow monks to communicate while maintaining a vow of silence. Two-handed fingerspelling was first revealed in print in 1698 by an unknown author in London, England.

Most ASL dictionaries describe the American manual alphabet as being composed of 26 handshapes. But with just a look at the difference between the letters "K" and "P" we see that these two letters actually use the same handshape; the two are differentiated by palm orientation, not handshape. William Stokoe (1965) identified a mere nineteen handshapes, which accounted for the entire manual alphabet as well as all of the signs of ASL. By using the Liddell and Johnson transcription system (explained previously in this chapter) we would understand the manual alphabet to be composed of as few as 12 and as many as 15 different finger configurations (the difference based on individual variation of performance). If the American manual alphabet were produced as pictured in figure 5.18, it would require the full fifteen distinct finger configurations in combination with different thumb positions and different kinds of bending of the extended fingers. Liddell and Johnson notation is provided beneath each handshape pictured below.

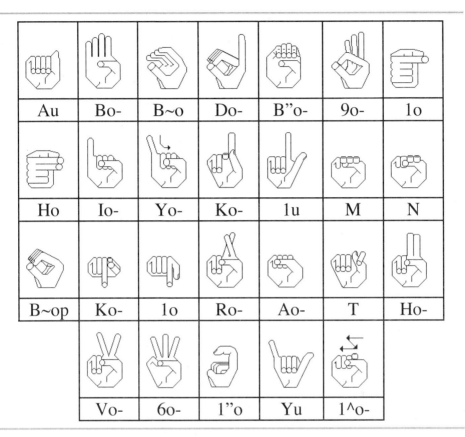

Au	Bo-	B~o	Do-	B"o-	9o-	1o
Ho	Io-	Yo-	Ko-	1u	M	N
B~op	Ko-	1o	Ro-	Ao-	T	Ho-
	Vo-	6o-	1"o	Yu	1°-	

Figure 5.18 - American Fingerspelled Alphabet

The two-handed fingerspelling of Great Britain and Australia uses pointing to the digits of the non-dominant hand to represent vowels and other configurations to represent consonants. A single letter, "C", is actually one-handed while all remaining letters require contact between the dominant and non-dominant hand.

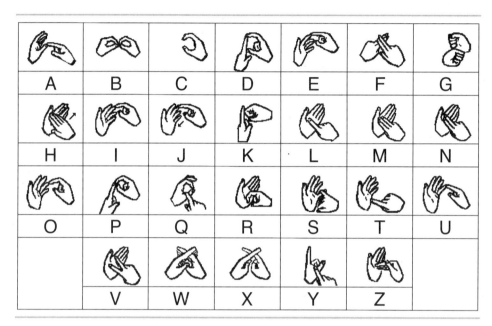

Figure 5.19 - British/Australian Fingerspelled Alphabet

5.4.4 Morse Code

In 1836 Samuel F. B. Morse invented the telegraph but he had been using his encoding system, *Morse Code*, for years with his wife, who was deaf. He would tap out messages to her using his finger on her hand (tactile communication). On May 24th, 1844, Morse sent his famous message, "What hath God wrought?" across telegraph lines which stretched from the Capitol building in Washington, DC to Baltimore. Some of the lines crossed over Amos Kendall's farmland. Kendall was Morse's financial manager (they both profited significantly from Morse's inventions) but also would later establish a school for deaf children on part of his farm land and then even later hire Edward Miner Gallaudet, Thomas Hopkins Gallaudet's son, to manage the school. That school is now known as Gallaudet University. Thus, Morse code is connected indirectly to the deaf community by at least two threads: communication with a deaf person (Morse's wife) and the financial gains it provided for Gallaudet University's benefactor, Amos Kendall.

Like fingerspelling and Braille, Morse encodes the written channel of language. Morse code uses two different symbols to build its representation of the alphabet. These symbols are dots and dashes. Since it is possible to use Morse code in all three of the primary communication modes (image, sound, and texture) it is helpful to understand dots as short symbols and dashes as long symbols. Visually these can be written with a dot (.) or a dash (-), which is where the names come from. But they can also be represented by how long the signal lasts: a relatively brief signal being a dot and a dash being three times as long as a dot. Thus is it possible to use a flashing light, an audible tone, or physical touch to encode via Morse.

The two symbols (dots and dashes) are arranged in different patterns to represent each letter of the alphabet with a gap as long as a dot between each of the symbols composing the letter. Longer gaps of silence lasting three dots in length indicate the completion of a set of symbols for any given letter. Gaps equal to the length of seven dots indicate separation between words. Traditional telegrams use the word STOP to indicate the end of sentences. Errors can be indicated by a series of eight dots (........), which means the last word sent should be deleted.

•-	-•••	-•-•	-••	•	••-•	--•	••••	••
A	**B**	**C**	**D**	**E**	**F**	**G**	**H**	**I**
•---	-•-	•-••	--	-•	---	•--•	--•-	•-•
J	**K**	**L**	**M**	**N**	**O**	**P**	**Q**	**R**
•••	-	••-	•••-	•--	-••-	-•--	--••	•----
S	**T**	**U**	**V**	**W**	**X**	**Y**	**Z**	**1**
••---	•••--	••••-	•••••	-••••	--•••	---••	----•	-----
2	**3**	**4**	**5**	**6**	**7**	**8**	**9**	**0**

Figure 5.20 - Morsed Alphabet

5.4.5 Semaphore

Semaphore is a visual encoding system for the written channel that uses combinations of two flags or arm/hand postures to indicate each letter of the alphabet. When flags are used they are usually square, divided diagonally with red in the upper section and yellow in the lower.

Each flag is held in one of five positions: down, low, out, high, and up. Six letters require one hand to be brought across the body so that both flags are on the same side. Numbers 1 through 9 are represented by the letters A through I respectively. The letter J can be used to indicate a shift from numbers to letters. The number 0 is represented by the letter K. Errors are indicated by raising both flags and then lowering them together. Figure 5.21 (below) shows the correct positions for semaphore from the viewer's perspective.

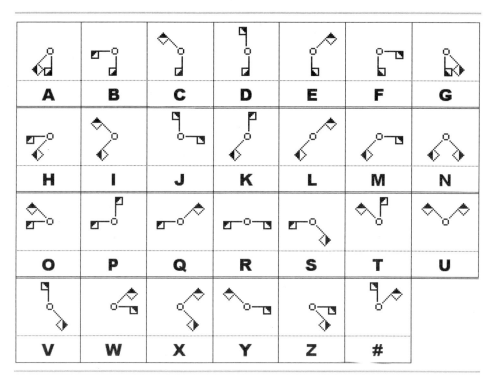

Figure 5.21 - Semaphored Alphabet

5.4.6 Secret Codes

Most secret codes of any fame are based on encoding alphabetic letters. The most simple codes merely require a rearranging of standard alphabetic characters following a fixed order. These are called *Ciphers*. A *Rail Fence Cipher* divides a written message into two, placing every other letter into either the first or second part of the message. If we were to encode the message "This message is in code" we would begin by omitting the spaces between letters and then rewrite the message in two parts: THISMESSAGEISINCODE. Next this string of text would be split in two so that every other letter was in one group and the remaining letters in another group: TIMSAESNOE and HSESGIICD. A person receiving this message would write the first letter of the first set of letters followed by the first letter of the second set of letters and keep working back and forth until the letters were all placed in the right order. The receiver of the message will still need to know the source language of the message in order to make any sense of the resulting string of characters.

A *Twisted-Path Cipher* uses a grid to arrange the letters of a message. The letters are then rewritten following a specific path through the grid. This requires the sender and receiver to know both the size of the grid and the path taken within the grid to encode/decode the message. Our secret message this time will be "This message is also in code" and it is placed into a five-by-five grid from left to right in Figure 5.22, below (the letters "XY" are added as needed in this case to fill the grid completely):

T	H	I	S	M
E	S	S	A	G
E	I	S	A	L
S	O	I	N	C
O	D	E	X	Y

Figure 5.22 - Secret Code Grid

For this example we will use an encoding path which moves in an inward spiral from the upper left corner down to the lower left corner, then across the bottom, up the right side, backwards across the top and continuing on toward the center space in the grid. Writing these letters in order would result in one long string of twenty-five letters: TEESODEXYCLGMSIHSIOINAASS. This could then be broken into random lengths to further confuse people who might incidentally see the message: TEE SOD EXYC LGM SI HSIO I NAASS. The decoder would need to know the grid size and path to follow, would then write the letters along the same spiral path in the grid, and then read the letters from left to right down through the grid. Again, knowledge of the source language will ensure that the decoder knows how to separate the pieces into words and where the extra "filler" letters are used.

More difficult ciphers will substitute the alphabetic letters with other characters. The *playing card cipher*, used in the dialogue opening this chapter, uses standard playing cards to encode the alphabet. What is important to understand about all encoding systems is that each system encodes at a *phonological* level. *Manual Cues* encode information on a *speech-sound*-for-*speech-sound* level. *Braille, Fingerspelling, Morse, Semaphore*, and *Secret Codes* all encode information on a letter-for-letter level. None of these codes attempt to encode at a meaning-for-meaning (morphological) level and that is why all of them are truly *encoding systems* of languages. Each *language encoding system* has its own phonetics (muscle movements); but it is possible to have a variety of different phonetic activities (muscle movements) that encode the same linguistic system from the phonological level to the stylistic level. Thus fingerspelling, Morse code, Braille, cursive writing, and printing may make use of different phonetics (muscle movements) but still encode the same language beginning at the phonological level.

The next chapter explores the creation of new languages through pidginization and creolization and also explores the creation of educational *Artificial Pidgins*, which have been mislabeled as codes. While *natural pidgins* stay within the same *Language Encoding Modality*, *Artificial Pidgins* mix modalities by using both manual signs and lip movements as the encoding systems. The mouth encodes English, but the manual signs encode a different linguistic activity, which is neither English nor ASL.

5.5 Summary

All languages are encoded. Signed languages use handshapes, locations, palm orientations, movements and mouth configurations. Spoken languages use expressed-air, vibrating vocal cords, tongue placement, and mouth configurations. Written languages use graphic symbols. Spoken languages may also be encoded by graphic symbols or by manual cues. Signed languages can be encoded by graphic symbols. Written languages may also be encoded via textural or auditory symbols.

The most versatile of all the language channels is the *Written Channel* because it may be encoded by all three of the primary language-encoding modalities: image, sound, and texture. *Image* and *Texture* can each encode all three channels: signed, spoken, and written. *Sound* generally only encodes the spoken channel (although it can encode written language via Morse code or spelling aloud). At the time of this writing, the only way that sound is used to encode the signed channel is by reading a transcription aloud.

Many specialty-encoding systems have been developed. *Manual Cues* are used to visually encode the spoken channel. *Braille, Morse code*, and *Semaphore* are all used to encode the written channel: *Braille* encodes via texture, *Morse* generally encodes via image or sound, *Semaphore* encodes via image. *Secret Codes* also provide for systematic encoding of the written channel but they are generally developed for private communication and do not represent natural language encoding mechanisms.

5.5.1 Review Questions
1. What are the five primary parameters for signed language phonology?
2. Which of these five primary parameters does not play a role in lexical distinction for ASL?
3. Identify five different signs that use the 1o- handshape.
4. Identify five different signs that are produced at the SF location.
5. Identify three of the factors that combine for the creation of spoken language phonology.
6. Identify three different pairs of English phonemes that are identically produced except for vocal cord movement (one member of each pair has vocal cord movement while the other does not).
7. What are the primary factors that differentiate English vowels?
8. What are the three different *kinds* of writing systems?
9. Which language channel do *manual cues* encode?
10. Which language channel do Braille, Fingerspelling, Morse code, and Semaphore encode?

5.5.2 Suggested Activities
1. Identify all of the signs you can think of which use each of the *handshapes* defined in the Liddell & Johnson Handshape Transcription Chart.
2. Identify all of the signs you can think of which use each of the *locations* defined in the Liddell & Johnson Location Transcription Chart.
3. Identify all of the letters that you can think of that phonemically represent each English sound in the Spoken English Consonants Chart.
4. Identify all of the letters that you can think of that phonemically represent each English sound in the Spoken English Vowels Chart.
5. Practice encoding spoken English words using manual cues. How many sounds does each handshape represent?
6. Practice encoding written English with each of the following encoding systems: Braille, American Fingerspelling, Australian/British Fingerspelling, Morse code, and Semaphore.
7. Create a new *substitution cipher* where each letter of the alphabet (or each possible speech sound) is represented by a new symbol. Encode a message using your new code.
8. Practice a fingerspelling alphabet other than one you already know. Use it to generate messages between yourself and other students.
9. Generate a *secret message* of your own using the handshapes of signs to spell one message while the signs generate an entirely different message. In other words, create a sign story such that each handshape that you use spells a secret message in the midst of your signing.

Chapter 6
Pidgins, Creoles & Other Things

"Pidgins, Creoles, and Other Things"

Timoth stared at the conversation partners as Rasmus generated OSL signs with odd handshapes. The visitor also signed with similar oddities.

When the visitor left, Timoth asked, "What language was that?"

Rasmus, still standing by the door, turned to face Timoth, "Well, technically it was not a language."

"Not a language? Then how did you communicate?"

"Timoth! Surely you know by now that language is not at all required for communication."

"I knew that as soon as I said it. But if you weren't using language then how certain can you be that you understood each other accurately?"

"There is always the possibility of misunderstanding, even when we do use language as part of our communication."

"OK... but what was it that you were using to communicate? They looked like OSL signs but, different somehow."

Rasmus reached for a book from the shelves. "That is what its inventors called 'Manually Emitted Signed Speech'. Here's the manual."

Timoth looked through the book, "It looks like they attempted to match spoken-language words with OSL signs."

"That's right. They used different handshapes for similar signs to distinguish various spoken words with similar meanings. But the result is neither spoken language nor OSL. It is a linguistic mix containing elements of both languages, but in the end it does not actually meet the definition of language."

"Why not?"

"Because the first generation models only used it to communicate with Deaf students, not with each other. Without a community of models, our visitor took this input, made his own modifications, and generated his own unique, personal pseudo-language. He is the only one on this planet to use his particular mix of OSL and spoken language. Since he completed school and found the Deaf community he has begun re-modifying his communication toward the signing used by the Deaf community."

Timoth continued to look through the book. "Why did anyone choose to invent such a thing?"

"The goal was to teach Deaf children. There was a time, not so long ago, when OSL was banned from educational settings with Deaf children. The inventors knew OSL and tried to use OSL signs to encode spoken language. In doing so they were able to sneak a portion of OSL back into the classroom for Deaf students."

"But if it's not a language, what good is it?"

Rasmus gazed at the ceiling and paused. "That is a very good question. It served a political purpose in its time, but it still causes so much division within the Deaf community."

Timoth looked at Rasmus. "So why were you using it with the person who was just here."

"In a sense, I was being polite, by using the same means of communication that our visitor prefers and uses every day."

"You mean that he doesn't know OSL?"

"Well, he knows parts of OSL, but not the entire language. Likewise he knows parts of spoken language, but is unsuccessful in lipreading alone. My goal was to communicate with him so I adopted a more mutually similar approach to our communication."

"Will I need to learn how to communicate that way?"

"You will encounter people with similarities to his communication style in the community. You may wish to learn about the system. Just be careful to keep it from influencing your OSL fluency."

Chapter 6 – Pidgins, Creoles & Other Things
"Be Careful What You Wish For, You May Get It!" - Willy Wonka

6.0 Overview
In Chapter Three we discussed *Language Variation* and how two languages in contact may vary between grammatical and ungrammatical forms. In Chapter Four we learned that all languages are expressed through encoding systems. Encoding systems may encode signed languages, spoken languages, or written languages; but any given encoding system is not actually limited to encoding only one specific language. In other words, written alphabetic letters may encode written French, written Spanish, written Welsh, and so on. Speech sounds may encode spoken Swahili, spoken Dutch, spoken Chinese, etc. Manual Cues may encode spoken English, spoken German, spoken Russian, etc. Handshapes, Locations, Movements, Palm Orientations, and Mouth Movements may encode British Sign Language, Auslan, American Sign Language, etc.

This chapter explores a phenomenon originally known as Manually Coded English (MCE), but which we shall see is not truly English, nor even a language. These manual English "codes" combine a remnant of speech encoding (mouth movements) with handshapes, locations, movements, and palm orientations to create a mixture of English, ASL, and manual inventions, which can only be accurately be classified as an *artificial pidgin*. In order to understand this analysis it will be necessary to understand how natural pidgins develop and that is where we will begin.

6.1 Natural Pidgins and Creoles
Pidgins are organized human communication, created from multiple languages which draw their vocabulary from one language, and their syntax and pronunciation from the remaining languages. Pidgins naturally occur when people need to communicate but no majority of people share any one language. This might happen if people of multiple language backgrounds move to a sparsely populated but economically prosperous region (such as newly discovered diamond mines or oil fields). It might also happen when people of multiple language backgrounds are forced to live together through war, imprisonment, or slavery.

Of the multiple languages feeding into a pidgin, one will be the *superstrate* and the others will be *substrates*. The *superstrate language* is the language of economic or social power; it provides the *vocabulary*. All the remaining languages that influence the pidgin are *substrate languages*; they provide the *grammar and pronunciation*.

If the circumstances that bring these people together lasts long enough, the people will develop a new communication system based on the languages that they know. This creation of a new communication system is called *Pidginization*. In order to determine whether a pidgin is a language, we need to remind ourselves of the definition of language. *Language is the systematic use of symbols to express and perceive information between members of a community, in which the system is rule-governed, has infinite production possibilities, is intergenerational, and changes over time.*

The result of pidginization will meet all of the requirements of a language except that it is not yet *intergenerational*. In fact, there is a different label used to differentiate a first-generation pidgin from subsequent generations. A *Creole* is a pidgin that has been passed on to a second generation who grow up using the pidgin as a native language. Once a pidgin has been *creolized*, it completely satisfies the definition of language.

Chapter 6 – Pidgins, Creoles & Other Things   113

6.1.1 Spoken Language Pidgins

Spoken *Pidgins* and *Creoles* have developed throughout the world. Many use English as the superstrate language, such as *Tok Pisin* of Papua New Guinea, *Solomon Island Pidgin*, *Cameroonian Pidgin*, and *Gullah* of the Sea Islands off of South Carolina and Georgia. Other pidgins use other European languages, such as Portuguese, Spanish or French as superstrates (often due to colonization efforts). Still other pidgins and creoles have developed from such diverse superstrate languages as Ngbandi, a west-central African language, and Lower Chinook, a Native American language.

Bloomfield (1933) was the first to distinguish between the labels of Pidgins and Creoles. Hymes (1971) refers to them as marginal languages: "Both are marginal, in the circumstances of their origins, and in the attitudes towards them on the part of those who speak one of the languages from which they derive." (Hymes, 1971: 3) The numbers of people who use *Pidgins* has been estimated to be at least two million while the numbers of people who use *Creoles* has been estimated to be at least six million (DeCamp, 1971).

6.1.2 Signed Language Pidgins

Pidgins have also developed within and between signed languages. The requirements are the same, however: organized human communication, drawn from multiple languages, which draw their vocabulary from one language, and their syntax and pronunciation from the remaining languages. International conferences of deaf people are the most common modern-day settings where the early beginnings of a pidgin are generated by the time the conference concludes. Since the conferences are temporary by design, these emerging pidgins never become fully developed.

Historically, most national signed languages in Europe are the result of pidginization. Prior to the founding of schools for deaf children, deaf people were widely scattered and had little ability to locate other deaf people. This meant that any sign-based communication would very likely have significant differences from one city to the next. If a location had a particularly large population of deaf people, then that city would be more likely to develop a more common, uniform, signed language. Otherwise each signed language that developed may have only a handful of people who used it. Once deaf people from different cities came together to be educated in a school, these smaller signed languages would merge, most likely with the language of the teacher, into a new regional or national signed language.

It is by gathering deaf people together that residential schools for deaf children throughout Europe and the United States helped to establish national signed languages. The most widely known signed language is American Sign Language (ASL). ASL was born" in 1817 in school classrooms in Hartford, Connecticut.

Prior to 1817 there was only one location with significant organization within the American Deaf population: Martha's Vineyard, Massachusetts. Martha's Vineyard had a very high ratio of genetic deafness such that one out of every 155 people on the island was deaf (Groce, 1985). This high proportion of deafness on the island lead to an interesting phenomenon: most of the hearing people knew some amount of sign language. Elsewhere in the United States, however, there was no other documented deaf community with a widespread use of signed language.

Beginning in 1817, Deaf people had a place and a reason to gather together from diverse communities: The place was the American School for the Deaf in Hartford, and the reason was to receive an education. ASL developed from the interaction of 1) the head teacher's native French Sign Language, 2) the Martha's Vineyard signing of several students, and 3) several other forms of home signs from each of the remaining students. This mix of people and languages lead to the creation of a new sign-based pidgin. The young children coming into the school quickly creolized the pidgin and thus was born ASL as a full-fledged language. Some remnants of this initial mixture of language can be seen in the ASL numeric symbols where the handshapes for the numbers one, two, four, and five all come from American signing/gesture while the handshapes for the numbers three, ten, and the twenties all come from French signing/gesture. It has been estimated that even today as much as seventy percent of French Sign Language signs overlap with ASL signs.

6.1.3 Summary of Natural Pidgins

So far we have explored the development of Natural Pidgins. Pidginization is a naturally occurring phenomenon that is entirely directed by humans in contact with other humans. Children born into an environment that uses a pidgin will naturally creolize the pidgin into a full-fledged language. We will next explore two creations of pidgin-like communication systems: *Esperanto* and *Gestuno*. The pidgin-like creations of *Esperanto* and *Gestuno* serve as pre-planned communication systems for people who anticipate short-term interaction with other people who otherwise share no common communication system (usually for international conferences). These communication systems are never anyone's native language and do not meet the definition of language. What is worth noting, however, is that all the natural pidgins and creoles are *intra*modal, meaning that either spoken language elements merge with each other, or that signed language elements merge with each other. Natural pidgins, and even the creations of Esperanto and Gestuno, are never *inter*modal; in other words, they never mix elements spoken languages with elements of signed languages.

6.2 Esperanto, Gestuno and International Signing

As mentioned in the section above, international conferences often provide the interactive settings for pidgin-like communication. Because these conferences only last for a short amount of time (usually only about a week), the developing communication does not become systematic enough to be considered a pidgin, but it does reveal the ability of humans to modify their communication very quickly to accommodate people with various linguistic backgrounds. In an effort to standardize this accommodation process, a vocabulary of about 1,500 signs was developed and published in 1973 by a special commission of the World Federation of the Deaf to serve as an initial starting base for international signed communication. This system was called *Gestuno* and followed some of the guidelines of those who created the international spoken language called *Esperanto*.

Esperanto is no-one's native language, but was created by Polish physician Ludwig L. Zamenhoff in 1887 to facilitate ease of communication among people who otherwise shared no common language. The strategy for developing this communication system was to take widely shared root morphemes (usually from romance languages such as Spanish and French) and reduce their pronunciation to the most commonly shared speech sounds. Through simple, regular rules of grammar, Esperanto allows the creation of new and original sentences. Esperanto is not a language, however, because it has no viable interactive community of users and is not intergenerational.

Gestuno parallels Esperanto in that it takes common elements of signed language vocabulary (usually from European signed languages historically linked to French Sign Language) and produces these signs with basic handshapes, movements, locations, and palm orientations which are common to most signed languages. The grammar of Gestuno is unspecified, but Subject-Verb-Object (SVO) is a fairly common word order for most spoken and signed languages and works well for users of Gestuno. What is fairly common, however, is that this base of communication will quickly become modified as the people using it add new signs and modifying existing ones. These modifications are most commonly related to the signed language surrounding the conference, but may also be influenced by American Sign Language since it is the most widely known signed language worldwide.

International Signing is the more natural development between signed-language users from various countries using their own natural gestures and signs to communicate with each other, regardless of the vocabulary identified as Gestuno. *International Signing* was already a common practice during international gatherings of the Deaf community, prior to the World Federation of the Deaf officially exploring standardization through Gestuno. *International Signing* in Europe can typically be tied to French Sign Language roots, but it is always completely dependent upon the choices made by the people using it for conversations.

6.3 Artificial Intermodal Pidgins

Beginning in the 1960's educators of deaf children attempted to create a new teaching tool to help their students improve their fluency in English. The idea was to use American Sign Language vocabulary (with some modifications) in English word order so that the student could *see* the vocabulary without ambiguity. This process of language mixing, when it naturally occurs, is called Pidginization. Because these Pidgins of ASL vocabulary and English syntax did not occur naturally, they are in fact Artificial Pidgins. The popular terminology for these Artificial Pidgins is "Manually Coded English." The use of the word "English" at the end of this label has fooled educators and parents alike into thinking that the Pidgins actually encoded English. A more accurate arrangement of these words is "Manual / English Code" or MEC.

Before we explore *Artificial Pidgins*, it would serve us well to review what we know about natural Pidgins. *Natural Pidgins* develop when the people who use at least three or more languages come into prolonged, interactive contact with each other. The majority of language users must not share any one of the languages, however. If the majority of people in contact share a single language, then there is no need to develop a pidgin since a language already exists that can handle the interaction between the majority of participants. The remaining people would simply need to learn the majority language.

Pidgins develop precisely because there are not enough people who share a common language. One of the languages will serve as the *superstrate*, or target language. The *superstrate language* is perceived as the language of power and provides all of the vocabulary for the Pidgin. The remaining *substrate languages* all contribute to the word order and pronunciation of the superstrate vocabulary. Pronunciation and Grammatical rules are reduced to the common elements between the substrate languages (usually resulting in a Subject-Verb-Object grammar). If the Pidgin remains stable enough for a generation of children to be born into it, those children will use their human brains to *creolize* the Pidgin into a brand new human language.

Manual English codes are composed of three elements. Two of these are natural languages: ASL and English. The third is the reason that MEC's are *artificial*: manual *inventions*. These three elements (ASL signs, English mouth movements, and manual inventions) are put into general English word order. Following what we know about natural Pidgins, this places English as one of the *substrate languages*: a language being adapted in order to move toward the *superstrate*, or target, language. What is potentially confusing for the deaf student is that both ASL and English are being presented simultaneously as a superstrate language. The *signs* indicate that ASL is the target language; but the *mouth movements* indicate that English is the target language. The simultaneous use of natural English mouth configurations and ASL signs provides a highly unnatural model of either language. It should not be a surprise to see that the result of showing deaf students a mixed language is that the students acquire a *mixed language* – neither ASL nor English. Figure 6.1 identifies ASL as the basis of various American manual English codes, identified here as *artificial pidgins*.

Figure 6.1 – Modifications of ASL to Create Artificial Pidgins

Manual English codes are incomplete representations of ASL. The only way they present a model of English is if the deaf student learns to ignore the manual component and relies on the mouth configurations representing English as they are presented in English word order. This process is called *De-pidginization*, but it is by no means guaranteed. If the deaf child has some useable hearing then it is more likely that she will be able to de-pidginize the visual information she is seeing. Some students are outstanding lipreaders and even without sufficient hearing they can successfully de-pidginize manual English code. For all of the remaining deaf students exposed to manual English codes, they face the reality that they will *creolize* the artificial pidgin into their own artificial creole, perhaps shared by their immediate classmates, but likely to have significant variation from school to school. In other words, they will develop language *mush*, which means that they will not be able to express themselves clearly through signs, speech or writing. If these deaf students are not exposed to a visually encoded interactive language before puberty, they will be language impaired for the rest of their lives. This is the danger in the use of manual English codes: not all of the students exposed to these codes will be able to successfully de-pidginize them into either ASL or English.

6.3.1 The Origins of American Manual English Codes

In 1962 **David Anthony** got the inspiration to develop a visual system for encoding English. Anthony was the deaf son of deaf parents and a teacher of mentally retarded deaf children in Michigan. He knew it was difficult for deaf children to learn English because his native ASL did not match up well with English syntax and oral approaches to teaching deaf children were largely ineffective. *Signing Essential English* (SEE) was his original name for the system he developed, which also served as the subject of his Masters Thesis at Eastern Michigan University.

SEE used modified ASL signs and manual inventions to represent English morphemes. In SEE, a single "word" could be composed of more than one sign. Take "boyishly", for example. That word would be broken down into the morphemes: "boy," "ish," and "ly," and three different signs would be used in sequence. (Gannon, 1980: 370)

By January of 1969 Anthony had moved to California to teach deaf children at the Brookhurst Junior High School in Anaheim. There he gathered a group of other educators and interpreters for deaf children who were likewise concerned about the English language development in deaf children. The group began with Anthony's system, which he had renamed *Seeing Essential English* (he changed the *Signing* to *Seeing* in order to de-emphasize the signing and encourage more parents to learn the system). As discussions progressed three distinct approaches developed.

6.3.2 LOVE, SEE1, and SEE2

The group divided into three smaller groups. **Dennis Wampler**, a child of deaf adults and a teacher of deaf children, believed that the vocabulary should be represented using William Stokoe's sign notation system instead of using pictures. Since few people are skilled at reading Stokoe's notation system, few people took the time to learn to read the descriptions of each sign. Wampler named his system the *Linguistics Of Visual English* (LOVE) but it was never widely implemented. The two remaining groups chose a more standard approach to describing their system and published dictionaries with pictures of the signs.

David Anthony led the group which eventually called their system *Seeing Essential English* which is now known as SEE1. SEE1 primarily allocates a single sign to each English morpheme. Each sign may be based on an ASL sign, which only has accurate meaning for the primary sense of the English word. This means that secondary or idiomatic uses of the English word will still use the same sign. Two common examples are the signs used for "butter" and for "fly" combined to represent the word "butterfly;" and the signs for the English words "car" and "pet" combined to represent the word "carpet." Although the results appear to be nonsense ASL signing, the SEE1 system actually maintains the closest link to the phonology of English. It still mixes ASL and English elements, however, and cannot be considered to be a true English encoding system.

The remaining splinter group from David Anthony's original group of educators modified their approach to include the *meaning* of the English word in the selection of the ASL sign. While this made the code appear more meaningful and pleasing to native ASL signers, it further *removed* it from representing English phonology. This group included **Gerilee Gustason** (a deaf teacher of deaf children), **Donna Pfetzing** (an interpreter with a deaf child), and **Ester Zawolkow** (an interpreter with deaf parents). They called their code *Signing Exact English* (SEE2).

SEE2 stays more morphologically true to the ASL meanings of signs while adding specific separate signs for English morphology. As an example, the SEE2 production of "going" would combine a sign for "go" and a sign for "ing." The SEE2 signs for "looked" would combine a sign for "look" and a sign for "ed." SEE2 would also add the past-tense marker to irregular verbs such as the following English words: went, saw, saw, ate, drove, and bought. These productions of a regular form in ASL to represent irregular forms in English imply that these words should be spelled "goed, seeed, sited, eated, drived, and buyed." While SEE2 attempts to maintain ASL morphology, it does so at the expense of English morphology and results in a significant mixing of the two languages that represents neither language accurately.

We already mentioned the Linguistics of Visual English as one of the three original splits from the groups that created SEE1 and SEE2. Several other systems have been developed, but none as deeply structured as these initial three attempts at creating manual English codes.

6.4 Summary

Natural Pidgins develop where a community comes together without a majority knowing any shared language. Elements of their languages combine with one another to create a business language, called pidgins. Pidgins become languages when the next generation of users interact with and "fix" the pidgin through a process called creolization.

Invented Pidgins have been created to assist people in international gatherings. *Esperanto* is the most organized invented pidgin and mixes elements of spoken languages. *Gestuno* is essentially only a vocabulary of 1,500 signs and does not specify grammatical rules. *International Signing* is a spontaneous means of communication, which is natural, not invented.

The creation of manual English codes represents the introduction of *Artificial Pidgins* to deaf children. Some of these deaf children will successfully de-pidginize this input toward either ASL or English. The remaining deaf children exposed to manual English codes will creolize their own, new language, which is neither ASL nor English. These children risk being permanently language impaired if they are not exposed to visually clear interaction in one or the other language prior to puberty.

6.4.1 Review Questions

1. How do natural pidgins develop?
2. What is the difference between a pidgin and a creole?
3. How are *Esperanto* and *Gestuno* similar to and different from pidgins?
4. When were *Esperanto* and *Gestuno* created?
5. How is *International Signing* different from *Gestuno*?
6. Which encoding mechanisms represent elements of *English* in manual/English Artificial Pidgins?
7. Which encoding mechanisms represent elements of *ASL* in manual/English Artificial Pidgins?
8. Who was the initial creator of American manual English codes?
9. What was the original name of the first American manual English code and what was it later changed to?
10. Why do manual English codes not actually encode English?

6.4.2 Suggested Activities

1. Make up a (pseudo) pidgin language of your own. Take the vocabulary of a spoken language (such as French, German, or Spanish) and put them in English word order. Change the pronunciation to American English speech patterns.
2. Find a guidebook for either SEE1 or SEE2 (or another *Artificial Pidgin*) and figure out how to express the following sentences using them:
   a. Yesterday I saw five goats.
   b. I finished eating two hours before I swam.
   c. The darkness of the coming night made us feel sheepish.

Chapter 7
Transcommunication

"Transcommunication"

Rasmus watched as Timoth gazed past Rasmus' shoulder. Timoth nodded and then tapped the shoulder of the person seated behind Timoth. Timoth pointed across the room and two conversations began.

"Well, you have become quite a transcommunicator, Timoth" Rasmus said.

Timoth stared across the table "What makes you say that? What's a 'transcommunicator'?"

"A transcommunicator is one who mediates the exchange of information between two other parties."

"Um... Isn't that the same as an interpreter?"

"Interpreters are transcommunicators, yes, that is true. But you just successfully transcommunicated a message and no interpreting took place!"

"And just where and how did I accomplish this amazing 'transcommunication' thing?"

"Just now, when that fellow behind me waved at you and you tapped the shoulder of that woman next to you. All he did was raise his eyebrows, look at you, and point at her."

"Hmm... That's right... no signs, no words"

"But significant communication none the less! You understood his message to mean he wanted her attention."

"So I turned, tapped her shoulder, looked at her and pointed to him."

"Transcommunication!"

"But how does interpreting fit into that?"

"The difference, Timoth, is that interpreting adds language to the communication."

"Adds language? You mean replaces communication with language."

"Oh no, I mean adds." Rasmus pulled out a book and turned a few pages, then gazed at the book and continued "Language is simply a small part of the many ways we communicate."

Timoth looked at the book in Rasmus' hands, pointed to it and said, "Is that written in there? What book is that?"

Rasmus gazed again at Timoth "Hmm?... is *what* written *where?*"

Timoth reached across the table and grabbed the book. "This is a *novel!* Why were you looking at it when you said 'Language is simply a small part of the many ways we communicate?'"

Rasmus slowly reached over and took the book back from Timoth. "And why did you think that I was reading aloud to you?"

Timoth smiled "Because you didn't look at me. You shifted your eye gaze toward the book."

Rasmus nodded "And the fact that I was holding a book combined with my shift of eye gaze toward it meant something to you, didn't it?"

"I thought you were quoting some authority on the subject of communication. That way I'd be more likely to accept your argument without any more questions."

"You thought all of that... But I didn't say I was reading aloud to you. You paid attention to much more than merely the words I was using. So do you agree with my statement now?"

Timoth leaned back in thought. "Your eye gaze and posture told me that what you were saying was perhaps very important and that maybe I should remember it." Timoth's gaze returned to Rasmus, "You communicated with much more than just language."

Rasmus smiled and put the book away.

Timoth smiled. "I will remember the lesson."

Chapter 7 – Transcommunication
"Language is Science, Language-Use is Art, and Interpreting is Both." - 1999 BC

7.0 Overview
Unit One identified the essential linguistic tools for successful interpreting. In Chapter 1 we introduced three variables that influence communication: *Intention*, *Immediacy*, and *Interactivity*. In Chapter 2 we gained an understanding of the differences between *Communication* and *Language*. We also learned that there are only three *Channels* for languages: signed, spoken, and written; and Chapter 5 revealed that each of these *Channels* may have a variety of *Language Encoding Systems* (such as typed symbols, written symbols, signed symbols, spoken symbols, Brailled symbols, fingerspelled symbols, Morse code symbols, and palm printed symbols). We performed an extensive analysis of the different components of language by means of the *Linguistic Pyramid* and in Chapter 3 we explored pragmatics and discourse, which are essential for successful interpreting.

Chapter 4 explored language variation in both spoken and signed languages, particularly American Sign Language. Languages can vary in dialect, sociolect, and register. Language use can also vary based on the bilingual skills of the people communicating (Language Contact) and this leads us now to the work of communicating a message between two languages. It also leads to the work of communicating a message within a single language but using different *Language Encoding Systems*.

Unit Two explores the work of *transcommunication*. This chapter will explore the transcommunication work of interpreters, translators, and transliterators. We begin by introducing the term "transcommunication" and then review the labels for extralinguistic (outside of language) work. Next we will explore intralinguistic (within one language) work, such as "transliteration". Finally we explore interlinguistic (between two languages) work, such as "translation" and "interpreting".

7.1 Transcommunication
Before we can move forward we need to define the word which captures all of the different kinds of work that can be done between any two communication system (including two different languages or just two different *Language Encoding Systems* for the same language): **Transcommunication**. *Transcommunication* is any kind of mediation where one person communicates another person's message to a third person.

Transcommunicators must understand information and do something with it. We will use the word "text" to refer to the information that a person produces. This includes the basic pieces of meaning as well as the cultural expectations surrounding the message and the manner in which it is generated. Transcommunicators work between two basic kinds of texts. *Source Texts* are created by people other than the transcommunicator. *Target Texts* are created by the transcommunicator. Figure 7.1 represents the sequence of a *Source Text* followed by a *Target Text*.

Figure 7.1 - Source and Target Texts

Transcommunication includes 1) basic communication without using any language (such as waving to get someone's attention on behalf of another person), 2) communication within a single language (such as reading a written message aloud to another person) and 3) communication between two languages (such as translating information from one language to another). We will begin with transcommunication without language, referred to here as *elucidation*.

7.2 Extralinguistic Transcommunication: Elucidation

Extralinguistic Transcommunication means that one side of the communication event does not use a language. Earlier in Unit One we introduced the concepts of communication and semiotics. Through semiotics it is possible to understand how we can communicate without language. This communication may be accomplished through vocalizations, gestures, body postures and facial expression as well as graphic symbols (such as an arrow). If the communication system is shared by members of a community in which the system is rule-governed, has infinite production possibilities, is intergenerational, and changes over time, then we can consider the communication system to be *linguistic*.

If each side of the communication event meets the definition of language then the transcommunication between the two will be *bilingual* if the languages are different; if both parties *share* the same language then the transcommunication is *monolingual*. We will explore both bilingual and monolingual transcommunication later in this chapter. If just one side of the communication event does not meet these requirements (such as the use of basic gestures, natural pidgins, or artificial pidgins) then any transcommunication between the two will be called *Elucidation*.

There are many people who are faced with the need to communicate without sharing any common language between themselves and the people around them. This can even be the case for locally available professional interpreters when a person's native language is not known to anyone locally or, in some cases, when a person is not fluent in any language at all. In order to serve these people it is common practice to employ gestures and more dramatic enactment of the ideas that need to be conveyed. Because this gesturing does not constitute an actual language, none of the terms we will learn later in this chapter can be applied to the process of elucidation. *Elucidation* is the transcommunication of a message between a language and something other than language.

Elucidation does not include communication between two people who use gestures to directly communicate with each other. Such forms of communication may commonly take place in business exchanges where pointing gestures, written or signed numbers, and the exchange of money ensures sufficient communication to transact a sale between people who do not share any language. Such direct exchanges of communication are not likely to be enhanced by a third person who also shares no language with either of the other two people. Therefore we shall not further explore transcommunication that makes use of no languages whatsoever.

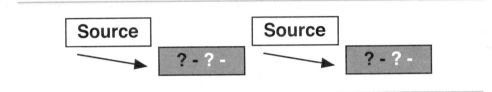

**Figure 7.2 - Elucidation (consecutive) of Monologic Discourse
from *Language* to *Less-Than-Language***

Elucidation can occur with *monologic* or *dialogic* texts and can be *simultaneous* or *consecutive*. Figure 7.1, above, shows consecutive *monologic* elucidation, Figure 7.2, below, shows consecutive *dialogic* elucidation. By definition, a language has a community of people who share the language. There should be many people in the language community who can directly communicate with each other. Most non-language consumers of elucidation services will not have such a community with shared knowledge of the communication system. Therefore a transcommunicator will likely require highly stylistic adjustments in order to meet the non-linguistic consumer's individual idiosyncrasies and preferences. These stylistic adjustments will require additional time and will be best accommodated by a *consecutive* approach to the work.

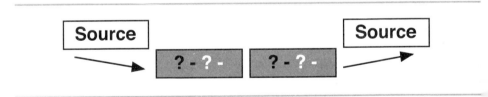

Figure 7.3 - Elucidation (consecutive) of Dialogic Discourse

Elucidation as a process requires 1) a language user (or a linguistic text, such as a magazine article, an audio book, or a videotape), 2) a transcommunicator who knows the same language as the language user (or linguistic text), and 3) a non-language user, who must communicate without using a language. A "linguistic text" is simply a document, which might be in a written language (such as a medical history form) or a signed language (such as a videotape). An elucidator may read the medical history form, and then attempt to convey the items on the form *gesturally* (but not truly *linguistically*) to the non-language user. The elucidator would then determine the meaning of any responses from the non-language user and write them down on the form. This process is possible because communication does not require language; but the danger is that without language it can be very difficult to be certain that the questions and answers are accurately understood. Because languages are very refined forms of communication, transcommunication will always be more accurate when it makes use of language at both ends.

7.2.1 Elucidation of Environmental Stimuli

One consideration when transcommunicating for deaf people is providing access to auditory environmental information in addition to the linguistic information. Hearing people who use interpreting services are still generally able to determine who is speaking, what noises exist in the environment, and other auditory information. A deaf person does not always have access to these important parts of the overall communication. Likewise a blind consumer of interpreting services needs to have access to visual environmental information, such as people entering or leaving a room, gestures, diagrams, charts, and facial expressions. DeafBlind consumers obviously need access to both auditory and visual environmental stimuli.

The deaf consumer may not hear the vocal inflections or the speaking rate of people using a spoken language. These elements of spoken communication, however, do have direct linguistic counterparts in signed languages (such as facial expression and signing speed). When deaf people take a turn in a conversation using a signed language, they produce visually clear information such that there is no doubt about who has the floor; but the visual information available from people who are only speaking is comparatively minimal. Deaf consumers of interpreting services are most commonly the minority members of the communication event. Therefore they are at a disadvantage for receiving visual information that helps them identify who is speaking. This means that the interpreter must also convey information about who has the floor when there is possible confusion. Lectures generally do not shift frequently between speakers (except if the lecturer is being heckled or taking questions from the audience), but group discussions and brainstorming sessions often include rapid-fire exchanges between several people and the interpreter will have to constantly work to identify who is speaking with every turn taken.

In addition to identifying who is speaking, the interpreter needs to be aware of the sounds within the environment: microphone feedback, squeaking noises, alarms, bells, buzzers, sirens, air conditioners, and even the sudden silence of electrical devices that stop making noise when they are turned off. Hearing people are all aware of changes to the environmental sounds. Sometimes the hearing people will react to those sounds. Deaf consumers of interpreting services may be confused about these reactions if they did not have access to the environmental sound in the first place. Just like understanding a joke is different than having one explained to you, the deaf person should be able to react to environmental sounds as they occur rather than having the reaction of hearing people explained after the fact.

Consistency in conveying environmental sounds requires that the interpreter first notice the sounds. This can be difficult when the pressures of regenerating the spoken information may be overwhelming to the interpreter. The way to start is to notice sounds at first during down time when there is relative silence. Just expressing the fact that no one is talking can be a starting point. People clearing their throats, pencils dropping or other apparently trivial noises may be very useful information: we often remind people to say things or indicate that we want to say something by clearing our throats. A pencil drop may be the first step in attempting a diversion from the topic of discussion. Once we condition ourselves to notice the sounds we must have strategies to represent the sound. First we need to indicate the source of the noise. This might include identifying the direction as well as the distance (inside the room, outside the room) or even a particular location (air vents, Bob's desk). The next part is either identifying what the cause of the noise is (a furnace turning on, or a fire truck passing by), identifying what the noise sounds like (a *boom*, or a *pop...* perhaps the cause is unknown), or providing a combination of these two.

Environmental sounds are often left out of the interpreting process but in order to provide comparable access to the environment, they need to be considered. With practice noticing the noises, and with careful thought about how to efficiently represent the environmental sounds to deaf consumers, interpreters can ensure that their deaf consumers receive the most complete interpretation possible.

7.2.2 Elucidation of Visual Gestural Communication

Some people are *semilingual*, meaning that they have some useable knowledge of two different languages, but do not have fluency in either one. Other people are truly *alingual*; meaning that they may be able to communicate, but have no language fluency at all. Somewhere between these two kinds of linguistic ability are many deaf people who may neither comprehend the standard productions of a signed language nor any written language. Some deaf children and adults do not have fluency in any language at all; either because they have yet to be exposed to an accessible language, or they grew past puberty before being exposed to an accessible language, or they have experienced some form of brain damage or mental deficiencies. It is still possible to communicate effectively with alingual or semilingual people through *Visual Gestural Communication* (VGC). VGC uses the widely accepted gestures of the hearing society as its base and includes significant use of facial expression, body postures, mime, and acting. VGC may also be used between people who actually have fluency in various languages, but do no share any *common* languages.

When using *Visual Gestural Communication* as either a source or target text it is important to remember several aspects of VGC. 1) VGC requires both parties to wish to communicate. If only one party wishes to communicate, VGC (or, for that matter, any other means of communication – including language) will fail. 2) VGC generally requires a repeating of a message to confirm mutual understanding. Often the person perceiving the source message does the repetition. Therefore, VGC takes significantly more time than the use of standardized language. 3) Abstract concepts *can* be expressed but will require *significant time* to explain the abstractions as compared to concrete noun or actions. A demonstration using actual objects may not be necessary, but may prove to be helpful and speedy. 4) If both parties are in regular contact for an extended time then familiar topics should require less time to discuss than newer, less-familiar topics. 5) A person with significant experience and practice communicating via VGC will generally be more effective than a person who has had limited VGC experience and practice.

7.2.3 Elucidation of International Signing and Gestuno

Communication between deaf people who do not share a common signed language is likely to begin via *Visual Gestural Communication*. Most European signed languages share some historical link to the Abbé de L'Epée's school in Paris. The result is some amount of similarity between certain signed language vocabularies across Europe. This set of similarities, combined with regular encounters between deaf people and their signed languages (such as the biennial conferences of the World Federation of the Deaf), have helped to create some generally agreed-upon vocabulary items which some people refer to as *International Signing*. *International Signing* still makes use of many aspects of VGC, but works in less of a vacuum for vocabulary, and may include fingerspelling some vocabulary using a widely known written language such as English or French.

A formal effort was made to standardize some of these vocabulary items and was published as *Gestuno*. While *Gestuno* is no one's native language, it represents an effort within the international Deaf community to streamline the time needed to develop a pidgin language for international gatherings of deaf people. The process of transcommunicating with *Gestuno*, or the broader category of *International Signing*, remains an act of *Elucidation*, since neither *Gestuno* nor *International Signing* constitute actual languages.

7.2.4 Elucidation of Natural and Artificial Pidgins

A *Pidgin* is a stabilized conglomerate of three or more languages, which is used for interaction among people who do not share a common language. Natural pidgins have typically sprung up initially as spontaneous trade jargons for economic reasons where several different cultures are found among people brought together (such as at gold mines, diamond mines, and in the slave trade of the European powers and their colonies). Pidgins are regularized "business" communication, which merge the vocabulary of the dominant culture's language[18] (Portuguese, for example) and the pronunciations and grammars of the various non-dominant cultures' languages.[19] Pidgins do not meet the definition of language established in *Unit One* because they have yet to show historical change and be passed from one generation to another.

If the economic and social circumstances are maintained for several years, then a second generation will be born into this community. This generation will "fix" the pidgin by wrapping their human brains around the pidgin. This process is called *creolization*. Once the second generation has creolized a pidgin, the resulting creole does indeed satisfy the definition of *language*. Therefore the following terminology correctly applies: Transcommunication between a language and a *Creole* is bilingual, such as *Interpreting* or *Translating*. Transcommunication between a language and a *Pidgin* is not bilingual, and therefore adopts the previously mentioned label of *Elucidation*.

Artificial Pidgins are created by intentionally merging the vocabulary of one language with the grammar of another along with at least one other modification. Most artificial pidgins have been created for the purposes of educating deaf children. Typically the vocabulary of a signed language is modified and then molded onto the grammar of a spoken language. The educators adopting the use of these artificial pidgins typically

---

[18] The dominant language in a pidgin is known as the "superstrate" language.

[19] The non-dominant languages in a pidgin are known as the "substrate" languages.

believe these mergings somehow represent the fullness of the language supplying the grammar (the substrate language). The reality is that children who are exposed to these artificial pidgins will attempt to *creolize* them toward the language supplying the vocabulary (the superstrate language) (Supalla, 1991). *Artificial Pidgins* (i.e. manual English codes) are not languages; therefore neither the label *Interpreting* nor *Transliterating* can be correctly applied to any work that involves a manual English code. The label of *Elucidation* is all that can be correctly applied to any work involving a manual English code[20] (such as SEE2).

7.2.5 Summary of Extralinguistic Transcommunication

Extralinguistic Transcommunication simply means that one side of the communication event did not use a language. In Chapter One we introduced the concept of communication and the terms *semiotics* and *pragmatics*. Through semiotics it is possible to communicate without language. This may be accomplished through vocalizations, gestures, body postures and facial expression as well as graphic symbols. The key factor to consider is whether both kinds of communication are shared by members of a community in which the system is rule-governed, has infinite production possibilities, is intergenerational, and changes over time. If just one side of the communication event does not meet these requirements (such as the signals of alarm clocks, the use of basic gestures, natural pidgins, or artificial pidgins) then any transcommunication between the two will be called *Elucidation*. If *both* sides of the communication meet the definition of language, then the transcommunication between the two will be described in the next sections of this chapter.

7.3 Monolingual Transcommunication: Shadowing & Transliteration

There are many possible reasons that a professional language specialist would be hired to work within a single language. Some of these reasons are related to the need to create reliable documentation of human interaction. Others are related to the need to provide access to an activity as it takes place. Four labels apply to *intralinguistic transcommunication*.

1) *Recited Reading* is the process of creating, within the same language, a spoken or signed target text from a written source text.

2) *Transcription* is the process of creating, within the same language, a written target text from a spoken or signed source text. Transcription also requires that the final product is fixed, or recorded, in some way (such as on paper, on videotape, or electronically in computer memory).

---

[20] Various manual English codes have been created. *Signing Essential English* (Anthony) ever underwent a name change to *Seeing Essential English* (SEE 1) to obfuscate the fact that it was composed of modified ASL signs. Another system, entitled Signing Exact English (SEE 2) held closer to ASL semantics and thus drew greater acceptance, even though it actually had less similarity to English than SEE 1.

3) *Transliteration* is the process of creating a target text in a different *language encoding system* but within the same language and channel (written, signed, or spoken), as the source text. An example of transliteration would be the changing of a written message from the language encoding system of *Typed English* (image) to *Brailled English* (texture).

4) *Shadowing* is the process of creating a target text in the *same* language encoding system and within the *same* language and channel (written, signed, or spoken), as the source text. Shadowing may be verbatim repetition or paraphrased. One practical application of shadowing, also known as *mirroring,* would be watching a source text produced in signed ASL by an audience member (that the general audience cannot easily see) and then repeating the same message in signed ASL from the stage (so that all the audience members can see the same message).

It is important to remember that all four of these labels are related to *intralinguistic transcommunication*, meaning that only one language is involved. The following grid organizes these intralinguistic (monolingual) activities for spoken and written English.

Intralinguistic Activities Involving English		
Source Text Channel	**Target Text Channel**	
	Spoken English	**Written English**
Spoken English	*Transliteration or Shadowing*	*Transcription*
Written English	*Recited Reading*	*Transliteration or Shadowing*

Figure 7.4 – Interlinguistic Transcommunication Labels

7.3.1 Recited Reading
    Recited Reading is otherwise known as reading aloud. **Recited Reading is the monolingual transfer of a written-channel source text to a spoken-channel or signed-channel target text.** *Recited Reading* requires at least literacy in the source language but can employ significant qualities of stylistics and register variation. An effective actor or storyteller can bring much expression to recited readings. *Recited Reading* may serve as an effective part of a battery of tests to determine the language processing skills of a potential student interpreter. Likewise, *Recited Reading* may help to serve as part of self-improvement techniques to enhance spoken-channel target text performances.

7.3.2 Transcription

Transcription is merely the reverse of *Recited Reading*. **Transcription is the monolingual transfer of a spoken-channel or signed-channel source text to a written-channel target text.** Transcription may be accomplished through handwriting, fingerspelling, using Braille, Morse code or semaphore; but it is most commonly done in one of three basic ways. 1) *Verbatim Typing*, which requires a fast typist to transcribe a spoken text as it is produced. Typing speeds of between 150 to 200 words per minute may be required to perform this service. 2) *Shorthand*, which also requires special training but results in a text that actually represents speech sounds and still needs to be retyped before transcription is complete. 3) *Machine Shorthand*, which is used for Court Reporting. This too requires special training and again results in a text that actually represents speech sounds and still needs to be retyped before transcription is complete. 4) *Computer Aided Real-time Transcription* (CART) which begins with *Machine Shorthand* but uses a computer to continue the process immediately into completed typed text. CART technology is often employed in real-time captioning on television[21]. CART is also used at conferences to provide visual access to the proceedings of business meetings and lectures.

7.3.3 Transliteration

Transliteration has traditionally meant the changing of letters in a word from one alphabet system to another. The point of *transliteration* is access: to allow a person who can read one alphabet to access a language that uses a different alphabet. **Transliteration is the monolingual transfer of a source text in one modality to another modality while maintaining the same language channel.**

Here is an example: If you went to Russia and encountered the words "POCTOb HA ΔONU" you would need to know the Cyrillic alphabet in order to pronounce the words correctly. If I transliterate those words to "Rostov Na Donu" it still doesn't tell you what the words mean, but you now have access to the words through a writing system you know. Only when I tell you that this is the name of a town in South Western Russia and that it is generally written in English as "Rostov on Don" because it is on the Don River, do you understand its meaning because I have translated it into a language you know.

Because Russian is written using the Cyrillic alphabet it takes an extra step to know how to read the letters as compared to reading French, Spanish or Italian, which each share (for the most part) the Roman alphabet. Both the Cyrillic and Roman alphabets are encoding systems for written languages. It is possible to encode English with Cyrillic letters and, likewise, it is possible to encode Russian with Roman letters. The process of substituting one encoding system for the other is the process of *transliteration*. The grid below shows three Russian words written in the Cyrillic alphabet, the *transliteration* of each into the Roman alphabet, and then a *translation* of each into an equivalent English word.

---

[21] There are some amazing typists who actually perform live captioning via verbatim typing.

Russian Word	Transliteration	English Translation
МОЛОКО	Moloko	*Milk*
СОК	Sok	*Juice*
ГРАНАТ	Granat	*Pomegranate*

Figure 7.5 – Russian-English Transliteration & Translation

As you can see, the first column contains some letters that you are not likely to recognize correctly. The transliteration column transforms each word to Roman alphabet versions, but still does not reveal what the *meaning* of the word is. The value of the transliteration is to allow you to approximate the pronunciation of the Russian word. **Transliterations never reveal meaning between two languages;** it is the *translation* between languages that reveals the basic meaning of the word in the above examples.

Transliteration may play a significant role in working with deaf, blind, and/or DeafBlind consumers who are fluent in a language but need the language encoding system changed to one which they can understand in their perceptive modality. Deaf consumers will need images, blind consumers will need sounds or texture, and DeafBlind consumers will depend entirely upon texture to perceive communication. Transliteration options for deaf people include changing spoken English to cued English. Blind and DeafBlind consumers may have written English transliterated into Brailled English. Transliteration is not the only access option, but certainly should be considered as one of many choices to accommodate a specific consumer's needs.

Transliteration can occur in either monologic or dialogic forms. Figure 7.6 shows the simultaneous processing (but slightly delayed presentation) of simultaneous transliteration for monologic discourse.

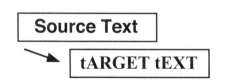

Figure 7.6 - Transliteration (simultaneous) of Monologic Discourse

Figure 7.6 represented *simultaneous monologic transliteration*. Figure 7.7 represents *simultaneous dialogic transliteration*. Consecutive processing is also possible, but usually is reserved for processing written transliterations where an entire text is completed before the transliteration process begins. Figures 7.6 and 7.7 both represent transliterations that are generated spontaneously *with consumers of each language modality physically present*.

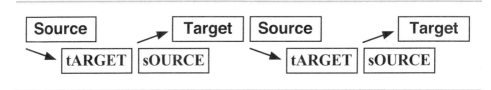

Figure 7.7 - Transliteration (simultaneous) of Dialogic Discourse

The point to remember is that transliteration provides *access*, but does not cross the "language barrier." That is, even though the *forms* of the word or words have changed, the *language* remains the same. You must know something about that language to understand a text that has been transliterated from a form that you *do not* have access to (such as Cyrillic) to a form that you *do* have access to.

The concept of transliteration has been expanded from its origins (related to written languages) to the presentation of spoken language in accessible forms for deaf people. *Oral Transliteration* is the presentation of spoken English into what has been called "Visible English" which is simply a controlled and clear presentation of lip movements, facial expression, and natural gesture which allows a deaf person with lip-reading skill to have access to the spoken language version. In this example, both the source text and the target text share the same language – English – but they make use of different encoding modalities.

Another version of transliteration is *Cued Language Transliteration* (generally known as Cued Speech). Cueing presents spoken language phonology through combinations of lip movement, eight handshapes, four locations, and three movement patterns, plus epenthetic movement. *Cued Language Transliteration* makes use of the cueing system to present the phonology (speech sounds) of spoken languages to a consumer who also knows (or is learning) the cueing system. Once again, there is no change in language: both the source and target texts use the same language.

Transliteration also occurs with ASL. DeafBlind people who attend conferences often receive either *tactile transliteration* or *reduced-space shadowing* when a source text is presented in ASL. Tactile transliteration / interpretation is used by deaf people who do not have usable vision and requires physical / tactile contact between the DeafBlind consumer and the transcommunicator. Deaf people who have limited usable vision (such as tunnel vision) use reduced-space shadowing/interpretation. The interpreting versions of these will be presented in the next sections of this chapter, which addresses bilingual transcommunication. If the source language and target language are both ASL, then the task is either *tactile transliteration* or *reduced-space shadowing*, even though the end result looks the same as the interpreting versions. The key difference is whether the source and target languages are the same or different. Many people who provide tactile transliteration or reduced-space shadowing for DeafBlind people are deaf themselves. They may use the services of another interpreter to regenerate a spoken English text into ASL. This ASL text now becomes the source text for a tactile transliteration or reduced-space shadowing for DeafBlind consumers. This form of *relayed interpreting* will be further defined later in Chapter 8.

Notetaking is also a form of transliteration if it takes a spoken form of language and represents it in writing. Notes might be in shorthand, which is a phonetic representation of the source text, or in long hand (standard written English, for example). Notes could be typed or word-processed. The most technical of all transliterations is *Computer Assisted Real-Time Transcription* (CART), which starts with a phonemic encoding of a spoken language (much like the use of cues or shorthand) and then generates written English words and punctuation through computer software.

It is entirely possible for each of these forms of transliteration to be used as a part of interpreting. The determining factor is whether the language barrier is crossed; if so, then the act is one of *interpreting*. A German source text presented in lip-readable French would be an *Oral Interpretation*. A British Sign Language source text presented in cued English would be a *Cued Language Interpretation*. A Spanish source text presented in tactile ASL would be a *Tactile Interpretation*. An English source text presented in reduced-space ASL would be a *Reduced-Space Interpretation*. A Russian source text entered into a computer as encoding for spoken English and then processed by computer into written English would be a *Computer Assisted Real-Time Transcription Interpretation*. While all of these variations are possible, most of them do not occur very often. The key to remember here is that *Tactile* and *Reduced-Space* forms will be *transliterations* when the source and target languages are the same; they will be *interpretations* when the source and target languages are different.

7.3.4 Shadowing

While *Transliteration* creates target texts in different *language encoding systems* of the same language channel, *Shadowing* maintains the same *language encoding system*. *Shadowing* **is the monolingual transfer of a source text in one modality to the same modality and the same language channel.** At first it may not be obvious what value there is in taking a text from signed ASL to signed ASL or from spoken English to spoken English. The practical application is when a cons0umer does not have direct access to the source text. This is a frequent occurrence in audience situations such as when an audience member asks a question (whether signed or spoken) which can be seen or heard by a lecturer on stage but cannot be seen or heard by the majority of the audience. The lecturer will often shadow, or repeat, the question before answering it. Interpreters are likely to perform shadowing themselves in just this situation if the lecturer needs interpretation in order to understand the question.

Shadowing can be accomplished with a range of performances. ***Mirroring*** is considered to be a more literal copying of the source text while ***Processed Shadowing*** focuses on the meaning of the source text and may or may not use any of the original words of the source text. *Processed Shadowing* is still an intralinguistic task that uses the same *Language Encoding System* of the source text, but it allows significantly more freedom from the word choices and word orders of the source text.

7.3.5 Summary of Intralinguistic Transcommunication
   This part of Chapter Seven has reviewed four different ways to regenerate a source text into a target text without changing the language. Two of these, *Recited Reading* and *Transcription*, change between written and non-written channels of the same language. *Transliteration* changes the *language encoding system* within the same channel, while *Shadowing* maintains the same *language encoding system* and the same language channel. Two distinctions of *Shadowing* include *Mirroring* and *Processed Shadowing*. *Mirroring* is a more word-for-word repetition of the source text. *Processed Shadowing* provides a greater range of variation from the source text while attempting to generate the same meaning as the source text. All four serve as potential options for providing access to information for various consumers, including deaf, blind, and DeafBlind people. Each may also be used for assessment purposes prior to second-language training for potential interpreters or as part of self-assessment and self-improvement strategies for working interpreters.

7.4 Bilingual Transcommunication: Interpreting and Translating
   One important thing to understand is that there have been heated debates about just what professional interpreters are supposed to do in various situations and even about the basic definition of interpreting. Part of this argument has been the paradigm of "conduit" as a framework for understanding how an interpreter works. In the *conduit* framework, language is a package that contains ideas. On one end of communication people put their ideas "into" word packages. The words then travel somehow to other people who then "extract" meaning from the word packages and perhaps send a reply.
   Within this framework interpreters are considered to be one more handler of the package (the words). The notion is that the interpreter extracts the meaning from the words (the first container), finds equivalent words in the other language (a new container) and then sends the re-packaged message to the intended receiver. If everything goes smoothly, no one needs to know the interpreter was ever involved; but this framework ignores the complexity of communication both through and beyond language. Eye contact, body posture, vocal intonation, and cultural expectations can all influence how we understand a message. Interpreters must include this kind of information in their interpretations. In other words, the interpreter not only replaces the container (the words), but also has to be concerned about how that container is wrapped (formal/informal; vocal inflection/facial expression), who is sending it, who is to receive it, how it is delivered, at what speed, and so forth. In addition to all of these factors, the very notion that a message can be "contained" or "packaged" into words is inaccurate since we know that communication requires background knowledge and a physical context. Every message is different and even multiple interpretations of the same message are possible, sometimes even necessary. Interpreting is a very interactive process that requires the interpreter to constantly make decisions.
   Section 7.1 introduced the concepts of *Source Texts* and *Target Texts*. Another variable in describing texts is whether the texts are variable or fixed. *Variable Texts* are spontaneously created and produced. *Fixed Texts* are either prepared or recorded (by writing, audio recording, video recording or any other means of documentation).
   It is possible to record a spontaneous, variable text; but the recording itself becomes a fixed text because it will be the same every time it is reviewed. One of the key factors to consider when determining whether a text is fixed or variable is the notion of being able

to interrupt and redirect the message. It is not usually possible to interrupt a text written in a book or performed on videotape (other than to stop reading or to turn the VCR off). Modern innovations in interactive media, such as CD-ROMs and DVDs allow the viewer to interrupt and redirect the message so we need to introduce the other key factor: is the text the same each time it is presented? Each time a section of a CD-ROM or DVD is played it is the same as before (or one of a very few variations which will eventually repeat after several viewings). In other words, a person could *memorize* the patterns because they don't change (or only change in predictable ways). Books, CDs, DVDs, videotapes, and any other forms of a recording are all examples of the ways that messages are *fixed* (made permanent).

Most of the time we would consider a live presentation to be spontaneous. But if the person is performing in a play, their performance is a prepared version of a fixed text (although you *could* try to interrupt and ask a question). Live presentations are considered to be spontaneous, *Variable Texts* unless they are memorized or scripted, in which case they are (relatively) *Fixed Texts*.

With this understanding of what interpreters work with, we can now define the process of interpreting. **Interpreting is an interactive exchange of information between two languages in which the interpreter actively creates spontaneous target texts that maintain the information and intent of their respective variable source texts.** So if you thought interpreting was simple, now you know that it has a very complex definition. Let's examine the pieces one at a time.

1) *Interpreting is an interactive exchange of information.* This means that the interpreter is just as much involved in the exchange of information as every other person who is participating. In fact the interpreter usually participates at least as much as every other person *combined.* Every message each person sends must be understood, analyzed, and regenerated by the interpreter. It is for this reason that phrases such as "*conveying* an interpretation" or "*delivering* a message" really are inadequate and this book has instead talked about "creating" interpretations or "regenerating" messages.

2) *Interpreting exchanges information between two languages.* This may seem obvious now, but it is an essential part of the definition. Different labels apply to other kinds of work that exchange information within the same language or when something less-than-language is involved.

3) *Interpreters actively create spontaneous target texts.* Our previous definitions indicated that interpreters are the people who create target texts but a key word related to interpreting is that the target text is spontaneously produced. If the target text is prepared or rehearsed and then recorded (written, typed, videotaped, etc), then we would probably call it a *translation.* In addition, the words "actively create" reveal that interpreters do not merely *convey* another person's thoughts. Interpreters must first bring their own knowledge and source language abilities to the understanding of the source texts. They then *create* their target texts based on that knowledge and their target language abilities.

4) *Interpreters maintain the information and intent of the source texts.* This means that the audience reaction to the interpretation *should* be the same as the reaction would be to the original message. This is tricky work because it requires the interpreter to make judgments about the meaning of the information and the speaker's intentions – often without being able to directly ask the creators of the source texts about the meanings of their messages.

Interpreting requires that two languages be involved. One language is related to the source text; the other language is related to the target text. The source text is variable and so is the target text. The process includes more than just repackaging words; it requires the interpreter to actively participate in the communication process. Because each interpreter has different experiences and skills, this means that no two interpreters can ever create identical target texts from the same source text. Even if two interpreters managed to use identical words, their inflection, volume, timing, and other stylistic features would still be different.

7.4.1 Translation

Another word commonly exchanged for "interpreting" is the word "translating". Interpreting is different from translating. While interpreting depends on variable (non-fixed) source texts and the immediate creation of variable target texts, translation is a slower process that exchanges information from a fixed source text to a fixed target text. **Translation is the extensive review and evaluation of a fixed source text in one language and the creation of a fixed target text, in a different language, which maintains both the information and intent of the source text.** For example, a written English document may be reviewed and evaluated over the course of several days and an ASL version of the same information can be prepared and even recorded onto videotape. It is possible to produce several drafts of the ASL version and choose one as the final translation of the original English text. The process may be very similar to interpreting, but the key differences are 1) the source text is fixed, 2) the target text is fixed, and 3) there is sufficient time to review the source text many times and revise the target text many times before the process is completed.

7.4.2 Simultaneous Interpreting

Now that we know what interpreting is, and what it isn't, we can expand the definition even more. There are two distinct approaches to interpreting. *Simultaneous Interpreting* occurs when the target text is created while the source text continues to be expressed. Simultaneous interpreting is common for monologic discourse, where one person will present a single source text (such as a lecture). Figure 7.8 indicates that the interpreter's target text begins before the source text is complete. It also suggests that the target text will probably conclude just after the source text is complete.

Figure 7.8 - Simultaneous Interpretation of Monologic Discourse

Simultaneous Interpreting can also occur when two (or more) people interact with each other. Each target text is created while the source text continues to be expressed. Figure 7.9 indicates that the source text in one language begins before the target text in another language. That language is then used to create a new source text, which is interpreted into the first language, and so on. Notice that there are time delays between the production of the source text and the production of the target text in both languages.

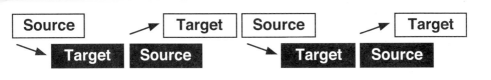

Figure 7.9 - Simultaneous Interpretation of Dialogic Discourse

The time delay between the source and target texts in each language can be problematic because the speaker who has just completed a source text may misunderstand the silence as an opportunity to take another turn. This means that the interpreter has to work to preserve the ability for the second language user to take a turn. This may mean that the interpreter explains the problem to the communicating parties. Other strategies exist for preserving the turn exchange, too. The main point here is that the interpreter must do more than merely "repackage" each message.

7.4.3 Consecutive Interpreting

Consecutive Interpreting requires that the production of the source text is suspended while the target text is produced. Upon completion of the target text the next portion of the source text may be produced. Consecutive Interpreting is fairly common in settings where two or more people alternate in their creation of multiple source texts (such as a job interview).

Historically consecutive interpreting has been done for monologic discourse but usually when the guest speaker (such as a business executive or an evangelist) uses one language to address a large audience who all share a language different from the speaker. This approach is only effective if the source text speakers agree to break-up their presentation into segments. Figure 7.10 shows this one-way use of consecutive interpreting for monologic discourse.

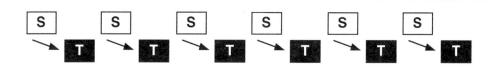

Figure 7.10 - Consecutive Interpretation of Monologic Discourse

One of the most practical applications of consecutive interpreting is for legal interpreting of witness testimony in a court of law. Each question to the witness is completed before the interpretation begins. Likewise each answer is completed before its interpretation is generated. Figure 7.11, below, shows the patterns of consecutive interpreting for dialogic discourse.

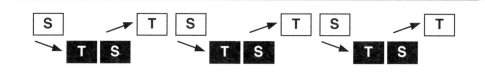

Figure 7.11 - Consecutive Interpretation of Dialogic Discourse

One strong advantage of consecutive interpretation for dialogic discourse is that each participant (including the interpreter) is able to give full attention to each participant during each conversational turn. This allows full access to the semiotic information surrounding the language and provides a greater likelihood for the subtleties of communication to survive the transcommunication process.

7.4.4 Site Translation

Two combinations of interpreting and translation also exist. *Site Translation* is the spontaneous creation of a target text based on the information in a fixed source text while maintaining both the information and intent of the source text[22]. For example, an interpreter reads a medical intake questionnaire, printed in English. The interpreter then, piece by piece, regenerates that information in Mandarin Chinese. In this instance, the interpreter is usually able to take as much time as is required to review and understand the source text before producing the target text; but the target text is not extensively revised or documented ("fixed") in any way. The result is actually a spontaneous and variable text. Please note that in the example above there is only one fixed text – the medical intake questionnaire. If the interpreting writes down the responses to the site translation, then that process is called "Recorded Interpretation".

---

[22] Traditionally this has been called "sight" translation, but is being replaced here with the more accurate word, "site", because the process need not depend on vision and is more related to the performing of the task "on location" or live, rather than depending upon using one's eyes.

7.4.5 Recorded Interpretation

Another combination of interpreting and translating is called *Recorded Interpretation* and it begins with variable source texts (without extensive review and evaluation) and results in fixed target texts, which have not had the benefit of revision or preparation. *Recorded Interpretation* is the documentation of an otherwise spontaneous interpretation of a spontaneous source text. The documentation of interpreted answers on a medical intake questionnaire is one example of recorded interpretation. Another example would be videotaping an interpreter's performance during a training session so that future deaf employees can have access to the same information via the videotape[23]. An alternative form of *Recorded Interpretation* is if the interpreter is creating a written document as the direct result of the interpreting process. This may take place in business settings where the business is being conducted in one language, but someone needs to have documentation of the activity in a language other than the one used to conduct business. The minutes of meetings conducted in ASL are commonly written in English and the recording secretaries are actually performing *Recorded Interpretation*, although their finished product is likely only to be a summary of the source texts. Because the recording of the interpreter's work can be used later as a document of the participants' communication, *Recorded Interpretation* should only be done by agreement of all participants: especially, but not limited to, the interpreter.

7.4.6 Performed Translation

A third variation is the simultaneous delivery of a *Performed Translation* at the same time that the source text is presented. This happens often with performances of plays that are interpreted for the benefit of deaf audiences. In most professional settings, the plays are actually translated prior to the performance and the interpreter is actually creating a performed translation at the same time that the actors on stage deliver their rehearsed lines. If the actors drop lines or ad lib new ones, the interpreter will need to deviate from the performed translation in order to keep the access equivalent. The whole process looks like the spontaneous interpretation of a spontaneous, variable source text; but in reality it is the creation of a performed translation that occurs at the same time as a prepared source text. The target text is considered "fixed" because it is rehearsed and *relatively* non-variable.

---

[23] Note that, technically, any deaf person viewing the videotape will not have complete access to the information originally presented because the videotape cannot reveal all of the original physical context, nor can the presentation be interrupted for clarification by a deaf viewer, etc.

7.4.7 Summary of Interlinguistic Transcommunication
This portion of Chapter Seven has explored some of the differences between source texts and target texts that do not share a common language. A significant distinction for *interlinguistic* transcommunication is whether the source and target texts are fixed or variable. The resulting interaction of these possibilities have given us the following terms: *Interpreting, Consecutive Interpreting, Simultaneous Interpreting, Recorded Interpretation, Translation, Site Translation,* and *Performed Translation.* It is important to remember that these labels are only related to *interlinguistic* activity, meaning that at least two different languages are involved. The following grid organizes the interlinguistic activity that has been described:

Interlinguistic Transcommunication Activities		
	Target Text Variable	**Target Text Fixed**
Source Text Variable	*Interpretation*	*Recorded Interpretation*
Source Text & Target Text Overlap	*Simultaneous Interpreting*	*Recorded Simultaneous Interpreting*
Source Text & Target Text Alternate	*Consecutive Interpreting*	*Recorded Consecutive Interpreting*
Source Text Fixed	*Site Translation*	*Translation*
Fixed Source Text Is Performed "Live"	*Interpretation* (if interpreter has no previous access to source)	*Performed Translation*

Figure 7.12 – Interlinguistic Transcommunication Labels

7.5 Summary of Transcommunication

This chapter has reviewed three kinds of transcommunication: *Extralingual*, *Monolingual*, and *Bilingual*. Extralingual transcommunication, which involves something other than a language on one side, is identified as *Elucidation*. The chart below identifies the various labels for the remaining two kinds of transcommunication that are either *intralinguistic* (monolingual) or *interlinguistic* (bilingual) between signed ASL, spoken English, and written English.

Interlinguistic and Intralinguistic Activities Involving English and ASL

Target Source	Target Text Signed ASL	Target Text Spoken English	Target Text Written English
Source Text Signed ASL	*Transliteration or Shadowing*	*Interpreting or Translation*	*Translation or Recorded Interpretation*
Source Text Spoken English	*Interpreting Site Translation or Translation*	*Transliteration or Shadowing*	*Transcription*
Source Text Written English	*Site Translation or Translation*	*Recited Reading*	*Transliteration or Shadowing*

Figure 7.13 – Interlinguistic & Intralinguistic Transcommunication Labels

Note that three of the above spaces in the grid are identically labeled as "Transliteration or Shadowing". The single factor that determines which label to be used whether the *Language Encoding System* was identical between the source and target texts (shadowing) or different (transliterating).

Let's look at the middle row of "Source Text: Spoken English" with the assumption that our source text is a video recording of a spoken-English lecture. A video recording of a spoken English text will be the same every time it is played; therefore this kind of source text is "fixed." Because the source text is *fixed* as a recording on videotape, it cannot be identified as *Interpreting*. If the target text is spontaneously signed ASL, we might have a *Site Translation* because the source text is fixed but the target text would be unrehearsed. If the target text is rehearsed but generated simultaneously with the source text, then we have the presentation of a *Performed Translation*. If the target text is rehearsed and then recorded on videotape then we have a standard *Translation*. If the translation is for a DeafBlind consumer, then only the first two of these are likely to be presented through tactile signing (although current technology does provide the *possibility* of having mechanical hands reproduce a recorded ASL translation).

Shadowing would take place if the same source text were repeated in spoken English. *Transliteration* would be the appropriate label if any of the following *Language Encoding Systems* were employed: 1) a Phonetic Alphabet, 2) Manual Cues, 3) Mouth

Movements without vocalization, 3) Fingerspelling, 4) Palm Printing, or 5) Tactile Fingerspelling 6) Tadoma, or 7) Tactile Manual Cues.

The same source text could be *Transcribed* by any of the following *Language Encoding Systems*: 1) Written Symbols, 2) Typed Symbols, 3) Morse Code Symbols, 4 Semaphore, 5) Brailled Symbols, 6) Raised (three dimensional) Letters.

Now let's twist everything sideways and replace our source text with a spoken French lecture, but have all of our target texts either as ASL or English. This twist means that the labels of Shadowing, Transcription, and Transliteration cannot apply. These three labels are all restricted to *intralinguistic* (within one language) activity, and we have just reset this sample task as completely *interlinguistic* (between two or more languages). The result is that every target text in the middle row of the grid will be some kind of translation; either a *Site Translation, Performed Translation*, or a standard *Translation* We would then specify both the language and *Language Encoding System* used in the source and target texts. Here are a few of the many possible kinds of target text resulting from a fixed spoken-French source text:

- Site Translation to English palm printing
- Site Translation to signed ASL
- Performed Translation to English Mouth Movements without vocalization
- Performed Translation to tactile ASL
- Standard Translation to Manually Cued English (recorded on videotape)
- Standard Translation to signed ASL (recorded on videotape)

If the source text were live and spontaneously delivered then we could replace the first two words in each of the above examples with Interpretation (note that the last two examples would be correctly identified as *Recorded Interpretations*). In truth, we could additionally distinguish between *Simultaneous* and *Consecutive* interpretations in each category.

7.6 Summary

This chapter explored the work of interpreters, translators, and transliterators. We began by introducing the term "transcommunication" and then reviewed the label for *extralinguistic* (outside of language) work – *Elucidation*. Next we explored the labels for *intralinguistic* (within one language) work – *Transliteration, Shadowing, Recited Reading*, and *Transcription*. Finally we explored the labels for *interlinguistic* (between two languages) work – *Interpreting, Consecutive Interpreting, Simultaneous Interpreting, Recorded Interpretation, Translation, Site Translation*, and *Performed Translation*.

.6.1 Review Questions

. What are the definitions of *Source Texts* and *Target Texts*?
. What label is used to describe extralingual transcommunication?
. What four labels are used to describe monolingual transcommunication?
·. What two primary labels are used to describe bilingual transcommunication?
. What are the two kinds of interpretations possible, based on the amount of time between the presentation of the source text and the creation of the target text?
. What kind of translation results from the spontaneous interpreting of a fixed text?
. What are the definitions of *Fixed Texts* and *Spontaneous Texts*?
. What is the correct label for the 'fixing' of a spontaneous text?
. What is the difference between interpreting and translating?
0. Provide an example scenario of a performed translation.

.6.2 Suggested Activities

. Take a children's story (with lots of pictures) and provide an elucidation of it that uses no more than five actual words or signs from any language. Use these words only to identify the actors or a few objects in the story. Use gestures, body posture, facial expressions to convey the actions of the characters, the plot, and any other details of the story.

. Take one or two sentences from the US Constitution (in Appendix C) and transliterate them into two or three of the encoding systems described in chapter four. As an example, take the preamble and fingerspell the entire passage, then write it out in Braille (using dots instead of raised bumps), then write it out again using Morse code.

. Perform a recited reading of one of the dialogues that open each chapter in this book. Read the lines for Rasmus and Timoth as though they are having a heated argument. Read the lines again as though they are exhausted and can barely concentrate. Read the lines a third time as though they can hardly keep from laughing. Now find a partner who will perform the lines of one character while you perform the lines of the other and mix the approaches (for example, Rasmus might sound tired while Timoth seems to think everything is funny).

Look at Article I of the US Constitution (in Appendix C) and rewrite it so that it is clearly understandable but still completely accurate. Now take this rewritten version (which is an idiomatic shadowing of the source text) and use it as the basis for a translation into another language that you know.

Obtain a recording of various *Sound Effects*. Listen to several sound effects and think about how you would represent them to a deaf person by 1) describing the actions that generated each sound (e.g. shooting a gun), 2) describing the sounds themselves (e.g. pop, bang, boom) or 3) doing both. Practice representing each sound during the same time that the sounds are generated on the recording.

Obtain a recording of a silent film (or an action film). Watch several minutes of the action in the film, then think about how you would represent the visual information and the actions to a blind person. Practice representing the visual elements and actions during the same time that the actions are generated in the film.

Chapter 8
Teamed Transcommunication

"Teamed and Relayed Transcommunication"

Timoth completed generating the target text, verified that the consumer was finished, and then hung up the phone. Timoth then returned to the second level of the convention center. Upon entering the grand ballroom Timoth noticed Rasmus at the foot of the stage chatting with another person. The two shook hands and parted as Timoth walked toward the stage. Rasmus was picking up notes and preparing to leave as Timoth approached.

"Well, there you are! How has your morning been?" asked Rasmus.

"A fine morning so far. I just completed interpreting a phone call and found it an interesting experience."

"Interesting, eh? What made it so interesting? You've certainly interpreted telephone calls before."

"This time there was an interpreter on the other end of the call. I had my consumer in front of me and the other interpreter had another consumer in front of her. That's the first time I ever experienced interpreting message to another interpreter."

Rasmus and Timoth turned toward the back of the grand ballroom and made their way to the doors in the back. "So you relayed your transcommunication." Rasmus said.

"Relayed transcommunication?" Timoth asked. Rasmus nodded but added no more explanation. Timoth sighed and thought for a moment as they exited the convention center. "Transcommunication is the work we do interpreting, translation, recited reading, shadowing, transcription transliteration, and elucidation. So relayed transcommunication requires two people?"

"At least two, yes," said Rasmus. "And this afternoon you shall see significant amount of relayed transcommunication during the plenary sessions. Did you see the person I was chatting with just before you came down to the stage? That's one of my interpreting teammates."

Timoth stopped and looked at Rasmus. "But you were using Our Sign Language to communicate with her!"

Rasmus' head shifted to one side while looking at Timoth. "Timoth, I hope you're not developing a language bias! I never noticed this in you before. What difference does it make which language I use to communicate with someone?"

"Well, I just assumed that using Our Sign Language meant that she was deaf. I guess I just don't think about using OSL except when deaf people are present."

Rasmus and Timoth entered the restaurant and were soon seated at a table. "Timoth, you are fluent in Our Sign Language. Here we are in an environment filled with many other people, also fluent in OSL; but some of the people here don't have access to spoken language. Doesn't it make sense that we should use the majority language for communication here?"

"Of course," Timoth replied, "I just thought it meant that your nterpreting teammate was Deaf."

"But she IS Deaf." Rasmus said, taking a sip of water.

Timoth sat for a moment. Rasmus looked at the menu for a moment, closed the menu, looked at Timoth and finally explained "I will be nterpreting from spoken language to Our Sign Language and she will be generating a processed shadowing to more idiomatic OSL on the stage. It provides an interpretation much closer to the quality we normally only achieve through translation. It's actually quite effective!"

Timoth smiled and nodded. "I see, so it works because two heads are better than one!"

Chapter 8 – Teamed Transcommunication

"One Person Can Have a Profound Impact on Another...
And Two People... Well, Two People Can Work Miracles."
- *Northern Exposure* Script -

8.0 Overview

Chapter Seven explored the individual work of interpreters, translators, and transliterators. After introducing the term "transcommunication" we then reviewed the labels for extralingual, monolingual, and bilingual transcommunication. This chapter builds on these various kinds of work by proposing appropriate practices for *Teamed Transcommunication* and then by introducing the concept of *Relayed Transcommunication*. Both of these variations require that two or more transcommunicators work together to provide coordinated services.

One of the first areas we explore is a physical reason for Teamed Transcommunication: *Overuse Syndrome*. Overuse Syndrome occurs from repeated use of the same muscle groups without sufficient rest. Spoken and signed language interpreters are both susceptible to overuse syndrome, but particularly if their work involves manual movements such as signing, typing, or writing. Related to this is the second significant reason for Teamed Transcommunication: reduction of mental fatigue. Research has indicated that after twenty minutes an interpreter's accuracy begins to decline (Brasel, 1976). It is essential for accuracy that mental fatigue does not set in. *Teamed Transcommunication* offers a way not only to reduce physical injury and mental fatigue, but it also provides an enhanced monitoring of the entire transcommunication process.

Teamed Transcommunication uses two minds to process a single source text. One person does the primary work of generating a target text while the other monitors both the source text and the target text to ensure accuracy and provide support as needed to complete the target text. In most circumstances, the two transcommunicators will then switch places and responsibilities as needed.

Relayed Transcommunication is another form of teamed transcommunication that uses one mind to process a source text into a target text which another mind then uses as its source text to generate yet another target text. This process is not as uncommon as it may seem. In multilingual conferences, one interpreter may generate an interpretation into one of the official languages for the conference. This interpretation may then serve as the source text for several other interpretations for consumers of other languages. DeafBlind people who depend on tactile communication are frequently the consumers of relayed transcommunication, especially during meetings and conferences of DeafBlind people where one person's message may be interpreted into signed ASL, which is then transliterated into tactile ASL by multiple transcommunicators (each with their own DeafBlind consumer) across the room. *Relayed Transcommunication* is also frequently used in courtrooms with defendants or witnesses who have very limited language skills of any kind.

This chapter begins with an investigation of *Overuse Syndrome*, introduces *Teamed Transcommunication*, explores *Relayed Transcommunication* (including a review of the historical uses of Relayed Transcommunication) and concludes with a review of the possible combinations of transcommunication that can be relayed.

8.1 Overuse Syndrome and Stress Management

Overuse syndrome is a potential hazard in any profession that requires repeated muscular movement. Assembly line workers, athletes, musicians, keyboard operators, and interpreters are all susceptible to injury through the repetitious movement of arm, hand, finger, leg, back, and neck muscles. The injuries that signed language interpreters face are most commonly related to the wrist, although fingers, upper arms, shoulders, and the neck may be involved as well.

There are many myths about overuse syndrome (O.S.) and signed language interpreters. Some people believe that native signers do not suffer from O.S. But there are indeed many native signers working as interpreters who do get O.S. Some people think that deaf people are immune or people who are both deaf and native signers are immune. The facts do not support these myths. Anyone can be susceptible to Overuse Syndrome simply by doing what its name says: over-use.

Similarly some people have assumed that an interpreter suffering from Overuse Syndrome is interpreting incorrectly. In one sense this is true, because correct interpretation will not overuse the interpreter's muscles but rather allow sufficient breaks for the interpreter to avoid injury. In this sense it is the lack of providing sufficient team members for assignments (or failure to request them) that lead to "incorrect" interpreting.

It is possible to generate a signed language (or for that matter, a spoken language) in ways that cause excessive stress. New learners of signed languages may generate extreme postures, particularly with wrist posture in fingerspelling, extreme muscle tension, or using larger signing space than is required for effective communication. Some nervous tendencies can also contribute such as repeated non-linguistic movement of the hands or "bobbing and weaving" side to side while signing. Overuse Syndrome can be reduced or prevented through careful attention to the phonetics of a person's signed language production.

The symptoms of Overuse Syndrome are simple enough: pain and then numbness. The levels of pain are progressive: 1) pain when the muscles are in use, 2) pain in between uses, 3) pain for several hours after use, 4) constant and unending pain during waking hours, 5) pain that is so severe that it disturbs sleep. The point at which you should become aware and begin to take action is the very first one, where pain occurs when the muscles are in use. If this pain continues for some time then it is possible that numbness will occur. One frequent experience of numbness is in the hand where the thumb, index finger, middle finger, and half of the ring finger become numb. Note that the pinky does not become numb in this situation. This specific form of numbness is tied to pressure in the carpal tunnel, which is a protective sheath around nerve tissue. The carpal tunnel travels through the wrist and pressure can be caused *directly* by severe or repeated bending or by pressing the base of the wrist against hard surfaces. Pressure can also be caused *indirectly* through swelling as a reaction to overuse or to repeated vibration, such as occurs when using electric hand tools (such as reciprocating saws and power drills). The solution to the problem is to immediately stop aggravating the situation. Through rest, the body should be able to repair itself, but the behavior that caused the numbness must be discontinued or significantly reduced.

If your muscles hurt just doing your job, then the way you do your job is probably causing the pain and needs to be reviewed. Do you put pressure on the base of your wrists? This might happen for keyboard operators who rest the weight of their hands on the base of their wrists while typing. While the fingers are typing, muscles and tendons are moving throughout the hand and wrists. With pressure being applied to the base of the wrists, this finger movement causes unnecessary friction, wear, and tear. The solution may be to reduce the pressure (by not placing weight on the wrists) and also, perhaps, to reduce the amount of time spent typing without a break.

Overuse Syndrome can come from cumulative trauma. Do you drive with your hands flexed back (thus increasing the pressure at the wrist)? Do you sleep with you head applying pressure to any part of your hands? Do you do keyboard work in addition to interpreting? Do you drive a stick shift car? Do you use the hand basket when shopping rather than a cart with wheels? Do you carry a heavy bag or purse for long periods of time (either over one shoulder or just in one hand)? Do you lift children or heavy packages frequently? Do shake your hand rapidly when you use a hairdryer? Do you use your hands or arms to support your head during classroom lectures? It is entirely possible that the act of using sign language by itself is not traumatic to your hands, wrist, arms, shoulders, or neck. The trauma may occur due to the *cumulative* effect of several factors.

The most obvious solution is to stop hurting yourself and to stop now. But in order to stop you have to catch yourself doing things that put you at risk. Think about what you are doing with your hands when you are not signing. How do you support your weight with your arms (elbows) and hands? Do you have any sensations of short and sharp pain, or even dull and prolonged pain? Determine what might cause the pain... can you change that behavior?

Another entire area of concern is emotional stress. When we are experiencing emotional stress, we tend to physically tense our muscles. The solution is the same: identify what causes emotional stress. Do you find yourself clenching your teeth in certain situations? Do you find yourself raising your shoulders toward your ears (especially while signing)? Determine what is causing you to become tense: the people you are with, the setting, the topic, and your comfort with your ability to do your job... all of these are potential stress-causing factors.

Next you should determine what things help to ease stress. Dancing, physical exercise, and listening to fast-paced music may relieve stress. Swimming, meditation, massage, and listening to slow, instrumental music may relieve stress. Become aware of the personal activities that help you to feel better about yourself and make the time to enjoy these activities. Become aware of the things that cause the stress and deliberately reverse them: Open your mouth from time to time instead of clenching your teeth; force your shoulders into a lower posture instead of raising them; stand with both feet slightly apart instead of locked together.

By paying attention to the way you do your work, and the way you do your relaxation, it is possible to prevent *Overuse Syndrome* and at the same time to better enjoy your work. An added benefit will be that your consumers are likely to be less tense because your work will appear more relaxed and natural. While some surgeries can reduce pain or provide some amount of comfort, there are few solutions as effective as prevention.

8.2 Teamed Transcommunication - Working Together

Teamed Transcommunication is a process whereby two transcommunicators work together in generating at least one target text. The target text(s) may be in the same language as the source text, or may be in any number of different languages. The team members providing the transcommunication may specialize in different portions of the transcommunication process or they may swap responsibilities back and forth as they take turns monitoring or creating the target text. In order to better understand the benefits and the complexities of *Teamed Transcommunication*, let's first explore the possible roles of the members of a transcommunication team.

8.2.1 "A", "B", and "C" Roles of Interpreters

Three labels help us define the roles of interpreters (or transcommunicators) within interpreting teams. The primary service providers at any moment are the "A" interpreters. If there is only one interpreter providing services then that person is by definition working as an "A" interpreter. If two people are hired to provide services, then the second person is likely to be functioning as a "B" interpreter. This means that the "B" interpreter is monitoring both the source text and the "A" interpreter's target text and is also prepared to provide clarifications or corrections to the "A" interpreter as needed.

The value of being able to provide clarification is that this reduces the need to interrupt the source text consumer. In some lecture settings, or especially with recorded source texts, it is not possible to interrupt. Without a team member the interpreter is left either guessing or omitting the information. Even if interruption is not a problem, it still takes time away from the communication surrounding an interruption. A team member who is monitoring the "A" interpreter's work is able to know immediately what the problem is and is either able to generate the missing information quickly and without disruption, or will confirm that the information was unintelligible. If the latter occurs, it is possible for the team member to generate the interruption[24] and ask for clarification, further reducing the burden on the "A" interpreter.

Generally the "A" and "B" roles are alternated as the two interpreters take turns providing the primary interpreting service. It is possible that team members will choose a different arrangement, however, based on the needs of the communication event. One interpreter may choose to provide "A" service for all interpreting from spoken language source texts while the other interpreter will provide "A" service when signed language source texts occur. Various factors may influence this decision, including the comfort and ease that each interpreter has for understanding the various consumers in a setting.

A "C" interpreter is one who is only observing the work of an "A" interpreter and is not directly involved in the interpreting process. Often interpreting students begin their practicum placements as "C" interpreters. There is value in having a "C" interpreter in that an observer may be able to identify both areas of excellence and areas of needed improvement which might be missed by the "A" and "B" interpreters. A "C" interpreter can also observe how the "A" and "B" interpreters work together as a team and then provide feedback to that team.

---

[24] This option should only be chosen at the direction of the "A" team member who is considered the executive in charge of the team's interpreting while in the "A" role.

A common practice in the early days of interpreting teams was for one interpreter to serve in the "A" role while the other "took a break". Both interpreters might have been physically present for the entire duration of the assignment, but only one was ever working at any given time. If the "A" interpreter needed any support to resolve ambiguity in the source message or to recapture a missing element, the other interpreter was not prepared or even paying attention. The result of such an arrangement is that each interpreter alternates in the "A" role, but otherwise is not participating in a team approach to interpreting (not even as a "C" interpreter). This arrangement has come to be known as "tag team" interpreting. Tag team interpreting is not professional and can lead to problems in justifying the expense of providing teamed interpreting.

8.2.2 Exchanging Team Member Roles
    The exchange of team roles (or "switching") should be as smooth as possible and cause little or no disruption to the main communication event. The methods vary depending upon the physical arrangement of the transcommunication team members. **NOTE: In every situation of exchanging team roles it is *always* the "A" team member who decides the moment of the exchange.**
    The best time to perform the exchange of roles is during some form of break in the source text. This may be as *obvious* as an exchange of source text presenters (or the source presenter pausing to take a drink from a glass of water). It may be as *subtle* as the use of a discourse marker such as "*So*" or "*Now*" which may indicate a change of topic. Exchange of roles should *never* occur prior to the completion of a sentence in the target text. Team members may choose to exchange roles based on regular time increment (such as every twenty or thirty minutes) but if the team members are comfortable and trust each other, they may choose not to depend on clocks but rather their sense of the difficulty of the source text and the accuracy of the target text. The "B" team member may be able to see minor flaws in the target text and indicate a need for exchanging roles. The "A" team member should understand this as a *positive contribution* to the team's overall effort (rather than a threat or challenge to the "A" team member's work). The "A" team member still holds the decision of when to make the exchange.
    The easiest exchange occurs when "A" and "B" team members are already seated side-by-side while providing spoken-language target texts. One example of this would be an ASL-to-English interpretation of monologic discourse, such as a conference presentation. The exchange of team member roles can be as simple as handing the microphone from one team member to the other. No other physical rearrangement should be required in such a situation, since both team members are already in their optimum position to visually access the source text. Target audience access to a spoken text may be through a public address system or, in smaller groups, may require the "A" team member to speak loudly to allow their target text to be heard in the back rows of the audience.
    Some interpretation from signed language source texts into spoken language target texts is intentionally not made available to the entire audience, since there may be non deaf people in the audience who are fluent in the signed language and cannot "block-out" the spoken interpretation, which interferes with their direct understanding of the source presenter. Private listening devices allow audience members with headsets to hear whispered (or quiet) interpretation into a microphone, which is then broadcast to the headset receivers. A less technological solution is to seat audience members who wish

access the interpretation near the interpreters. If this arrangement is provided for a single audience member, then it may be necessary for the interpreting team members to physically switch seats when exchanging the "A" and "B" roles of the team.

Another common exchange where the team members switch seats is for DeafBlind consumers. In these instances it is very important for the "A" team member to inform the DeafBlind consumer that a switch is about to occur[25]. Sometimes team members will be seated on either side of the DeafBlind consumer, who may choose to alternate their use of right and left hands to tactually perceive the interpreter's target texts. This specific arrangement, however, may function more like a "tag-team" if the team members cannot easily support each other's work because their consumer is physically between them. Another consideration for dividing the team's efforts this way is that each team member should have different hand dominance for producing the signed language. In other words, the team member to the DeafBlind consumer's left side should be right-hand dominant, while the team member to the right side of the DeafBlind Consumer should be left-hand dominant. Otherwise the DeafBlind consumer will not be able to access one-handed signs and signs that depend upon dominant-hand distinctions from the non-dominant hand.

Exchanging roles of the team members becomes more complex when the team members are not side-by-side, which is fairly typical for interpretations that have a significant amount of spoken-to-signed language work. The reason that team members would not already be side-by-side is so that the "B" team member can visually monitor and support the "A" team member's work. Thus the "B" team member will most frequently be seated across from, and facing, the "A" team member. If the "A" team member is standing, then the proper procedure has the "B" team member confirm that the "A" team member is prepared to exchange team roles. The "B" team member then moves so that they are behind, and not blocking, the "A" team member. The "B" team member then indicates readiness (either by a single touch to the "A" team's shoulder, a brief auditory cue, or some other agreed-upon signal). The "B" team member continues to monitor both the source and target texts and waits for the "A" team member to move to the side and/or step away from the location they have been working in. The "B" team member takes a step forward and then resumes the interpretation.

This exchange can be fairly quick for most classroom environments. It may take a longer amount of time if the "A" team member is working from an elevated stage, especially if the stage access is from the side or behind the stage. In such situations, it may be useful to add a "C" team member who takes on the "B" role while the "B" team member maneuvers to take the "A" role. A three-person team would continue this exchange, where the "A" team member is allowed to rest from their recent work by taking the "C" role, the "C" team member begins to intensely monitor both the source and target texts (and thus prepare for the "A" role), and the "B" team member moves into the "A" role fully prepared and aware of the recent communication prior to the exchange.

---

[25] NOTE: if there are multiple DeafBlind consumers in the same room, it may be essential to request a suspension of the communication so that the "A" and "B" members of multiple teams can switch at the same time. A coordinated switching of multiple team members will reduce the likelihood that other people's sight lines will be disrupted during a switch and ultimately cause less confusion and disruption to the overall proceedings.

If the "A" team member is seated (which is fairly common in lengthy classroom lecture settings, especially if the instructor is also seated) then the exchange of "A" and "B" team members is generally a simultaneous movement where both stand, they exchange places (without bumping into each other!) and the transcommunication resumes. Again, the initiator of the actual exchange is always the active "A" team member. The "B" team member may indicate readiness for the exchange by leaning forward, with direct eye gaze to the "A" team member, and signing "SWITCH?" The "B" team member must wait for a confirmation from the "A" team member before moving. The signal in this situation is likely to be as simple as returned direct eye gaze and a head nod toward the "B" team member.

8.2.3 Teaming Based on Language Fluency

The members of a transcommunication team may divide the overall work of the transcommunication process based on the individual language fluencies and/or background knowledge of the team members. A generally accepted principle for spoken language interpreters is to produce target texts in one's native language. This allows the transcommunicator the best possibilities of producing natural-sounding, idiomatic sentences that sound less like an interpretation and more like a source text created in the target language. Recent graduates of interpreting programs may still be developing their full range of fluency in ASL. Some signed language interpreters are children of Deaf adults (CODAs) and have native fluency in ASL; but some CODAs may struggle with generating effective CALP[26] target texts in spoken languages. An interpreting team may choose to assign its members so that they provide the bulk of primary services with the best language fluencies matched to the output: the target texts generated by the team.

Teams may also include Deaf transcommunicators who are able to generate a idiomatic target text based on a hearing transcomunicator's target text. This specific arrangement has an added benefit because it can reduce the likelihood of syntactic interference from the source language, especially if the deaf transcommunicator attempting to generate an idiomatic target text (as opposed to a more literal target text *Relayed Transcommunication* will be further explored later in this chapter.

8.2.4 Procedures for Teamed Transcommunication

These procedures are designed to provide guidance to members of *Transcommunication Team*. They are intended to establish a set of expectations for a members of the *Transcommunication Team* that will lead to efficiency, accuracy, and professional growth. All members of the team should agree to these procedures before they are implemented.

1) Pre-conference the team - agree what the goals of the team are, how feedback and corrections to the message will take place, how signals for assistance and replacement will be given, general time intervals for each of the team members to serve as "A" transcommunicators.

2) Pre-conference the consumers - team members discuss the communication goals and the procedures that are required for accurate and efficient transcommunication with the primary consumers of each language. In one-on-one settings, one team member may pre-conference with one consumer or consumer group while another team member works

---

[26] Cognitive Academic Language Proficiency was identified and discussed in Chapter Three.

with the other consumer group. If separate and simultaneous pre-conferencing takes place, then the team members will need additional time to debrief after pre-conferencing with the consumers.

3) Prepare the environment - team members ensure that the physical set-up of the room meets the needs of both consumer groups and also the needs of the transcommunicators to perform their services. Whether the team members move chairs and other furniture or some other person rearranges the environment depends on the services available in the environment. It is the team's responsibility to ensure that the environment satisfies the interpreting needs of the people within it (to the best extent possible).

4) Prepare the team - team members take their places before the communication event begins. Ensure that there are no problems that remain to be solved. If there is a problem, then agree upon how the problem will be solved and take appropriate action.

5) Perform the transcommunication - team members work together to ensure that the message is as accurate as possible and meets the communication needs of the consumer groups in the environment. Replacement of team members between the "A" and "B" roles should be smooth and organized with minimal distraction to either consumer group.

6) Complete the task - all team members should continue providing appropriate services until it is clear that both consumer groups no longer require services.

7) Re-establish the environment - undo the environmental changes which were made to accommodate the transcommunication process if necessary and reasonable.

8) De-brief the consumers - team members discuss the communication event and the result of the transcommunication with the primary consumers of each language, seeking feedback regarding what worked well and what seemed not to work. Team members should listen to the entire comments of the consumers and take notes, offering explanations only after the entire question, comment, or complaint has been expressed and noted. Questions from consumers should be answered as completely as possible while remaining faithful to the Code of Ethics.

9) De-brief the team - team members review their notes and memories of the communication event. Problems should be explored with the intention to find solutions. Feedback on performances should be constructive and increase the trust team members have for each other.

8.3 Relayed Transcommunication

Now that we have an understanding of the varieties of transcommunication and of transcommunication teams, we can expand yet again and combine two different transcommunicators into a *relayed* transcommunication team, which has (at least) two people working as "A" transcommunicators processing the same message from the source to the final target form. This is generally referred to as *Relayed Interpretation*, since the most common applications among spoken-language interpreters involve interpretations between three or more languages. One example would be a conference with an official language of English where a lecturer is presenting in spoken French. One interpreter (or team) would provide interpretation into spoken English. Another interpreter (or team) may take the English message into another language, such as Arabic, for one or several consumers who know Arabic, but do not know either English or French.

Switching members of a team for relayed transcommunication should be coordinated so that all the members of a relay team are switched at the same time. This means that a second team of relay members would switch into the roles of the current team. In organized conferences this may be done by requesting a suspension of the proceedings in order to make the switch (or using existing pauses, such as changes in speakers). If it is not possible to suspend the proceedings then team members will need to switch while the source text continues. Because the work of relayed teams is somewhat consecutive, the Hearing team members should switch first, followed by the Deaf team members. The point in the message where the Hearing team members switched can then serve as the break in the discourse for the Deaf members to make their switch. The switch may be initiated by either "A" team member of the active team, or by a "C" coordinator of relayed services. Figure 8.1 identifies several possible combinations of relayed transcommunication between spoken and signed communication.

Source Language & Channel	Processing of Team Member 1	Processing of Team Member 2	Final Target Language & Channel	Overall Team Processing
Spoken English	*Interpreting* English to ASL	*Transliterating* from ASL to Tactile ASL	Tactile ASL	*Relayed Interpretation*
Spoken English	*Interpreting* English to ASL	*Elucidating* From ASL to Gestures	Gestural Communication	*Relayed Elucidation*
Spoken English	*Interpreting* English to ASL	*Interpreting* From ASL to LSQ	Signed Quebec Sign Language	*Relayed Interpretation*
Spoken English	*Transliterating* Spoken English to Cued English	*Transliterating* to Lipreadable English	Lipreadable English	*Relayed Transliteration*
Signed ASL	*Mirroring* of ASL for audience access	*Transliterating* from ASL to Tactile ASL	Tactile ASL	*Relayed Transliteration*
Signed ASL (but disfluent)	*Processed Shadowing* of ASL	*Interpreting* From ASL to Spoken English	Spoken English	*Relayed Interpretation*
Gestural Communication	*Elucidating* from Gesture to ASL	*Transliterating* from ASL to Tactile ASL	Tactile ASL	*Relayed Elucidation*

Figure 8.1 – Some Varieties of Relayed Transcommunication

Relayed Interpretation also takes place between signed and spoken languages and often includes Deaf interpreting team members. One common use of this form of relayed interpreting is provided at conferences that have significant attendance from Deaf participants. If the source text is presented in spoken English then a hearing team member will provide the first link in the relayed interpretation, generating a target text in the signed language. From the hearing team member's target text, the Deaf team member then generates a *Processed Shadowing*[27], which is more idiomatic (natural) and therefore less demanding upon the Deaf audience members.

There are countless varieties of relayed transcommunication. The overall work being accomplished by the team defines the kind of relay work being done. In other words, the forms of the source message and the final target message determine the label for the team's work. If the source and final target are different languages then the team members are involved in either *Relayed Interpretation* or some form of translation. If the source message and the final target message share the same language, but different forms, then the team is involved in *Relayed Transliteration*. If one side of the interpreting process involves something less than language then the process is *Relayed Elucidation*. Within the overall team process, each team member will be responsible for contributing a specific portion of the team's overall process.

8.3.1 Relayed Elucidation

There is a fairly common practice for interpreting in the Deaf community that is more appropriately identified as *Relayed Elucidation*. These instances involve one team member working between English and ASL (interpretation) and the other team member working between ASL and something less than language, such as *Visual Gestural Communication* (elucidation). This service may be performed for Deaf people who were not consistently exposed to any accessible language prior to puberty, or for Deaf people who have moved to a language community where the local interpreters do not know the deaf person's native language. In these situations, the hearing interpreter would interpret spoken information from English into ASL. The Deaf interpreter, working from the first interpretation, would then create a gestural message in an attempt to allow the Deaf consumer to understand the essence of the original source text. The process would also work in the opposite direction. The Deaf interpreter would regenerate any gestural reply from the deaf consumer into ASL. The hearing interpreter would then complete the process by interpreting from ASL to English.

Relayed Elucidation occurs any time that the source or target text is generated in something other than a language. This is most common with deaf consumers who do not know a standard signed language or any written or spoken language. This service is essential for ensuring justice in the legal system.

8.3.2 Relayed Transliteration

Relayed Transliteration occurs most commonly at conferences or meetings within the DeafBlind community. These instances involve one team member, near the podium, shadowing a question or comment from the audience. This ASL message is then transliterated into tactile ASL for DeafBlind audience members. Another related form is *Relayed Shadowing*, which would be identical except for the final version being a shadowing (either *Mirroring* or *Processed Shadowing*) for a DeafBlind consumer with usable, but limited vision. Since the final product shares the same *Language Encoding System*, it is identified as shadowing instead of transliterating. A third related form would be *Transcribed Interpretation*, in which Computer Aided Real-time Transcription

---

[27] *Processed Shadowing* was defined in Chapter Seven.

(CART) is used to generate a visual, typed English transcription of a message that has been interpreted into English.

<u>8.3.3 Relayed Interpretation</u>
Relayed Interpretation is the process where one person conveys a source text into a target text, which then serves as another person's source text in order to generate a second target text. Relay interpreters have been doing their work for at least several decades, yet their work has only recently been extensively researched or even documented (Cerney, 2004).

The Registry of Interpreters for the Deaf (RID) began evaluating and certifying interpreters in 1972. Among the people receiving certification were deaf adults who were fluent in both English and American Sign Language. They were eligible to receive a certification known as the "Reverse Skills Certification" or RSC. RSC certification indicated that the interpreter had achieved at least a 70% accuracy rating in conveying signed language source texts into spoken English. The RSC was awarded as a partial certification for hearing interpreters who had not demonstrated an overall 80% rating in the three areas required for "Comprehensive Skills Certification" (CSC). The other two areas required for the CSC, were called "interpretation" and "transliteration" and required the candidate to be able to hear. Therefore deaf interpreters with an RSC were considered *fully* certified.

The practice of using a hearing member and a Deaf member in an interpreting team is known as relayed interpreting. The process of relayed interpreting is as follows: One of the consumers produces a source text. For this explanation, let's start with a spoken English source text. The hearing interpreter would then provide an interpretation into American Sign Language. The deaf interpreter would then treat this interpretation as a source text and provide a version of the message that the deaf consumer could more readily understand. When the deaf consumer produces a message, the deaf interpreter then provides a version in ASL designed to allow the hearing interpreter to provide an interpretation into spoken English. Generally this process is consecutive for dialogic discourse so that each piece of information is relayed completely before the next piece is attempted.

8.4 Summary
This chapter explored teamed transcommunication, where two people work together to generate a single target text. The team may work in different roles, such as "A" and "B" roles where the "A" role is actively generating the target text and the "B" role actively monitors and corrects (as needed) the work of the "A" team member. An additional "C" role in a team provides a means of monitoring the entire interpreting process, including the effectiveness of the team. These roles can be maintained o exchanged throughout a transcommunication event. One major reason to exchange these roles is to reduce the risk of overuse syndrome.

Overuse syndrome occurs when various muscles and parts of the body are over-used and/or moved with extreme stress. The primary symptoms of overuse syndrome include pain and numbness of the affected areas. Other symptoms include redness or swelling o the affected areas. The most effective treatment for overuse syndrome is resting the injured areas along with recognition of the behaviors causing the injury and modifying those behaviors to prevent or diminish further injury.

Relayed Transcommunication requires a team, but in these instances, both team members are working simultaneously in the "A" role, actively generating target texts. The reasons for providing *Relayed Transcommunication* are multiple. They include simultaneously meeting the physical communication needs of multiple DeafBlind consumers; providing efficient linguistic access for Deaf people who are not fluent in a signed language; and providing comfortable access to conference proceedings for large numbers of Deaf participants.

8.4.1 Review Questions

1. What causes overuse syndrome?
2. What are the most common symptoms of overuse syndrome?
3. How can overuse syndrome be treated or prevented?
4. What is teamed transcommunication?
5. How can teamed transcommunication reduce overuse syndrome?
6. What are the "A", "B", and "C" roles in a transcommunication team?
7. Which team role directs when a switch is made?
8. What order should team members switch if there are "A", "B" & "C" members on a team and they are all exchanging roles?
9. What is relayed transcommunication?
10. Provide an example of relayed elucidation.

8.4.2 Suggested Activities

1. Find a person to work with. Take turns shadowing either a spoken or signed text with one person monitoring both the source text and the shadowing. Discuss how the texts were similar and different before switching roles.
2. Find a person to work with. Take turns relaying either a spoken or signed fixed text (audio or video recording) where one person has direct access to the text (by restricted viewing or headphones) and the other person only has access to the first person's output. Record the second person's output and then compare with the source text. Switch roles and repeat the process. Try to use material that is new to both of you so that you are not overly advantaged by your memory of the text.
3. Repeat the task in Activity #2, using the same material, but now try to summarize and anticipate the message to create "bursts" of information that alternate with pausing so that the second person has time to regenerate the message without looking at the first person or overlapping your output.

Chapter 9
Processing Levels

"Processing Levels"

Timoth stared into empty space. "How will I ever learn enough words?"

Rasmus looked across the table at Timoth and said "Enough words?"

"To convey the meaning of every message I hear. I can't see how I will ever learn enough words to capture every meaning, every shade of nuance, every detail. It just seems impossible."

"Timoth, do you think the work of a Server is accomplished only through words?"

"What do you mean? Of course, Rasmus. Words hold the meaning, we express our thoughts to each other in words."

"And those two over there aren't communicating at all?"

Timoth looked across the room at a couple holding hands and staring silently into each other's eyes. "But they're not even using language. They're just staring at each other."

Rasmus tried again. "So language is the key to our work?"

"Of course"

"And it makes no difference how we send the message, as long as we use the right words?"

"And I will never learn enough words!"

"Well," said Rasmus, "You are right about that. You will never learn enough words."

"So I will never be adequate in my work."

"Why do you draw that conclusion?"

"You just agreed that I would never learn enough words. I understood you to mean that I would never gain the fluency needed. So I might as well stop here and find some other way to serve."

"Is that what my words said? Listen to yourself. 'I understood you to mean that....' How did that happen if words are the key? You didn't pay attention to the words I used and you ignored most of the message I have been sending. Timoth, words only hold part of the meanings we share with each other. How we send the meaning is very important, sometimes even more important than the words."

"You mean that I might still succeed in this work?"

"Finally you are listening to my message and not just my words! Yes. Think about how you communicate with a child. Do you use every one of your precious words in that kind of communication?"

"Of course not! The child is still learning language."

"And are *you* still learning language?"

"Yes, but that's different."

"What makes it so different? Are there any people here who know every word of their own language? Is there any moment in life that we can say 'I have finally completed the learning of my language'?" Rasmus leaned back, "If *words* were the key, we'd only be able to communicate with children if they were born with a complete lexicon in their brains. We'd never be able to learn any other language."

Timoth smiled. "So there's hope for me yet?"

"You must focus on the message, not the words."

Chapter 9 – Processing Levels
"Make Sure You Know The Rules Before You Play Another Person's Game."
- 1997 BC

9.0 Overview
It is possible to match (or mismatch) the interpreting process to the needs of the consumers. One clear example is the difference between consecutive and simultaneous interpreting. Consecutive interpreting requires more time and therefore causes the interpretation to be generated at a later time than simultaneous interpreting would provide. The benefit for consecutive work is that, if done properly, consecutive interpreting can be much more accurate than simultaneous interpreting. The interpreter must assess which need is greater: accuracy or timeliness. The resulting interpretation format should reflect the needs of the consumers as well as the interpreter[28].

All communication situations are altered when they are interpreted. In other words, there is no such thing as a "normal" communication situation when that communication is being interpreted, even if the interpretation is for the benefit of a very small minority of people. Therefore the perceived need for both speed and accuracy *must* be adapted *because* interpreting is taking place.

9.1 Consecutive Versus Simultaneous Processing
In some situations, only one choice is clear. For example, if the only way to understand the source text is to devote 100% of your attention to it, then consecutive interpreting will just *have to be* acceptable, otherwise the consumers should seek a different interpreter or a different arrangement of interpreters. One example of this is providing elucidation in a legal setting such as a deposition or witness testimony[29]. A Deaf consumer who does not have regular language fluency presents an overwhelming challenge to ensuring accuracy in the interpreting process. An interpreter doing such work without a team member will not likely be able to ensure accuracy with simultaneous processing. In fact, even working consecutively may take significant time because there is likely to be a need to clarify and confirm the side of the message that is without language. Providing a relay team member allows a division of the interpreters' responsibilities so that the task of understanding the message is largely one interpreter's responsibility while the language transfer is largely the other interpreter's responsibility. The overall processing of a relay team should be faster than a solo interpreter; and yet the accuracy of the message will still depend on some ability to process at a consecutive pace.

Consecutive interpreting is the most logical choice in naturally dialogic situations. During a doctor's examination, for example, both participants are generally communicating only with each other, taking turns asking and answering questions. While the consumers may be in a hurry, they generally will wait for questions to be

---

[28] The interpreter may need to involve the consumers in the decision process, but ultimately the interpreter is the professional who will be making decisions about the interpreting process. If consumers are resistant to using consecutive interpreting then they should be presented with choice of their priorities: accuracy or timeliness.

[29] All interpretation as part of witness testimony should be done consecutively. This is the common and accepted practice for spoken language interpreters in court settings.

completed before answering them and likewise will wait for answers to be completed before asking a new question. Within this situation, a consecutive interpretation is very logical. The additional time is not significant and accuracy is maintained at a high level.

Simultaneous interpreting may be the most logical choice in some situations. During an academic lecture, for example, there may be little interaction between the presenter and the audience members. The audience might even be physically distanced or even separated from the speaker, perhaps even depending upon a public address system to amplify the presenter's message so that the entire audience can hear it. The expectation in such a setting is that the presenter will not be interrupted. In this setting, a consecutive interpretation is rarely appropriate, unless a concerted effort is being made by the presenter to accommodate the interpreting process. If the presenter is using visual aids, a simultaneous interpretation may be *essential* simply because a delay in processing the message may mean that the appropriate visual aids have disappeared by the time the accompanying message is produced.

These situations tend to provide clear distinctions that help to determine which approach to interpreting will best meet the communication goals of the participants. Other situations may not be so clear. During a group discussion, for example, there may be several deaf and several hearing people. If all the participants know ASL, then the best solution is for the participants to choose to use ASL for the discussion. But if any member of the group will depend upon interpreting services, then the goals of the communication must be considered. Is the discussion a series of prepared presentations? If so, accuracy may be a key factor and turn taking, or the overlapping of turns, may not interfere with your work. If the participants are brainstorming ideas, however, the need for speed may be much greater than the need for accuracy.

The differences between literal and idiomatic interpreting also play a role. As people try to figure out what it is they are trying to say in a brainstorming session, an idiomatic interpretation would require that the thought be completed before it could be understood sufficiently for interpretation. A literal interpretation is less dependent on understanding the whole message, but will be less comprehensible to a consumer who does not know significant portions of the source language.

A final consideration is the hearing ability of the deaf consumer. If the consumer is hard of hearing then the interpretation may need to be provided as a constant "backup" so that if information is missed, the deaf consumer can immediately look to the interpreter and expect to see the missed word immediately within a literal, simultaneous interpretation.

The choice of consecutive or simultaneous processing, therefore, depends on several factors: 1) communication goals and abilities of the source-text consumers, 2) communication goals and abilities of the target-text consumers, and 3) comprehension and production abilities of the interpreter.

9.2 Communication Variables and Transcommunication Choices

Back in Chapter One we identified three variables in communication: *Intention*, *Immediacy*, and *Interaction*. These variables play a significantly increased role in transcommunication because there are two people communicating with and through a third person. In other words, Person A is communicating with the Interpreter and *also* with Person B; Person B is communicating with Person A and *also* with the Interpreter;

and the Interpreter is communicating with Person A and *also* with Person B. The graph below identifies the variations of *intention, immediacy,* and *interactivity* for these lines of communication.

Intentional Source Presenter / Transcommunicator	Immediate Source Presenter / Transcommunicator	Interactive Source Presenter / Transcommunicator	Transcommunication Examples
+ / +	= / +	= / +	Talking with someone face-to-face via interpreting or transliterating
+ / +	- / +	- / +	Talking with someone by phone via interpreting or transliterating
= / =	= / +	= / =	Attending an interpreted or transliterated lecture or performance
= / =	= / +	- / -	Watching an interpreted live satellite broadcast or television show (interpreter is at broadcast source)
= / =	- / -	- / -	Hearing / watching a recorded interpretation or transliteration
- / +	= / +	+ / +	Receiving interpretation or transliteration of *other* people conversing
- / +	- / +	- / +	Receiving a *Site Translation* of written or recorded information
- / =	- / +	- / =	Receiving a live performance of a *Prepared Translation*
- / =	= / +	- / =	Watching an interpreted live satellite broadcast or television show (interpreter is at downlink site)
- / =	= / +	- / =	Watching an interpreted live satellite broadcast or television show (interpreter is at origin site)
- / =	- / -	- / -	Reading, hearing, or watching a completed translation
- / -	= / +	- / +	Secretly monitoring a private interpretation

KEY: "+" means the condition is present, "-" means the condition is absent, "=" means the condition is present for some elements and absent for others.

Figure 9.1 - Intentional, Immediate, & Interactive Aspects of Transcommunication

This chart is more complicated than the one presented in Chapter One. The main complication is that the access to two people is identified in each space: Access to the source text presenter and access to the transcommunicator. Let's work through an example to gain a better understanding. The first example says "Talking with someone face-to-face via interpreting or transliterating". This means that the Target consumer is relying on a transcommunicator for access to the source text presenter during a face-to-face interaction.

The target consumer is an intentional recipient of both the source presenter and the transcommunicator. (Intention: [+ / +]).

The target consumer is only able to immediately access the semiotics surrounding the source presenter's linguistic message but has full and immediate access to the transcomunicator's message. (Immediacy: [= / +]).

The target consumer may be able to directly interrupt the source presenter but contributions to the discussion will rely on interaction through the transcommunicator. (Interactivity: [= / +]).

9.3 Literal Processing, Idiomatic Processing & Cultural Adjustment

While it might seem perfectly confusing to have as many labels as we already do so far, there are still several very important variables that need to be accounted for. The transcommunication processes of interpreting, translating, transliterating, transcribing, shadowing, and recited reading may all be either *literal* or *idiomatic*. In fact these two labels (*literal* and *idiomatic*) belong on a continuum because there are different degrees to which a target text may be literal or idiomatic, even within a single sentence. A *Literal* process is one in which the original word order (syntax) is maintained (or approximated) in the target text. An *Idiomatic* process is one in which more natural word orders are generated within the target text, and perhaps the entire text is restructured as well. The *Literal* end is easier to predict because the word order to be used is already presented in the source text. The *Idiomatic* end has much more variation because things that are "more natural" or "appropriate" will be different based on who is providing the service and who the consumers of the service are. This gives rise to the concept of *unduly free* processing where the target message may be very idiomatic, but is no longer an *accurate* representation of the concepts presented in the source message. On the other side is "transliteration" which no longer makes use of the target language and instead merely provides monolingual access to the source language, such as through fingerspelling or mouth movements.

Figure 9.2 – Literal and Idiomatic Processing Continuum

If a variety of consumers are being served, then a mixture of literal and idiomatic processing may appear in the target text. It is even possible that some parts of the message will be presented twice so that consumers receive both literal and idiomatic versions in the same target text. In addition, many bilingual deaf adults may express a preference for a "Middle of the Road" (MOR) interpretation, especially for work or school settings so that many of the concepts represented in the interpretation can be more readily matched to the written and spoken language of the setting.

Another way to think of these two extremes is called *Cultural Adjustment*. A *Literal* processing provides a certain amount of access to the culture of the source text while making little effort to make it accessible to members of the target culture. An *Idiomatic* processing would reduce the access of the source culture while making the target text more accessible to members of the target culture.

9.4 Information Processing Levels

There are six levels of information processing tied to these concepts: *Phonological, Lexical, Syntactic, Semantic, Pragmatic,* and *Stylistic*. A representation of these variables and their relationship to the concepts of literal versus idiomatic processing is presented below.

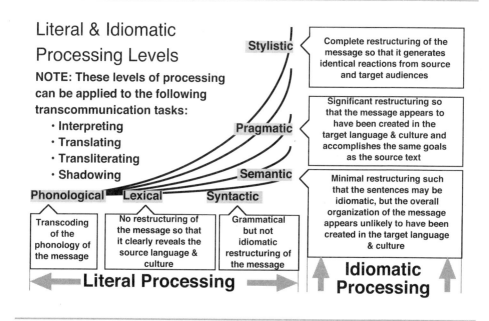

Figure 9.3 - Processing Levels Between Source and Target Texts

9.4.1 Phonological (Sublexical) Processing

Phonological processing can occur when an unfamiliar term is presented in a source text or when the interpreter is simply inexperienced in the target language and does not yet know the conceptually accurate vocabulary. The interpreter may focus on *how* the words are produced, rather than *what they mean.* Phonological processing is most likely done by novice/untrained people who are not fluent in both the source and target languages. Phonological processing may occasionally be of value for experienced interpreters when faced with examples from a third, unknown language:

Hypothetical Source: "and then he said 'C'est la guerre', but I don't speak Chinese!"

Hypothetical Target: "MAN SAY SOUND SIMILAR QUOTE SAY L-A G-A-R-E QUOTE DIFFERENT 1PP NOT TALK CHINA"

It is possible that the consumer of such an interpretation may know both English and French and recover the intended joke[30] of the source text. Phonological processing allows for an interpreter to convey information, including jokes, even if the interpreter is unaware of the meaning of the message. But the success of phonological processing depends on the target consumer being able to *reconstruct* the intended message. In essence, it requires the *consumer* to be the actual interpreter and therefore phonological processing is not generally seen as a targeted level for information processing.

9.4.2 Lexical Processing

The *Lexical* level focuses on words so that conceptual accuracy is maintained between the source and target texts, but not much more adjustment is made.

Hypothetical Source: "and then he said C'est la guerre, but I don't speak Chinese!"

Hypothetical Target: "MAN SAY QUOTE #CEST #LA #GUERRE QUOTE DIFFERENT 1PP NOT UNDERSTAND CHINA LANGUAGE".

The processing in this example would require the interpreter to know enough French to be able to spell the French phrase correctly. The result would not be sound-based but would still require the *consumer* to understand written French in order to recover the joke. In fact, because this example requires awareness of multiple languages, even for source language audiences, it may be impossible to provide an effective interpretation that maintains the joke without directly explaining the joke. Some things just don't survive interpretation very well.

---

[30] "C'est la guerre" is a French phrase, not Chinese.

9.4.3 Syntactic Processing

The *Syntactic* level includes the juxtaposition of words within grammatical relationships so that conceptually accurate words are also used in their correct grammatical category.

> Hypothetical Source: "the test was proctored by the librarian."

> Hypothetical Target: "LIBRARY AGENT SUPERVISE TEST".

The processing in this example restructures the source text to eliminate the use of passive voice. Syntactic processing can also include the insertion of a "dummy" subject when the source text is not specific as in the following example: "Mistakes were made." An English restructuring of this sentence might be "(Someone) made mistakes". One hypothetical target text of this sentence would be "SOMEONE ERR/WRONG"

9.4.4 Semantic Processing

The *Semantic* level includes the organization of phrases into complete and coherent sentences and connections between sentences. This results in complete thoughts being organized the way those ideas would normally be organized within the target language. The following example was chosen because it makes use of a feature not present in the source text – CLassifiers.

> Hypothetical Source: "the clock is on the wall."

> Hypothetical Target: "WALL, TIME CL-disc, CL-placed-above".

The processing in this example sets up the signing space so that a surface is identified prior to placing an object on that surface. An alternative – but somewhat more syntactic – version would be to use a rhetorical question: "TIME CL-disc WHERE? WALL THERE".

9.4.5 Pragmatic Processing

The *Pragmatic* level includes the organization of the entire text so that it would appear that the target text was in fact *originally created* in the target language and that the source language & culture had not been involved at all.

> Hypothetical Source: "Most people remember where they were and what they were doing when Kennedy was assassinated."

> Hypothetical Target: "LONG-AGO, 1963 SOMEONE KILL PRESIDENT J-F-K. MOST PEOPLE REMEMBER THAT DAY. WORK, PLAY, SCHOOL, NO-MATTER, MOMENT HEAR JFK DIE, DO-DO (topicalized), REMEMBER THAT WILL (head-nod)".

The processing in this example restructures the source text to provide the full meanings of "when Kennedy was assassinated" This includes establishing the contextual time of "1963", identifying the "dummy" subject of "SOMEONE", shifting the final verb in the original ("assassinated") into the introduction of the topic, and identifying which

Kennedy is implied: "PRESIDENT J-F-K". The concept of "where they were" is presented as a short list of likely examples. The final product is composed of three sentences instead of only one, therefore it moves beyond syntactic processing. *Conceptually*, however, the source and target texts remain identical.

Main points in the source language should remain main points in the target language; supporting details in the source should remain supporting details (not main points) in the target. Comparisons and contrasts should also be maintained. Organizationally, the style of the source text should be culturally matched in the target text. If the source language and culture makes regular use of performed dialogues as an expected part of lectures, but the other language and culture do not use that mechanism, then a pragmatic adjustment needs to be made in generating the target text.

9.4.6 Stylistic (Whole-Text) Processing

The *Stylistic* level includes the processing of the entire text so that it reveals equivalent elements of the speaker's organization and personality.

It is difficult to clearly exemplify differences in idiolect of a text because such stylistic differences are individual and performance-based. In other words, two different people reading the same text will generate stylistically different performances. Stylistic processing means that beyond all of the other levels of processing the final product also provides access to some (or many) aspects of the performance style of the source text presenter. The value of this is to allow the audience of both the source text and the target text to reach the same conclusions about the personality of the speaker. In other words, one group might really dislike the speaker while the other thinks the speaker (via transcommunication) is a really pleasant person[31].

The ability to match the stylistics is very likely to depend on the inherent stylistics of the interpreter generating the target text. This is one reason why people may express a desire to have an interpreter who is the same gender and/or ethnicity as the source text presenter. It also may be an issue for why some deaf students prefer educational interpreters who share their preferences for clothing, and conversational style as a reflection of themselves to their hearing peers.[32]

Another aspect of stylistic processing is that it considers the entirety of the source text. Stylistic parity (matching the style of the source text) can appear repeatedly throughout a target text; but full stylistic processing can only be achieved as a full-text, consecutive task, such as translation. In other words, it is *possible* to match the style of the source text during a semantically processed interpretation; but a *stylistically processed* interpretation must also consider the entirety of the text so as to make it appear as complete and accurate as possible while also appearing to be an original message produced in the target language rather than an interpretation.

---

[31] In fact, Dennis Cokely's (1983) research indicated this kind of difference in audience perceptions of source text presenters and interpreters. Cokely's research on metanotative features of interpretations is reviewed in the next chapter.

[32] Janet Cerney (2005).

9.4.7 Summary of Processing Levels

The six processing levels of *Phonological, Lexical, Syntactic, Semantic, Pragmatic,* and *Stylistic* can also be related to the kind of work being done. Standard translations may generate a target text at any of the top four levels (syntactic and beyond). The key factor for success in translation is that the *entire source text* can be analyzed before any part of the target text is created. This allows the freedom to rearrange the entire text and to ensure that it is organized in a way that the target language would organize an original text. Therefore the process of translation (including *Performed Translation* and *Site Translation*) allows *Pragmatic Processing* to take place (and *Stylistic Processing* to at least be attempted.

It is also possible to accomplish these higher levels of processing with *Consecutive Interpreting*, but only if the entire source text is completed before the target text is attempted. Since there is less time to make adjustments and no time to consult additional resources, it is more likely that a *Consecutive Interpretation* will be processed somewhere between the *Syntactic* and *Pragmatic* levels. *Simultaneous Interpreting* reduces further the amount of time for analysis and readjustment of the target text and therefore is likely to result in processing somewhere between the *Lexical* and *Semantic* levels. If the interpreter can make significant predictions about the source text, then it is possible to expand, at times, into more idiomatic target language structures and exceed the *Semantic* level of processing.

The *Lexical* level of processing is always available and may be chosen even in a translation if the goal is to provide access to the *original structure and culture* of the source text. *Lexical* and *Phonological* levels of processing also may be generated during interpretations if the source text is not well understood by the interpreter, if the interpreter is becoming exhausted, or if the interpreter is not adequately fluent in the target language to process at any higher level.

9.5 Labels Within the Profession of Interpreting

An important development in the profession of interpreting was the founding, in 1964, of an organization of signed language interpreters that came to be called the Registry of Interpreters for the Deaf (RID). When the RID was first established it was composed of people who worked in professions involving Deaf people, primarily the fields of education and vocational rehabilitation; but these people only worked as interpreters on a volunteer basis. In other words, there was no such thing as a *professional* interpreter working in the Deaf community in 1964.

Just four years prior to the founding of the RID, William Stokoe had published the first scientific analysis of the structure of American Sign Language and claimed that it was indeed a language, separate and distinct from any other language. Stokoe also noted the variety of *language use* within the deaf community that was well known to the founding members of the RID.

The original members of RID were focused on finding more qualified people to provide interpreting services rather than academics or linguistic analysis. They identified two varieties of signing - one which was understood to be a mixture of ASL and English and the other more true to ASL without influences of English. Working between spoken English and the mixed version was initially called "translation" while the other kind of work was called "interpretation". Years later the word "transliteration" replaced the use of "translation" as people gained a better understanding of these technical terms. And ye the revised label remains inaccurate. In fact the two processes that RID certifies are both interpreting: one being *Idiomatic Interpreting*, the other *Literal Interpreting*.

9.5.1 Literal and Idiomatic Interpreting

In general, the act of interpreting is known to be the transformation of a message from one language to another language without altering the meaning of that message. Translation is known to be the transformation of a fixed (documented) message from one language to another without altering the meaning of that message. There remains some additional variation in the use of these terms and one area of specific concern is how these acts are performed when the consumer of the services knows both the source and target languages. In other words, if the deaf person knows both ASL and English, then there are additional options in how to perform interpreting services.

The field of translation recognizes the extreme ends of this variation as "literal translation" and "idiomatic translation." *Literal Translations* transfer the meanings of the words but do not make grammatical or cultural adjustments in the process. *Idiomatic Translations* are so natural that they do not appear to be translations at all but instead they seem to have been created originally in the target language. Literal translations are useful for people who either *know* about the grammar and/or culture of the source language or *want to know* about the source language and culture. Idiomatic translations are useful to people who either don't know about the grammar and/or culture of the source language or don't *need* to know that information.

These ideas of variation can be applied to interpretation as well. In other words, a deaf person who knows both ASL and English may *desire* a literal interpretation. A literal interpretation would use ASL signs for access to *information* but it would arrange those signs in the same (or nearly the same) grammatical order as the original spoken English message. Bilingual Deaf people can use their knowledge of English grammar to resolve any mismatching of ASL grammatical information and English information. The deaf person would also use knowledge of English to fill in gaps created because English marks its grammar in ways that ASL has no vocabulary to represent.

This task of performing literal interpretations is the same task that the Registry of Interpreters for the Deaf certifies as "Transliteration." Technically the term "Transliteration" is incorrect, but it does mark a distinction between idiomatic interpreting and literal interpreting. *Transliteration* is known to be taking a message from one form of one language into another form of the same language. Literal interpretation actually does change the language, but not into the most natural-sounding variety of language. The RID originally called this task "Translation", then changed it to "Transliteration". In reality, the process is correctly identified as *Literal Interpreting*. This means that one of the certifications still being issued by RID at the time of this writing still has an inaccurate label: the Certification of "Transliteration" is actually a certification of *Literal Interpretation*.

9.5.2 Reasons to Choose Literal Interpreting

Literal interpretations may be very useful for bilingual deaf people. The notion of *Register Variation* can be applied to this task in that the appropriate use of ASL for a given Person, Setting, and Topic may include more linear productions of ASL or even include influences uniquely related to English.

- Person: English may be the dominant language for the Deaf person. In this case ASL is a means of accessing information but the Deaf person prefers to have the information arranged in English grammatical structures.

- Setting: The environment surrounding the communication may be academic or business oriented, both of which tend to make extensive use of written languages for books, assignments, and computers. References to written materials may require *Literal Interpretation*.

- Topic: The topic may be information that will appear on an examination or may be expected to be reproduced in the minutes of a meeting or in company reports, etc. Some technical topics may require Literal Interpretation for jargon and phrases that are specific the field being discussed.

Being able to perform both idiomatic and literal interpretations is important. So which is easier? Many people have misunderstood literal interpreting to be the easier task. Literal interpreting requires conceptually accurate sign production within grammatical structures that are not efficient in ASL. This means that the hands will be moving much more quickly to generate the information, more fingerspelling will be required to fill in gaps for grammatical relationships, and the interpreter's mind will be very busy processing the meaning while also remembering the grammar used to generate the source text. In short, literal interpreting, done correctly, is much harder physical and mental work than idiomatic interpreting.

Generally a literal interpretation is done with very little processing time because the human brain cannot retain both the meaning and the source text grammar for extended periods of time. In other words, *Literal Interpretation* most commonly requires *Simultaneous Interpreting* and is very rarely seen as a part of *Consecutive Interpreting*. This increases the chance for the interpreter to generate errors, to misrepresent meanings, or to become overwhelmed, stop, and begin again after missing a portion of the source text. People pursuing certification should consider beginning with certification in idiomatic interpreting. Once that ability is proven, then it should be possible to move on to certification in literal interpreting.

9.6 Summary
This chapter has presented aspects of communication and transcommunication related to information processing. We began with a discussion of simultaneous versus consecutive processing, and then reviewed the three factors of *Intention*, *Immediacy*, and *Interactivity* (and how these factors interface with transcommunication). We then explored the six processing levels: *Phonological* (Sublexical), *Lexical*, *Syntactic*, *Semantic*, *Pragmatic*, and *Stylistic* (Textual). We continued with a discussion of *literal* versus *idiomatic* work and how the six processing levels interact with those labels. The next chapter will review interpreting history and research.

9.6.1 Review Questions
1. What factors influence the decision to use *consecutive* or *simultaneous* processing?
2. What does "unduly free" mean?
3. Provide an example of a transcommunication event that is not immediate, not intentional and not interactive between the source and target consumers.
4. What are the *six levels* of information processing?
5. Why might an interpreter deliberately choose to use lexical processing?
6. What is the difference between *literal* and *idiomatic* processing?
7. Why might a consumer of interpreting services prefer literal processing?
8. What kinds of considerations may influence the interpreter's decision to choose literal processing?
9. What is the correct label for work that the RID certified as "Transliterating"?
10. Which levels of information processing are more likely for simultaneous interpreting versus translating?

9.6.2 Suggested Activities
1. Take a children's story (with lots of pictures) and generate three different versions in your second language: a) a word-for-word processing, b) a semantic processing of each paragraph of the story, and c) a complete recasting of the entire story that may not match the sequencing of the original story.
2. Generate a translation of one of the dialogues that open each chapter in this book. Work toward making a stylistically processed translation.
3. Choose one of the Codes of Ethics presented in Appendix B and generate a monolingual syntactic-level processed rewording of each of its tenets. The result should represent the same meanings, but use different word orders than the original text.
4. Choose one of the Codes of Ethics presented in Appendix B and generate a semantic-level translation of each of its tenets using another language that you know. The result should represent the same meanings, but use appropriate grammatical structures and vocabulary of the target language.
5. Generate a translation of the Preamble to the US Constitution (located in the appendices to this book). Ensure that you process at least to the semantic level by providing contextual information so that the resulting translation makes sense to someone who does not have extensive knowledge about the founding of the United States.

Chapter 10
Interpreting History & Research

"Interpreting History and Research"

Timoth sighed.

Rasmus asked, "What's wrong?"

Timoth closed the book and set it down. "I've come to the boring part of the book. It's all about history and research."

Rasmus sat next to Timoth. "I see... nothing new, just old information, eh?"

"I'm trying to improve my skills. How can research make any difference in my own work?"

Rasmus picked up the book and flipped through the pages. "Wouldn't you say this entire book is a matter of history? It's certainly been a while since it was printed."

"Yes, of course; but I don't need to review things even older than this book is. I just want to know about the new and useful things."

"Aha. New and useful things. There's your answer right there?"

"Rasmus, why do you torture me like this?"

"Because when you find your own answers you appreciate them more and remember them better than if I simply tell you how the world works."

"But I'm tired of thinking so hard. Can't you just explain it to me?"

"You'll still have to think to accept the argument. If you refuse to think, I might waste my time presenting my case with you just nodding and saying 'oh, I see' at the end just to make me change topics. Right?"

Timoth smiled "I guess you do know me pretty well, huh?"

"I have a long history of experience as a Mentor, Timoth. I have evidence for what works and what doesn't."

"OK. You just used the word 'history' so I better analyze your last sentence. Let me think for just a moment." Timoth's eyes closed. "History tells you where you have been and what progress has been made. It helps you appreciate the advances of more recent times and lets you know that you are doing things well."

"Good, keep on going."

"Keep on going? I thought I was finished." Timoth sat for a moment in silence.

Rasmus maintained both silence and eye contact with Timoth.

Timoth leaned forward, "You know, Rasmus, this behavior of yours borders on being psychopathic."

Rasmus smiled and leaned back in the chair.

Timoth looked at the ground and thought a little longer. "OK, you said something about evidence. So research provides evidence and unless we have evidence we are only making judgments on opinions and personal biases. So research keeps us 'professional'. How's that?"

"Well done!"

Timoth stared at Rasmus, "I hate it when you make me do that."

"You were the one who brought it up."

"I brought it up? You were the one who asked me 'what's wrong'."

"But you were the one who let out that 'sigh for help'."

Timoth smiled. "Well, I will admit you have raised my curiosity about this next chapter."

Chapter 10 – Interpreting History and Research

"Those Who Are Ignorant of Their Past Are Doomed to Repeat It." - Georg Santayana

10.0 Overview

This chapter begins by establishing the historical framework for the use of interpreting. Only after the field of interpreting was established was there any need to conduct research of it. The first research studies were experimental in nature, meaning that artificial circumstances were created and an interpreter was asked to perform interpreting within these settings, usually without any actual consumers of their service present at all. More recently, observational studies have been conducted which have allowed researchers to at least begin to acknowledge the influences of consumers upon the work of interpreting.

Many of the researchers proposed models of interpreting. Some of these models are as basic to the interpreting process as "something in, something done, and something out". More complex models have been built on the earlier ones which acknowledge the complexities of understanding the words, structure, meaning, and intentions of one message while simultaneously constructing a message with similar or identical intention and meaning within the words and structure of another language. Some of these models are presented in Chapter Eleven. The rest of this chapter summarizes key research in the interpretation of spoken languages and the interpretation of signed languages.

10.1 The Profession of Spoken-Language Interpreting

The history of interpreting will never be fully known. There has been a need for interpreters ever since there have been people who wished to communicate, but did not share the same language. Prior to the 1940's, most professional interpreting was done consecutively. That is, one person would produce a message (or part of a message) and then stop, momentarily, while the interpreter produced the same message (or part of the message) in another language. There was very little simultaneous interpreting happening at international business and political events because there was no easy access to private electronic sound systems. Without a private electronic sound system, a simultaneous interpretation would require that the speaker and the interpreter talk at the same time. This would be too distracting to the audience and the speaker. Widespread use of simultaneous interpreting would require a way of sending the interpretation to the listener without interrupting the main speaker.

It is often said that the mother of invention is necessity. When World War II ended and four major governments began investigating the activities of German leaders, it became necessary to interpret the proceedings in four languages: English, French, German, and Russian. Traditional (consecutive) approaches to interpreting between four languages would have extended the trial proceedings greatly. The *need* was for simultaneous interpreting and the *invention* was a four-channel electronic sound system provided by IBM.

When the *Nuremberg Trials* began, and judges from four different countries began to ear testimony regarding the war crimes of German leaders, a select group of people egan providing simultaneous interpreting services. The procedures they developed ould become the model for interpreting services at the United Nations and a wide ariety of international events. Siegfried Ramler (1988) was one of the interpreters for e Nuremberg Trials, which began in 1946:

> We required teams of 12 interpreters for the trials, with three persons on each of four language microphones located in booths divided by glass panels. Thus the English channel would require one person to interpret from German into English, one from French in to English, and one from Russian into English. The same pattern continued for the other channels, so that, for example, the Russian booth would have three individuals translating from German into Russian, English into Russian and French into Russian. The eight members of the tribunal, the prosecution and defense staffs, the defendants and the audience in the courtroom wore earphones and were provided with a selector switch at each seat, allowing the listener to tune in to any of the four languages he wanted to hear. The original language spoken on the courtroom floor would, of course, come through "verbatim" on a given channel. This technology, with equipment which would be considered primitive by today's standards, was supplied by I.B.M. After the trial started, Hermann Goering was overheard to say: "This system is very efficient, but it will also shorten my life!" (Ramler, 1988: 437-438)

> In addition to providing simultaneous interpreting there were transcripts made of the proceedings in each language. Once interpreters had completed interpreting several hours of sometimes shocking testimony they had to verify the transcripts of their interpretations by comparing them with audio recordings of the trial. Even with all of this checking and double checking there were still disputes about the details of the interpretations, especially with terms which had rather neutral meanings in German but had taken on specific meanings under Nazi use: A well-known example is the term 'Endlösung,' final solution, an innocuous term in ordinary use, but in the Nazi context indicating annihilation, as in 'the final solution of the Jewish problem.' (Ramler, 1988: 439).

For all of their hard work, however, the importance of the interpreters' work was not st on the people coordinating the trial. In post-World War II Germany there were great ortages of many things including motorized transportation, fuel, and food. Yet the erpreters were not only paid but were also provided with transportation, luxurious commodations and good meals for the duration of the trial proceedings. The IBM hnology would later be further enhanced and expanded to serve the needs of the ited Nations where many of the practices established at the Nuremberg trials are still ployed to this day.

.2 The Profession of Signed/Spoken-Language Interpreting

There was a time, not long ago, when even the people who were doing the work of erpreting did not think of interpreters as "professionals". While foreign language nference interpreting had been widely regarded as *professional* work, community erpreting did not hold this status. Community interpreting with deaf people was seen being charitable rather than anything professional.

10.2.1 The Registry of Interpreters for the Deaf

Interpreting between a signed and spoken language as a profession has its origins i the 1963 founding of the Texas Society of Interpreters for the Deaf. The following yea the need for interpreters received national attention. A group of educators, interpreter and rehabilitation counselors gathered at Ball State University in Muncie, Indian between June 14 and June 17 in the summer of 1964. One evening they gathered for a impromptu meeting to address the need to identify practitioners of interpretin nationwide. This meeting ended up establishing the roots for the Registry of Interpretel for the Deaf. A national organization of interpreters was proposed and was establishe initially with the name "National Registry of Professional Interpreters and Translators fc the Deaf."

The people providing interpreting services in 1964 were generally volunteers. The provided services to friends and were rarely reimbursed for their efforts at that tin (Fant, 1990). The meeting in Muncie was simply an attempt to solve the problem c identifying qualified interpreters nationwide but it ended up being the beginnings of th first national professional organization of Signed/Spoken Language Interpreters. Th people in attendance certainly did not regard it as historic:

> In my conversations and correspondence with some of the other participants, I am of the opinion that the occasion was not very dramatic nor exciting. It was not even a scheduled event on the agenda, and happened only because two participants, Edgar Lowell and Ralph Hoag, came up with the idea.
>
> Lowell, then the Administrator of The John Tracy Clinic, knew no sign language and nothing about interpreting. He did, however, possess a keen mind and by questioning the participants, especially Hoag, the son of deaf parents and an accomplished interpreter, he acquired an understanding of the problems we were having in the field of interpretation. The major problem was the shortage of competent interpreters, so recruitment of interpreters and people to become interpreters were priority matters. Following hard on the heels of this would come the matter of training new recruits to become interpreters. Lowell and Hoag, then the administrator of the Grants-in-Aid Program for Training Teachers of the Deaf, U.S. Office of Education, agreed that some kind of organization seemed needed that could assess interpreter competency and maintain a registry of them so consumers could be assured of receiving quality service. (Fant, 1990: 1-2)

The meeting lasted two and a half hours and resulted in the election of an Executi Board which consisted of a President (Kenneth Huff, the superintendent of the Wiscons School for the Deaf in Delevan, Wisconsin), a Vice President (Dr. Elizabeth Benson, tʰ Dean of Women at Gallaudet College), a Secretary-Treasurer (Virginia Lewis Youngstown, Ohio), and two members at large (Frank Sullivan of the National Fratern Society of the Deaf, and Lillian Beard of Houston, Texas).

The five-member board took their positions as they were elected. Participants we asked to identify themselves as members of the new organization, if they desired, and so to identify themselves as interpreters or as sustaining members. Forty-two of th participants identified themselves as interpreters and twenty-two others as sustainin members (although seven of these indicated that they could interpret). Thus began th National Registry of Professional Interpreters and Translators for the Deaf (NRPITD).

In less than a year (January of 1965) the Executive Board would rename tʰ organization "The Registry of Interpreters for the Deaf" and by the early 1970's the Rᴵ had established a national office, become incorporated, and was beginning to perform certification examinations nationwide. While most of its members still provided interpreting work only on a part-time basis, the roots of professionalism had been planted.

The RID was initially supported by a Rehabilitation Services Administration grant administered by the National Association of the Deaf (NAD). The NAD provided office space and support services through this time. This funding lasted until 1972 when the RID became an incorporated organization. The purpose of the organization had originally been to recruit, educate, and maintain an updated listing of signed language interpreters. The first national convention was held in Delevan, Wisconsin (where Wisconsin's residential school for deaf children is located) in 1970. Meetings were held every two years after that until 1982, then were shifted to odd-numbered years beginning in 1983. RID had grown in membership and also in scope: it is now concerned with certification standards and testing, certification maintenance through education, and the publication of research and theory related to the interpreting profession.

A board of directors consisting of a president, vice-president, member-at-large, secretary/treasurer, and five regional representatives governs the RID. An executive administrator and the RID office staff manage the RID on a daily basis. The National RID office used to be located in Silver Spring, Maryland, which is also where the National Association of the Deaf has its national offices. The national office was moved to Alexandria, Virginia after the RID purchased its own building there. The national office staff has specialized areas of responsibility for certification exams, certification maintenance, membership services, and publications.

The *National Testing System* (NTS) coordinator is responsible for ensuring the quality of the certification exams, the training of the raters, establishing testing sites, and scheduling and tracking candidates for certification. The *Certification Maintenance Program* (CMP) coordinator is responsible for coordinating the approval of educational offerings for *Continuing Education Units* (CEUs) in five categories of training, coordinating the sponsors of CMP educational offerings, and tracking the progress of all certified members toward maintaining their certification within the program. Membership services maintain the list of RID members for publication in the annual RID membership directory, collects membership dues and issues membership cards. RID publications include the RID *Views*, which is the monthly newsletter containing reports from the board, regional representatives, and committees. It also lists upcoming certification exam testing dates, approved sponsors for the CMP, advertisements for interpreting products and employment, and articles of interest to the membership. The RID also publishes *The Journal of Interpretation*, which includes theory and research in the field of interpreting.

With approval of the national membership, the RID publishes various position papers, which reflect the official recommendations of the RID for various issues such as Team Interpreting, Mentoring, and Business Practices. There is also an *Ethical Practices System* (EPS) in place to review ethical practices of interpreters. This system allows consumers of interpreting services to file complaints about unethical interpreters. The review board has the authority to issue penalties to interpreters found to be in violation of the code of ethics, including the revocation of certification.

Within the membership of RID there are Special Interest Groups (SIGs) which can be formed either to address particular issues in the profession (such as the Educational Interpreters of the RID [EdITOR] and the Mental Health SIG), or to address specific groups of members (such as the Interpreters/Transliterators of Color [ITOC], and Hearing Interpreters with Deaf Parents [HIDP]).

RID national conferences occur every odd-numbered year, while RID regional conferences occur every even-numbered year. Conferences provide the opportunity for the membership to propose and vote on motions during business meetings, attend educational workshops, and develop or strengthen professional contacts with other people in the field. The membership of RID consists of both certified and non-certified interpreters. Non-certified interpreters of RID are called *Associate* members and make up over half of the total membership in the RID.

10.2.2 The Association of Visual Language Interpreters of Canada

The beginnings of professionalism in Canada are linked to the Registry of Interpreters for the Deaf, with Provincial chapters of the RID being incorporated in Manitoba (1976) and in Alberta (1977). In 1979 a conference was held in Ottawa that led to the establishment of a Canadian national organization. Supporting funding was obtained from the National Department of Health and Welfare, the Canadian Hearing Society, the Canadian Association of the Deaf, the Western Institute for the Deaf, and the Canadian Coordinating Council on Deafness. The *Association of Visual Language Interpreters of Canada* (AVLIC) had its first organizational meeting in November of 1979 in Winnipeg.

AVLIC chose its name carefully. 1) They wished to avoid choosing a name that identified only a portion of the consumers of interpreting services (RID and AVLIC members interpret for both Deaf and hearing people). 2) They wished to avoid identifying specific languages since a large number of members may be working between any of the following four languages: American Sign Language, English, French, and Quebec Sign Language (LSQ).

A board of directors consisting of a president, vice-president, secretary, and treasurer governs AVLIC. The *Canadian Evaluation System* (CES) provides for testing and certification of visual language interpreters in Canada.

10.3 Research on the Interpreting Process of Spoken Languages

Eva Paneth (1957) was among the first people to provide any analysis of spoken language interpretation and observed that interpreters would generally produce elements of their target texts between two and four seconds after those elements had been presented in the source text. Thus began the identification of an important difference between interpreting and translating. Translations could be done across any range of time (minutes to years) but this time lapse was nothing of importance for research. Consecutive Interpretation allowed the interpreter to take as long as needed to convey the entire text (or portion of a text). Paneth's observations focused on simultaneous interpreting, where the timing of source and target texts becomes a significant issue.

Simultaneous Interpreting first became a practical option during the Nuremberg trials after World War II (Bowen and Bowen, 1987; Ramler, 1988). Advances in technology allowed for headphones to provide private access to one of several interpretations in different languages. Since the interpretations were perceived privately, they did not interfere with the source text. This meant that the interpretation could be generated at the same time as the source text. The advent of technology and simultaneous interpreting placed the interpreter in a battle of time between the source presenter and the target audience. It became common practice to move the interpreters away from the presenters and isolate them with headphones and microphones in soundproofed interpreting booths. These booths were generally in the back of the proceedings hall and had glass windows, which allowed a view of the presenter and audience, but no means of interaction, other than a light-based signaling system[33]. Now source speakers would proceed with their texts as though no interpreter were present and the need to "keep up" with the source presenter became a concern of utmost importance to professional interpreters.

Further research of the time difference between the presentation of source and target texts was conducted by Oléron & Nanpon (1965), who were among the first to conduct experimental studies on the interpreting process. Their work demonstrated that the processing time (sometimes referred to as "ear-voice span") of interpreters ranged between two seconds and ten seconds. This research established that *Simultaneous interpreting* is not completely simultaneous.

David Gerver (1969) investigated the effect of presentation speed (between 95 and 165 words per minute) on the accuracy of the interpretation. His results indicated that increased source-text speed had an adverse effect on target-text accuracy and that the optimum rate for interpreting (specifically from spoken French to spoken English) was 100 words per minute. In the same study, Gerver also investigated the transliteration process of shadowing (trans-communicating a message into the same language and the same *language encoding system* in which it was presented) and determined that the optimum rate for shadowing spoken French was at 130 words per minute. He identified several categories for errors: omissions (of words, phrases, or larger strings of eight or more words), substitutions, and corrections. Gerver's research began the analysis of errors in determining accuracy of interpreting.

Oléron & Nanpon's 1965 work demonstrated the processing delay in simultaneous interpreting, but questions remained about how much true simultaneous work was being done during simultaneous interpreting. Gerver, in another experiment (1974), determined that interpreters working from spoken French into spoken English both listened and spoke simultaneously for 65% of the texts they interpreted, which lasted between five and twenty minutes. This meant that the remaining 35% of the time was spent either listening or speaking in isolation without overlap between the source presenter and the interpreter. This demonstrates that interpreters are very busy both attending to the source text and producing a target text simultaneously for about 65% of the time. Therefore simultaneous interpreting is not so much a label for how quickly the target text is produced, but rather a description of the activity of interpreters: they produce target texts while simultaneously attending to other portions of the source texts.

Barik (1969) determined that source-text pausing played a significant role in how interpreters analyzed the source text. The pausing structure of the source text was often understood by interpreters as being meaningful divisions of main points; therefore the

---

[33] The light-based feedback from the interpreters was generally three options, such as green for "go", yellow for "slow down", and red for "stop". Because the light system is much less forceful than a human request, there have been stories of interpreters banging on the glass panels of the booth when the red light had been ignored for too long!

interpreters would divide their target texts in similar ways. With further research, Barik (1973) discovered that interpreters generally make such use of pauses in the source text but also determined that the overall pause time in interpretations was less than those of the source texts (meaning that the interpreters generating target texts had talked for more of the time than the source text speakers had talked). Barik also included analysis of errors in determining accuracy. His categories for errors included omissions, additions, and substitutions (remember that Gerver included "corrections" but did not include "additions").

Goldman-Eisler (1972) also investigated pausing structures and identified three strategies employed by interpreters: 1) they may match the pausing structure in their target texts; 2) they may begin their target text before the source text pauses; 3) they may string together several segments without reflecting the source-text pauses. In other words, interpreters may or may not use identical pausing as compared to the source presenter.

Part of the value of this information was the understanding that interpreters are directly in charge of the work they produce. Various metaphors for interpreting have previously suggested that the interpreter only repackages the information from its source form to its target form while doing nothing else to its organization; but research from the early 1970's began to build a case contrary to this view. Seleskovitch (1978) provided different metaphor than that of a "conduit:"

> The interpreter is an intermediary, like the actor whose style of acting complements the playwright's script. And like the actor, he knows that to put his message across successfully, he must not be self-effacing but, on the contrary, make his presence very much felt. Like the actor, the interpreter is good or not so good and, like him, his presence is always felt. (p 112).

All of the experimental studies of the 1960s and early 1970s used audiotape recordings of source texts rather than live, spontaneous presentations. They provided the bulk of scientific research on interpreting when David Gerver (1976) performed a extensive review of research on the interpreting process between spoken languages. At that time there had been little research conducted by linguists, psychologists or teachers of interpreting. Gerver's explanation for the paucity of research included the relative youth of the profession (it had only been thirty years since the *Nuremberg Trials*) and the complexity of the process. The studies were divided into two different approaches: analyzing the time lapse between source and target texts as well as the percentage of correctly interpreted words; and 2) analyzing the errors generated along with personality measures and factors causing stress during the interpreting process (e.g. noise level).

Soon afterward Chernov (1979) proposed that the key to successful interpretation was the accuracy of *predictions* interpreters make about the source text. He credited semantic and pragmatic knowledge as the essential elements of predictability, but primarily analyzed the semantic realm of source language texts and how semantic propositions were conveyed between spoken languages. In other words, the interpreter must understand the meaning of the source text and the intentions of its presenter to efficiently generate an equivalent target text. The ability to make predictions requires that the interpreter understand a source text's meaning beyond its words. Seleskovitch (198? suggested that linguistic meaning is not as important as the "sense" conveyed in a text. This is an argument against finding merely lexical and semantic equivalents between anguages. Instead the interpreting process should be a search to understand the message ully (to discourse and stylistic levels) and build one's interpretation from that nderstanding.

Wilcox & Wilcox (1985) defined the process of interpreting in terms of schema heory where the interpreter plays an active role in constructing meaning. They emonstrated that a part of constructed meaning comes from being able to make accurate redictions about the source text. One factor influencing predictions of source texts is the ocial context surrounding the source text. Tannen (1984) stated that as the nderstanding of linguistics grew to include studies of meaning, linguists began to nderstand that all meanings are influenced by their social contexts:

> In fact, there can hardly be any meaning other than social meaning. As a generation
> of generative semanticists discovered (with the result that they metamorphosed into
> pragmatists), hardly a sentence can be seen as having a crystalline meaning that cannot be
> changed by the positing of a different context for it. (p 7).

Gregory & Carroll (1983) address these issues as they relate to the process of anslation:

> There has been a growing awareness that translation is not just a matter of item-to-
> item equivalence, or indeed of group of items to group of items, or structure to structure;
> rather it is a matter of text-to-text equivalence which involves variety and register
> considerations. (p 95).

).4 Research on the Interpreting Process Including a Signed Language

Research on interpreting including a signed language did not begin until the 1970s. ost of the early studies of sign language interpreting investigated variables outside of e interpreting process. Quigley, et al, (1973) and Schein (1974) both investigated rsonality traits of interpreters but both failed to draw any correlations between rsonality traits and competency. Other research on student comprehension of terpreted texts (Caccamise & Blasdell, 1977; Jacobs, 1977; Newell, 1978) did not port on the performance of the interpretations.

Brasel's research (1976) determined that after twenty minutes of interpreting, the curacy of the target text is significantly diminished. This information revealed the ensity of the work of interpreting and the need to have teams of interpreters providing rvice in order to maintain accuracy. Other factors also impact the accuracy of terpretations. Llewellyn-Jones (1981) studied interpreters working between British gn Language (BSL) and English. He found that linguistic abilities in both the *source* d *target* languages were two areas that strongly influenced the resulting interpretations. other words, greater linguistic skill in both English and BSL provided more accurate terpretations. Hurwitz (1980) demonstrated that experienced interpreters out- rformed inexperienced interpreters (as would be expected) when interpreting from nerican Sign Language to English. As predictable as this result would seem it clearly ntifies that interpreting is a complex process not easily mastered in a short time.

Cokely (1986) investigated processing time (the time between the production of the source text and the interpreter's production of the target text) and miscues (errors)[34] Cokely found an inverse relationship between processing time and miscues. This mean that the greater the length of time between the production of an element in a source text and its equivalent production in the interpreter's target text, the more likely it was to be correct[35]. While popular belief might hold that an ideal interpretation should be produced with very little processing time (so that it appears nearly simultaneously with the source text) Cokely's research found that such an interpretation is likely to be replete with errors.

The research on the timing of interpreting was also a first step in demonstrating that interpretation is done differently by different people who make decisions about the work that they are doing. Various researchers have explored coping strategies used by interpreters. Napier (2002) explored the idea of interpreters using linguistic coping strategies to succeed in the process of interpreting. In reviewing Cokely's 1986 research Napier suggested that interpreters might *deliberately* use omission at times as an *intentional* coping strategy rather than merely an error.

Related to the concept of processing time is the overall processing *strategy* for interpreting, which can be generated either simultaneously with the source text or in consecutive bursts of information which alternate between source text productions and target text productions. Russell (2002) investigated simultaneous and consecutive interpreting[36] within legal settings and discovered that consecutive interpretation provided greater accuracy overall, particularly when the messages being interpreted contained technical terminology or content not well known to the interpreters:

> Overall, the interpreters recognized that the quality of their interpreting was better when they used consecutive interpreting, but consistently they said that they needed to have more practice with consecutive interpreting in order to have the process go more smoothly for all participants. The interpreters also identified how they need to employ more consecutive interpreting into their regular work. (Russell, 2002: 177)

Pausing structures in source texts and their target texts also have relevance to the simultaneous or consecutive nature of interpreting. Gee and Kegl (1983) determined that the use of pausing in American Sign Language narratives was related to the internal structure of those narratives and that longer pauses occurred at organizational junctures within the narratives. Their work suggests that the use of pauses as an *organizational* component in a source text may be essential for an interpreter to replicate in a target text. Cokely (1983) investigated metanotative features of interpretations as they compared the same features in the source presentations. *Metanotative features* reflect the organization of a text and the presenter's attitudes and personality. Cokely found the interpretations appeared to produce more positive metanotative features than the source presentations, even though the source and target texts themselves contained equivalent content. This is to say that the *way* things were conveyed differed between the speaker and the interpreters while the *content* of the information being conveyed remained the

---

[34] Note that processing time and errors are the two areas that Gerver found the majority of prior research to focus on. Cokely's research *tied* these two areas together and found a *correlation*.

[35] Cokely identified the optimum time frame to be between four and six seconds.

[36] See Chapter Seven for definitions of consecutive and simultaneous interpreting.

ame. Cokely suggested that ideal interpretations should allow the Deaf consumers to
raw the same conclusions about how information was conveyed as well as ensuring that
he information was also identical.

Beyond pausing and metanotative features, discourse markers also provide essential
organizational information and need to be represented in target texts. Wilbur and Petitto
(1983) found that the organization of ASL discourse parallels that of spoken language
iscourse, with both *linguistic* and *non-linguistic* features. Maintaining or gaining the
oor is achieved primarily through raising the hands and averting eye gaze (except for
uestions) while terminations of conversational turns may be marked by such lexical
ems as "WELL," or "FINISH." Zimmer (1989) analyzed the interpretation of dialogic
iscourse (an interview) and found that while interpreters readily use turn holding
trategies (um... er... well...) they rarely made use of turn maintenance strategies (I see...
h-huh... sure...). The hearing consumers of the interpretation – who heard silence
stead of reassuring feedback – frequently attempted to repeat information or otherwise
lled the silence because they perceived them as informational pauses. This caused
terference and delays of the turns taken by the interpreter. Roy (1989) identified
veral strategies used by interpreters during overlaps of dialogic turn-taking such as
ssigning a turn (usually to the person of higher status), *retaining* information for
sertion into the next turn, and *omitting* the information of both parties during the
verlaps. Zimmer's and Roy's research indicate that the interpreters function as a
ommunication manager during dialogic discourse but are hard pressed to provide access
overlapping information such as turn-maintaining feedback or competition for taking
e next turn.

Metzger (1995) specifically examined this role of the interpreter as a manager of
alogic discourse and found two primary forms of influence: 1) *direct insertions* of
terpreter-generated content and 2) *misrepresentations* of the participant's perspectives
ithin otherwise accurate interpretations. Metzger's work and Cokely's metanotative
ork indicate that the interpreter's personal perspective and personality can directly
pact an interpretation.

Roy (1987) and Gish (1987) emphasized the need for the interpreter to be aware of
ch things as discourse markers, contextualization cues[37], and constructed dialogue[38].
y suggested that bilingual interpreters are more likely to focus on the lexical items and
eanings when reviewing an interpretation; but they often ignore the use of discourse
atures in the source language and whether an appropriate match was found in the target
xt. Her study indicated that mismatches between an ASL source text (which used
nstructed dialogues) and an English interpretation (which inappropriately used
nstructed dialogues) lead monolingual English users to understand a lecture for adults
the source language (ASL) to be a children's story in the target language (English).

---

[37] John Gumperz (1971) identified the notion of *Contextualization Cues*, which include
osodic features, such as the rhythm, intonation and tempo of communication; and also include
nverbal features, such as eye gaze and gestures.

[38] *Constructed Dialogue* occurs when a language user represents both the parties in a dialogue.
s typical in signed languages for contrasting space to represent the participants such that one side
the signing space represents one participant addressing the other. In English the exchange of
ns in constructed dialogues is typically marked with phrases such as "he said" and "she said".

Gish (1987) suggested an approach for text analysis that combines the interpreter's prio knowledge with the incoming information of a source text so that interpreters ca determine the main points and secondary points. A target text which merely relates, bu does not organize, these points is likely to be less useful than one which clearly states th main points and omits some amount of secondary points. Armed with this understandin of the organization of the text, interpreters should be better able to present a target tex that shares similar organization to the source text. Once interpreters have understood th organization of the source text they also should make correct inferences when explici information is not presented in the source text.

Cultural differences between the source text language and the target text language ar another consideration in the ability to create equivalent meaning in the interpretin process. Even lexical items may evoke different meanings in different cultures. Cokel (2001) had ASL/Interpreting students research how non-deaf people associated meaning to eight specific English words[39]. These words were chosen as a subset of English word that have specific cultural meaning to deaf people. The non-deaf people involved in th study did not have any significant contact with the deaf community. The resul indicated that the English words frequently used to identify culturally rich concepts in th Deaf community (especially when interpreting from ASL to English) did not successfull convey these concepts for the non-deaf consumers. In other words, interpreters workin to express these culturally rich concepts through only lexical equivalence are likely t fail.

10.5 Components of the Interpreting Process

Isham (1986) proposed six parameters which are essential to the interpreting proces 1) content (morphology and semantics), 2) function (pragmatics), 3) register, 4) affect, contextual force (discourse), and 6) metanotative qualities (stylistics). Witter-Merithe (1987) identified four parameters necessary for text analysis in the interpreting proces 1) content (morphology and semantics), 2) context (discourse and register –how, wh what, and where), 3) function (pragmatics), and 4) style (stylistics). These four overl for the most part with Isham's six parameters:

> CONTENT: analyzing what is being talked about, the topic, the general information being communicated. This stage of analysis usually provides understanding of the surface meaning of a message.
> CONTEXT: analyzing the circumstances or situation in which a particular text occurs. This includes an examination of the people involved, as well as the environment and setting in which the text occurs. This is the part of analysis that examines what surrounds the words used in the message and leads to the deeper level of meaning.
> FUNCTION: analyzing the purpose, function, object of the text. Understanding the goal of the message enables students to identify specific relationships, comparisons and contrasts in the message.
> STYLE: analyzing the structure, register and manner in which a text is expressed or executed. Looking at the distinctive ways in which one expresses oneself. Often, how interpreters weight information during an interpretation deals more with their own background and style than their understanding and recognition of the speaker's background and style. (Witter-Merithew, 1987: 78-79)

---

[39] The eight words in Cokely's study were as follows: *mainstreaming, cochlear implant, si language, ASL, Gallaudet, hearing, hard of hearing,* and *deaf.*

Witter-Merithew (1987) presents a five-part "Core Meaning Model" which includes 1) attending to the source message, 2) analysis of the source text, 3) transferring to basic meaning elements, 4) restructuring of the basic meaning into the target language, and 5) production of the target text. These elements help to merge with and fill in the spaces between the five key elements in Colonomos' (1989) model[40] of 1) *Concentrating* on the source message, 2) considering its *Source Frame*, 3) *Representing* the message, 4) *Generating* a the *Switch* into the Target language, and 5) *Planning* and delivering the target text.

10.6 Register Variation and Interpreting

While language varieties are generally cultural, register varieties may be more individual. One way to view pragmatic meaning is as a combination of "cultural convention and personal choice" (Zimmer, 1992: p 83). The present text considers cultural convention as *discourse*, and personal convention as *stylistics*: the unique but frequently repeated choices made by individuals in their speaking habits.

Two early studies of register in the interpreting process between ASL and English both focus on English as the target text. June Zimmer (1990) compared two performances of simultaneous interpretation into English. Both interpretations were performed during the presentation of the ASL source text with the expectation that neither interpreter would interrupt the presenter. The source text and both interpretations were recorded on videotape and are commercially available. Zimmer noticed differences in spoken English productions between the two interpretations. One interpreter tended to use more colloquial terms, shorter, simpler and sometimes incomplete, sentence structures. The other interpreter used more technical terms, and longer, more complex and nearly always complete sentence structures. Zimmer concluded that although there was variation between the two interpretations, the register of both appeared to nearly match the source text with one interpretation being slightly less formal than the source text and the other being slightly more formal than the source text.

Risa Shaw (1987) conducted another significant study of register in ASL to English interpreting. Her research used samples from the same data tapes that Zimmer used in her study[41], but also sampled elements from another Deaf person providing a more formal lecture. Shaw's results indicated that a variety of variables (words per minute, pausing, false starts, enunciation, complexity of sentence structures, vocabulary choices) were juggled between the two performances such that, even with differences between the interpreters, they both accomplished effective matching between the source text and target text registers. Zimmer's and Shaw's research both indicate that interpreters are able to match register in the process of interpreting but that this match is achieved through *personally unique* choices by each interpreter. In other words, individual and personal style of an interpreter will influence and infuse every target text that interpreter creates.

---

[40] Colonomos' model is based on concepts presented by Danika Seleskovitch (1978).

[41] The videotapes used in Zimmer's and Shaw's research are commercially available through gn Media Incorporated ("Interpreting Model Series" Item #301).

10.7 English-Influenced ASL Variation and Interpreting

Within American Sign Language (as with any language) there is significant variation for a variety of reasons. One kind of variation is known as *Contact Signing* (Lucas & Valli, 1992) where elements of English directly impact the productions of ASL. This phenomenon is sometimes desired by bilingual Deaf consumers of interpreting services who make use of the visual nature of ASL to make the message accessible while desiring the organization of the message to reflect the English structures of the source text. The Registry of Interpreters for the Deaf certifies this kind of interpreting with the title "Transliteration" (See Chapter 9, Section 9.4). It may be referred as "English-Influenced Interpretation into ASL" or in the present text as "*Literal Interpreting*" since the target language is not a form of English but rather is a variety of ASL.[42]

Hoffmeister & Shettle (1983) present evidence that deaf adults who are bilingual in ASL and English will vary their communicative behavior depending upon their audience, whether native ASL users or people who have learned ASL later in life. Cokely (1984) addresses a similar issue in the frame of *Foreigner Talk*. While the visual-gestural language contact that can often occur between deaf and hearing people exhibits aspects of both English and ASL, Cokely attributes this to foreigner talk (the signing of Deaf people who are talking to non-native hearing signers) and learner's grammar (the signing of non-native hearing signers who are talking to Deaf people). In other words, a hearing person who knows English will generate signs using an interlanguage grammar based on English. The deaf person communicating with this hearing person will make grammatical simplifications in order to assist the hearing person's comprehension of a signed discussion.

Lucas and Valli (1992) call this entire process "contact signing," which they propose is what occurs both between hearing and deaf people and also on occasion between fluent deaf people and less-than-fluent deaf people. Contact signing has various features of both ASL and English, but is not entirely predictable: "There is a set of predictable linguistic features that do constitute a system, but there also seems to be a great deal of individual variation due to differences in linguistic background. This means that the contact signing input that second-language learners are exposed to may also be highly variable." (Lucas & Valli, 1992; p 118).

Winston (1989) investigated English-Influenced Interpretation into ASL (identified in the study as "transliteration") and discovered five strategies relevant to successful interpretation in this manner: 1) Sign Choice, 2) Additions, 3) Omissions, 4) Restructurings, and 5) Mouth Movement patterns. *Sign Choices* were conceptually accurate, based on semantic relationships of secondary or figurative meanings rather than phonological relationships to only a primary sense of the word. *Additions* were used to idiomatically clarify portions of the interpretation that were otherwise very literal and potentially confusing. *Omissions* were generally of morphological elements unique to English. *Restructurings* involved combinations of Sign Choice with grammatical structures in ASL that more clearly represented relationships than the syntax of the source text. *Mouth Movements* were used to disambiguate specific English words within

---

[42] Note that a language can include varieties that are ungrammatical or disfluent, such as those produced by non-native users of the language. ASL signs presented in English word order may not be grammatically accurate ASL, but the result remains distinct from the language of English; just as putting French words into English word order would not be considered to be a form of English.

the source text where a single conceptually accurate sign might have several possible English equivalent words.

Ingram (1988) investigated the differences between listening, literal interpreting and idiomatic interpreting and their effect on memory for syntactic and semantic information in the source texts. He found that interpreters could much more readily recognize the meaning of source texts after generating *idiomatic* interpretations. This result directly contrasted the results of similar research done with spoken language interpreting (Lambert, 1983; Gerver, 1974) which indicated a deficit for memory after interpreting as compared to only listening. The Lambert and Gerver studies also investigated shadowing, or verbatim repetition of the source text, and found that this had the most negative effect on memory as compared to just listening or interpreting. Ingram considered the literal interpreting task (which he labeled as "transliterating") initially to be a task similar to shadowing, but it showed improvement on memory over listening alone, indicating that it was indeed very different from shadowing. Ingram explains his improved results in part as being related to a reduction in interference since the source and target texts are expressed in different, non-competing modalities. In other words, the interpreter's production of the source text (signed ASL) does not interfere with the perception of the source text (spoken English).

Siple (1993) analyzed the use of pausing within spoken discourse in relationship to the task of literal interpretation from spoken English to English-influenced ASL. The results of Siple's study indicated that spoken texts with random pausing disrupted the target transliteration more than spoken texts with normal speech pausing. This clearly indicates that literal interpreting is not merely a word for word lexical matching but enters into semantic processing. Another implication is that the manner in which a text is performed has an impact upon the way it is understood in the interpreting process and that source texts that maintain connections between ideas are more successfully interpreted than those which do not. In other words, the accuracy of the *interpretation* can be influenced by the clarity and cohesion of the *source* text.

Livingston, et. al. (1994) compared idiomatic interpreting and literal interpreting of both *narrative* and *lecture* source texts. Forty-three Deaf subjects responded to questions after receiving one or the other stimuli. Results indicated that students receiving idiomatic interpretations performed better, even if the students had previously indicated a preference for literal interpreting. The authors analyzed the differences in the performances of literal and idiomatic interpretations. They found that the need to maintain the general syntax of the source text in the literal interpretations results in a very limited amount of processing time between hearing the source text and generating the target text. The limited processing time meant that message processing was generally at the *lexical* level, which prohibited a deeper understanding of the source text prior to generating the target text. This limited understanding of the source text had less of an impact upon the interpretation of the narrative than it did the interpretation of the lecture. The authors conclude that the meanings of syntactically complex lectures are not adequately conveyed via literal interpretation.

It is interesting to note that for both of RID's generalist certification exams the ASL to English requirements are identical except for the provision of additional processing time for the idiomatic interpreting task. This indicates that the Deaf community has need for both literal and idiomatic interpretations into signed languages while the hearing community benefits primarily from interpreting into idiomatic spoken language. This can be explained logically in that the Deaf community members are much more likely to be bilingual in both ASL and English and may desire to know the original structure of an English source text. The hearing community members are much more likely to have little or no knowledge of ASL and therefore have little need to know the original structure of an ASL source text.

Kelly (2001) provides an overview of the traditional views of "transliteration" as being a form of signed English. While several different specific manual English codes are identified as the possible result of the work of a "transliterator" Kelly's research focuses largely on the work done into what is called "Conceptually Accurate Signed English", which by Kelly's own definition is essentially ASL restructured to fit the grammatical patterns of English. Kelly's work largely reinforces the concepts that the work of "transliterators" is actually *literal* interpreting (as contrasted with *idiomatic* interpreting), but Kelly makes no attempt to reassign these labels.

These pieces of research represent the scientific investigation into the differences of *literal* and *idiomatic* interpretation into ASL. The Registry of Interpreters for the Deaf has also issued guidelines for successful completion of their performance exams for literal and idiomatic interpreting (see Appendix A). These guidelines indicate essentially the same five variables that Winston's 1988 research identified as elements of successful English to ASL "transliteration" (literal interpretation).

10.8 Relayed Interpreting

Relayed interpreting occurs when the target text of an interpretation serves as another interpreter's source text. Janet Altman (1990) included relayed interpreting in a survey of ninety-four European conference interpreters (spoken language interpreting) and found overwhelming *negative* response to its use. Three questions on the survey were as follows (Altman, 1990: 32):

11. What is the effect of relay interpreting on the communication process?

very positive	positive	neutral	negative	very negative
2%	13%	28%	50%	7%

12. What is the effect on your work when you know you are being used as a relay?

very positive	positive	neutral	negative	very negative
4%	46%	38%	12%	0%

13. I prefer working on relay to interpreting "direct"

often	occasionally	hardly ever	never
2%	6%	26%	65%

Figure 10.1 – Altman's (1990) Survey Questions on Relayed Interpreting

While interpreters generally felt that serving as an early link in the process of relayed interpreting had a positive effect on their own work (50% responding either "very positive" or "positive" to question #12), they overwhelmingly agreed that relayed interpreting was detrimental to the overall communication and that they did not prefer relayed interpreting to "direct" interpreting.

The use of relayed interpreting within the American Deaf community differs from its general use in spoken-language settings. Spoken-language interpreters who are part of relayed interpreting are likely to have a large number of direct consumers of their services, meaning that an interpretation from Arabic to French might serve a large number of French-speaking audience members at the same time that it serves as the source text for several relay interpreters working into English and German, for example. This means that the Arabic-to-French interpreter is not monitoring the English or German interpretations. In contrast, relayed interpreting within the Deaf community generally works between only two languages and the first interpreter is at least potentially able to monitor the production of the relayed target text and may in fact have only the relay interpreter as the consumer of the initial interpretation. This allows for much more feedback and interaction between the interpreters and therefore is likely to create greater confidence in the accuracy of the final interpretation. There are very few formal papers on *Relayed Interpretation* that discuss the use of relayed interpretation where a signed language is involved.

Bienvenu & Colonomos (1990) describe relayed interpreting within the American Deaf community as involving a minimum of four parties: Hearing Consumer, Hearing Interpreter, Relay Interpreter (Deaf), and the Deaf Consumer. In the spaces between each party they identify the language options being employed in the relayed interpreting process: Spoken English used between the Hearing Consumer and the Hearing Interpreter, "preferred Sign Variety" between the Hearing Interpreter and the Relay Interpreter, and then four options between the Relay Interpreter and the Deaf Consumer based on the consumer needs): Foreign Sign Language, Idiosyncratic Sign/Gesture, ASL for monolinguals, and Native/Complex ASL (Bienvenu & Colonomos, 1990: 70). The first two of these are further explained within their article:

> A serious problem occurs when the person who requires relay interpretation has no formal language. In training, we must come up with strategies for communicating in gestures and mime. In some situations, this is not a difficult task, but, particularly in legal matters where the consequences are severe and the ideas are not concrete, it's very hard to come up with successful ways to communicate. It's important to keep in mind that some D/deaf people who come from other countries, will be relying on a much different gestural system than what is commonly used in America... If the D/deaf consumer is using foreign signs, that will give the relay interpreter a clue that there can be a basis for communication. (Bienvenu & Colonomos, 1990: 75).

Bienvenu & Colonomos identify legal, medical, mental health, psychiatric, and drug/alcohol treatment programs as settings where relayed interpreting may be essential for effective communication, especially when the Deaf consumer has little usable language and the information is complex. "Legal dialogues often have little to do with concrete and material things (i.e. the Miranda Warning), and it is difficult to convey abstract concepts using gestures." (p 77). Bienvenu & Colonomos also identify the use of relayed interpreting for public events:

For years it has been standard practice to [provide idiomatic and literal interpreting simultaneously with two interpreters] for an event, whether it be a lecture, rally, performance, etc. A number of Deaf people in the audience have not always been able to follow the [literal interpreters] and some [idiomatic] interpreters have been equally unclear. An alternative to this would be to have a hearing [literal interpreter], in clear view of the relay interpreter, who would then take that [literal interpretation], and provide an [idiomatic] interpretation for the Deaf audience. (Bienvenu & Colonomos, 1990: 77).

Carolyn Ressler (1999) produced the first published research of relayed interpretation using ASL. Her study investigated only the Hearing interpreter's work and compared the differences between the Hearing interpreter's target text production when working as part of a relay team and when providing direct, solo interpretation of the same text (specifically, the hearing interpreter was asked months later to reinterpret the same material but not as part of a relay team). The source text was a videotaped message in spoken English and the setting was a research lab without any consumers of the interpreting work being done. Results indicated a few differences between the performances of the hearing interpreter performing direct and intermediary interpreting. These differences included significant direct eye gaze directed toward the deaf interpreter while working as a team (compared to much less "audience" eye gaze in the direct interpreting). The interpreting as part of a team had more head nodding (as part of monitoring the Deaf Target Text), had fewer signs per minute, and had greater use of fingerspelling. The teamed interpretation made significant use of pausing and clarification strategies (communication between the team members about the information being interpreted). Ressler's research did not investigate the differences between the Hearing interpreter's interpretation and the Deaf interpreter's target text within the relay team.

Whynot (1999) compared the roles of interpreters and ethnographers and found similarities in how both approach their work. One key area of similarity was that the members of the minority culture must trust the interpreter. Interpreters can enhance this sense of trust by increased association with minority culture members and thus gaining an inherent respect and desire to convey the meanings of the culture with accuracy. These concepts can help to explain the popularity of relayed interpreting with Deaf team members because a member of the minority culture is generating the final target text thereby immediately increasing the trust that the minority culture members will have in that interpretation.

10.9 Relayed Interpretation From English To American Sign Language Via A Hearing And A Deaf Interpreter (Cerney, 2004)

The research in this study specifically investigated two interpreters, one hearing and one deaf, who were both actively involved in the process of taking a message from English to ASL during the opening business meeting at an RID conference. Conference proceedings are generally monologic in nature and therefore the use of relayed interpreting at conferences tends to be unidirectional. In this case the hearing interpreter, working from English to ASL, sat in the front row of the audience and faced the stage. The deaf interpreter, standing on the stage with a clear view of the hearing interpreter, performed processed shadowing of the first interpreter's message, generating a more cohesive and culturally appropriate target text than the hearing interpreter's text. Both portions of this form of relayed interpreting occurred simultaneously with the on-going source text; however each team member's portion of this work was generally accomplished through a series of (mostly) consecutive performances (with overlaps at the beginnings and ends of nearly every segment).

Throughout this process, both interpreters were functioning in the "A" role. At first it may seem redundant to have two interpreters providing the primary service but there are very good reasons to use the service for specific consumers or settings. The hearing interpreters generally have English as their "A" language and ASL as their "B" language. The Deaf interpreters generally have ASL as their "A" language and therefore are more likely to make better cultural adjustments to the message. The ultimate result is a more idiomatic and cohesive message in the target language.

The choice to use simultaneous relayed interpreting may also be influenced by the nature of the communication. Monologic discourse of a technical nature, such as court proceedings and conference lectures, may be best conveyed through relayed interpretation. The reason being that the Hearing Interpreter can provide a partial adjustment of the source language and culture to the target language and culture; then the Deaf Interpreter may be able to bring further adjustment in the final target message so that the deaf consumer(s) need not struggle to understand the resulting interpretation. The chart below provides a graphic representation of the process.

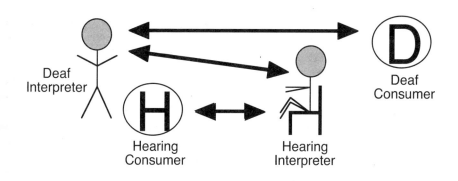

Figure 10.2 – Physical Arrangements of Relayed Interpreting Participants

The scope of this study was limited to the use of relayed interpreting within a conference setting for four significant reasons: 1) it is ethically difficult (if not impossible) to perform research on actual court use of relayed interpreting since the introduction of researchers to the situation will not only distract the consumers and interpreters but may directly impact the result of the communication being interpreted. 2) the recording of a performance of interpreting designed for a large audience creates little distraction and should have a minimal impact upon the communication. 3) Investigating this complex process in a unidirectional form reduces the total number of variables involved in the process, thus increasing the chances of accounting for the most significant factors. 4) Future research on the relayed interpretation of complex dialogic discourse will need a base, which this research provides.

10.9.1 Research Methods

From a set of recordings of seven interpreters providing relayed interpreting at a National Convention of the Registry of Interpreters for the Deaf, one team of two interpreters (one Hearing, one Deaf) were selected for intensive study. The team interpreted a ten-minute set of introductions and announcements during a plenary session. Video recordings were made, one of each interpreter. Video recordings were digitally edited and synchronized to allow both interpreters to appear in a split screen arrangement. The data set was then transcribed using *SignStream* software which allowed a frame-by-frame identification of fourteen variables including the Source text words, Audience reactions, ASL vocabulary generated for the dominant and non-dominant hands for both interpreters, head postures, eye gaze, eye brow postures and additional notes for each interpreter. A total of 18,015 frames were transcribed for each of the fourteen variables. Analysis was accomplished using *HyperCard* and *Microsoft Excel* software on *Macintosh* computers.

10.9.2 Summary of the Research Results

This research provides only a first look at the process of relayed interpreting. Only one team of interpreters was investigated and only the first ten minutes of their work was explored. It is the intention of the author that this research serves as a starting point for further investigation. There are many questions that the present study does not address even if the practices of relayed interpretation have not changed in the time between the data collection and publication of these results. How do other teams of interpreters perform relayed interpreting? Why do Deaf consumers of this service indicate a preference for relayed interpreting? How is relayed interpreting different for consumers who have limited ASL skills as opposed to consumers who are fluent in ASL? These are some of the questions that the next generation of researchers may choose to explore as they continue to learn more about the interpreting process.

10.9.3 Message Accuracy

Jacobs (1977) estimated that only 80% of a message survived the interpreting process. The first area of investigation in the present study was the representation of key concepts and of nouns between the Source Text, (ST), Hearing Target Text (HTT) and the Deaf Target Text (DTT). Results revealed that the HTT generated between 89% and 95% accuracy in the interpretation from English to ASL. Furthermore the DTT maintained this level of accuracy or slightly improved upon it. It is possible to use more detailed but less objective, ways of determining message accuracy, such as using propositional analysis. This study made use of more objective measurements – the use of nouns and of key concept words – to establish a baseline measurement of accuracy. Message accuracy is only a minor portion of this research and the results indicated acceptable levels of accuracy given previous research and estimates.

10.9.4 Processing Time

The second area of exploration was the timing required to generate the key concept words and the nouns of the Source Text, (ST), in the Hearing Target Text (HTT) and the

Deaf Target Text (DTT). Paneth (1957) observed interpreters generating concepts between two and four seconds after their appearance in the source text. Oléron & Nanpon (1965) indicated an "ear-voice span" of between two and ten seconds. Cokely (1986) determined an optimum processing time of between four and six seconds.

Results of the present study indicated that the HTT required an average of just less than 5 seconds of processing time to be generated. This is centered within Cokely's (1986) suggested optimum processing time. The DTT required, on average, less than 1.5 additional seconds, meaning that the entire process from Source Text to Deaf Target Text could be accomplished, on average, in less than 6.5 seconds, well within the processing times observed by Oléron & Nanpon (1965) for standard simultaneous interpreting. These results indicate that the time required to generate relayed interpreting takes only slightly longer than non-relayed interpreting and still falls within the same time ranges as expected for non-relayed interpreting.

Variation in the processing time is to be expected, but the longest instance of processing time was less than 15 seconds from the ST to the DTT[43]. More interesting is the fact that information was predicted, or anticipated, by both the Hearing and the Deaf interpreters such that some elements of the ST were predicted by several seconds[44]. In other words, not only was the Hearing interpreter able to anticipate some elements of the ST but the Deaf interpreter was also able to anticipate some elements of both the ST and the HTT. Chernov (1979) identified the ability to make predictions about the Source Text as an essential component of successful interpretation. The ability of the Deaf interpreter to anticipate the presenter of the Source Text is part of the evidence that the Deaf interpreter is processing the information as an interpreter and not merely mechanically reproducing or mirroring the HTT.

The most interesting aspect of the processing was the tendency for the interpreters to work somewhat consecutively. As the Source Text moved into new topics, the Hearing interpreter generally began with fixed eye gaze toward the source text presenter while hands were held together in what was transcribed as "PAUSE". As eye gaze moved to the Deaf interpreter and hands were raised, the Deaf interpreter focused eye gaze on the Hearing interpreter. The Hearing interpreter would generate at least several signs before the Deaf interpreter moved from PAUSE and began signing, while still maintaining eye contact with the Hearing interpreter. Within a few more sign productions the Deaf interpreter would generate a head nod and shift eye gaze toward the audience. Sometimes the first portion of the DTT would rephrase the HTT, at other times the DTT began by shadowing the HTT. The DTT changed, however, when the Deaf interpreter appeared to have sufficient understanding of the message, produced the head nod and established eye contact with the audience.

At this point the DTT would generally begin to make use of greater signing space, even to the point of the Def interpreter moving slightly from side to side within the stage space. Even though eye contact between the interpreters was broken at this point, the

---

[43] The noun-based analysis generated the maximum time span between ST nouns and DTT nouns: 14.37 seconds.

[44] The key-concept analysis generated the minimum time span between ST key concepts and DTT key concepts: negative 3.2 seconds, meaning that the concept was actually represented in the DTT 3.2 seconds before the ST generated the same concept.

Hearing interpreter continued and completed the thought being expressed. The Deaf interpreter would make occasional eye contact with the Hearing interpreter through these potions of the process. Upon completion of a portion of the message the Hearing interpreter either returned hands to PAUSE (indicating the full completion of the message segment) or held the hands in either an anticipatory or residual hold[45] (indicating a more phrasal or conceptual boundary). When the Deaf interpreter had come to either a full or partial completion of the message segment then the Deaf interpreter generated either a PAUSE or a residual hold, and the process repeated. The end result was that the two members of the relayed interpreting team generated their target texts in a largely (though not purely) consecutive manner.

10.9.5 Differences in Grammar and Style

The DTT was not an identical regeneration of the HTT. In fact, less than half of the lexical choices were identical between the HTT and the DTT. The DTT included substitutions of homonyms, repetitions that were not present in the HTT, and additions for either grammatical or idiomatic reasons. The morphological complexity of the HTT was not very different from the DTT, however the DTT did provide more grammatical and conceptual clarifications as compared to the HTT. All of these differences provide further evidence that the DTT is not merely a mirroring of the HTT, but rather the Deaf interpreter is actively engaged in generating an original target text that maintains the accuracy of the HTT. The Deaf interpreter is an active participant in the overall interpreting process of both team members.

Stylistic differences between the two interpreters include the Hearing interpreter making greater use of indexing, topicalizations, and conditionals while the Deaf interpreter made greater use of lexicalized fingerspelling, classifiers, pronouns, rhetoricals and yes/no questions. These differences may be stylistic differences rather than general differences between Deaf and Hearing interpreters. The Deaf interpreter also made a greater use of the overall signing space, using the non-dominant hand for many ASL lexical items. This difference may be related to the greater ability to access distinct signing space because the Deaf interpreter was standing, unrestricted by any podium or furniture on stage while the Hearing interpreter was seated and therefore less mobile.

10.9.6 Private Communication Between the Team Members

There is a need for the team members to communicate with each other in order to work effectively as a team, and yet overt linguistic communication could easily be misunderstood as being part of the interpretation. Eye gaze and head nods served as the primary communication mechanisms between the Deaf and Hearing team members. Each interpreter directed his or her eye gaze to the other interpreter for just over fifty percent of

---

[45] *Anticipatory holds* occurred when the handshape of a sign was held at its starting point for an extended time prior to the generation of the sign. *Residual holds* occurred when the final handshape and location of a sign was held for an extended time after the sign had been completed.

the overall data set[46]. Their eye gaze was mutual for just less than twenty-five percent of the overall data set.

The Hearing interpreter generated multiple instances of repeated head nods while observing the Deaf interpreter. This feedback generally occurred during the Hearing interpreter's PAUSEs, residual holds, or anticipatory holds. This means that the feedback was given consecutively with the generation of various segments of the HTT. At no time did the Hearing interpreter simultaneously generate this form of feedback while still generating any portion of the HTT. A different pattern was evident from the Deaf interpreter who frequently began each portion of the DTT with a head nod, indicating comprehension of the HTT and readiness to begin generating the next segment of the DTT.

Any private message between the interpreters using signs during the interpreting would confuse the target audience and be misunderstood as part of the source presenter's message. The Deaf interpreter could misunderstand such communication from the Hearing interpreter as source text to be interpreted. Consumers of the DTT might misunderstand a message from the Deaf interpreter as being part of the final target text. Only one time, during an obvious shift between speakers, did the Hearing interpreter initiate linguistic communication with the Deaf interpreter. This communication was marked by the Hearing interpreter leaning forward and signing in lower-than-normal space. The Deaf interpreter responded, also using lower-than-normal space. Both interpreters maintained mutual eye gaze during this exchange[47].

10.10 Summary

Research on the interpreting process began with observations made by Paneth in 1957. In the 1960s research was primarily experimental in nature, which excluded the consumers of interpreting services. Observational studies began in the 1970s. Various models of interpreting have been proposed which currently leave us with the understanding of interpreting as an incredibly complex process primarily in the hands and mind of the interpreter.

The interpreting process has been previously assumed to be a simple matching of the meanings of words that is conducted automatically without conscious decisions being made by the interpreter. The research reviewed in this chapter indicates that interpreters are very much involved in making decisions regarding much of the communication process. Interpreters need processing time and vary the amount of processing time required to understand the source text and produce a target text (Paneth 1957; Oléron & Nanpon, 1965; Llewellyn-Jones, 1981, Cokely, 1986). They may even produce a target text that has larger units of message production than the source text (Barik, 1973). Interpreters simultaneously attend to a source text while producing a target text (Gerver, 1974) and serve both as audience to the source text and as presenter of the target text (Roy, 1989; Seleskovitch,1995) which means they are working at least twice as hard as

---

[46] The Hearing interpreter's eye gaze was directed toward the Deaf interpreter across 50.8 percent of the data set. The Deaf interpreter's eye gaze was directed toward the Hearing interpreter across 53.8 percent of the data set.

[47] The exchange itself was very brief and consisted of the Hearing interpreter asking "HEY-Dave, THUMB-UP, #OK?" and the Deaf interpreter responding "F-OKAY".

any of their consumers; and therefore interpreters can only work to their highest ability for a limited time (Brasel, 1976).

Interpreters with more language skills (Llewellyn-Jones, 1981) and with greater experience (Hurwitz, 1980) are more likely to provide accurate interpreting. Interpreters can improve their accuracy while interpreting if they allow themselves more processing time during the task (Cokely, 1986). The organization of target texts created by interpreters may be influenced by the pausing structures in the source text (Barik, 1969; Siple, 1993) but interpreters may impose their own organization (Goldman-Eisler, 1972). Interpreters must know the meaning of the source text in order to accurately construct an equivalent target text (Chernov, 1979). Interpreters need to have an understanding of the intentions and goals of the presenter to accurately construct an equivalent target text (Chernov, 1979; Seleskovitch, 1987).

Interpreters are communication managers who influence how participants take turns in dialogues while also directly influencing the meaning of the resulting message (Zimmer, 1989; Roy, 1989; Metzger, 1995; Cokely, 1983). Interpreters manipulate a variety of variables to create their own unique target texts (Zimmer, 1990; Shaw, 1987). Greater lengths of processing time and the use of consecutive interpreting provide for greater accuracy than shorter processing times and simultaneous interpreting (Cokely, 1986; Russell, 2002). Literal interpreting[48] shares many aspects with idiomatic interpreting and is significantly different from transliterating (Ingram, 1988; Winston, 1994; Siple, 1993). Idiomatic interpreting results in significantly better comprehension of complex source texts than Literal interpreting (Livingston, et. al., 1994).

Literal interpreting may play a part in relayed interpreting (Bienvenu & Colonomos 1990) but research by Cerney (2004) indicates that Deaf Target Texts are not mirrorings of the Hearing Target Texts (HTTs), but rather original processed shadowings in which the Deaf Interpreter accurately represents the concepts of both the source texts and HTTs while making distinct lexical, syntactic, semantic, pragmatic and stylistic choices as compared to the Hearing Interpreter.

---

[48] Literal Interpreting occurs when an interpretation places the target language words into word orders that parallel the structure of the Source Text.

0.10.1 Review Questions

1. What was the first major event to make significant use of simultaneous interpreting?
2. What technology allowed this simultaneous interpreting to take place?
3. What statewide interpreting organization was founded in 1963?
4. Where was the initial meeting that founded the RID and when did it take place?
5. How many seconds of time span between the source and target texts were reported by Paneth, and by Oléron & Nanpon
6. How many minutes did Brasel's research suggest that interpreters are able to maintain accuracy?
7. What were the six parameters that Ingram proposed as essential to the interpreting process?
8. What was the average processing time of relayed interpreting (in Cerney's 2004 study)?
9. How was private communication between team members accomplished (in Cerney's 2004 study)?

0.10.2 Suggested Activities

. Read an article in the most recent *Journal of Interpretation* (or a similar journal such as *Babel*). Identify the elements of the linguistic pyramid that the article mentions (either directly or indirectly). Determine the different kinds of transcommunication that are discussed within the article and the languages that are used.
. Perform an Internet search using the key words from one of the headers in this chapter. What new research has been done on the topic?
. Perform an Internet search to find the names of other interpreting organizations, either at a state/regional level or in other countries.

Chapter 11
Models of Transcommunication

"Models of Transcommunication"

Timoth's forehead lowered onto the book. "I'll never memorize all of these models!"

Rasmus stopped and faced Timoth, "Why are you trying to memorize them?"

"So I can be a better interpreter," Timoth met eyes with Rasmus.

"How will memorizing a model make you a better interpreter?"

"If I understand the model, then I can know more about the process. If I know more about the process, then I can work to improve my skills."

"Yes, that's all true. But I still don't know how memorizing the models fits into all of this. Can't you understand them without memorizing them?"

Timoth sat up. "But if I don't memorize them, I'll forget all the pieces that fit into each little box or triangle."

Rasmus walked over to the chalkboard on the wall and drew a square on one side and a circle on the other. "What do these stand for?"

"Well, some models use the circle for starting and stopping. Others use it to represent the human mind. Squares usually contain a process or a series of processes."

"No. The circle stands for understanding and the square stands for memorizing. You didn't even ask me what this was a model of. I never said it was a model of interpreting." Rasmus turned toward the board and started to erase it.

"So what is it a model of?"

"Its a model of your dilemma. You say you will never memorize all of the models but your goal is to understand them." Rasmus finished cleaning the board and faced Timoth. "My model showed memorizing and understanding as two separate tasks."
"But it was just a circle and a square. How can you call that a model?"

"Well, looks like you've got the memorizing part done already. But you still don't understand it, so it would seem we still need to work on the understanding."

"So your model simply showed that the two tasks were separate pieces. OK, so now I understand, but I first had to memorize, didn't I." Timoth looked back at the diagram in the book "I'm still stuck."

"What if I hadn't drawn the model at all? Could you still understand it without a picture?"

"Well, I suppose so. You mean that I could have understood the concept even without knowing what the model looked like? Well, if that's true then what do we need models for in the first place?"

Rasmus looked at Timoth and smiled.

Timoth leaned back into the chair "Because models can lay things out to help us understand complex concepts we wouldn't otherwise grasp."

Rasmus nodded, "So stop worrying about memorizing and start trying to understand."

Chapter 11 – Interpreting Models
"If a picture paints a thousand words, Then why can't I paint you?" – David Gates

11.0 Overview
A variety of researchers and practitioners of interpreting created the Transcommunication Models presented within this chapter. Each person brought their own insight into the creation of their model(s). Together they provide a fairly effective explanation of the key components for successful interpreting. Before we begin this review of models, we should understand two contrasting metaphors which frame our understanding of what an interpreter is supposed to be doing.

11.1 Metaphors for Interpreting
A *Metaphor* is stating that one thing is another thing. A related concept is called a *Simile*, which is almost the same except that it uses a word of comparison. Paul Simon's song "I Am a Rock" uses a metaphor to draw a comparison of the qualities of a rock with himself as he faces the breakup of a romance. If he had called the song "I Am Like A Rock" he would have used a simile, but he also would have really messed up the rhythm and rhyme scheme of his song.

Members of the Interpreting profession have proposed various metaphors as a means of helping them explain how the interpreting process works. Sometimes they have been referred to as "models" but these metaphors are not detailed models of how a process works; rather, they merely make comparisons. These metaphors have influenced not only how consumers perceive the work of interpreters but also how interpreters see themselves. These perceptions have significant implications on ethical practices in our field, so it is worth investigating the metaphors and their resulting influence.

11.1.1 The Helper Metaphor
During the beginning of the Registry of Interpreters for the Deaf (RID), the only guide to the goals of interpreting was the RID code of Ethics. The original Code of Ethics, introduced in the summer of 1965, included a guideline that interpreters "shall maintain an impartial attitude during the course of his interpreting avoiding interjecting his own views unless he is asked to do so by a party involved." (Fant, 1990: 135). Other portions of the original code's twelve tenets suggest that the interpreter should determine the fluency of the deaf consumer and inform court officials as to the type of interpreting being done based on the deaf consumer's ability to read and write; and to "take responsibility of educating the public regarding the deaf whenever possible recognizing that many misunderstandings arise because of the general lack of public knowledge in the area of deafness and communication of the deaf." (Fant, 1990: 136). This early understanding of interpreting is commonly referred to as the Helper Metaphor.

11.1.2 The Conduit Metaphor
The *Helper Metaphor* for interpreting was largely replaced by the *Conduit Metaphor* in the 1970's once various flow-chart models of the interpreting process had been proposed (Gerver, 1974; Moser-Mercer, 1976, 1978) and a new Code of Ethics had been adopted by the RID. The new RID Code of Ethics at that time included the following tenet: "Interpreters / Transliterators shall not counsel, advise, or interject personal opinions" which, combined with these orientations to interpreting, contributed to the

notion that an interpreter should behave as an unemotional conduit, or connection, between two people. Common comparisons were made to being a bridge or telephone such as this one from Sharon Neumann Solow (1981) in one of the first textbooks for teaching interpreting:

> The sign language interpreter acts as a communication link between people, serving only in that capacity. An analogy is in the use of a telephone – the telephone is a link between two people that does not exert a personal influence on either. It does, however, influence the ease of communication and the speed of that process. (1981: ix).

The *Conduit Metaphor* of interpreting suggests that the interpreter strive to have no influence on the communication being interpreted, to have no personal involvement of any kind, even to the extent of responding to questions asked of the interpreter. Neither the *Helper Metaphor* nor the *Conduit Metaphor* has any graphic chart explaining a flow of information from one side through an interpreter and to the other side. These metaphors are not models but simply orientations to understanding the role of the interpreter.

11.1.3 The Mediator Metaphor

Cynthia Roy's dissertation (1989) focused upon dispelling the *Conduit Metaphor* by analyzing the interpretation of an interactive conversation. She then described the allocation of turns by the interpreter between the two consumers. Roy's study of the turn exchanges within an interpreted conversation demonstrated that the interpreter plays a very active role in the interpreting process but does not act as an agent of any one consumer. Roy demonstrated that neither the *Helper Metaphor* nor the *Conduit Metaphor* are adequate in representing the process of interpreting.

Ford (1981) proposed the idea of communication facilitator or communication specialist where the interpreter receives, decodes, encodes, and transmits messages. These elements to some extent are represented in Robert Ingram's models (1974, 1980). Sherman and Phyllis Wilcox (1985) approached the process of interpreting from the perspective of schema theory. Within this framework they state that the conduit metaphor of interpreting with its notion that the interpreter merely conveys information without becoming involved is "impossibly idealistic" (1985: 89). Wilcox & Wilcox instead propose that the interpreter is indeed very active in the construction of meaning during the interpreting process and that the ability to make predictions in the source text is a significant indicator of interpreting ability. Specifically they suggest that schema theory provides a powerful representation of the interpreting process.

Schema theory suggests that instead of decoding language to determine its meaning we actively apply our perspective and knowledge to pieces of language. The application of schema theory to the interpretation process would mean that interpreters apply their own personal experiences and linguistic skill to understanding a source text before then creating the target text (which still reflects the personal experiences and language skills of the interpreter). Our personal experiences and our knowledge of the world are interconnected in "schemes." Schemes are organization strategies such as an understanding that when the phone rings, a person can pick it up, start talking into it, and another person is very likely to be connected and able to respond. What's more, that other person is usually someone known to the person who picked up the phone. If such a scenario seems unremarkable to you, then you already have this scheme as part of your understanding of how the world works. But to a person who knows nothing about phones, the notion of picking it up and talking to it may seem rather bizarre (it is, after all, just a piece of *plastic*).

The value of having schemes is that as we construct an understanding of a linguistic message we are able to make predictions about what the rest of the message is likely to be. These predictions will influence how we understand new portions of the message. If they fit easily into the emerging scheme then they are readily understood. If they do not fit easily then the scheme may be adjusted to accommodate the new portions or the new portions may be rejected as meaningless. Wilcox and Wilcox suggest that the constructors of target texts (interpreters) will be more successful if they are able to predict the next pieces to be added to the source text.

Danika Seleskovitch (1995) incorporated the notion of schemes and schematic association. She proposed that the interpreting process can be described as three essential elements: 1) merging elements of linguistic meaning with extra-linguistic knowledge to obtain sense; 2) deverbalizing that sense as it emerges; and 3) spontaneously expressing this sense linguistically. Step one requires the interpreter both to attend to the source text and to associate its meaning with the interpreter's own experiences (schemes) and knowledge of language use. In this way the interpreter very actively participates in determining the meaning of the source text. As this understanding is achieved, the interpreter must eliminate any dependence upon the words used in the source language so that they do not adversely influence the creation of the target text. Finally, the interpreter spontaneously produces the target text, meaning that interpreters actively create their own, unique target texts from their own understanding of the source text.

The *Helper Metaphor* suggests that the interpreter is involved in the process but also that the consumers are not able to fend for themselves and need additional assistance. The *Conduit Metaphor* suggests that the interpreter is only marginally involved and that the consumers had better be able to figure out all communication problems on their own. We have seen that neither of these orientations is an accurate perspective of the interpreting process. As mentioned previously, Ford (1981) used the term "Communication Facilitator," which had certain advantages over the other two metaphors. A facilitator is one who makes something easier or "facile". Interpreters accomplish a very complex skill, but do not necessarily make the communication itself any easier: the source consumer still has to figure out how to say what they want to say and the target consumer still has to figure out what the interpretation means. So *Facilitator* does not appear to be an adequate metaphor.

The terms "Helper" and "Facilitator" both imply interactivity with one or more parties. "Conduit" assures a connection between two elements (though not necessarily animate parties). The English word that incorporates the double connection between parties and the interactivity with both parties is "Mediator." Given the evidence of research in the interpreting process it appears that a *Mediator Metaphor* will lead us to a more accurate understanding of the interpreting process.

With a few more descriptors we can expand this metaphor to a descriptive label such as "Bilingual / Bicultural Communication Mediation" to describe interpreting. Bilingual means that there are two languages involved. Bicultural means that there are two cultures involved. Communication is what is being attempted between two parties. A mediator is a person who actively engages two parties to bring them to a mutual understanding. A

Bilingual / Bicultural Communication Mediator actively engages two parties, each with distinct languages and cultures, into a mutual understanding of their communication with one another. Likewise the notion can be adapted for transliteration as follows "Monolingual / Monocultural Communication Mediation." The more generic concept of transcommunication can be identified as simply "Communication Mediation."

11.2 Models of Interpreting

None of these models of interpreting are framed within the *Helper Metaphor*, but many are framed, at least in part, within the *Conduit Metaphor*. They regard the mechanics of interpreting as the essential essence of interpreting. Usually they do not recognize the impact of consumers upon the interpretation but rather begin with a source text and end with a target text; but source texts are created by people, and people have to interact with target texts in order for them to be useful. Many models of the interpreting process reflect the *Conduit Metaphor* simply because the models are attempting to show a process of "something in, something done, and something out."

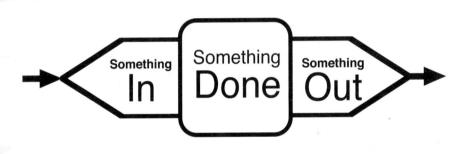

Figure 11.1 – Minimum Requirements for an Interpreting Model

The *Conduit Metaphor* does not explain *all* of the interpreting process, but it can usefully explain some essential parts of the process.

1.2.1 The Gerver Model

One of the pioneers of interpreting research was David Gerver. Gerver condensed his own research and that of others into a psychological model based on human information processing theories. Gerver (1976) suggested that interpreting is largely an interaction of memory of incoming information, memory of target and source languages, and encoding decoding strategies. Gerver's model was a flow chart, which identified "the processes involved in decoding the source language message and its subsequent encoding in the target language." (1976: 196). As decisions are made they influence the paths taken along the flow chart. The primary value of Gerver's model is to identify many of the decisions and variables that influence the interpreting process.

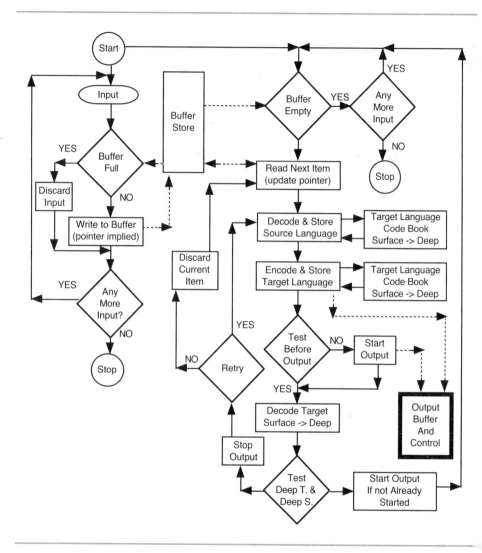

Figure 11.2 – Gerver's (1976) Model

11.2.2 The Moser-Mercer Model

Barbara Moser (1978) presented an information-processing model, which included more elements in the comprehension of the source language and the production of the target language than Gerver's (1976) model. Moser-Mercer's revision of her work (1983) outlines a processing model of interpreting which takes a message from auditory reception to a semantic understanding within context and then proceeds toward output in the target language. Also contained in the model are short-term memory and long-term memory, which interact with linguistic skills. Moser-Mercer suggested that the understanding of the source text is limited by short-term memory to seven (plus or minus wo) chunks of information[49]. She explains the difference between experienced and nexperienced interpreters as a function of the relative size of each chunk with more experienced interpreters being able to group larger sets of ideas into single chunks of neaning.

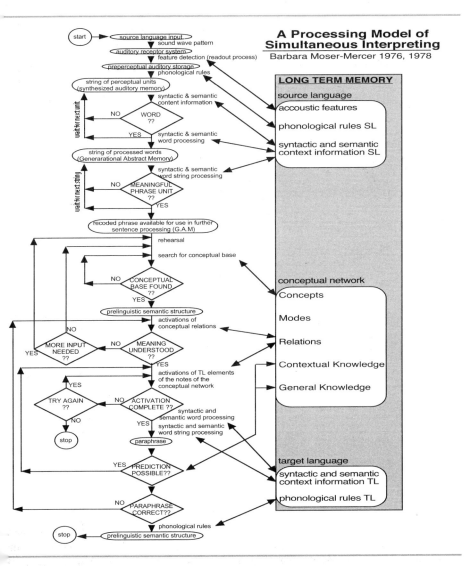

Figure 11.3 – Moser-Mercer's (1978) Model

[49] George Miller (1956) originally identified the patterns that the number seven had in sychological research, including short-term memory.

Smith (1983) reviewed Moser-Mercer's model and commented:

> There were several points of Dr. Moser-Mercer's model with which I was particularly struck: the simultaneity of a multitude of tasks, the importance of restructuring the way an idea is expressed, the need for rapid analysis, the place of public speaking skills, and the necessity of being able to work well under stress. (Smith, 1983:71)

Moser-Mercer's recognition that language and language processing rely upon long term and short-term memory is a significant contribution to the models of the interpreting process. Her hypothesis, that more experienced interpreters are able to group large portions of the source text into each meaningful unit, sheds light on the concepts of understanding a message. Is the message only understood to the lexical level (the words)? Are the sentences meaningful? Does the text "make sense" to the interpreter? The ability to understand the meaning of a message would have a significant impact on the ability to maintain accuracy through the interpreting process.

11.2.3 The Ingram Models

Robert Ingram (1974) proposed a model of interpreting whereby the interpreter served as a channel of communication between the presenter of a source message and the receiver of the target message.

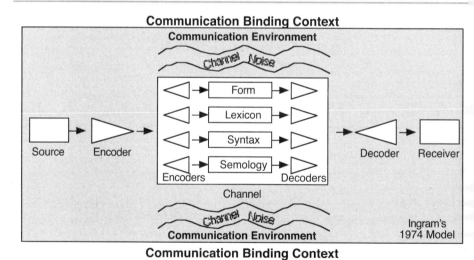

Figure 11.4 – Ingram's (1974) Model

In 1980 Ingram released a revised version of his model, which accounted for greater complexities in the understanding of multiple messages in the source text and the challenge of re-encoding all of these messages into the target text. His model is a one way process of encoding form, lexicon, syntax, and semantics from multiple potential codes within the source language into the multiple potential codes of the target language amidst whatever noise exists within the communicative context. Greater noise impacts e process by reducing the amount of information processed. Ingram's model set the age for an understanding of interpreting as being at least more complex than packaging a message between two languages because the interpreter had to understand e sense of the source text given its context.

It is worth noting that Ingram's models acknowledge several additional factors to the overall interpreting process: 1) Communication occurs within a physical context or etting, 2) All contexts have some amount of noise which may interfere with the language channels being used, 3) There are more people than just the interpreter involved in the rocess (the Source and the Receiver).

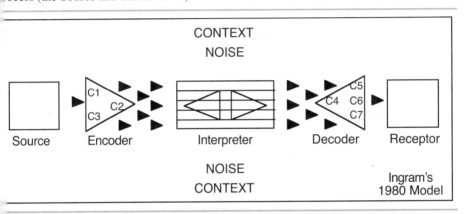

Figure 11.5 – Ingram's (1980) Model

.2.4 The Cokely Model

Dennis Cokely (1984) proposed that the act of interpreting was not merely formation processing, but rather the mediation of information "between two individuals d communities as well as mediating between two languages." (1984: 10). His ciolinguistic model of interpreting combines the features of memory with specific guistic abilities (similar to Ingram's model). The categories of linguistic skills that kely includes are syntactic, semantic, and contextual knowledge as well as a owledge of culture. These skills apply to both the source and target languages. Cokely ecifies three progressive levels of linguistic processing: 1) lexical & phrase level, 2) ntence level, and 3) discourse level. Finally, Cokely allows that the stages within the ocess of interpreting need not flow only in one direction, but that it can back up as eded in order to correct potential or realized errors. Cokely's model accounts for four nds of errors: 1) errors in perception, 2) errors in memory, 3) errors in production or 4) rors due to incomplete development of knowledge of the source language and/or target nguage.

Specifically, Cokely's model identifies seven stages to the interpreting process: 1) essage Reception, 2) Preliminary Processing, 3) Short Term Message Retention, 4) alization of Semantic Intent, 5) Determination of Semantic Equivalent, 6) Syntactic essage Formulation, and 7) Message Production. Each of these seven areas has related fluencing factors, which make connections to the interpreter's knowledge of the source

language and of the target language. Cokely's model is a flow chart in which the variou
pieces are interconnected in multiple ways.

Cokely's model focuses on the mental processes of the interpreter and does no
directly acknowledge the physical context nor the source and target consumers of th
interpreting process. Cokely's model does acknowledge that the movement betwee
various elements in the model is fairly fluid and unimpeded, as compared with Mose
Mercer's model, which dictates very clear lines of processing between stages. Cokely'
model recognizes that the human brain is actively involved in decision-making based o
a variety of factors.

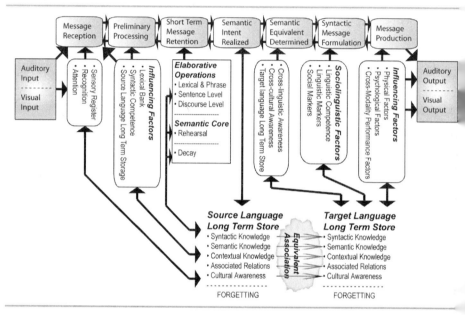

Figure 11.6 – Cokely's (1984) Model

11.2.5 The Llewellyn Jones Model

Peter Llewellyn-Jones (1981) investigated variation in interpreting between B!
(British Sign Language) and spoken English. He proposed several models. One of the
specifically addresses idiomatic interpreting while the others attempt to explain oth
aspects of more literal interpreting. The idiomatic model is presented here. It sugges
that proper interpreting requires an understanding of meaning, independent of languag
from which the target text is created. His other models will identify the form of t
message, rather than meaning, as a stumbling block for people who do not succeed in tr
interpreting.

Llewellyn-Jones' models address the issue of language fluency as an essenti
component of the interpreting process. Deficiencies in either the source language or t
target language will by necessity have a negative impact upon the interpretation.

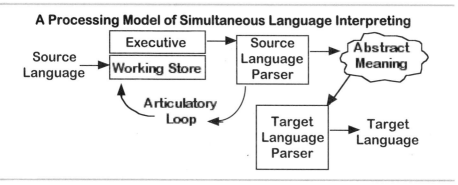

A Processing Model of Simultaneous Language Interpreting

Figure 11.7 – Llewellyn-Jones' (1981) Model of Idiomatic Interpreting

1.2.6 The Colonomos Models

Betty Colonomos (1987) developed a model of three major tasks (*Concentrating*, *Visualizing*, *Rehearsing*), which were connected by two additional variables (Source Frame and Target Switch). By 1992 she had revised this model slightly, using different descriptors (*Visualizing* was replaced by the term *Representing*, *Planning* replaced *Rehearsing*). *Concentrating* is essential to the process is comprehension of the source text which must first be attended to, then analyzed, and then understood without any dependence upon the particular words used. The *Source Frame* (who is speaking to whom, in what environment, and about what topic) guides this comprehension of the source text. *Representing* is how the interpreter finds a way to remember the information independent of the source language structures. This representation of the ideas moves through a *Target Switch* in which the ideas are brought into the second language. The final stage is *Planning*, during which the interpreter mentally assembles the target language structures (composition), mentally reviews the initial composition by making additions or corrections (revision), and then finally delivers the mental composition into a production in the target language (production).

Colonomos (personal communication) has used the model as a basis for interpreter training and has students apply the concepts initially in consecutive interpreting tasks where the sociolinguistic frame and communication goals are directly addressed prior to the presentation of the source text. Attention is drawn to the register and performance of the source and target texts as key elements of finding equivalence (beyond the words and sentences). Consecutive processing allows the students to anticipate portions of the source text, mentally represent those concepts without the competition of simultaneously perceiving them, actively plan and rehearse the target text with peer review, and then generate a final performance of the target text.

Pedagogical Model of the Interpreting Process

Betty Colonomos - 1989/1992/1997

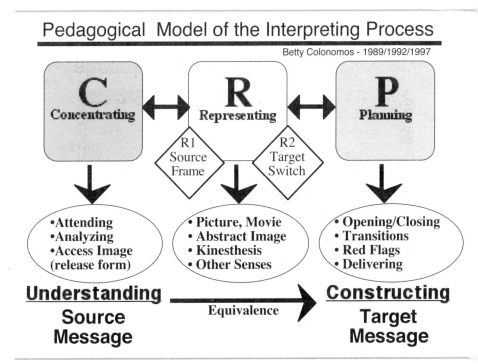

Figure 11.8 – Colonomos' (1997) Pedagogical Model

The simplicity of the model is somewhat deceptive because it is attempting to contai
most of the concepts addressed by the other models in this section. The most significa
additional contributions are the focus of the sociolinguistic frames of the source an
target consumers and their impact on the message. An interpreter who is disconnecte
from the community of either the source or target consumers will struggle to fir
equivalence in the interpreting process.

To further explain the complexity of the interpreting process represented in the abov
model, Colonomos generated two other models to accompany her *Pedagogical Mode*
The first supplementary model identifies the components of how a person construc
meaning from a linguistic message. These components include knowledge of th
language, the culture, the setting, and the participants, all contained within the context c
the communication itself. The interpreter determines meaning from all of these facto
but is also influenced by a variety of factors including their own culture, ideas, languag
abilities, feelings, personality, and the style of the presentation. Amid all of these facto
people determine their own understanding of the meaning of a message.

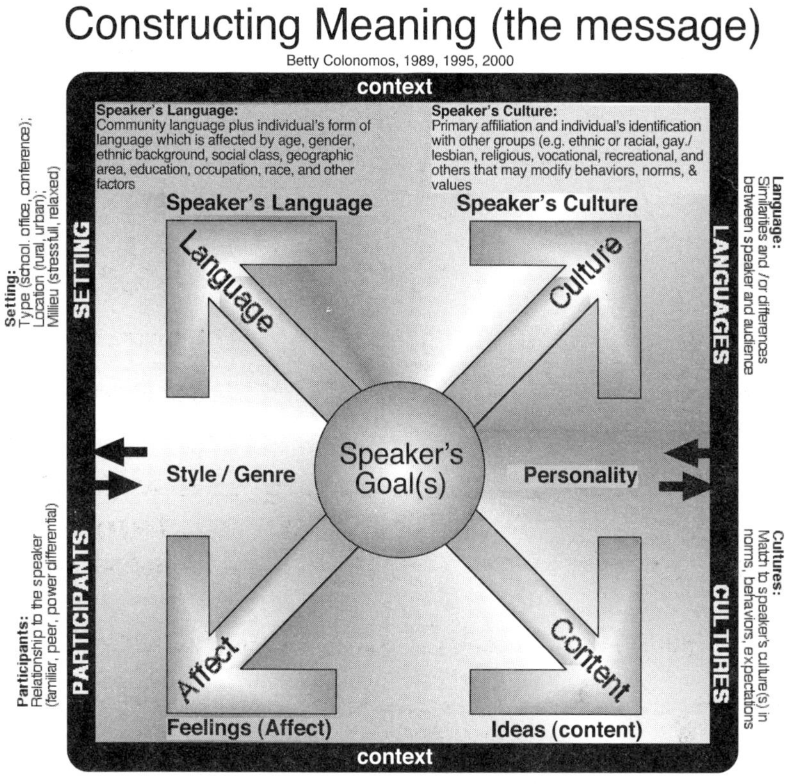

Figure 11.9 – Colonomos' (2000) Model of Meaning Construction

Colonomos then inserts this entire model of meaning construction into a larger frame explanation for the entire interpreting process. This process includes factors influencing both the analysis of the source text and the production of the target text. These factors include processing skills, process management abilities, competence in each language, general knowledge, specific preparation for the assignment, awareness and knowledge of the environment, and various filters.

The Interpreting Process

Betty Colonomos
1987/1992/1997

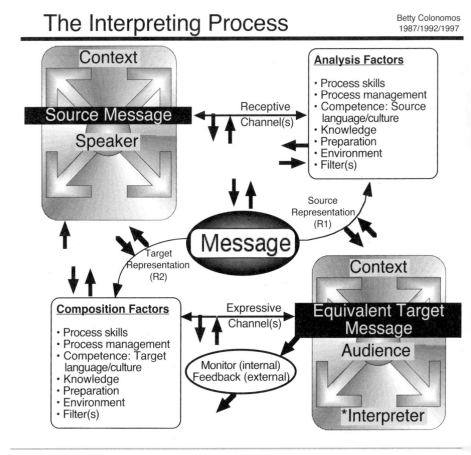

Figure 11.10 – Colonomos' (1997) Model of the Interpreting Process

11.2.7 The Kirchoff Model

All of these models mentioned so far focus on the interpreter as acting on source text and creating target texts. Aside from the Ingram models and the Colonomos model above, they consistently overlook the physical contexts and the consumers of the interpreting process. Someone had to create the source text and someone should be attending to the target text. Most of the models of the interpreting process make little mention, if any, of these consumers of the interpreter's services. Kirchoff's (1976) "Three-Party, Two-Language" model of interpreting makes a specific effort to include the consumers. The presenter of the source text is identified as having 1) an inherent nature, 2) a culture (including language), 3) a task to accomplish. The source consumer conceives of a concept or idea to be conveyed (Cs) which the source consumer encodes and expresses. The resulting message is recognized and decoded by the interpreter who registers the concept (Ci). The interpreter then encodes and expresses that concept as a new message, which the target consumer recognizes, decodes, and understands as a received or registered concept (Cr).

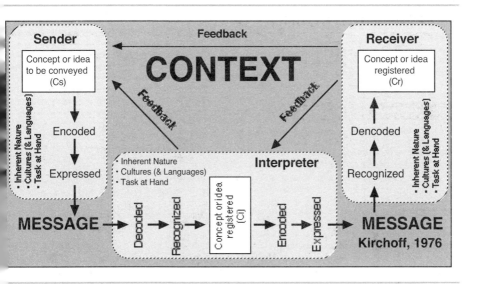

Figure 11.11 – Kirchoff's (1976) Model

Surrounding the interaction of these three participants are three forms of feedback: Target Consumer directly to Source Consumer, Target Consumer to Interpreter, and Interpreter to Source Consumer. It is important to note the first of these, because it is a form of communication that directly links the consumers without including the Interpreter. Kirchoff's is the only model to identify this direct link of communication between consumers, independent from the interpreter.

11.3 Models of Literal Interpreting

Betty Colonomos and Peter Llewellyn-Jones have both provided models of litera interpreting and models of failed interpreting that may approximate literal interpreting These are reviewed here to explain the concept of intentional monolingua transcommunication that provides greater clarity and/or access to another person' message.

11.3.1 The Colonomos Model

Colonomos' models are divided into transcommunicating that is either *Product-base* or *Process-based*. Colonomos identifies the *Product-based* efforts as successful an intentional attempts to generate the target text in the forms that are used, either idiomati ASL, or more linear, English-based productions of ASL or of manual English codes. Th *Process-based* efforts identify two different approaches: processing with attention to th *form* (coding) or processing with attention to the *meaning* (interpreting). Colonomc suggests that many attempts at interpreting are thwarted by inadequate competency in th target language and the attempts at *Process-based* interpretation fail to achieve a idiomatic result.

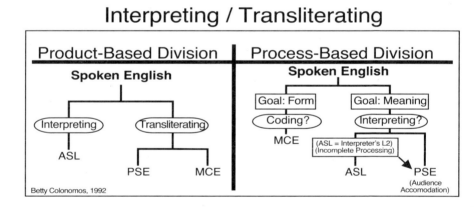

Interpreting / Transliterating

Figure 11.12 – Colonomos' (1992) Model of Literal Interpreting Options

The Colonomos model indicates two main pathways for literal interpreting: a) t interpreter is guided by a *Product-based* approach with intentional processing of t message to be a literal interpretation (identified in the graph as "transliterating") or b) t interpreter is attempting to be idiomatic, but through a *Process-based* approach, is falli short of that goal.

1.3.2 The Llewellyn-Jones Models

Llewellyn-Jones identifies these same concepts with three distinct representations: a) an intentional effort to provide a literal interpretation, b) an inadequate processing which focuses on the form, rather than the meaning, and c) an unintended literal processing due to lack of target language fluency. Llewellyn-Jones specifically identified the target language as BSL (British Sign Language), but the concepts can be applied to any signed language.

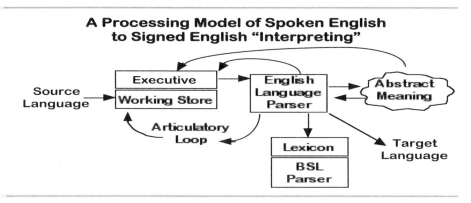

A Processing Model of Spoken English to Signed English "Interpreting"

Figure 11.13 – Llewellyn-Jones' (1981) Model of Intentional Literal Interpreting

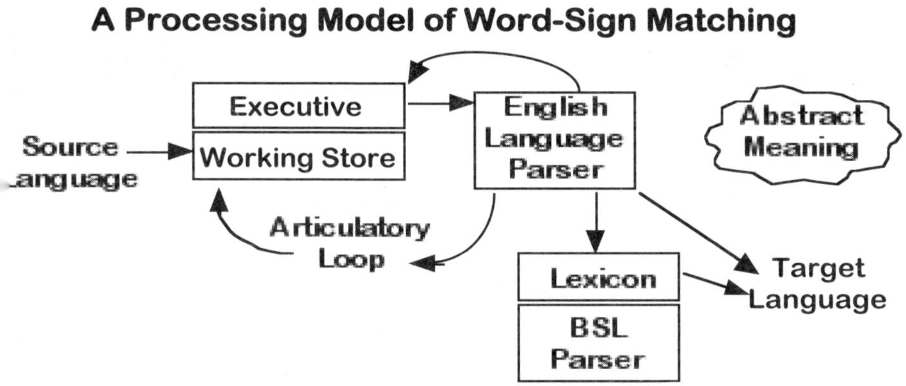

A Processing Model of Word-Sign Matching

Figure 11.14 – Llewellyn-Jones' (1981) Model of Inadequate Processing of Form

A Processing Model of Interpreting from BSL into English with an Inadequate BSL Repertoire

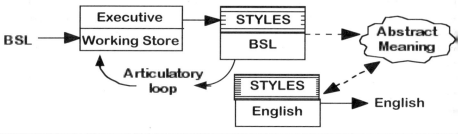

Figure 11.15 – Llewellyn-Jones' (1981) Model
of Unintentional Literal Interpreting

11.4 Summary

What remains to be acknowledged by any of these models of interpreting is the ability for the target consumer to receive some portion of source text information directly from the source consumer. Kirchoff's (1976) model comes closest by identifying a link of feedback from the consumer to the source presenter, but Kirchoff does not identify the possibility of the target consumer directly perceiving any source text elements, particularly paralinguistic elements such as gestures, facial expressions, or vocal intonations. Another factor not mentioned in any of these models is the familiarity that the source and target consumers have with each other and familiarity that each has with the interpreter, although Colonomos' models come close by addressing the sociolinguistic frames of the consumers and the interpreter. One common consideration in assigning interpreters is to determine whether the consumers have worked with specific interpreters before and if so, for which interpreters each consumer may have a preference. If these variables are so important for the scheduling of interpreters they ought to play some role in the interpreting process itself.

Various models of interpreting have been proposed which present interpreting as a complex cognitive activity (Cokely, 1984; Ford, 1981; Moser-Mercer, 1978, 1983; Gerver, 1976; Ingram, 1974, 1980). Kirchoff (1976) proposed a model of the interpreting process that includes consumers. While these processes and models may be assumed to be relevant, even duplicated, during teamed and relayed interpreting, there remains a need for researched models of teamed and relayed interpreting.

Several models of interpreting have considered memory as an integral factor within the interpreting process (Moser-Mercer, Cokely). Gerver (1974) demonstrated that comprehension memory is impeded during simultaneous interpreting as compared to listening without interpreting. Gerver further demonstrated that the task of shadowing further impeded comprehension memory. Ingram (1992) tested these findings with interpretations from spoken English into ASL. He analyzed the above pattern described by Gerver and also by Lambert (1983) for interpretations from spoken languages to other spoken language as well as shadowing within a single spoken language. Ingram found that idiomatic interpretations from spoken English into ASL yielded better semantic memory results than literal interpretations from spoken English into English-like signing. Ingram also discovered that listening alone resulted in lower semantic memory scores than either literal or idiomatic interpretation. Ingram concluded that literal interpreting (identified as "transliteration" in his research) is not merely an act of shadowing: there is a deeper level of language processing going on during "transliteration" than during shadowing[50].

Within the models previously presented, this difference is explained by recognizing the different levels of linguistic processing required for each task. The task of shadowing conversational speech need not be processed beyond the syntactic level, and perhaps can be accomplished at the morphological level. While it is possible to shadow phonemes in new languages, the level of accuracy at conversational speeds is likely to depend upon one's ability to predict patterns of sounds through word recognition and even recognition

---

[50] NOTE – This supports the findings in Chapter Four that "English-based" signing is actually a variety of ASL, not a variety of English.

of sentence patterns. Yet, at no point is it necessary for semantics to enter into the shadowing task. *Literal Interpretation*, in order to be *accurate*, requires at least processing to the *semantic level*. Llewellyn-Jones (1981) found some of the interpreters in his study of "transliteration" were processing the *information* while others were focused on processing the *words*. He explained that this was measurable due to the paraphrasing of information in the processed "interpretations" and by the word-for-word shadowing of the non-processed "interpretations." This evidence suggests that there is a difference based on the level of linguistic analysis applied to both the comprehension of the source text and the production of the target text. In order to remain accurate in extended discourse, literal interpretations should also be processed to the discourse and stylistic levels as well. Literal interpretations that are not processed to the discourse level are likely to have some deficits from the consumer's perspective. Llewellyn-Jones examples of the lexical-level processing (literal interpretations) demonstrate a failure to processs at the semantic level.

Llewellyn-Jones (1981) also found that limited knowledge of the target language will (logically) reduce the accuracy of the interpretation. This is to say that although an interpreter might understand a message beyond the semantic level, the resulting interpretation cannot be produced at a level beyond the interpreter's knowledge of the target language. The converse is true as well – inadequacies in knowing the source language will limit an interpreter's ability to produce a coherent target text:

> Much information is likely to be lost during this circuitous route through the processing system, and an interpreter intent on making sense of the original message may resort to filling in the gaps by guessing what is being missed. If the interpreter knows the deaf person and the topic well enough, his guesswork might be quite inspired and reasonably accurate, but the chances are slim.
> More often, the interpreter will give up trying to determine the meaning and produce instead a word for sign rendering of the incomplete message, so leaving the target audience to sort out the meaning for themselves. The result is an incomplete spoken gloss of the source message. (Llewellyn-Jones, 1981; p 57).

Cokely (1992) demonstrated that processing time impacts upon the accuracy of interpretation in such a way that longer periods of processing time yield more accurate interpretations. Cokely attributes this improvement to the interpreter having a better comprehension of the message.

Simultaneous interpreting and consecutive interpreting are most obviously different in the amounts of time and overlap that occur within them. Simultaneous interpreting requires that both the processes of understanding the source text and producing the target text happen more or less at the same time. Consecutive interpreting separates these two processes and allows greater time for either one to occur. Cokely's research indicates that greater accuracy should be achieved via consecutive interpreting.

<u>11.4.1 Review Questions</u>
1.   What are the three basic components of all of the models? (See section 11.2)
2.   Which two models identify the interpreting process with distinct "Start" and "Stop" points? (See sections 11.2.1 and 11.2.2)
3.   Ingram's models identify the consumers of interpreting within the model. Which other model also identifies the consumers as part of the process? (See section 11.2.7)
4.   What are the seven stages in Cokely's model? (See section 11.2.4)
5.   What are the five main components identified in Colonomos' model (See figure 11.8)
6.   Language, Culture, Affect and Content are elements of which part of Colonomos' models (section 11.2.6)
7.   Identify three of the factors influencing the analysis of source texts and the production of target texts in Colonomos' model of the Interpreting Process (Figure 11.10)
8.   What are the two results that Colonomos predicts for *Product-based* approaches to interpreting?
9.   What are the three results that Colonomos predict for *Process-based* approaches to interpreting?
10. What are the three explanations that Llewellyn-Jones offers for interpretations which are not idiomatic (section 11.3.2)

<u>1.4.2 Suggested Activities</u>
.   Take the models from any two different authors and compare them. What labels identify similar (or identical) components? What elements are present in one model but missing in the other?
2.   Create your own model of the interpreting process. What are the essential elements that you will include?

Chapter 12
Five More Models

"Five More Models"

Timoth dropped two tablets into a glass of water and then leaned forward while placing both hands on the desk... waiting for the tablets to dissolve and the tiny bubbles to fill the glass. "When will it end? Please... make it stop!"

Rasmus entered the room and sat on the desk, beside the glass of bubbling liquid. "Make *what* stop?"

"This pounding in my head, these endless models in the book, everything I can't take it anymore." Timoth grabbed the glass and quickly drank the liquid.

"I understand your predicament. I might even say that I feel your pain The interpreting process is rather complex. In fact, it is quite amazing tha it can be done at all!"

Placing the empty glass back on the desk Timoth shuffled over to the chair beside the desk. "I don't understand all of the complexities of th models presented in the previous chapters. How am I going to understan the next set of models?" Leaning forward, head over knees, with finger interlaced and resting firmly against back of head, Timoth slowly rocke forward and back while breathing very slowly and deeply.

"Have no fear, Timoth. The presentation of models in Chapter Eleven i intended only to be an overview, not a detailed exploration. The last fiv models in Chapter Twelve are based on the principles that you already know The important concepts have already been explained in the book."

Timoth stopped rocking and looked up at Rasmus. "Which concepts?"

Rasmus walked behind the desk and sat down. "What did you learn in th first few chapters?"

Opening the book to the Table of Contents, Timoth's finger traced a pat down several pages, "Well, first was Communication: Background Knowledg Semiotics, Physical Context, Pragmatics; then the Linguistic Pyrami language fluency, language variation and register, and language encodir systems."

Chapter 12 – Five More Models 221

"Yes. Good. All of those are essential elements in the final five models." Rasmus leaned forward and turned a few pages in the book. "See here where it identifies the models to be described?"

"Wait... There are more than five models!"

"That's right, but the first ones are just models of communication, the last five are models of *transcommunication*. So the author is working on a set of parallel concepts, building each model upon the previous one."

"So these last models will finally explain everything?"

"What, like the meaning of life and the origin of the universe? Is that what you mean?"

"No." Timoth smiled. "I just mean everything about interpreting."

"Timoth, I'm surprised that you even think it is possible. I haven't met a human being yet who knows everything there is to know about any single topic. I can't imagine that anyone could ever create a model that explains half of the complexity of interpreting."

"So you mean I'll still have to study even more models... I'm never going to be done learning?" Timoth stood and reached for the empty glass and started digging into a pocket for more tablets.

Rasmus took the glass from Timoth's hand and smiled. "Don't panic, my friend! You are undergoing intensive learning right now, but soon you will be an Independent Server. We must always strive to learn and improve – I am no exception. But the important thing right now is that you know *what* you need to learn and *how* to improve yourself. You have done well so far and I expect great things from you. Just take a moment to rest and clear your head. Then you will be ready to complete this part of your learning.

Timoth sat down again and leaned back into the chair "Thanks for calming me down. I just want to do a good job."

Rasmus nodded, "So recognize that you have already learned a great deal and now it is time to synthesize that knowledge into an integrated understanding of the work that we do."

Chapter 12 – Five More Models
"It ain't over till it's over" – Yogi Berra

12.0 Overview
The *Transcommunication Models* presented within this section are intended to be simple, even intuitive, and yet useful in providing direction for improving any potential interpretation and explaining possible sources of error in the interpreting process. Before we explore these final five transcommunication models, we will need to build a model of communication. The model of communication should be very familiar because it makes significant use of concepts that we have already learned in Unit One of this text. We will then make use of the *Model of Communication* in each of the five models of *Transcommunication*. Each model of Transcommunication will incorporate different concepts presented in Unit Two of this text.

12.1 The Need for Another Model of Interpreting
As we have just seen in the previous section, several models of the interpreting process have popped up since the 1970's. Most of these models have approached interpreting from a psycholinguistic view and attempt to get at the underlying processes that happen in the brain during the interpreting process; but models should also provide some amount of guidance for training and improvement of interpreters. This chapter presents several related models of various transcommunication processes in an effort to further our understanding and organize our efforts in teaching the interpreting process.

These models are not offered as a replacement for the models already presented in Chapter Eleven, but instead they are offered as further extensions of our understanding of a very complex process. In other words, consider the models you are about to see as containing *every element* presented in all of the models in Chapter Eleven. The point of these additional models is to focus on several more elements that play a role in the interpreting process.

The first element of focus of these models is *Language Competence,* following Llewellyn-Jones' observations that many problems with ineffective interpreting can be tied to insufficient fluency in one or both languages being interpreted. The second element of focus is the on *interpersonal communication.* Because language has value primarily in *social contexts,* these models require acknowledgement of *real people* within *real settings* who are attempting to communicate with each other. With this basis, these models can be categorized as *sociolinguistic* models of transcommunication.

Five related models are presented here (whole-text translation, consecutive, simultaneous, teamed, and relayed). Each is distinct because of both the timing of the task (delayed, alternating, and immediate) and the number of participants in each transcommunication task being accomplished (interpreter and text, interpreter and two consumers, two interpreters and two consumers). Other linguistic aspects (monolingual, bilingual, or even extralingual processing) are not specific to the models. This means that all of the models can be applied to interpreting, transliterating, or elucidation. The similarities for each model center on the communication process of producing and perceiving communication between all of the participants that are present within physical context. All five models share a majority of their components. These components have been previously identified in greater detail, but are briefly reviewed here.

12.2 Review of Communication and Language

Communication begins with the *intentions* to communicate. This requires intelligence and therefore a brain, or mind, capable of thought and knowledge. In order to communicate that mind must have knowledge of *how* to communicate, *what* can be communicated, *others* who might be able to understand the communication, and how the *physical environment* will permit the communication to take place. The mind must have some idea or notion to be communicated, whether conscious or unconscious. In the transcommunication models, a sphere will represent each human participant, or mind, which contains all of the above-mentioned elements.

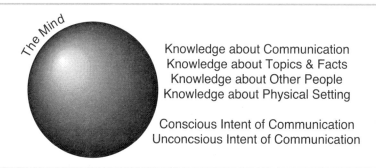

Knowledge about Communication
Knowledge about Topics & Facts
Knowledge about Other People
Knowledge about Physical Setting

Conscious Intent of Communication
Unconcsious Intent of Communication

Figure 12.1 – The Mind

Next the mind must have avenues of expressing and perceiving the communication. Communication expression requires muscle movements. Communication perception requires actively functioning senses.

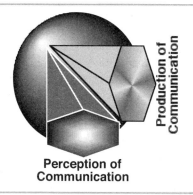

Perception of
Communication

Figure 12.2 – The Communicating Mind

Finally, there must be another mind to perceive the communication productions and perhaps produce a communication response. Both communicators should be able to perceive (monitor) their own communication production. Both will also be able to influence and perceive the physical environment surrounding the communication. The physical context is assumed to be accessible and influenced by all participants in these transcommunication models. Because the physical environment acts as a kind of filter in the communication process, we must also recognize that there will be *noise* (visual noise, auditory noise, tactile noise, etc) that can interrupt or interfere with each mind's ability to communicate with the other.

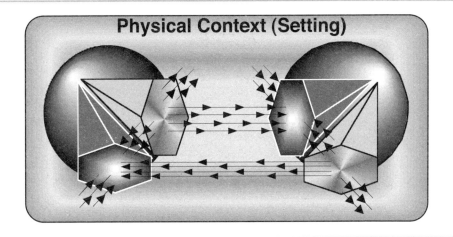

Physical Context (Setting)

Figure 12.3 –Communicating Minds Within a Shared Physical Setting

12.2.1 Review of the Linguistic Pyramid
    Language is the use of symbols to convey information between members of community, in which the system is rule-governed, has infinite production possibilities, i intergenerational, and changes over time. Language has a series of levels that overla and build one upon another. At the bottom-most, basic level is *phonetics*, which identif the basic building blocks of language. The rules that guide how the building blocks ar put together are the realm of *phonology*. The study of the smallest units of meaning an how they combine to make words is *morphology*. The rules of word order are calle *syntax*. These basic levels of language are essential building blocks but they ar insufficient when talking about language fluency and the interpreting proces. Interpreting does not begin until we rise to the next levels in the pyramid.
    Semantics is the contextual meaning of words and sentences. We need *discourse* an *pragmatics* to know how our consumers are using the words they use; and we need t know the appropriate ways to say those kinds of things in the target language. Knowin these things about language also helps us to make predictions about what someone leading to, what the real point is, and why they want to tell us about it. This is where re interpreting takes place.
    There is one more level toward perfection: *stylistics*. When we understand th message well enough not only to adequately predict where it is going; but we als understand the person creating the message well enough to know her purpose, h tendencies, her idiosyncrasies of language use; then we have entered a stylist

understanding of the source text. If we are further able to reproduce equivalents of these individual linguistic tendencies in the target language, then we are being about as accurate and perfect as we can ever be when we interpret.

Reaching across all of these levels of linguistic ability is the concept of *register variation*, which accounts for how we modify our language use based on the participants, settings, topics, and methods of communication (who, where, what and how).

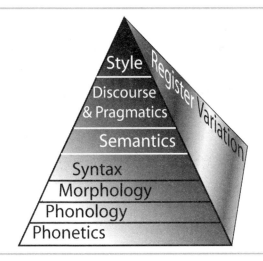

Figure 12.4 - The Linguistic Pyramid

12.2.2 Review of Language as a Subset of Communication

With all of the layers of the *Linguistic Pyramid* in place we should also recognize that language, as a specific subset of communication, includes both production and perception. Phonetics (the most basic layer of the *Linguistic Pyramid*) is the production of all language elements. All of the remaining layers of the *Linguistic Pyramid* are built on that base for both production of language and the perception of language. The *perception* of a linguistic message depends upon active senses matched to the modality of the message being produced (hearing to perceive a spoken language, vision to perceive a signed language, etc.) The *production* of a linguistic message depends upon muscles moving human anatomy.

If these movements (or they're resulting evidence, such as writing) are then perceived by another mind, the perceiving mind begins with only the result of muscle movement. The mind can then reconstruct the message by applying successive layers of the *Linguistic Pyramid* to the incoming pieces. Additional elements of communication will generally accompany the use of language, such as gestures, vocal intonation patterns, facial expressions, etc. We will assume that each human mind in these transcommunication models will be able to produce and perceive both linguistic and paralinguistic communication. The graphic below places the linguistic pyramid within the previous representation of communication, including both the perception and productive influence of the physical environment.

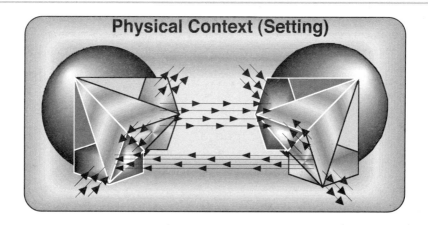

Figure 12.5 - Linguistic Communication Within a Physical Setting

The physical setting influences the clarity of the communication. Both participants generate movement, which may be part of communication or may add to the visual or auditory noise in the environment. Participants also have some ability to monitor their own production of communication, language, and noise. The process of self-monitoring can *reinforce* the communication or *interfere* with a person's own communication.

The visual elements of a source text play a significant role in the production of the target texts and in the feedback given to the source presenter by the audience. Regulations of the International Association of Conference Interpreters require unobstructed view of the speaker and audience (Buhler, 1987). Jumplet (1987) explains the need as follows:

> Interpreting includes the perception of events that are accessible only visually, such as the interplay of gestures between speaker and listeners, certain events taking place in the hall that are reflected in the speaker's response, request for the floor through the raising of hands, and visual aids (overhead projectors, graphs) that "speak for themselves" but without which the speaker cannot be understood even in his original language. (Jumplet, 1987: 84).

Viaggio (1997) indicates that producing gestures, as part of the target text, can be important, even if the audience does not see your efforts:

> Intonation and gestures are bound to be coherent (in spontaneous speech, words can easily be wrong, but, in normal circumstances, there is no such thing as the wrong intonation or the wrong gesture)...they follow the stream of thought and thus create their own inertia: The interpreter who catches himself in the midst of the wrong gesture or intonation, knows for sure that he is not saying what he should. (Viaggio, 1997: 290).

Expression of communication does not *ensure* an audience's comprehension of that communication. It is important to note that whatever comprehension does take place, it is unique to each mind engaged in the communication. One mind might focus on the words used; another mind may give more emphasis to the manner in which the message was performed. This is how a variety of witnesses can see the same event and yet report different information about what they saw. It is essential to understanding the interpreting process that each interpreter has a mind of their own, unique and different from both the source presenter's mind and also different from the target text perceiver's mind.

The four previously mentioned variables of knowledge[51] help to explain greater similarity or greater distance in how each person's mind is engaged in the communication process. Transcommunication requires at least three participants: source presenter, transcommunicator, and target perceiver. It facilitates their mutual communication if all of these participants share the same physical environment, have enough background knowledge to understand each others' likely topics of discussion, have at least some experience communicating with members of each others' language communities, and are able to keep track of the conversation as it takes place. As fewer of these variables are present then the task of transcommunicating a conversation between two people becomes progressively harder.

12.3 From the Mind to a Text

The process of expressing communication involves more than just a mind and muscles. Four essential factors are identified here: *Sociolinguistic Frame, Productive Semiotics, Monitor,* and *Errors.* Each has direct impact on the creation of a *Linguistic Text,* which is surrounded by the semiotics of expressed communication. Neurologists may be able to identify other parts of the process (neurons and synapses, chemical and electrical processes in the brain, etc). Our focus instead is on the outward, observable aspects of the interpreting process.

2.3.1 Sociolinguistic Frame

In addition to the seven levels of the *Linguistic Pyramid* are a set of factors called the *Sociolinguistic Frame,* which is primarily composed of the *Culture, Setting, Participants,* and *Background* information. The *Background* information has been previously reviewed in Chapter One as a part of the mind's ability to communicate. The *Settings* and *Participants,* too, have been previously reviewed in Chapter Two as part of *Register Variation.* The remaining factor is *Culture,* which is the set of social norms and expectations that surround the language users of a community. *Culture* overlaps, to some extent, with *discourse, pragmatics,* and *stylistics*; but culture is not limited to linguistic elements. *Culture* includes the attitudes, beliefs, expectations, and morality of a community. While *Culture* is a shared and social phenomenon, it may be realized in each person in unique and individual ways. In these models, *Culture* will be identified as *Personal Biases and Opinions.*

All communication both reflects and influences the *Sociolinguistic Frame.* The *Sociolinguistic Frame* influences the linguistic choices that a person makes; it is the stimulus that the mind responds to by creating *Register Variation.* In the models of

---

[51] The four kinds of communication knowledge are 1) knowledge of *what* can be communicated (background information), 2) knowledge of *how* to communicate, 3) knowledge of *other people* involved in the communication, and 4) knowledge of the *physical setting.*

transcommunication we will represent the *Sociolinguistic Frame* by using a larger triangle that surrounds the linguistic pyramid.

Sociolinguistic Frame

Figure 12.6 – Sociolinguistic Frame and Language Competence

12.3.2 Message Preparation and Productive Semiotics
    As the mind works to produce a linguistic text, sections may be mentally rehearsed or revised prior to production while other portions may be relatively spontaneous. The mind begins to instruct muscles to move and begin generating communication. Some of this movement may be linguistic (phonetic), but all of the muscle movement is potentially symbolic (semiotic).
    Semiotics, as mentioned in Chapter One, is the study of signaling systems, or symbols. A smile, a wave of the hand, rapid breathing, clenched teeth, or a person's posture all have the potential of communicating some information even though they are not linguistic. *Productive Semiotics* is the movement of muscles that in any way relate to communication, conscious or unconscious.

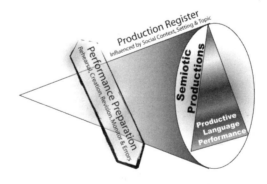

Figure 12.7 – Message Preparation and Productive Semiotics

12.3.3 Monitor

The mind is also aware of the movement that it causes. This self-awareness is called *Monitor* and can vary from a heightened sense of self-awareness to very low levels. *Monitor* allows a person to catch their own misproductions and correct them, or to adjust volume for the noise level in a room. High self-awareness can also cause interference in communication if the mind is focused too much on its own production and not on the communication and feedback coming from others. High self-awareness is common for second language learners and can inhibit the development of language fluency.

Monitor requires a certain amount of mental attention; therefore high self-awareness will reduce the amount of mental attention that can be applied to other tasks. One reason[52] that many interpreters experience greater frustration working into spoken languages (as opposed to working into a signed language) is that they cannot prevent hearing themselves speak. This creates a kind of feedback loop in simultaneous interpreting where the interpreter is initially able to attend to a source text but that attention is diminished as soon as the interpreter begins to speak while the source text continues. This mental competition is identified here as *Monitor Interference*.

12.3.4 Errors

There may be *linguistic errors* in the text because the human body has physical limitations responding to the mind's directions, or because the mind's directions may generate ungrammatical or disfluent actions (in other words, the body may respond correctly to incorrect instructions). All of the movement made – whether accurate or inaccurate, intentional or unintentional, linguistic or extra-linguistic – becomes part of the semiotic message generated by the body in response to the stimulus of the mind.

There is an additional aspect of errors to consider. Suppose the interpreter is from a language community that commonly uses pronunciations or grammatical structures that are considered non-standard or even ungrammatical. An interpreter who uses these pronunciations or structures with someone outside that community might be considered to be generating errors; but would they be errors if used among the members of the interpreter's community? In other words, if the interpreter's dialect or sociolect has non-standard components, must the interpreter always avoid those components when working with all consumers or should the interpreter still work to match the language styles of the consumers that they serve? The essential question is this: Who decides that something is an error?

Remember, so far we are only talking about generating a message, not the interpretation of that message. These errors are just in language use, not message equivalence. The semiotic message will occur within a physical setting, social context, and history of communication topics prior to it. These factors are part of a person's *semiotic Productions*, which may include errors.

---

[52] There are *many* possible reasons why some interpreters struggle to work from signed languages to spoken languages. The most obvious question is whether they have sufficient fluency in the source language. Many interpreters working with signed languages are native spoken-language users. Their internal sense of grammar for the spoken language is higher than their internal sense of grammar for the signed language. As a result, their signed productions may be reasonably fluid, but less grammatical (unfiltered and uncorrected) than their spoken productions.

12.3.5 The Eight Cs of Linguistic Texts

If language is part of this message then it is interwoven with all of the other elements in the semiotic productions of the text. The resulting *Linguistic Text* will have at least eight distinct qualities to it which can be documented or recorded to various extents: 1) its channel (spoken language, written language, signed language), 2) its clarity of articulation (phonemics and phonology), 3) its pace or rate of information, 4) its lexical content or vocabulary, 5) its grammatical accuracy, 6) its cohesion across the duration of the text, 7) the confidence of its creator, and 8) various cultural factors regarding values and beliefs. The figure below attempts to represent all of these elements:

Linguistic Text

Channel
Clear Articulation
Comfortable Pace
Conceptual Vocabulary
Complete Clauses
Cohesion
Confidence
Culture

Figure 12.8 – The Eight Cs of Linguistic Texts

The concept of a *Linguistic Text* is actually a step removed from the act of communication. It is not possible to document or permanently record all of the factors surrounding communication. A video recording may capture more elements of the communication than a written transcript can, but the participants, setting, and especially the time (temporal context) of the communication will no longer be identical. Direct interpersonal communication does not require the concept of a *Text*, but linguists have adopted the concept of *Text* as a helpful tool for linguistic analysis of monologues and dialogues. Likewise interpreters and interpreter educators will talk about *Source Text* and *Target Texts* because a documented text is more concrete and definable than the immediate act of interpersonal communication.

12.3.6 Summary of Expressed Communication

Figure 12.9 combines all the elements discussed in this section. Linguistic communication begins with the mind, represented by a sphere on the left side. The mind has knowledge of communication, topics & facts, participants, and settings. It has linguistic knowledge (represented by the Linguistic Pyramid)), which is surrounded and influenced by the *Sociolinguistic Frame* (culture, setting, participants, background knowledge – represented by the larger triangle). The *Semiotic Productions* (the cylinder expanding rightward from the mind's components) are filtered by mental rehearsal and revision, *Monitor*, and mental/physical *Errors* (represented in the elongated hexagon attached to the *Sociolinguistic Frame*). The *Semiotic Productions* may include language (represented by another *Linguistic Pyramid*, contained within the *Semiotic Production* cylinder). The result of all of these efforts is a *Linguistic Text*, which can be recorded or documented (to a limited extent) and is represented by the abstract oval on the right. A *Linguistic Text* contains eight definable/measurable components: the language *Channel*, the *Clarity* of its articulation, the relative *Comfort* in its pace, the *Conceptual* accuracy of its vocabulary, the completeness of its grammatical relationships or *Clauses*, the overall *Cohesion* of the message, the amount of *Confidence* with which it is presented, and the amount of *Cultural* information it expresses or requires for accurate comprehension.

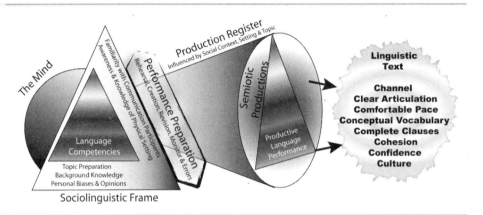

Figure 12.9 – Moving Communication from the Mind to a Linguistic Text

12.4 From a Text to the Mind

From the semiotic productions of the first person's mind we can document a *Linguistic Text*. Whether the second person engaged in communication is reading a printed text, watching a video recording, or directly perceiving the first person's communication, that person must begin by *concentrating*, or attending to that communication. It is only possible to attend to *all* of the semiotic productions by reviewing a very detailed *Linguistic Text* several times[53]. Therefore direct perception of a live semiotic production can never be complete; some portion will be missed or overlooked. It is possible, however, that some amount of a person's semiotic productions will be *unconsciously* perceived. These unconscious perceptions help to explain the sense" that people may either trust or distrust a person's message.

2.4.1 Comprehension of a Linguistic Text

We can use the levels of the linguistic pyramid to categorize the level of *linguistic* concentration, or attention to the text generated by each mind perceiving communication. If the message is comprehended only at the phonological level, then it is being processed

---

[53] The reality is that it is really *impossible* to capture *all* of the semiotic productions in a *Linguistic Text* in the first place; but imagine a video recording of a person from at least three angles plus sensor readings on their respiration and all muscle movements. From such a text, it is theoretically possible to attend to all of the semiotic productions after a close viewing of each video angle plus a review of the sensor reading data.

sub-lexically. The result would be confusion in the perceiver about what had been said and whether the message was even in a language known by the perceiver.

Morphological comprehension equals lexical processing, where the perceiver would recognize words but not understand the meanings of the sentences. Syntactic comprehension would allow some understanding of the sentences but no strong understanding of what the message is. Semantic processing would provide some understanding of the points but some doubt about the presenter's intentions. Pragmatic processing would provide a clear understanding of the intentions and goals of the presenter but may leave some confusion about the organization of the text and the idiosyncrasies of the presenter. Stylistic processing would provide a fairly complete understanding of the message. These are imperfect descriptions of reality, but they are offered here as a means of attempting to organize and describe essential elements of the communication process. Figure 12.10 reviews these six processing levels that were previously introduced in Chapter Nine.

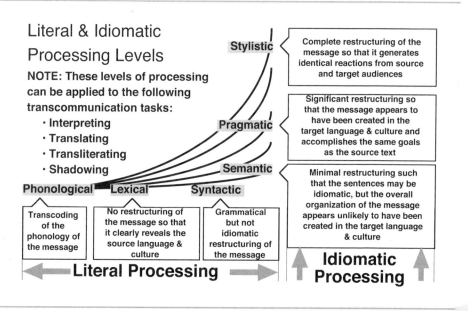

Literal & Idiomatic Processing Levels

NOTE: These levels of processing can be applied to the following transcommunication tasks:
· Interpreting
· Translating
· Transliterating
· Shadowing

Stylistic — Complete restructuring of the message so that it generates identical reactions from source and target audiences

Pragmatic — Significant restructuring so that the message appears to have been created in the target language & culture and accomplishes the same goals as the source text

Semantic — Minimal restructuring such that the sentences may be idiomatic, but the overall organization of the message appears unlikely to have been created in the target language & culture

Phonological — Transcoding of the phonology of the message

Lexical — No restructuring of the message so that it clearly reveals the source language & culture

Syntactic — Grammatical but not idiomatic restructuring of the message

← Literal Processing →   ↑ Idiomatic Processing ↑

Figure 12.10 - Processing Levels Between Source and Target Texts

The level of comprehension (and its associated processing level) is relevant to the interpreting process because it provides insight to how a person's focus on a source text will directly impact their production of a target text. A message processed at lower levels cannot be intentionally accurate[54] at any higher level in the target language.

---

[54] It is certainly possible that a person can be *accidentally* accurate, but this does not fall in the realm of being a reliable and professional transcommunicator.

12.4.2 Noise, Clarification Requests, and Feedback

The physical environment has a direct impact upon the concentration and the perception of a message. The acoustics of a room, the amount of lighting, visual distractions (*visual noise*) or the amount of auditory distractions (*auditory noise*) can enhance or interfere with concentration and the perception of the message. The physical and mental ability to perceive another person's semiotic information *(Semiotic Perception)* is individual to the mind doing the perceiving and the physical abilities of the body housing that mind. In other words, hearing loss, vision loss, and other mental or physical conditions (including stress and emotional state) can enhance or interfere with different kinds of perception.

If there is direct interaction between the communication participants then *Clarification Requests* can also be generated back to the first communication partner, which may generate additional *feedback* between the communication participants. Knowledge of the *social context*, awareness of the *setting* and of the *topic* all can enhance the perception of the message. Potential errors include *misrepresentation* of perceived information, *miscomprehensions* of that information, and failure to remember some elements of the communication.[55] The understanding of the message will further depend on the language competencies of the receiving mind (filtered through the *Sociolinguistic Frame* of the person) along with familiarity with the other person, familiarity with the topics being discussed, general background knowledge, and personal biases. The figure below attempts to represent all of these elements:

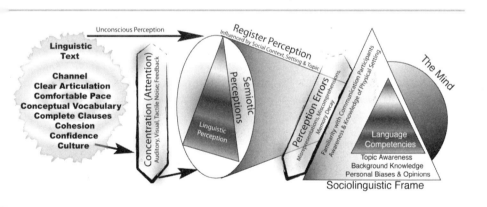

Figure 12.11 – Moving Communication from a Linguistic Text to the Mind

---

[55] An example of *misrepresentation* would be correctly understanding a word (e.g. "boat"), but creating incorrect images in your mind ("speedboat" as opposed to "ocean cruiser"). *Miscomprehension*, or misunderstanding, is a replacement of correct concepts with incorrect concepts, such as misunderstanding "moat" for "boat".

12.5 Proposed Models of Linguistic Communication

Figure 12.12, below, displays all of the components we have covered, but without labels. See if you can identify all of the components before we move on.

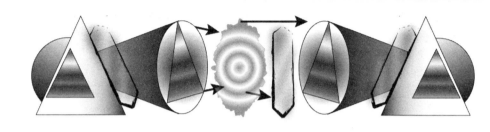

Figure 12.12 – Components of Communication

The complex concepts that we have just discussed in the previous sections will now be represented in a much more compact graphic. The main reason for doing this is to focus on other key concepts without shrinking the images to the point that you would need a magnifying glass to see all of the parts. So far we have identified the components of communication in a one-way arrangement. The following models will also reveal the two-way ability for a single mind to both produce and perceive communication. Lines will show the connections of produced and perceived semiotic communication (linguistic, paralinguistic, and non-linguistic) between the minds and also to and from the physical environment. Note also that each mind producing communication is able to perceive, or *Monitor,* its own productions.[56] The first model, below, shows the first mind's creation of a linguistic text, which a second mind then perceives without direct access to the first mind. The second model will show direct communication between two minds within a shared physical environment.

Figure 12.13 represents communication between two minds that are not in direct contact with each other. The only point of contact between these two minds is a *Linguistic Text* (such as a book, letter, email, signpost, etc). The circumstances and physical setting of the mind that created the text is represented with a white background. The circumstances and physical setting of the mind that perceives the text is represented with a gray background. The *Linguistic Text* is the only element that connects the mind in this model.

---

[56] *Monitor* is always available to some extent even if the mode of production is not matched directly by a sensory mode of perception. For example, Deaf people who are speaking may not be able to monitor their own speech by sound (auditory perception) but will still have some tactile (points of articulatory contact and vibrations) sense of their own speech productions.

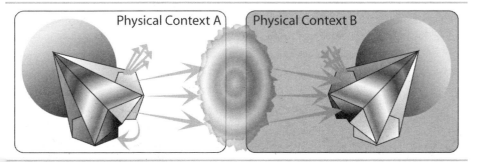

Figure 12.13 – Reduced Model of Communication via a Linguistic Text

Figure 12.14 represents communication between two minds that are in direct contact with each other. This means that there is no *Linguistic Text* involved in the communication. It is possible to make a *Linguistic Text* through video or audio recording, but that text would not be a mechanism in the direct communication between the two minds being recorded. The circumstances and physical setting is shared between both minds. Beyond all of these factors, the communication is two-way, rather than one-way, so that each mind can both initiate communication and perceive the other mind's communication.

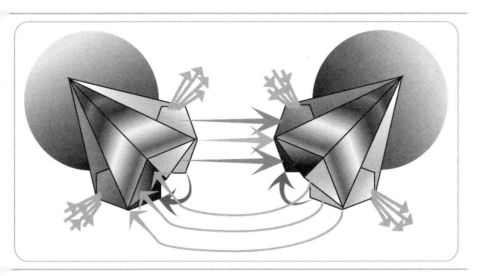

Figure 12.14 – Reduced Model of Direct Interactive Communication

In the next several sections we will expand and modify these representations of linguistic communication into various models of transcommunication. The key factor in *transcommunication* is that there will be at least *one more mind* involved in the process.

12.6 Five Proposed Models of Transcommunication

Specifically these models attempt to represent key components of 1) Translation, 2) Consecutive Transcommunication, 3) Simultaneous Transcommunication, 4) Teamed Transcommunication, and 5) Relayed Transcommunication. All of these models will build upon the base models of communication presented in Section 12.5.

12.6.1 Proposed Model of Translation

The first model put forth is for translation. Translation is the regeneration of a fixed text into a language other than that of its origin. Fixed texts can be written text, or other recordings of a performance, such as videotape. Translation has several significant advantages over interpreting because a) the text can be previewed multiple times, b) the pressure of time is reduced, c) multiple advisors or team members can be brought into the task, and d) draft translations can be reviewed and revised before target consumers ever see them. Some major disadvantages with translation involve the fact that the source text is not interactive with its audience. Translations are typically monologic in nature, meaning that the work is one-way, from one language to another, not vice versa.[57]

The creation of a *Linguistic Text* requires at least one mind and some physical effort. Translators (or members of a translation team) begin the translation process as direct readers (perceivers) of the *Linguistic Text* in the source language. They must then work to regenerate the message in the target language. It is important to note that this text regeneration is a creative process, controlled by the translator and not by the original author. Likewise the target consumer is not typically involved in the translation process.

Although Figure 12.15, below, may seem fairly simplistic, please remember the complexity previously discussed regarding the production and perception of communication between minds. All of those elements are implied, but not directly identified in the figure. It is also worth noting in this representation of translation there is no direct interactive communication between any of the parties. This arrangement is parallel to that represented in Figure 12.13. Each participant in the process is either producing and/or perceiving a *Linguistic Text* without feedback or response from any other party. The impact of each participant upon the physical environment and the perceptions of that environment are the only other lines of communication in these models.

---

[57] Translations may make use of "back translations" to verify the accuracy of a translation, but back translations are generally only part of the translation process and are not generated as the final target text for consumers.

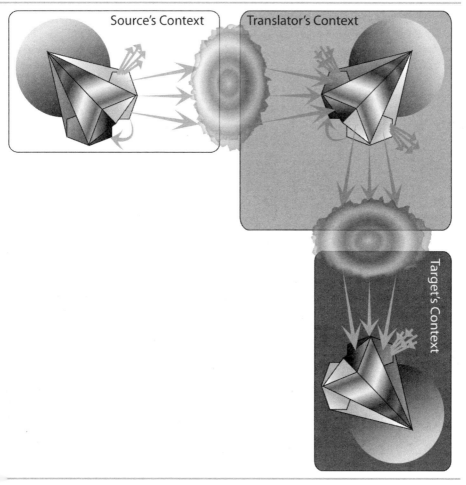

Figure 12.15 – Reduced Model of Translation

2.6.2 Proposed Model of Consecutive Transcommunication

Consecutive interpreting takes place when the source and target messages are performed in alternating, not overlapping, segments. The amount of interactive communication changes greatly once the source and target consumers share the same physical space. Not only is the interpreter able to give and receive feedback to each participant, but the source and target consumers also have access to each other directly, even if not linguistically. One significant advantage to consecutive interpreting is that each consumer's focus shares the same object at any given time. When the source consumer initiates communication, both the interpreter and target consumer can attend to that message, even though the target consumer may not understand much (or any) of the *linguistic* portions of that source message. When the interpreter regenerates the source message, both the source consumer and target consumer can attend to the interpreter's message. In other words, all of the participants can focus on the communication of each participant separately, rather than simultaneously dividing their attention between participants. The following sample model of consecutive interpreting assumes dialogic discourse, but the first two steps could be used to represent a consecutive interpretation of monologic discourse.

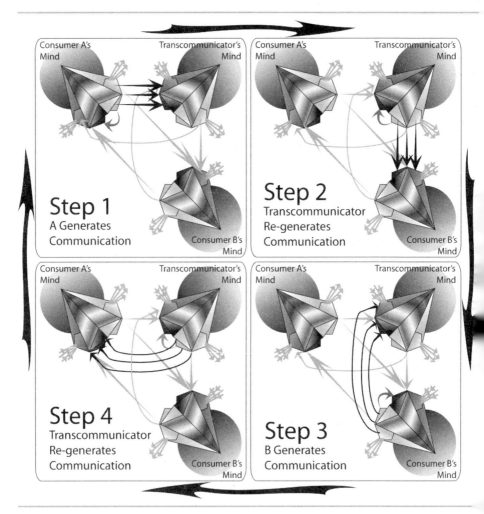

Figure 12.16 – Consecutive Transcommunication of Dialogic Discourse

<u>12.6.3 Proposed Models of Simultaneous Transcommunication</u>
   The process becomes more complex (and more prone to errors) when interpreter perceive a source message at the same time that they are generating a target message The interpreter's mind must concentrate on the source message, overcome interferenc from auditory and visual noise in the environment, and come to an understanding of th various meanings that have been perceived, both linguistic and extra-linguistic. Durin

he construction of the target message the interpreter must continue to monitor the source ext while simultaneously monitoring the production of the target text. The interpreter nust also monitor feedback from the consumers and respond appropriately to that eedback. Ultimately the interpreter will also generate some amount of auditory and/or 'isual noise, which has the potential of creating additional interference in monitoring the ource text.

The three components of *Monitor*, *Feedback*, and *Noise* function as a first filter in oth the comprehension of the *Source Text* and in the production of the *Target Text*. deally, the source *Sociolinguistic Frame* would be the same as the target *Sociolinguistic 'rame*, but when communicating between different cultures, there are, by definition, ifferences between the source and target *Sociolinguistic Frames*. In addition to all of ie stress of simultaneous processing, it is important to remember that we can never itentionally provide an accurate interpretation that is any better than our understanding f the source text. Figure 12.17, below, is a graphic representation of the key elements in imultaneous Interpreting of dialogic discourse.

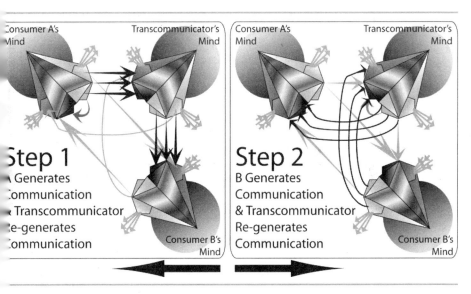

Figure 12.17 – Reduced Model of Dialogic Simultaneous Transcommunication

At first you might look at Figure 12.17 and think, "this looks easier than the nsecutive model." Remember that these models are not attempting to define what ppens in the brain when we do all of this; the models are guides to let us examine the miotic and linguistic information which is available, and better understand different erpreting situations. The key difference between consecutive and simultaneous erpreting is the timing of the process. All four steps of the consecutive process tween consumers must now take place within only two steps for a simultaneous ocess. This includes working with two different minds, two different languages, and two different *Sociolinguistic Frames* at the same time. The result is that the interpreter must do *more than twice as much work* because of the difficulty added by doing all three tasks (understanding the source, finding equivalence, and regenerating that message simultaneously. The consumers of the services are also less able to directly monitor each other. The overall result of simultaneous processing is that the interpreter is more likely to make errors while the consumers are even more dependent upon the interpreter because each consumer has reduced access to the semiotic information that the other consumer is producing.

Part of this added burden on the interpreter is the negotiation of when each speaker' turn ends and the other person can begin to say something. Consecutive interpreting allows each consumer to complete a thought before the other consumer begins. When the interpreter takes turns with each consumer, there is no overlap between any two people Simultaneous interpreting, by definition, ensures overlap between the interpreter and a least one other person. This largely leaves the negotiation of turns to the interpreter rather than to the consumers (Roy, 1989b. 1992).

The next figure is provided to remind the reader of the many of the details required i the simultaneous interpreting of monologic discourse. Notice that the transcommunicating mind (in the upper right corner) is performing double duty, bot perceiving the source presenter's "text" and generating a target "text" for the target consumer. The main addition to these elements of communication is the thin rectangle which bisects the mind of the transcommunicator. This thin rectangle represents the search for equivalence between the source and target messages. All of the elements of the six *Processing Levels* (Figure 12.10) fit within this rectangle as part of the search for equivalence. There are multiple possible results of the search for equivalence for each of the six processing levels:

1) - Success at both understanding the source and at generating a match
   (or "equivalence") in the target language
2) – Success at understanding the source but failure to generate a match
   a) because of *omissions* (deleting information that was present in the source)
   b) because of *intrusions* (source language adversely affecting the target)
3) – Failure to understand the source but success at generating at least a mismatch
   c) because of *substitutions* (deleting information and replacing it)
   d) because of *additions* (adding information not present in the source)
4) - Failure at both understanding the source and at generating an understandable
   mismatch
   e) because of *anomalies* (other errors with no obvious explanation)

Each of these possible results can be applied to each level of the six *Processing Levels* so that a message could be successfully equivalent at a semantic level but fail achieve equivalence at the pragmatic and stylistic levels, for example. This complex interaction allows for a deeper analysis of an interpreter's work that marks the success an interpreter is having while also pinpointing the most urgent areas for improvement Instead of saying that a message was not equivalent, this model allows a more specific point of feedback such as "You successfully achieved semantic equivalence (correct conceptual vocabulary choices) but at the pragmatic level the equivalence was lost due intrusion from the source language." Of course, the specific examples would need to provided, followed by a discussion of how the speaker's goals are more natural

:hieved by users of the target language. Providing such detailed analysis to interpreters and interpreting students) will require significant thought and practice.

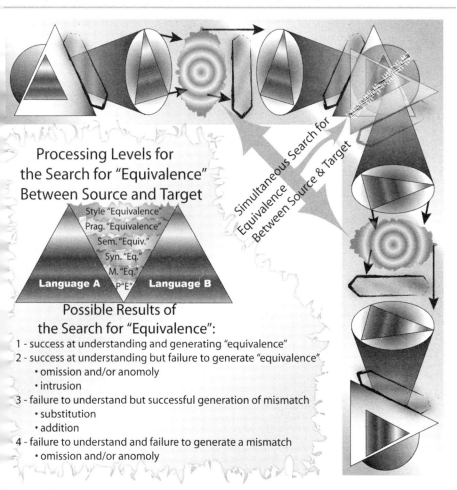

Processing Levels for
the Search for "Equivalence"
Between Source and Target

Style "Equivalence"
Prag. "Equivalence"
Sem. "Equiv."
Syn. "Eq."
M. "Eq."

Language A   P "E"   Language B

Simultaneous Search for
Equivalence
Between Source & Target

Possible Results of
the Search for "Equivalence":
1 - success at understanding and generating "equivalence"
2 - success at understanding but failure to generate "equivalence"
  • omission and/or anomaly
  • intrusion
3 - failure to understand but successful generation of mismatch
  • substitution
  • addition
4 - failure to understand and failure to generate a mismatch
  • omission and/or anomoly

Figure 12.18 - A More Detailed Model of Monologic Simultaneous Transcommunication

Figure 12.18 provides more information than the model presented in Figure 12.17. It isits the elements of the mind, expressive language, etc but it also represents one-way, monologic, processing. One thing that is absent from this version is the direct nmunication between the source and target minds. That communication is not :sented here because the focus of the model is on the interpreter's need to divide their ntal efforts between comprehending the source text while generating a target text that intains "equivalence" to the source text. Interpreting is a complex task and the ability represent it in two-dimensional models in a book is difficult at best. Just keep on)lying every model to an ever-growing master-model in your mind.

12.6.4 Comprehension and Production
    Figure 12.19 compares the 8 Cs of a source text with the 10 Cs of a target tex
Notice that the two additional features are identified in the oval representing the Targe
Message: *Comparable Affect* (style & register) and *Correctness* (or accuracy). Althoug
the interpreter creates the target message, the whole point of creating that message is *
faithfully represent the concepts of the source message and the intentions of the sourc
consumer.   The first requirement for accuracy is that interpreters must understand
source message if they are to reproduce that message accurately in the target language.
interpreters fail to achieve the highest level of comprehension, then their interpretatior
can only be accurate to the linguistic level that was comprehended.   Differer
participants, settings, and topics are likely to yield different levels of comprehensic
(based on the interpreter's communication knowledge).   A person may be able *
comprehend and produce both languages fully to the stylistic levels in casu
conversations, yet be limited to syntactic levels or lower during a business briefing f*
IBM, a lecture on fusion for graduate physics students, or a briefing on economic trac
sanctions at the State Department.   The basic premise of these models is that the targ*
text can be accurate only to the level that the source text was comprehended.

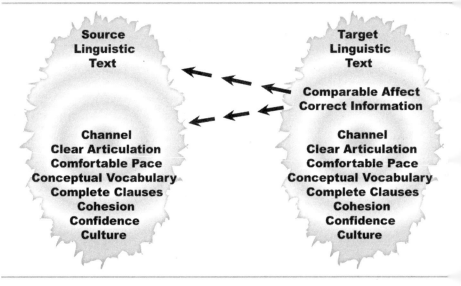

Figure 12.19 – Source Text's 8 Cs Compared to the Target Text's 10 Cs

2.6.5 Proposed Model of Teamed Transcommunication

The process continues to gain complexity when two interpreters work together to
ing a source message into a single target message. One of the key motivations for
oosing to do this is to ensure accuracy in the target text. This is accomplished
imarily in two ways.

1) The "B" interpreter provides additional and external monitoring of both the Source
d Target texts. If the team members have experience working together and have
veloped a trusting relationship, then this external monitoring provides an opportunity
r the "A" interpreter to devote more mental energy to other tasks, such as higher
ocessing levels in the understanding of the Source Text and greater planning and
ental rehearsal before generating the Target Text. If there is distrust among the team
embers, however, *Teamed Transcommunication* may actually cause increased mental
ess for the "A" member. The team members must agree to function as a team in order
receive the benefits of *Teamed Transcommunication.*

2) The "B" interpreter is able to provide quick corrections, either to replace erroneous
ormation in the Target Text or to fill a gap in the accurate perception of the Source
xt in order to generate the Target Text. Making corrections is necessary if essential
ints are misstated in the Target Text. The misstatements may be due to
srepresentations or miscomprehensions. A simple example is saying that something
ists when the speaker's intention was to say that it does *not* exist. Missing a single
rd in the Source Text can cause the Target Text to generate an opposite meaning. A
" team member of a *Transcommunication Team* can quickly offer a correction to the
" team member. It is important to recognize that the "A" team member then makes the
ision in how to implement the correction (or whether it is worth making the correction
the first place). Similarly, if a gap in the perception or understanding of the Source
xt occurs, the "B" team member may be able to supply the missing information or
aphrase its meaning. Of course it is also possible that the "B" team member also
sed the information or is equally confused about the Source Text's meaning. Having
B" team member provide the information allows a much more seamless approach than
rrupting the Source Text presenter for the information. Figure 12.19 represents a
plified representation of simultaneous teamed interpretation of monologic discourse.

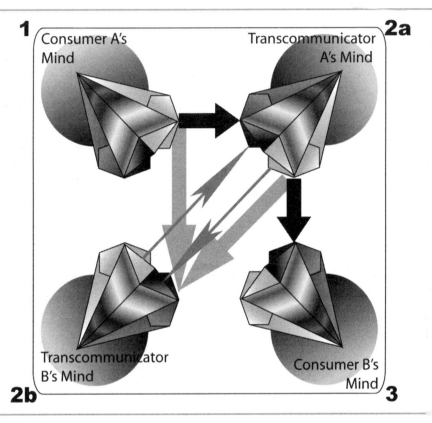

**Figure 12.20 – Simplified Model of Teamed Simultaneous
Transcommunication of Monologic Discourse**

Notice that there are two different lines of communication between the two memb__
of the Transcommunication Team. The thick lines represent source and target messag__
The thin lines represent relatively private communication between the team memb__
This can most effectively be accomplished if different language channels or modali__
are used for this communication. When transcommunicating between Deaf and Hear__
consumers, the Source language and the Target language are already in differ__
modalities (visual versus auditory).   It is possible for the B Transcommunicator __
provide feedback and corrections to the A Transcommunicator through a visual moda__
when the Source Text is presented in an auditory modality.   Likewise the __
Transcommunicator may be able to provide feedback and corrections to the __
Transcommunicator through an auditory modality when the Source Text is presented __
visual modality. Regardless of the modality of this private communication it is import__
to emphasize that the communication between the team members is PRIVATE. T__
requires the B team member to be positioned either directly in front of the A member __
visual communication or next to (and perhaps slightly behind) the A team member __
auditory (whispered) communication.

The simplified version shown in Figure 12.20 does not represent the additional lines
f communication and feedback that remain available between the consumers and the
anscommunicator. Likewise the access to, and impact upon, the physical context is not
presented in the simplified version. Also not represented are the stages of the
anscommunication process, including the search for "equivalence" mentioned in the
evious section. As with all of the models presented in this chapter, each builds on the
ncepts that have previously been presented in the entire text, so continue to build the
ll representations in your mind. You should quickly come to the understanding that
ch model presented in this chapter is more complex than prior models.

The increasing complexity of the models is intended to be representative of the
mplexity of the transcommunication processes being described. Thus the least
mplex process is translation, followed by consecutive transcommunication, and then
nultaneous transcommunication, then teamed transcommunication, and finally relayed
nscommunication.[58]

.6.6 Proposed Model of Relayed Transcommunication

The process continues to gain complexity when two interpreters work together to
ing a source message into a single target message. One of the key motivations for
oosing to do this is to provide a matched set of *Sociolinguistic Frames*: The Hearing
erpreter and the Hearing Source Consumer both share significant portions of their
ciolinguistic Frames. Likewise the Deaf Interpreter and the Deaf Source Consumer
ll share significant portions of their *Sociolinguistic Frames*. The *Sociolinguistic
ames* are a key filter in how a person understands the communication surrounding
m. Matching the *Sociolinguistic Frames* between interpreters and consumers should
vide significant benefit to the transcommunication process. The model below
resents a simultaneous relayed transcommunication of monologic discourse.

---

[58] The levels of complexity do not completely reflect an increasing challenge to accuracy. The
dle process of lone simultaneous transcommunication is the most prone to inaccuracies, simply
ause there is only one mind attempting to do all of the transcommunication work with the added
ssure of limited time and simultaneous processing. Translation provides the greatest *potential*
complete accuracy. Consecutive transcommunication comes next, with Teamed and Relayed
scommunication as close contenders with consecutive work for accuracy. The chapter
mary will review the relative accuracies of each approach with more detail.

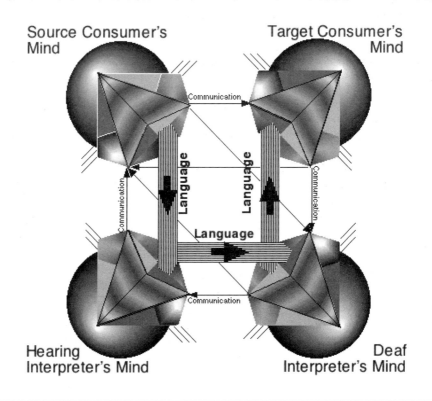

Source Consumer's Mind

Target Consumer's Mind

Hearing Interpreter's Mind

Deaf Interpreter's Mind

Figure 12.21 – Reduced Model of Relayed Simultaneous Transcommunication of Monologic Discourse

Notice that the lines of communication remain intact between all of the participa_ except for two: the Hearing Interpreter and the Target Consumer. The break in this li of communication is deliberate because the alternative would be distraction and excess noise. The arrangement depicted in Figure 12.21 specifically depends upon differ channels of language operating simultaneously. The source presenter in the arrangem depicted above is using spoken language to generate the source message, which Hearing Interpreter regenerates using a signed language. The channels of spoken a signed languages do not cause significant mutual noise.[59] The Deaf Interpreter mainta the channel of signed language. If the target consumer were able to view both Hearing Interpreter's message and the Deaf Interpreter's message then the result wo be competing messages in the same channel: signed language. In order to eliminate form of visual noise, the Hearing Interpreter should be located out of the perceptual ra

---

[59] This is not to say that consumers will not be distracted by visual elements of a spo message or auditory elements of a signed message. The point is that there is no inherent confli the one person's physical production of a spoken message and another person's physical produc of a signed message occurring simultaneously.

the target consumer. The research regarding the effectiveness of relayed anscommunication was reviewed previously in Chapter Ten.

2.6.7 Linguistic Processing Within the Models

As stated previously, the intentional accuracy of interpreters is limited to the linguistic level that they comprehend the source message. Other factors can also contribute to diminished accuracy, but weaknesses in language fluency cannot be otherwise counterbalanced. The six processing levels, identified previously in Chapter 9 and again at the beginning of this chapter are as follows: 1) Phonological (sub-lexical), 2) lexical (morphological), 3) Syntactic, 4) Semantic, 5) Pragmatic and 6) Stylistic (whole-text). Here are some hypothetical examples.

The similarities or differences in the sociolinguistic frames have a significant impact on the expected success of achieving cohesion across every one of the six processing levels. For monolingual and monocultural transcommunication (transliteration or shadowing), both sociolinguistic frames are either identical or very similar. A fluent and experienced transcommunicator should not be overwhelmed *linguistically*, but if the task involves *simultaneous processing* then the transcommunicator will still face a challenge. This challenge is greater if the transcommunication is bilingual and bicultural (interpreting) because the sociolinguistic frames will be different. Greater differences between the source and target sociolinguistic frames will present greater challenges, especially when combined with simultaneous processing. The greatest challenge to finding equivalence is in *elucidation* situations where one consumer does not have a language because he is alingual, semilingual, or using an artificial pidgin such as SEE. Such consumers have a diminished/damaged sociolinguistic frame, which is not likely to be shared by the transcommunicator. These challenges can best be met by using both a consecutive approach and a *relay team* where one of the interpreters has significant experience with the alingual/semilingual consumer's sociolinguistic frame.

How does the pressure of *simultaneous processing* impact the search for equivalence across the six processing levels? Suppose we are interpreting for a dear old friend giving a lecture. We know every thing about his lecture topic, his lecture style, the phrases he tends to use, the kinds of jokes he tells, everything. Assuming that we have the sociolinguistic skills necessary to convey this kind of information in the target language (and having such skills is not a trivial point) then we can expect to be able to produce a target-language text that is just as stylistically rich as the original text. This doesn't guarantee that the interpretation will be perfect; it only means that given the interpreter's level of source language comprehension and the interpreter's ability to produce messages in the target language, the interpreter has every possibility of reproducing that message the same way it was intended, but in a different language.

Every possibility exists except for one problem. Assuming that the task is a simultaneous interpretation and that the information in the source message is not old news to the interpreter, then the act of interpreting *simultaneously* may be mentally taxing enough to prevent the interpreter from reaching the stylistic level of target text construction. In other words, the process of monitoring the ongoing interpretation as well as monitoring the ongoing source message is enough to keep the interpreter's best level of production at least one level below the highest comprehension level, which in this case is the pragmatic level. Thus, the mental processing prohibits consistent access to a equal level of processing between the source and target texts.

Here is another hypothetical example, continuing with the assumption that th interpreter has complete linguistic ability all the way to the stylistic level in both of th languages in the interpreting situation. A person is giving a lecture on a topic that somewhat familiar to the interpreter, but the lecture contains mostly new information. A the beginning of this task, the interpreter can make no predictions about the lecturer style; but the interpreter can make some predictions about what kinds of things are likel to come up in the lecture. We can now set the highest level of comprehension at th pragmatic level. This may increase to the stylistic level over time as the interpret becomes familiar with the speaker's style, but for now, at the beginning of the lecture, th highest level of comprehension is at the pragmatic level.

Because this interpreting event is a simultaneous task, it will require a certain level simultaneous attention to both the source and target texts. This level of interference likely to bring the interpreter's overall interpretation down at least one step – into th semantic level. This does not mean that the interpreter will not have short bursts (or eve extended periods) of accuracy to the pragmatic level during target text productions. only means that the best level of accurate interpretation that can be consistently expecte is at the semantic level. When the interpreter can begin to make predictions about t speaker's style, then we can increase our expectations of consistent accuracy in t interpretation to the pragmatic level.

Suppose we have an interpreter who is native in one language but is still facing sor fluency problems with a second language. Let's say that this interpreter is able consistently produce semantically accurate messages in the second language but or occasionally maintains pragmatic accuracy. If this interpreter is working in the "dear c friend" scenario that we described above, then what predictions can we make about t overall accuracy of the resulting interpretation?

We can begin by predicting that the target text can be accurate only to the seman level simply because the interpreter cannot consistently produce texts which are accur beyond that level, even in casual conversation. So even though the interpre comprehends the message to the stylistic level, it is still *impossible* for that interpreter intentionally achieve an interpretation consistently accurate at any level higher than semantic level, which in this case is two levels below the level of comprehension.

It gets worse, however, because the interpreter is performing a simultaneous task t involves new information and the interpreter must therefore devote mental attention both the target and source texts. This extra mental energy to processing will reduce attention to language fluency and therefore we must reduce the expected accuracy of resulting interpretation to being no better than at the syntactic level. This means that interpreter is no longer *interpreting*. All the work that the interpreter is going throu will only be useful if the consumers of the interpretation have enough skill in the sou language to *reconstruct* the original source message. And that means the consumers at best gaining *access* to the source text while doing a lot of the actual interpret themselves. Colonomos and Llewellyn-Jones both provided models, in the last part Chapter 11, which exemplify this kind of failed interpretation as a function of insuffici fluency.

Lets review the last example, using the interpreter who has a full stylistic ability in interpreter's native language but is only consistently accurate at the semantic level of second language. Let's have this interpreter working from the second language for the source message and the target language is the interpreter's native language. Since the source language comprehension is only consistently accurate at the semantic level, it will be impossible for the interpreter to produce a target text that is accurate above the semantic level. The semantic level would be the best we could expect; but the task of simultaneous processing, including the monitoring of both the source and target texts, will reduce our expectations back down to the syntactic level. This interpreter, however, appears to be producing fluid interpretation at the pragmatic level. How can this be? The answer is that the interpreter is not consistently accurate. This does not mean that the interpreter is making it all up; only that we cannot depend 100% on the accuracy of the information conveyed in the target language. Bits and pieces of accuracy may pop up now and again, but when the target-text production level exceeds the source-text comprehension level then the resulting interpretation cannot be trusted to be consistently accurate. Even if the resulting interpretation was consistent and fluid (i.e. *Cohesive*) at the semantic level, we would be forced to conclude that it will not be consistently accurate because the act of monitoring both the source and target texts should drag the interpretation accuracy down to no better than the syntactic level.

Suppose the interpreter has different levels of comprehension and production of the same language – let's say of the interpreter's second language – then what? The answer depends on which task the language skills are applied to. If the interpreter has better comprehension than production in a second language, then the interpreter will have better results interpreting from that language to the native language. If for some reason the interpreter has better second-language production than comprehension[60], then the interpreter will find better results moving from the native language to the second language.

Note: the above examples focus on simultaneous interpretations. If the interpreting task is not simultaneous, but is instead a consecutive task, then the burden of the monitor is reduced and it should be possible to accurately render the target text at the same level that it was understood. Likewise translation work and teamed transcommunication can exceed the separate fluency limitations of the various team members involved.

2.7 Applications of the Models

How are the concepts presented here useful? Let's start with evaluating an interpreted performance, whether for personal improvement, educational assessment, or certification purposes. These models focus on the parts of interpreting that are to some extent measurable. We can combine the explanations made possible by the models with actual performance measurements and provide recommendations for improvement or decisions of acceptable performance.

First, it is worth knowing to what level an interpreter can both comprehend and produce any given language. To that end we can develop tests that measure the semantics, pragmatics, and to the extent possible, the stylistics of both the production and

---

[60] New second-language learners often begin with a greater ability to produce elements of their new language rather than to understand their new language. Typically this indicates an overall fluency below the semantic level. If this is the case then such a person is not qualified to be interpreting.

comprehension of each language an interpreter intends to work with. We already have a great tool that helps us to get at some of these issues in comprehension: the *cloze test*. In the cloze test we (generally) take an actual text, taken from some real-life situation, and methodically remove elements from it. We then see if the person being tested can replace those gaps with the same bits we took away, or at least with reasonable substitutes.

On the other side of the interpreting process we can measure directly the accuracy and cohesion of the target text production. Keeping the goal of a 100% accurate target text in mind, we can see that to be stylistically accurate, the interpretation must also be accurate to at the pragmatic level, which means it must also be semantically accurate and so on. An interpreter can be less than 100% stylistically accurate (and this probably happens most of the time) and still demonstrate wonderfully long stretches of accuracy at pragmatic, semantic, and syntactic levels. But any errors in a lower level will negatively influence our accuracy at all higher levels.

When we attempt to measure our production accuracy it might well be worth investigating areas such as syntax and morphology in addition to the semantic, pragmatic and stylistic levels. Since the task of simultaneous interpretation nearly precludes the ability to produce stylistically accurate target·texts, it might be more fruitful to delete the stylistic level from target-text analysis and use it only when analyzing consecutive interpretations. We can analyze target texts by examining the syntax, by comparing the propositional[61] content with the propositions within the source text, and by examining the register to ensure it matches the register of the source text.

When we are discussing interpreting, we must at least be able to deal with language at the semantic level. Processing at anything less than the semantic level does not constitute *interpreting*, and at best can be described as some form of *transcommunication*. Interpreting begins where the meaning conveyed by a language can be understood and used to reconstruct that meaning within the target language. To this extent, the models helps us know when a training program can start to move beyond teaching language and can begin to teach interpreting. Specifically, we can see that if we only want minimal interpreting then we should only teach and/or verify language skills up to the semantic level. But if we want interpreters to have the opportunity to reach 100% accuracy then we must teach and/or verify skills all the way through the stylistic level. We can also see that it is inappropriate to begin instruction in interpreting until the student exhibits at least semantic abilities in both languages. It is probably best to teach interpreting to people who command both languages fully to the stylistic level, but it is perhaps more likely that we will have students who exhibit a mixture of skills between the semantic and stylistic levels. The models suggest that there is value in teaching the art and science of interpreting to such students, but that significant language fluency is a pre-requisite to interpreter training.

Not every interpreting assignment is a communication event that requires interpreting at the stylistic level. The most obvious places that would require stylistic interpretation are dramatic performances and political campaigns. But an interpretation at the pragmatic level may be fine for a performance review with the boss. A semantic interpretation may even suffice within certain highly predictable situations. The point here is that many interpretations can be considered successful even when accomplished

---

[61] Propositions are the combinations of concepts with EVENTS or STATES and were briefly defined in Chapter 8.

below the stylistic and even pragmatic levels. Our goal should generally be stylistic "equivalence", but true failure only occurs when the processing is below the semantic level.

12.7.1 Boundaries

There are many boundaries that may exist within a communication event. With the different levels of interpretation described above, an interpreter will rarely stick to just one level all the way through, never wavering, as though the interpreter were a well tuned automobile running down an empty highway and set on cruise control. Very few communication events are this easy all the time. It is far more likely that the interpreter will be shifting between levels depending upon a variety of factors. The boundaries within and between levels help us to predict where some shifting is likely to occur.

The most obvious source of boundaries is the *person*. When different people provide source texts then the target text stylistics should also change. When Mr. Smith finishes his announcements and Ms. Jones begins her keynote address, we have a change in the speaker, and therefore a change in the stylistics of the source message. This is one *boundary*. This notion of the *boundary* can help us to analyze the effectiveness of an interpretation at various points within the interpreting process. Suppose that Smith mumbles and produces other noise to the source message such as rustling papers or creating a number of false starts or partial repairs. Jones on the other hand may be one of the best speakers ever to hit the lecture circuit. The task of interpreting the source texts produced by these two people is going to be very different and the results are likely to be better for Jones' message than for Smith's.

This expectation could be reversed if Smith's style was the same but his message was highly predictable by the interpreter, but Jones' topic was completely unknown to the interpreter. Interpreting is such a complicated process to describe because of the multitude of simultaneous possibilities within any given message. Smith may be dull, inarticulate and clumsy, but Smith's message may still be understood and reproduced at the stylistic level. Jones may be interesting, articulate, and precise, but Jones' message may challenge those who are totally unfamiliar with the topic of, say, quantum mechanics, and leave the interpreter struggling to construct a target text at even the semantic level.

But suppose that Jones did both the announcements and the lecture on quantum mechanics and that Jones was interesting, articulate and precise throughout the entire communication event. So within the same speaker we could see a clear discourse boundary due to the *topic*. The target text construction of the first part may be stylistically "equivalent" while the target text construction of the second part may be merely semantically accurate.

Beyond these obvious boundaries, other factors may influence differences in potential interpretations such as changes in the physical environment, changes in register, and changes in discourse strategies. These are all areas within pragmatics; but what about the lower levels? Are there semantic boundaries in communication events? I would offer that boundaries only exist at the pragmatic and stylistic levels. At the semantic level we are focusing primarily on words. If we start setting up boundaries every time the interpreter encounters an ambiguous word, we will have so many subdivisions in the source text that we'll have to hire a zoning clerk to make sense of it all.

The value of the boundary concept is that it allows us to break up the communication event and determine the general level that an interpretation is at within certain boundaries. The notion that an interpretation will be at a stylistic level, for example, is theoretical in nature. In other words, we may see an interpretation at the stylistic level that is somehow less than perfect. The imperfections that enter into the interpretation might only be occasional glitches or they could be absolute drops in the interpretation level.

Let's say that Jones is on stage giving the keynote address to the International Quantum Mechanics Association and we are providing interpretation services for this communication event. Let's also assume that we have the same level of general knowledge about quantum mechanics as most audience members. Jones is making her third primary point in the keynote address and we misunderstand some small piece of information, the name of a physicist, for example. We produce the information in our target text but we remain unaware that we misunderstood it in the first place. This is a glitch within the interpretation. This disruption to the interpretation is at the semantic level, but it alone does not prevent us from producing an overall stylistic interpretation.

Now let's suppose that while Jones is lecturing someone begins to cough violently for a few moments, interrupting our ability to understand the source message. Here we have a discourse boundary within the communication event. The physical environment has been temporarily altered with a burst of noise and with that noise has come two new boundaries: the onset of that noise and the conclusion of that noise. The noise segment between these two boundaries may still be interpreted at the stylistic level or perhaps it is not interpreted at all. The point is that this piece of the communication event is different from the other pieces of the same communication event. Any difference in the processing level that takes place *between* these boundaries should be considered separate from interpreting *outside* of those boundaries. This way of dividing a communication event can help us understand what factors have the strongest influences on any given interpreter's work.

With these models of interpreting to provide guidance, we should be able to better describe where an interpretation succeeds, where it falls short, and provide suggestion for how to make improvements. We can make predictions about a given interpreter's likely success in specific contexts and appropriately match interpreters of different skill to a variety of interpreting situations.

12.7.2 Four Predictions for Bilingual Transcommunication

Here are four proposed predictions about an interpretation based on knowledge about the source text comprehension level and the target text production level:

1)   Target text construction at levels beyond source text comprehension will cause fabrications (logical extensions or outright errors). These kinds of interpretations may appear to be fluent, but they constitute *deceptive interpretation,* which is unethical behavior for any professional interpreter.

2)   Attempting to produce a target text at the same level as source text comprehension, in a simultaneous interpretation, is likely to co-occur with enough stress to cause production errors in the lower regions of language production (phonological errors, morphological errors, and syntactic errors).   The resulting non-linguistic noise may be sufficient to make the target text incomprehensible to the target language consumers.

3)   Deliberately attempting to produce a target text at one level below the level of source text comprehension, in a simultaneous interpretation, is likely to reduce the stress enough to allow a consistent interpretation without production errors in the lower regions of language production (phonological errors, morphological errors, and syntactic errors).

4)   A consecutive interpretation will not have the same stress factors as simultaneous interpretations and therefore target text construction can better be generated at the same level as source text comprehension (ie. consecutive interpretations will yield better results than simultaneous interpretations).

From the last two of these predictions, let's paint a possible scenario for a consistent simultaneous interpretation at the pragmatic level (this is called "armchair linguistics". Real data would be much more valuable). Let's have Mr. Smith be an articulate, well-organized speaker who will be making a presentation about the impact of the latest Government budget upon the cost of living in our region. The interpreters have pre-conferenced with Smith and have begun to know his conversational style and also understand the introductory information that will occur at the opening of the presentation.

As the interpretation begins it functions nearly as a consecutive task because all of the information in the opening remarks is already known to the interpreters.   Yet the interpreters still need to get used to Smith's lecture style, and therefore they only comprehend Smith's message to the pragmatic level.   Following prediction number four it is possible that as long as the interpreters continue to comprehend Smith's message to the *pragmatic* level, they have every possibility of accurately constructing target texts that are also at the *pragmatic* level, since the content of the message is entirely old information. As Smith continues to lecture, the interpreters become familiar with Smith's lecture style. Although the interpreters are now encountering new information in Smith's message, they now understand the message at the *stylistic* level. Following prediction number three, the interpreters have every possibility of comfortably interpreting at one level below their level of comprehension.   In this case, they could still produce an interpretation at the *pragmatic* level.

We must remember that these are predictions about the best possible *consistent* level of interpretation. There may be bursts of stylistic interpretation. There may be glitches, fatigue, distractions, and any number of other factors that will prevent the interpreter from producing a target text consistently at the predicted level. The point of the prediction is to provide a target level of reasonable expectation when we analyze our own work or the work of other interpreters. It also helps interpreter trainers to narrow their focus of instruction on the elements that can be more immediately "fixed", rather than stressing the interpreting student with feelings of inadequacy. It is where an interpretation deviates from the predicted level that we find areas of interest for further study.

The likelihood that stylistic "equivalence" will almost never occur in simultaneous work helps us to better understand why consumers of interpreting generally prefer direct communication rather than interpretation, when it is possible. The impact of an interpreted education for Deaf students in mainstreamed settings must, by these definitions, be less than the impact of direct instruction in Deaf settings. If the interpreters in a mainstreamed educational setting have sufficient fluency in both the spoken and the signed languages of their consumers, then pragmatic processing is possible and provides the possibility of only a slightly diminished education. But if the interpreters' skills are lower, then the resulting interpreted education will fall further from the potential that non-Deaf students have.

12.7.3 Transcommunication Errors

Production errors are accounted for in these models as primarily due to stress. Stress is expected when production occurs at the same time and at the same level as source text processing. Without the monitor being fully able to analyze whether the interpretation is accurate, the interpreter will feel as though he or she is barely able to keep up. Production errors are likely to go uncorrected, and most likely, unnoticed by the interpreter[62]. In non-simultaneous interpreting (which includes both consecutive interpreting and rehearsed interpreting) then the target production can be relatively error free.

Errors of inaccurate additions or substitutions (fabrications) are likely to occur when production levels exceed levels of source processing. A sense of overconfidence may prevail in the interpreter and technical production errors are likely to be few. The interpreter will look believable but the interpretation will not be true to the source message.

An interesting problem (especially for mental health interpreting) is when the interpreter processes the source language to deeper levels than the speaker intended or than is fully possible from the source text that was produced. In other words it would be a problem if a consumer's language production was only coherent at the morphological or syntactic level, but the interpreter imposed meaning on it to higher levels and produced

---

[62] But errors can be more readily caught and corrected if an interpreter is working with a team member who is providing an external monitor of both the source and target texts. A team member providing this extra support provides the advantage not only of capturing un-intended errors, but also can provide repetitions and/or clarifications of portions of the source text, thus allowing the source presenter to continue without interruption while the interpreting team maintains higher levels of accuracy in simultaneous interpreting.

a target text beyond the source production levels. The result would be processing an incoherent source message to that it appears to be coherent in the target language. In psychotherapy these alterations in meaning might have serious implications about the patient's future, the form of treatment that will be prescribed, perhaps even whether the patient should be incarcerated or put to death. In such serious situations the most obvious solution would be to eliminate the interpreter from the situation by finding a psychotherapist skilled in the source language of the consumer. Since this is not always possible, an alternative might be to video tape the interview and review the tape with the therapist in private in order to reveal those areas where the interpreter imposed cohesion upon the source message.

12.7.4 Measuring Performance

Choosing a target processing level for analyzing an interpreter or student should be guided by the purpose of the evaluation. Admission to a general interpreting program or basic certification of an interpreter should require consistent accuracy at the semantic level.[63] For graduation from an interpreting program or for certification within specific realms of interpreting, consistent accuracy at the pragmatic level is a good goal. A stylistic analysis of source and target texts may help someone who is already a very good interpreter become an excellent interpreter, or even determine which of two or three candidates is best for a long-term interpreting assignment for a government diplomat or business executive. This chapter makes no attempt to define the actual means of assessing semantic, pragmatic, and/or stylistic levels of processing. Indeed, assessments may need to vary based on the content areas that are of value (general educational topics, medical topics, legal topics, etc.)

One significant part of evaluation remains to be defined: just what is meant by the words "consistent accuracy." "Consistent" should mean no less than 50% of the interpretation is accurate within the targeted processing level. If the analysis is indeed being done statistically, then this measure can be achieved with some degree of objectivity. We may wish to tie the percentage to the level that most consumers would be willing to accept within certain contexts. While the interpretation of non-critical community events might be acceptable when 60% of the message is reproduced with semantic accuracy, the expectations in a legal situation might be for the pragmatic level to be at 90% (or beyond).

Why not go for 100%? That is the understood goal of all interpreting. These models suggest that when we comprehend information at higher levels, then the production in the lower levels can be more accurate. If we can comprehend the source text to a stylistic level, we should experience less stress in the production of the target text. Therefore we should be able to reduce the number of errors we make while we construct our target text.

---

[63] Remember that this work suggests that processing below the semantic level should not be identified as "interpreting". Therefore the training in interpreting should be withheld until a student has demonstrated bilingual fluency at the semantic level or beyond.

The problem of creating an interpretation that is 100% error free is that 1) there must be no ambiguities in the source text, 2) we must be able to find exact counterparts of meaning for every concept between the source and target languages, 3) we must have target language equivalents for every discourse feature that occurs in the source text, and 4) we must be so much like the speaker of the source text that people would think we were the speaker of the source text. It is unlikely that we can fulfill all four of these requirements in any simultaneous interpretation task. If we really wanted to be 100% fair to a defendant who is charged with a felony, then we ought to pursue getting a judge and jury who use the defendant's language and forget about the interpreter. Likewise, if we want to provide 100% access to an educational setting, then the teachers, administrators, and peers of a linguistic-minority student should all use that language at the school and leave the interpreter to work elsewhere. Until people demand and require 100% access, these things will not likely happen (and interpreters will still have work for years to come).

These models are intended to provide some basic guidelines for interpreter training and for establishing testable parameters that can predict current interpreting limits and suggests specific areas of improvement to both interpreters and interpreter trainers. They also offer the potential for providing a more extensive certification system for interpreters both of signed languages and spoken languages. As with all models, these cannot even attempt to be complete and comprehensive explanations of the process, but rather they are offered in the spirit of being a few more perspectives that will be of benefit to some people but not to others. As Marina McIntire once said[64]: "Interpreting is impossible… so get better!"

---

[64] Personal communication from a 1997 workshop co-presented with Gary Sanderson.

12.8 Summary

This chapter has presented five related models of transcommunication, all based on the principles presented throughout this book, beginning in Chapter One. The primary elements are three (or more) minds engaged in communication within at least one physical setting. It is important to remember that in face-to-face communication settings, the target consumer is generally able to receive some portion of source text semiotic information directly from the source consumer.

Translation typically does not provide shared access to a physical setting, nor does it provide shared access between the minds of the source text creator, the translation team, and the target language audience. The other four models were all generated with the assumption that the source creator, transcommunicator(s), and target audience all do share the same physical setting. It is not actually a requirement that the physical setting be shared. One obvious example is video relay interpreting where one consumer using a signed language through an internet video link is in one physical setting (such as an office or living room), another consumer is using spoken language through a telephone in a different setting, and a video relay interpreter is in a call center providing interpretation between the other two parties. The basics of these models can be applied and modified to fit any number of specific conditions.

Translation allows for broad variation in the amount of time required to complete the transcommunication task. Simultaneous interpreting and consecutive interpreting have greater limits on the amount of time available to complete the transcommunication task. They are most obviously different in the amounts of overlap that occurs between the source and target texts. Simultaneous interpreting requires that both the process of understanding the source text and the process of producing the target text happen more or less at the same time. This adds stress and mental fatigue to the transcommunication process, which both limits the level of consistent processing and increases the likelihood of errors.

Consecutive interpreting separates the two processes of source comprehension and target production, and allows greater time for either one to occur. Consecutive interpreting provides for less stress and mental fatigue and the potential to generate fewer errors.

The final two models presented introduced the use of transcommunication teams. Teamed simultaneous interpreting and relayed simultaneous interpreting (with consecutive processing between the relay team members) provide greater potential for higher processing levels and fewer errors. Relay work has the greater advantage because the *sociolinguistic frames* are better matched between the consumers and the members of the relay team.

Figure 12.22, below, identifies the expected potential processing levels for each kind of transcommunication identified in the five models. The lighter *Linguistic Pyramids* (in the background) indicate the source text production. The darker *Linguistic Pyramids* (in the foreground) represent the expected potential for each form of transcommunication.

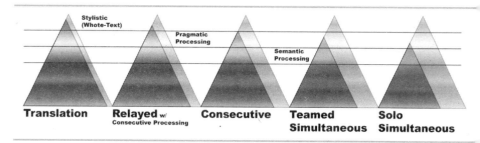

Figure 12.22 – Potential Processing Levels

The images presented in figure 12.22 indicate that the target text is unlikely to generate 100% "equivalence" to the source text, but that Translation provides the greatest opportunity in generating "equivalence" to the stylistic, or whole-text, level. Notice that as each type of transcommunication falls to slightly lower expectations in achieving stylistic or pragmatic equivalence, the target texts also generate less equivalence across all of the lower levels. In other words, the best expectations for consistent processing through teamed simultaneous interpreting would be at the pragmatic level; yet there would be some short-comings in semantic equivalence, syntactic equivalence, etc. This is true even for monolingual transcommunication such as verbatim shadowing. The reason being that it is not possible to generate (or even document) an exact match of every nuance of the source text performance (including all of the productive semiotics). Therefore we understand that 100% "equivalence" will generally be a goal for transcommunication, but technically it will always be an unachievable goal.

There may be times where a transcommunicator intentionally attempts processing below a semantic level. Generally, however, we recognize that such work is more likely to be accidental in nature, and probably generated by a transcommunicator who does not have sufficient fluency in either the source or target languages (or both). Such work cannot be identified as Translation or Interpreting and instead should be identified as "Transcoding" where elements of the *target language encoding system* are used to attempt to represent elements of the *source language encoding system*. This kind of work may be useful to target language consumers who are fluent in the source language, but unable to directly access it, such as late-deafened adults. All other consumers of such work will struggle to force their own understanding upon the target text, which may generate serious misunderstandings. Figure 12.23 identifies the three forms of transcoding: syntactic transcoding, lexical transcoding, and phonological transcoding.

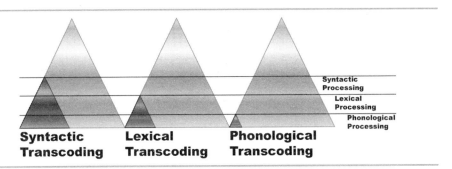

Figure 12.23 – Three Levels of Transcoding

12.8.1 Review Questions
1. What are the main components of communication upon which all five models are based?
2. What are the primary components of the "Sociolinguistic Frame"?
3. What are the eight components of a "Linguistic Text"?
4. What is the minimum number of participants (or "Minds") involved in Transcommunication?
5. What two additional components of "Linguistic Texts" are related to the creation of a target text (beyond the eight Cs of a source text)?
6. What prediction is made about attempting to simultaneously create Target Texts at *higher levels* than the Source Text comprehension?
7. What prediction is made about attempting to simultaneously create Target Texts at *equal* levels to the Source Text comprehension?
8. What prediction is made about attempting to simultaneously create Target Texts at *exactly one level lower* than the Source Text comprehension?
9. What prediction is made about attempting to create Target Texts *consecutively* with the Source Text?
10. Sequence the following types of transcommunication from highest expected target text processing to lowest: Consecutive, Relayed, Solo Simultaneous, Teamed Simultaneous, and Translation.

12.8.2 Suggested Activities
1. Videotape your own transcommunication work. Be sure that the recording documents both the source text and your production of the target text. Analyze the source text for the following variables:
    1) its channel (spoken language, written language, signed language),
    2) its clarity of articulation (phonemics and phonology),
    3) its pace or rate of information,
    4) its lexical content or vocabulary,
    5) its grammatical accuracy,
    6) its cohesion across the duration of the text,
    7) the confidence of its creator, and
    8) various cultural factors regarding values and beliefs.
2. Continuing with the text used for Activity #1, use the *Ten Cs Target Text Evaluation Form* (in Appendix D) to analyze your target text for the following variables:
    1) its channel (spoken language, written language, signed language),
    2) its clarity of articulation (phonemics and phonology),
    3) its pace or rate of information,
    4) its lexical content or vocabulary,
    5) its grammatical accuracy,
    6) its cohesion across the duration of the text,
    7) the confidence of its creator (you),
    8) various cultural factors regarding values and beliefs,
    9) Comparable Affect (style and register) to the source text, and
    10) Correctness or accuracy of the target text as compared to the source.

Conclusion (?)

"The End Is Only a Beginning"

Rasmus took a step back from the artwork hanging on the wall. "What does this say to you?"

Timoth glanced up from the theory book. "Is that another print by M.C. Escher? I just love waterfalls."

"How much do you know about water?"

"Ah, Rasmus. You are trying to trick me into thinking that you are really asking me about water when something else is up your sleeve."

Rasmus placed a marker in Timoth's book and closed it. "Now I know that you really have been paying attention all this time. Are you going to answer my question?"

"In a moment." Timoth looked closer at the print on the wall. "Hey, this waterfall never stops. It's both the beginning and the end of the stream. So maybe its like the water cycle where the amount of water on the planet finite and it simply recycles."

"Recycles? It's just a print: it's ink and paper. How can anything recycle on a fixed document?" Rasmus started to grin.

"What's that thing in your hands right there?"

"This? This is your book, 'The Interpreting Handbook'. What does this have to do with art?" Rasmus' grin became a smile.

"Does the book still have any value to you? Do you ever re-read portions of it?"

"Well, it's not exactly a page-turning novel. But it contains useful information about the profession of interpreting... so, yes, I guess I re-read sections once in a while."

"So a book's information can be recycled. But who is doing the recycling?"

"Who is doing the recycling? Um.... well, I'm the one reading it."

"Yes, and I hope you keep on reading; so even though it is just a book – ink on paper – it's contents can still be used more than once"

"You mean the words?"

"Sure... the words. But also the author's intentions, the meanings tha you have derived from it, the figures... all of it."

"Well, of course. So this work – this book – is somehow like that prin that I just put up in the room?"

"And that other print you put up of the *Hand With Reflecting Sphere*."

"Sometimes you surprise me Timoth. I really am proud of you observational skills and your ability to apply your observations to you continued growth," Rasmus placed a hand on Timoth's shoulder.

"I've learned that we communicate in different ways. What we do, ho we do it, how we arrange our physical settings, the books we read, the ar we look at, the things we create. Everything about us communicate something to everyone we encounter. Even if they encounter the things w have created years later, we continue to communicate even to people we wi never meet."

"So, in other words, even though you are just now finishing your theor book, you recognize that none of us is ever finished learning?"

"Well put. Now, give me back my book."

M.C. Escher's *"Waterfall"* (1961)

BIBLIOGRAPHY

Alegria, J., C. Dejean, J.M. Capouillez, & J. Leybaert. 1990. Role Played by the Cued Speech in the identification of written words encountered for the first time by deaf children. *Cued Speech Journal, 4.*

Alegria, J., J. Lechat, & J. Leybaert. 1990. Role du LPC dans L'Identification de Mots chez L'Enfant Sourd: Theorie et donnees preliminaries. *Cued Speech Journal, 4.*

Allsop, L., B. Woll, & J. Brauti. 1995. International sign: The creation of an international Deaf community and sign language. In H. Bos & T. Schermer (eds.), *Sign Language Research 1994 Proceedings of the 4th European Congress on Sign Language Research, Munich, September 1 - 3, 1994.* Hamburg: Signum Press.

Altman, J. 1990. What helps effective communication? Some interpreters' views. *The Interpreter. Newsletter*, 3: 23-32.

Altman, J. 1994. Error analysis in the teaching of simultaneous interpreting: A pilot study. In Lambert, S. & B. Moser-Mercer (eds.), *Bridging the Gap: Empirical Research in Simultaneou Interpretation.* Philadelphia, PA: John Benjamins Publishing Company.

Anderson, B. 1976. Perspectives on the role of the interpreter. In *Translation: Applications and Research.* R. Brislin (ed.), New York, NY: Gardner Press, Inc.

Anderson, B. 1978. Interpreter roles and interpretation situations. In D. Gerver & H.W. Sinaike (eds.), *Language Interpretation and Communication.* New York, NY: Plenum Press.

Anderson, E. 1990. Speaking With Style: The Sociolinguistic Skills of Children. New York, NY Routledge.

Anderson, L. 1994. Simultaneous interpretation: Contextual and translation aspects. In Lambert, S & B. Moser-Mercer (eds.), *Bridging the Gap: Empirical Research in Simultaneou Interpretation.* Philadelphia, PA: John Benjamins Publishing Company.

Anthony, D. 1971. *Seeing Essential English.* Anaheim, CA: Educational Services Division Anaheim Union High School District.

Antia, S. & K. Kreimeyer. 2001. The Role of Interpreters in Inclusive Classrooms. *America Annals of the Deaf,* 146: 355-365.

Aramburo, A. 1989. Sociolinguistic aspects of the Black Deaf community. In C. Lucas (ed.), *Th Sociolinguistics of the Deaf community.* San Diego, CA: Academic Press.

Arjona, E. 1984. Education of translators and interpreters. In M. McIntire (ed.), *Proceedings of th Fourth National Conference of Interpreter Trainers: New Dialogues in Interpreter Educatio.* Silver Spring, MD: RID Publications.

Arjona-Tseng, E. 1994. A psychometric approach to the selection of translation and interpretir students in Taiwan. In Lambert, S. & B. Moser-Mercer (eds.), *Bridging the Gap: Empiric Research in Simultaneous Interpretation.* Philadelphia, PA: John Benjamins Publishing Co.

Atwood, A. 1984. Mental processes in voice interpreting. In P. White & B. Kondrotis (eds. *Proceedings of the 8th National Convention of the Registry of Interpreters for the Deaf: Gold Opportunities in Interpreting.* Siver Spring, MD: RID Publications.

Atwood, A. & D. Gray. 1986. Interpreting: The culture of artful mediation. In M. McIntire (ed. *Proceedings of the 1985 RID Convention: Interpreting: The Art of Cross Cultural Mediatio.* Siver Spring, MD: RID Publications.

Austin, J. 1962. *How To Do Things With Words.* Cambridge, MA: Harvard University Press.

Bahan, B. 1991. ASL literature: Inside the story. In *Deaf Studies: What's Up?* Washington, DC Gallaudet University College for Continuing Education.

Bahan, B., Kegl, J., MacLaughlin, D. and Neidle, C. 1995. *Convergent Evidence for the Structu of Determiner Phrases in American Sign Language.* Paper presented at FLSM VI, Indiar University, Bloomington, IN.

Bailey, J. 1993. Mentoring and Meetings. *RID Views,* 16:10.

Baker, C. 1976. Eye openers in ASL. In *California Linguistics Society Conference Proceeding* San Diego, CA: San Diego State University

Baker, C. 1977. Regulators and turn-taking in American Sign Language Discourse. In L. Friedman (ed.), *On the Other Hand: New Perspectives on American Sign Language*. New York, NY: Academic Press.

Baker, C. 1980. Sentences in American Sign Language. In C. Baker & R. Battison (eds.), *Sign Language and the Deaf Community: Essays in Honor of William C. Stokoe*. Silver Spring, MD: National Association of the Deaf.

Baker, C. & D. Cokely. 1980. American Sign Language: A Teacher's Resource Text on grammar and Culture. Silver Spring, MD: T.J. Publishers.

Baker-Shenk, C. 1985. The facial behavior of Deaf signers: Evidence of a complex language. *American Annals of the Deaf*, 130: 297-304.

Baker-Shenk, C. (ed.), 1990. A Model Curriculum for Teachers of American Sign Language and Teachers of ASL/English Interpreting. Silver Spring, MD: RID Publications.

Baker, M. 1993. *In Other Words*. New York, NY: Routledge.

Bakhtin, M. 1986. *Speech Genres and Other Late Essays*. Austin, TX: University of Texas Press.

Barik, H. 1994. A description of various types of omissions, additions, and errors of translation encountered in simultaneous interpretation. In Lambert, S. & B. Moser-Mercer (eds.), *Bridging the Gap: Empirical Research in Simultaneous Interpretation*. Philadelphia, PA: John Benjamins Publishing Company.

Bennett, A. 1981. Interruptions and the interpretation of conversation. *Discourse Processes* 4:2: 171-88.

Bienvenu, M. & B. Colonomos. 1990. Relay interpreting in the '90's. In Laura Swabey (ed.), Proceedings of the Eighth National Convention of the Conference of Interpreter Trainers, The Challenge of the 90's: New Standards in Interpreter Education. CIT Publications. 69-80.

Blattberg, S., L. Byers, E. Lockwood, & R. Smith. 1995. Sociolinguistic variation in American Sign Language: Phonological variation by age group in fingerspelling. In L. Byers, J. Chaiken, & M. Mueller (eds.), *Communication Forum 1995*. Washington, DC: Gallaudet University School of Communication.

Borden, B. 1996. *The Art of Interpreting*. Plymouth, MI: Hayden-McNeil Publishing.

Bowen, D. & M. Bowen. 1987. The Nuremberg trials (communication through translation). *Readings in Interpretation*. Montclair, NJ: Educator's Pedagogical Institute.

Brasel, B. 1976. The effects of fatigue on the competence of interpreters for the deaf. In H.J. Murphy (ed.), *Selected Readings in the Integration of Deaf Students at C.S.U.N. Centre on Deafness series (#1)*. Northridge, CA: California State University.

Bridges, B. & M. Metzger.1996. *Deaf Tend Your: Non-Manual Signals in ASL*. Silver Spring, MD: Calliope Press.

Brown, P., S. Fischer,. & W. Janis. 1991. Pragmatic and linguistic constraints on message formulation: A cross-linguistic study of English and ASL. *Journal of Speech and Hearing Research,* 34:. 1346-1361.

Brown, P. & S. C. Levinson. 1987. *Politeness: Some Universals in Language Usage*. Cambridge: Cambridge University Press.

Bühler, H. 1987. Conference interpreting: A multichannel communication phenomenon. *Readings in Interpretation*. Montclair, NJ: Educator's Pedagogical Institute.

Burch, D. 2002. Essential education for sign language interpreters in pre-college educational settings. *Journal of Interpretation,* 125-149.

Cartwright, Brenda. 1999. *Encounters with Reality: 1,001 Interpreting Scenarios*. Silver Spring, MD: RID Press.

Cavell, J. & M. Wells. 1986. The interpreter as cross-cultural mediator: How does a student learn to do it? In M. McIntire (ed.), *Proceedings of the 1985 RID Convention: Interpreting: The Art of Cross Cultural Mediation*. Siver Spring, MD: RID Publications.

Cerney, B. 1987. *Numeral Incorporation in British Sign Language*. Unpublished Manuscript. Gallaudet University.

Cerney, B. 1987. *A Reader's Guide to an International Study of Seven Signers.* Unpublished Manuscript. Gallaudet University.

Cerney, B. 1989. *The Deaf Adult Learner.* Unpublished Manuscript. University of Maryland.

Cerney, B. 1993. *The Self-Concept of Deaf Children in Residential and Mainstreamed Environments.* Masters Thesis. University of Maryland.

Cerney, B. 1996. Interpreters as cultural allies. *RID Views*: February.

Cerney, B. 1996. Interpreter working conditions: Sharing the vision. *RID Views*: February.

Cerney, B. 1996. Don't quit, we need you" *RID Views*: March

Cerney, B. 1996. Language acquisition, language teaching, and the interpreter as a model for language input. *RID 1995 National Convention Proceedings.* Silver Spring, MD: RID Publications.

Cerney, B. 2000. Models and paradigms. *RID Views*: March

Cerney, B. 2000. The ten c's of effective target texts. *Journal of Interpretation,* 131-149.

Cerney, B. 2004. Deaf History Notes. Colorado Springs, CO: Hand & Mind Publishing.

Cheng, Y. 1994. Consecutive interpretation: How to use your symbols intelligently. In Richard Seymour & C.C.Liu (eds.), *Translation and Interpreting: Bridging East and West.* Honolulu, HI: University of Hawaii Press.

Chernov, G. 1979. Semantic aspects of psychological research in simultaneous interpretation. *Language and Speech,* 22:3: 277-295.

Chernov, G. 1994. Message redundancy and message anticipation in simultaneous interpretation. In Lambert, S. & B. Moser-Mercer (eds.), *Bridging the Gap: Empirical Research in Simultaneous Interpretation.* Philadelphia, PA: John Benjamins Publishing Company.

Chernov, G. 1996. Taking care of the sense in simultaneous interpreting. In Dollerup, Cay & Vibeke Appel (eds.), Teaching Translation and Interpreting 3: New Horizons. Papers from the Third Language International Conference, Elsinore, Denmark 9-11 June 1995. Philadelphia, PA: John Benjamins Publishing Company.

Clark, T. 1993. Views from a mentee. *RID Views,* 16:10.

Cokely, D. 2001. Interpreting culturally rich realities: Research implications for successful interpretation. *Journal of Interpretation,* 1-45.

Cokely, D. 2000. Exploring ethics: A case for revising the code of ethics. *Journal of Interpretation,* 131-149.

Cokely, D. 1992. *Interpretation: A Sociolinguistic Model.* Burtonsville, MD: Linstok Press.

Cokely, D. 1986. The effects of lag time in interpreter errors. *Sign Language Studies,* 53: 341-376.

Cokely, D. 1984a. Towards a Sociolinguistic Model of the Interpreting Process: Focus on ASL and English. Doctoral Dissertation. Washington, DC: Georgetown University.

Cokely, D. 1984b. Foreigner talk and learner's grammar. The Reflector: A Journal for Sign Language Teachers and Interpreters, 8: 23-30.

Cokely, D. 1983. Metanotive qualities: How accurately are they conveyed by interpreters? *The Reflector: A Journal for Sign Language Teachers and Interpreters,* 5: 16-21.

Cokely, D. 1982. The interpreted medical interview: It loses something in the translation. *The Reflector: A Journal for Sign Language Teachers and Interpreters,* 3: 5-10.

Colonomos, B. 1987. Various Handouts.

Colonomos, B. 1992. *Processes in Interpreting and Making Them Work for You.* Riverdale, MD: The Bicultural Center.

Commission on Education of the Deaf. 1988. *Toward equality: education of the deaf.* Washington, DC: US Government Printing Office.

Coppock, P. 1991. Interpreting discourse: Signs for the future? In J. Plant-Moeller (ed.), *Expanding Horizons: Proceedings of the Twelfth National Convention of the Registry of Interpreters for the Deaf.* Silver Spring, MD: RID Publications.

Corina, D. & J. Vaid. 1994. Lateralization for shadowing words versus signs: A study of ASL-English interpreters. In Lambert, S. & B. Moser-Mercer (eds.), *Bridging the Gap: Empirica*

Research in Simultaneous Interpretation. Philadelphia, PA: John Benjamins Publishing Company.

Cornett, R. & M. Daisey. 1992. *The Cued Speech Resource Book For Parents of Deaf Children*. Raleigh, NC: National Cued Speech Association.

Coulter, G. 1990. Emphatic stress in ASL. In S. D. Fischer & P. Siple (eds.), *Theoretical Issues in Sign Language Research, Volume One*. Chicago, Il: University of Chicago Press.

Crystal, D. 1987. *The Cambridge Encyclopedia of Language*. Cambridge: Cambridge University Press.

Cummins, J. 1979. Linguistic interdependence and the educational development of bilingual children. *Review of Education Research*, 49:222-51.

Cummins, J. 1984. Bilingualism and Special Education: Issues in Assessment and Pedagogy. Clevedon, U.K.: Multilingual Matters.

Daro, V. 1990. Speaking speed during simultaneous interpretation: A discussion on its neuropsychological aspects and possible contributions to teaching. In L. Gran & C. Taylor (eds.), *Aspects of Applied and Experimental Research on Conference Interpretation*. Udine: Campanotto.

Daro, V. 1994. Non-linguistic factors influencing simultaneous interpretation. In Lambert, S. & B. Moser-Mercer (eds.), *Bridging the Gap: Empirical Research in Simultaneous Interpretation*. Philadelphia, PA: John Benjamins Publishing Company.

Davis, J. 2000. Translation techniques in interpreter education. In C. Roy (ed.), *Innovative Practices for Teaching Sign Language Interpreters*. Washington, DC: Gallaudet University Press.

Davis, J. 1989. Distinguishing language contact phenomena in ASL interpretation. In C. Lucas (ed.), *The Sociolinguistics of the Deaf Community*. San Diego, CA: Academic Press.

Dawn Sign Press. 1998. Numbering in American Sign Language: Number Signs for Everyone. San Diego, CA: Dawn Sign Press.

DeCamp, D. 1971. Introduction: The study of pidgin and creole languages. In D. Hymes (ed.), *Pidginization and Creolization of Languages*. New York, NY: Cambridge University Press.

DeGroot, A. 1997. The cognitive study of translation and interpretation. In J. Danks, G. Shreve, S. Fountain, & M. McBeath (eds.), *Cognitive Processes in Translation and Interpreting*. Thousand Oaks, CA: SAGE Publications, Inc.

Department of Linguistics. 1991. *Language Files, Fifth Edition*. Columbus, OH: Ohio State University Press.

Dillinger, M. 1994. Comprehension during interpreting: What do interpreters know that bilinguals don't. In Lambert, S. & B. Moser-Mercer (eds.), *Bridging the Gap: Empirical Research in Simultaneous Interpretation*. Philadelphia, PA: John Benjamins Publishing Company.

Dodds, J. M. 1989. Linguistic theory construction as a premise to a methodology of teaching interpretation. In L. Gran & J. Dodds (eds.), *The Theoretical and Practical Aspects of Teaching Conference Interpretation*. Udine: Campanotto.

Duncan, S. 1972. Some signals and rules for taking speaking turns in conversations. *Journal of Personality and Social Psychology*, 23:2. 283-292.

Duncan, S. 1974. On the structure of speaker-auditor interaction during speaking turns. *Language in Society*, 2: 161-180.

Ervin-Tripp, S. 1968. An analysis of the interaction of language, topic, and listener. In J. Fishman (ed.), *Readings in the Sociology of Language*. New York, NY: Mouton Publishers.

Fant, L. 1994. *The American Sign Language Phrase Book*. Chicago, IL: Contemporary Books.

Fant, L. 1990. Silver Threads: A Personal Look at the First Twenty-five Years of the Registry of Interpreters for the Deaf. Silver Spring, MD: RID Publications.

Flanagan, R., T. Garfinkle & S. Woods. 1995. Foreigner talk. In L. Byers, J. Chaiken, & M. Mueller (eds.), *Communication Forum 1995*. Washington, DC: Gallaudet University School of Communication.

Fleetwood, E. & M. Metzger. 1990. *Cued Speech Transliteration: Theory and Application.* Silver Spring, MD: Caliope Press.

Fleetwood, E. & M. Metzger. 1998. Cued Language Structure: An Analysis of Cued American English Based on Linguistic Principles. Silver Spring, MD: Caliope Press.

Frishberg, N. 1990. *Interpreting: An Introduction.* Silver Spring, MD: RID Publications.

Ferguson, C. 1964. Diglossia. In D. Hymes (eds.), *Language in Culture and Society.* New York: Harper and Row.

Ferguson, C. 1977. Baby talk as a simplified register. In C. Snow & C. Ferguson (eds.), *Talking to Children.* Cambridge: Cambridge University Press.

Ferguson, C. & C. DeBose. 1977. Simplified registers, broken language, and pidginization. In A. Valdman (ed.), *Pidgin and Creole Linguistics.* Bloomington, IN: Indiana University Press.

Gardner, M. 1972. *Codes, Ciphers and Secret Writing.* New York, NY: Pocket Books.

Gazdar, G. 1979. *Pragmatics.* New York, NY: Academic Press.

Gee, J. & J. Kegl. 1983. Narrative/story structure, pausing, and American Sign Language. *Discourse Processes,* 6: 243-258.

Gentile, A., U. Ozolins & M. Vasilakakos. 1996. *Liaison Interpreting: A Handbook.* Melbourne University Press.

Gerver, D. 1974. Simultaneous listening and speaking and retention of prose. *Quarterly Journal of Experimental Psychology* 26: 337-342.

Gerver, D. 1975. A psychological approach to simultaneous interpretation. *Meta* 20,2: 119-128.

Gerver, D. 1976. Empirical studies of simultaneous interpretation: A review and a model. In R. Brislin (ed.), *Translation: Applications and Research.* New York, NY: Gardner Press, Inc.

Gile, D. 1990. Scientific research vs. personal theories in the investigation of interpretation. In L. Gran & C. Taylor (eds.), *Aspects of Applied and Experimental Research on Conference Interpretation.* Udine: Campanotto.

Gile, D. 1994a. Methodological aspects of interpretation and translation research. In Lambert, S. & B. Moser-Mercer (eds.), *Bridging the Gap: Empirical Research in Simultaneous Interpretation.* Philadelphia, PA: John Benjamins Publishing Company.

Gile, D. 1994b. The process-oriented approach in translation training. In Dollerup, Cay & Annette Lindegaard (eds.), Teaching Translation and Interpreting 2: Insights, Aims, Visions. Papers from the Second Language International Conference, Elsinore, Denmark 4-6 June 1993. Philadelphia. PA: John Benjamins Publishing Company. p107-112.

Gile, D. 1995. *Basic Concepts and Models for Interpreter and Translator Training.* Philadelphia PA: John Benjamins Publishing Company.

Gile, D. 1997. Conference interpreting as a cognitive management problem. In J. Danks, G. Shreve, S. Fountain, & M. Mcbeath (eds.), *Cognitive Processes in Translation and Interpreting* Thousand Oaks, CA: SAGE Publications, Inc.

Gish, S. 1987. "I understood all the words, but I missed the point": A goal-to-detail / detail-to-goal strategy for text analysis. In M. L. McIntire (eds.), *New Directions in Interpreter Education. Curriculum & Instruction: Proceedings of the Sixth National Convention of the Conference of Interpreter Trainers.* Silver Spring, MD: RID Publications.

Goodman, D. 1993. The Complete HyperCard 2.2 Handbook: Fourth Edition. New York, NY Random House.

Green, A., J. Vaid, N. Schweda-Nicholson, N. White, & R. Steiner. 1994. Lateralization for shadowing vs. interpretation: A comparison of interpreters with bilingual and monolingual controls. In Lambert, S. & B. Moser-Mercer (eds.), *Bridging the Gap: Empirical Research in Simultaneous Interpretation.* Philadelphia, PA: John Benjamins Publishing Company.

Gregory, M. & S. Carroll. 1978. *Language and Situation: Language Varieties and Their Social Contexts.* Boston, MA: Routledge & Keegan Paul.

Grice, H. 1975. Logic and conversation. In Cole, P. & J. Morgan (eds.), *Syntax and Semantics Volume 3.* New York: Academic Press. pp. 41-58.

Grosjean, F. 1982. *Life With Two Languages: An Introduction to Bilingualism*. Cambridge, MA: Harvard University Press.

Guggenheim, L. 1993. Ethnic variation in ASL: The signing of African Americans and how it is influenced by conversational topic. In E. Winston (ed.), *Communication Forum 1993*. Washington, DC: Gallaudet University School of Communication.

Gumperz, J. J. 1971. *Language in Social Groups*. A.S. Dil, (ed.). Stanford, CA: Stanford University Press.

Gumperz, J. J. 1982. *Discourse Strategies*. Cambridge: Cambridge University Press.

Haas, Christopher. 1999. Sign language interpreters: simultaneous interpreting and memory. *Journal of Interpretation*, 21-36.

Haas, C., E. Fleetwood & M. Ernest. 1995. An analysis of ASL variation within Deafblind interaction: Question forms, backchanneling, and turn-taking. In L. Byers, J. Chaiken, & M. Mueller (eds.), *Communication Forum 1995*. Washington, DC: Gallaudet University School of Communication.

Halliday, M. 1968. The users and uses of language. In J. Fishman (ed.), *Readings in the Sociology of Language*. New York, NY: Mouton Publishers.

Halliday, M. 1978. Language as Social Semiotic: The Social Interpretation of Language and Meaning. Baltimore, MD: University Park Press.

Halliday, M. & R. Hasan. 1976. *Cohesion in English*. New York, NY: Longman.

Harvey, M. 2001. Vicarious emotional trauma of interpreters: A clinical psychologist's perspective. *Journal of Interpretation*, 85-98.

Hatch, E. 1992. *Discourse and Language Education*. Cambridge: Cambridge University Press.

Hatim, B. & I. Mason. 1990. *Discourse and the Translator*. New York, NY: Longman.

Hayes, L. 1993. Mentoring: Formalizing a unique part of RID history. *RID Views*, 16:10.

Hervey, S. 1992. Registering registers. *Lingua*, 86: 189-206.

Hoemann, H. W. 1975. The transparency of meaning of sign language gestures. *Sign Language Studies*, 7: 151-161.

Hoffmeister, R. J. & C. Shettle. 1983. Adaptations in communication made by deaf signers to different audience types. *Discourse Processes*, 6: 259-274.

Ioza, J. 1999. Saving face: The interpreter and politeness. *Journal of Interpretation:* 39-68.

Ioza, J. 1987. Pulling it all together: Activity ideas for comparative language study - ASL and English. In M. L. McIntire (ed.), *New Directions in Interpreter Education: Curriculum & Instruction: Proceedings of the Sixth National Convention of the Conference of Interpreter Trainers*. Silver Spring, MD: RID Publications.

Huber, M. 1993. Birth of a mentor at the National Center on Deafness. *RID Views*, 16:10.

Humphrey, Janice. 1999. Decisions? Decisions!: A Practical Guide for Sign Language Professionals. Amarillo, TX: H & H Publishers.

Hurwitz, T. 1980. Interpreter's Effectiveness in Reverse Interpreting: Pidgin Signed English and American Sign Language. Doctoral Dissertation. Rochester, NY: University of Rochester.

Hymes, D. 1971. Preface. In D. Hymes (ed.), *Pidginization and Creolization of Languages*. New York, NY: Cambridge University Press.

Hymes, D. 1974. Models of interaction and social life. In J. Gumperz & D. Hymes (eds.), *Directions in Sociolinguistics: Ethnography of Communication*. New York, NY: Holt, Rhinehart and Winston, Inc.

Ilic, I. 1990. Cerebral lateralization for linguistic functions in professional interpreters. In L. Gran & C. Taylor (eds.), *Aspects of Applied and Experimental Research on Conference Interpretation*. Udine: Campanotto.

Ingram, R. 2000. Foreword. In C. Roy (ed.), *Innovative Practices for Teaching Sign Language Interpreters*. Washington, DC: Gallaudet University Press.

Ingram, R. 1988. Interpreters' recognition of structure & meaning. *Sign Language Studies*, 58: 21-36.

270   The Interpreting Handbook (part 1)

Ingram, R. 1985. Simultaneous interpretation of sign languages: semiotic and psycholinguistic perspectives. *Multilingua,* 4:2: 91-102.

Ingram, R. 1980. *Linguistic and Semiotic Process of Interpretation.* Unpublished training materials. American Sign Language Associates.

Ingram, R. 1978. Sign language interpretation and general theories of language, interpretation and communication. In D. Gerver & H.W. Sinaiko (eds.), *Language Interpretation and Communication.* New York, NY: Plenum Press.

Ingram, R. 1974. A communication model of the interpreting process. *Journal of the Rehabilitation of the Deaf,* 7:3, 3-9.

Isham, W. 1986. The role of message analysis in interpretation. In M. McIntire (ed.), *Proceedings of the 1985 RID Convention: Interpreting: The Art of Cross Cultural Mediation.* Siver Spring, MD: RID Publications.

Isham, W. 1994. Memory for sentence form after simultaneous interpretation: Evidence both for and against deverbalization. In Lambert, S. & B. Moser-Mercer (eds.), *Bridging the Gap: Empirical Research in Simultaneous Interpretation.* Philadelphia, PA: John Benjamins Publishing Company.

Isham, W. & Harlan Lane. 1994. A common conceptual code in bilinguals: evidence from simultaneous interpretation. *Sign Language Studies,* 85: 291-316.

Jacobs, R. 1977. The efficiency of interpreted input for processing lecture information by deaf college students. *Journal of Rehabilitation of the Deaf,* 11: 10-15.

Jacobs, R. 1996. Just how hard is it to learn ASL? The case for ASL as a truly foreign language. In Ceil Lucas (ed.), *Multicultural Aspects of Sociolinguistics in Deaf Communities.* Washington, DC: Gallaudet University Press.

Johnson, K. 1991. Miscommunication in interpreted classroom interaction. *Sign Language Studies,* 70: 1-34.

Johnson, R., S. Liddell & C. Erting. 1989. *Unlocking the Curriculum: Principles for Achieving Access in Deaf Education.* Gallaudet Research Institute Working Paper 89-3. Washington, DC: Gallaudet University.

Joos, M. 1961. *The Five Clocks.* New York, NY: Harcourt, Brace & World, Inc.

Joos, M. 1968. The isolation of styles. In J. Fishman (ed.), *Readings in the Sociology of Language* New York, NY: Mouton Publishers.

Jumplet, R. 1987. The conference interpreter's working environment under the new ISO and IEC standards. Readings in Interpretation. Montclair, NJ: Educator's Pedagogical Institute.

Kalina, S. 1992. Discourse processing and interpreting strategies - an approach to the teaching of interpreting. In Dollerup, Cay & Anne Loddegaard (eds.), *Teaching Translation and Interpreting: Training, Talent, and Experience. Papers from the First Language Internationa Conference, Elsinore, Denmark 31 May - 2 June 1991.* Philadelphia, PA: John Benjamin. Publishing Company. 251-257.

Kalina, S. 1992. Discourse processing and interpreting strategies - an approach to the teaching of interpreting. In Dollerup, Cay & Annette Lindegaard (eds.), *Teaching Translation and Interpreting 2: Insights, Aims, Visions. Papers from the Second Language Internationa Conference, Elsinore, Denmark 4-6 June 1993.* Philadelphia, PA: John Benjamins Publishing Company. p225-232.

Kannapell, B. 1985. Language choice reflects identity choice: A sociolinguistic study of dea college students. Doctoral Dissertation. Washington, DC: Georgetown University.

Kelly, A. B.1995. Fingerspelling interaction: A set of deaf parents and their deaf daughter. In C Lucas (ed.), *Sociolinguistics of Deaf Communities.* Washington, DC: Gallaudet University Press. 62-73.

Kempson, R. 1988. Grammar and conversational principles. In F. J. Newmeyer (ed.), *Linguistics The Cambridge Survey II Linguistic Theory: Extension and Implications.* Cambridge: Cambridg University Press.

Kelly, A. B.1995. Fingerspelling interaction: A set of deaf parents and their deaf daughter. In C. Lucas (ed.), *Sociolinguistics of Deaf Communities*. Washington, DC: Gallaudet University. Press. 62-73.

Kelly, J. 2001. *Transliteration: Show Me The English*. Alexandria, VA: RID Press.

Kirchoff, H. 1976. Das Dreiliederge Zweisprachige Kommunicationssytem Dometschen. *Le Language et l'Homme*, 31: 21-27.

Klatt, D. 1980. Speech perception: a model of acoustic-phonetic analysis and lexical access. In R. Cole (ed.) *Perception and production of fluent speech*. Hillsdale, N.J.: Lawrence Erlbaum Associates.

Klima, E., & U. Bellugi. 1979. *The Signs of Language*. Cambridge, MA: Harvard University Press.

Klonowicz, T. 1994. Putting one's heart into simultaneous interpretation. In Lambert, S. & B. Moser-Mercer (eds.), *Bridging the Gap: Empirical Research in Simultaneous Interpretation*. Philadelphia, PA: John Benjamins Publishing Company.

Kondo, M. 1990. What conference interpreters should not be expected to do. *The Interpreters Newsletter*, 3: 59-65.

Kopczynski, A. 1994. Quality in conference interpreting: Some pragmatic problems. In Lambert, S. & B. Moser-Mercer (eds.), *Bridging the Gap: Empirical Research in Simultaneous Interpretation*. Philadelphia, PA: John Benjamins Publishing Company.

Kurz, I. 1992. 'Shadowing' exercises in interpreter training. In Dollerup, C. & A. Loddegaard (eds.), Teaching Translation and Interpreting: Training, Talent, and Experience. Papers from the First Language International Conference, Elsinore, Denmark 31 May - 2 June 1991. Philadelphia, PA: John Benjamins Publishing Company. 245-250.

Lambert, S. 1983. *Recall & Recognition Among Conference Interpreters*. Unpublished doctoral dissertation. University of Stirling.

Lane, H. 1984. *When the Mind Hears: A History of the Deaf*. New York, NY: Random House.

Larson, M. 1984. Meaning-based Translation: A Guide to Cross-language Equivalence. Lanham, MD: University Press of America.

LaSasso, C., K. Crain & J. Leybaert. 2003. Rhyme generation in deaf students: The effect of exposure to cued speech. *Journal of Deaf Studies & Deaf Education, 8(3)*, pp. 250-270.

Lechat, J. & J. Leybaert. 2001. Phonological effects in memory for serial order of cued speech. *Journal of Speech Language and Hearing Research, Vol. 44, #5*, pp. 949-963.

Leybaert, J. & B. Charlier. 1996. Visual speech in the head: The effect of cued speech on rhyming, remembering, and spelling. *Journal of Deaf Studies and Deaf Education, Vol. 1, #4*, pp. 234-248.

Liddell, S. 1977. An investigation into the syntactic structure of American Sign Language. University of California San Diego dissertation.

Liddell, S. 1980. *American Sign Language Syntax*. New York, NY: Mouton Publishers.

Liddell, S. & R. Johnson. 1989. American Sign Language: The Phonological Base. *Sign Language Studies*, 64: 195-277.

Livingston, S., B. Singer, & T. Abrahamson. 1994. Effectiveness compared: ASL interpretation vs. transliteration. *Sign Language Studies*, 82: 1-54.

Llewellyn-Jones, P. 1981a. Simultaneous interpreting. In B. Woll, J. Kyle & M. Deuchar (eds.), *Perspectives on British Sign Language and Deafness*. London: Croom Helm.

Llewellyn-Jones, P. 1981b. *Target Language Styles And Source Language Processing In Conference Sign Language Interpreting*. Presented at the Third International Symposium on Interpretation of Sign Languages. Bristol, England.

Lucas, C. 1995a. Sociolinguistic variation in ASL: The case of DEAF. In C. Lucas (ed.), *Sociolinguistics in Deaf Communities*. Washington, DC: Gallaudet University Press.

Lucas, C. 1995b. Sociolinguistic variation in ASL: The case of DEAF. In H. Bos & T. Schermer (eds.), Sign Language Research 1994: Proceedings of the 4th European Congress on Sign Language Research, Munich, September 1 - 3, 1994. Hamburg: Signum Press.

Lucas, C. & C. Valli. 1992. *Language Contact in the American Deaf Community*. San Diego, CA: Academic Press.

Lucas with Aramburo, Cerney, Jacobowitz, Levine, Patschke, Riley, Ward. 1987. Bilingualism & Deafness: An annotated bibliography. *Sign Language Studies*. 55:97-14.

Luciano, J. 2001.Revisiting Patterson's paradigm: Gaze behaviors in Deaf communication. *American Annals of the Deaf,* 146: 39-44.

Luftig, R & L. Lloyd. 1981. Manual sign translucency and referential concreteness in the learning of signs. *Sign Language Studies,* 30: 49-60.

Lyons, J. 1977. *Semantics:1*. Cambridge: Cambridge University Press.

MacWhinney, B. 1997. Simultaneous interpretation and the competition model. In J. Danks, G. Shreve, S. Fountain, & M. McBeath (eds.), *Cognitive Processes in Translation and Interpreting*. Thousand Oaks, CA: SAGE Publications, Inc.

Malloy, C. & J. Doner. 1995. Variation in ASL discourse: Gender differences in the use of cohesive devices. In L. Byers, J. Chaiken, & M. Mueller (eds.), *Communication Forum 1995* Washington, DC: Gallaudet University School of Communication.

Mansfield, D. 1993. Gender differences in ASL: A sociolinguistic study of sign choices by Deaf native signers. In E. Winston (ed.), *Communication Forum 1993*. Washington, DC: Gallaude University School of Communication.

Martinez, L. 1993. Eye-gaze as an element in Filipino Sign Language discourse. In E. Winston (ed.), *Communication Forum 1993*. Washington, DC: Gallaudet University School o' Communication.

Martinez, L. 1995. Turn-taking and eye gaze in sign conversations between Deaf Filipinos. In C Lucas (ed.), *Sociolinguistics in Deaf Communities*. Washington, DC: Gallaudet University Press

Massaro, D. 1975. *Relay Interpretation: An Exploratory Study*. Unpublished masters thesis University of London.

Matthiessen, C. 1992. Interpreting the textual metafunction. In M. Davies & L. Ravelli, ed: *Advances in Systemic Linguistics: Recent Theory and Practice*. London: Pinter Publishers.

Mayberry, R. & S. Fischer. 1989. Looking through phonological shape to lexical meaning: The bottleneck of non-native sign language processing. *Memory & Cognition,* 17 (6): 740-754.

McIntire, M. 1990. The work and education of sign language interpreters. In. S. Prillwitz & ' Vollhaber (eds.), Sign Language Research and Application: Proceedings of the Internationa Congress on Sign Language Research and Application, March 23-25, 1990 in Hambur; Hamburg: Signum Press.

Mellen, D. 1984. Selection and sequencing of texts for translation training. Conference c Interpreter Trainers Fifth National Convention: New Dimensions in Interpreter Education: Tas Analysis - Theory and Application. Silver Spring, MD: RID Publications.

Members of C.I.T. 1984. Task analysis of interpretation and response. Conference of Interpret Trainers Fifth National Convention: New Dimensions in Interpreter Education: Task Analysis Theory and Application. Silver Spring, MD: RID Publications.

Members of C.I.T. 1984. Task analysis of transliteration and response. Conference of Interpret Trainers Fifth National Convention: New Dimensions in Interpreter Education: Task Analysis Theory and Application. Silver Spring, MD: RID Publications.

Metzger, M. 2000. Interactive role-plays as a teaching strategy. In C. Roy (ed.), *Innovati* *Practices for Teaching Sign Language Interpreters*. Washington, DC: Gallaudet Universi Press.

Metzger, M. 1995a. Constructed dialogue and constructed action in American Sign Language. C. Lucas (ed.), *Sociolinguistics in Deaf Communities*. Washington, DC: Gallaudet Universi Press.

Metzger, M. 1995b. The Paradox of Neutrality: A Comparison of Interpreters' Goals with t Reality of Interactive Discourse. Doctoral Dissertation, Georgetown University, Washingto DC.

Metzger, M. 1993. Pronoun variation in formal and informal ASL discourse. In E. Winston (ed.), *Communication Forum 1993*. Washington, DC: Gallaudet University School of Communication.

Miller, G. 1956. The Magical Number Seven, Plus or Minus Two: Some Limits on Our Capacity for Processing Information. *The Psychological Review*, 63: 81-97.

Miller, K & M. Vernon. 2002. Qualifications of sign language interpreters in the criminal justice system. *Journal of Interpretation*, 111-124.

Miller, K. 2001. Access to sign language interpreters in the criminal justice system. *American Annals of the Deaf*, 146: 328-330.

Mills, C. 1984. Factors influencing manual sign learning in hearing adults. *Sign Language Studies*, 44: 261-278.

Mindess, A. 1999. Reading between the signs: A practical approach to cultural adjustments. *RID 1999 National Convention Proceedings*. Silver Spring, MD: RID Publications.

Moody, B. 2002. International sign: A practitioner's Perspective. *Journal of Interpretation*, 1-47.

Moores, D., Cerney, B., Garcia, M. 1991. School placement and least restrictive environment. In D. Moores, K. Meadow-Orlans (Eds.), *Research in Education and Developmental Aspects of Deafness*. Washington, DC: Gallaudet University Press.

Moser, B. 1978. Simultaneous interpretation: A hypothetical model and its practical application. In D. Gerver & H.W. Sinaiko (eds.), *Language Interpretation and Communication*. New York, NY: Plenum Press.

Moser-Mercer, B. 1983. Defining aptitude for simultaneous interpretation. *Proceedings of the 4th CIT Conventions*. Silver Spring, MD: RID Publications.

Moser-Mercer, B. 1994. Aptitude testing for conference interpreting: Why, when and how. In Lambert, S. & B. Moser-Mercer (eds.), *Bridging the Gap: Empirical Research in Simultaneous Interpretation*. Philadelphia, PA: John Benjamins Publishing Company.

Moser-Mercer, B. 1997. Beyond curiosity: Can interpreting research meet the challenge? In J. Danks, G. Shreve, S. Fountain, & M. McBeath (eds.), *Cognitive Processes in Translation and Interpreting*. Thousand Oaks, CA: SAGE Publications, Inc.

Napier, J. 2002. Linguistic coping strategies of interpreters: An exploration. *Journal of Interpretation*, 93-110.

Neidle, C., D. MacLaughlin, B. Bahan, R.G. Lee, and J. Kegl. 1997. *The SignStream™ Project. Report No. 5, American Sign Language Linguistic Research Project*. Boston, MA: Boston University.

Neidle, C., J. Kegl, B. Bahan, D. MacLaughlin & R. Lee. 1996. *Non-Manual Grammatical Marking As Evidence For Hierarchical Relations In American Sign Language*. Paper presented at the Fifth International Conference on Theoretical Issues in Sign Language Research. September 19-22. Montreal.

Newmark, P. 1981. *Approaches to Translation*. Oxford: Pergamon.

Nida, E. 1953. Selective listening. *Language Learning IV*. 3-4: 92-101.

Nida, E. 1964. Toward a Science of Translating with Special Reference to Principles and Procedures Involved in Bible Translating. Leiden: E. J. Brill.

Nishimura, J. 1993. Addressing professional development and staffing: Sign Language Associates' mentorship program. *RID Views*, 16:10.

O'Brien, S. & C. Steffen. 1996. Tactile ASL: ASL as used by Deafblind persons. In L. Byers & M. Rose (eds.), *Communication Forum 1996*. Washington, DC: Gallaudet University School of Communication.

O'Malley, J. & A. Chamot. 1990. *Learning strategies in second language acquisition*. Cambridge, England: Cambridge University Press.

Ochs, E., B. Schieffelin, & M. Platt 1979. Propositions across utterances and speakers. In E. Ochs & B. B. Schieffelin (eds.), *Developmental Pragmatics*. San Diego, CA: Academic Press.

Oléron, P. & H. Nanpon. 1965. Research on simultaneous interpretation. *Journal of Psychology and Pathology*, 62: 73-94.

Omaggio, A. 1986. *Teaching Language in Context: Proficiency-Oriented Instruction*. Boston, MA: Heinle & Heinle Publishers, Inc.

Padden, C. 1988. Interaction of Morphology and Syntax in American Sign Language. New York, NY: Garland Publishing.

Padden, C., & T. Humphries. 1988. *Deaf in America: Voices from a Culture*. Cambridge, MA: Harvard University Press.

Paneth, E. 1957. An Investigation into Conference Interpreting (with special Reference to the Training of Interpreters). Unpublished MA thesis, University of London.

Parsons, H. 1978. Human factors approach to simultaneous interpretation. In D. Gerver & H. Sinaiko (eds.), *Language Interpretation And Communication*. New York, NY: Plenum Press.

Patrie, C. 2000. Cognitive Processing Skills in English: Teacher's Guide. San Diego, CA: Dawn Sign Press.

Patrie, C. 2000. *English Skills Development: Teacher's Guide*. San Diego, CA: Dawn Sign Press.

Patrie, C. 2001. *Translating from English: Teacher's Guide*. San Diego, CA: Dawn Sign Press.

Peper, E. & K. Gibney. 1999. Psychophysiological basis for discomfort during sign language interpreting. *Journal of Interpretation*, 11-18.

Peterson, R. 2000. Metacognition and recall protocols in the interpreting classroom. In C. Roy (ed.), *Innovative Practices for Teaching Sign Language Interpreters*. Washington, DC: Gallaudet University Press.

Pollitt, K. 2000. Critical linguistics and cultural awareness: Essential tools in the interpreter's kit bag. In C. Roy (ed.), *Innovative Practices for Teaching Sign Language Interpreters*. Washington DC: Gallaudet University Press.

Poyatos, F. 1997. The reality of multichannel verbal-nonverbal communication in simultaneous and consecutive interpretation. In F. Poyatos (ed.), *Nonverbal Communication and Translation: New Perspectives and Challenges in Literature, Interpretation and the Media*. Philadelphia, PA: John Benjamins Publishing Co.

Preston, C. 1993. Mentorship at the National Center on Deafness. *RID Views*, 16:10.

Prince, E. 1988. Discourse analysis: A part of the study of linguistic competence. In F. J Newmeyer (ed.), *Linguistics: The Cambridge Survey II Linguistic Theory: Extension and Implications*. Cambridge: Cambridge University Press.

Quintos-Pozos, D. 2002. Interpreting for foreign language courses: The case of Spanish. *Journal of Interpretation*, 93-110.

Ramler, S. 1988. Origins and challenges of simultaneous interpretation: The Nuremberg trial experience. In D. Hammond (ed.), *Proceedings of the 29th Annual Conference of the American Translators Association*. Medford, NJ: Learned Information, Inc.

Reilly, J., M. McIntire, & H. Seago. 1992. Affective prosody in American Sign Language. *Sign Language Studies*, 75: 113-128.

Ressler, Carolyn. 1999. Comparative analysis of a direct interpretation and an intermediary interpretation in American Sign Language. *Journal of Interpretation*, 71-102.

Roberts, R. 1987. Spoken language interpreting vs. sign language interpreting. In D. Hammond (ed.), *Proceedings of the 28th Annual Conference of the American Translators Association*. Medford, NJ: Learned Information, Inc.

Rodriguez, E & A. Guerrero. 2002. An international perspective: What are ethics for sign language interpreters. *Journal of Interpretation*, 49-61.

Richards J. & T. Rodgers. 1986. *Approaches and Methods in Language Teaching: A Description and Analysis*. New York, NY: Cambridge University Press.

Richards J. & T. Rodgers. 2001. *Approaches and Methods in Language Teaching: Second Edition* New York, NY: Cambridge University Press.

Roy, C. 2000. Training interpreters - past, present, and future. In C. Roy (ed.), *Innovative Practices for Teaching Sign Language Interpreters*. Washington, DC: Gallaudet University Press.

Roy, Cynthia. 2000. *Interpreting as a Discourse Process*. New York, NY: Oxford University Press.

Roy, C. 1992. A sociolinguistic analysis of the interpreter's role in simultaneous talk in face-to-face interpreted dialogue. *Sign Language Studies*, 74: 21-61.

Roy, C. 1989a. Features of discourse in an American Sign Language Lecture. In C. Lucas (ed.), *The Sociolinguistics of the Deaf Community*. San Diego, CA: Academic Press.

Roy, C. 1989b. *A Sociolinguistic Analysis of the Interpreter's Role in the Turn Exchanges of an Interpreted Event*. Doctoral Dissertation, Georgetown University, Washington, DC. University Microfilms, Inc. DA064793.

Roy, C. 1987. Evaluating performance: An interpreted lecture. In M. McIntire (ed.), New Directions in Interpreter Education: Curriculum & Instruction: Proceedings of the Sixth National Convention of the Conference of Interpreter Trainers. Silver Spring, MD: RID Publications.

Rudser, S. & M. Strong. 1986. An examination of some personal characteristics & abilities of sign language interpreters. *Sign Language Studies*, 53: 315-331.

Rudser, S. 1986. Linguistic analysis of changes in interpreters' language 1973-1985. *Sign Language Studies*, 53: 332-340.

Russell, Debra. 2002. Interpreting in Legal Contexts: Consecutive and Simultaneous Interpretation. Burtonsville, MD: Linstok Press.

Sauerburger, D. 1993. Independence Without Sight or Sound: Suggestions for Practitioners Working with Deaf-Blind Adults. New York, NY: American Foundation for the Blind.

Schiffrin, D. 1987. *Discourse Markers*. Cambridge: Cambridge University Press.

Schjoldager, A. 1996. Assessment of simultaneous interpreting. In Dollerup, C. & V. Appel (eds.), Teaching Translation and Interpreting 3: New Horizons. Papers from the Third Language International Conference, Elsinore, Denmark 9-11 June 1995. Philadelphia, PA: John Benjamins.

Schwartz, S. 1996. Choices in Deafness: A Parent's Guide to Communication Options. Washington, DC: Gallaudet Press.

Searle, J. 1969. *Speech Acts: An Essay in the Philosophy of Language*. Cambridge: Cambridge University Press.

Seleskovitch, D. 1978. *Interpreting for International Conferences*. Washington, DC: Pen and Booth.

Seleskovitch, D. 1987. Take care of the sense and the sounds will take care of themselves (Lewis Carroll) or Why interpreting is not tantamount to translating languages. *Readings in Interpretation*. Montclair, NJ: Educator's Pedagogical Institute.

Seleskovitch, D. & M. Lederer. 1995. *A Systematic Approach to Teaching Interpretation*. Translation by Jacolyn Harmer. Silver Spring, MD: Registry of Interpreters for the Deaf.

Senter, E. 1993. Mentoring: Next to ideal. *RID Views*, 16:10.

Shapiro, E. 1993. Socioeconomic variation in American Sign Language. In E. Winston (ed.), *Communication Forum 1993*. Washington, DC: Gallaudet University School of Communication.

Shaw, R. 1987. Determining register in sign-to-English interpreting. *Sign Language Studies*, 57: 295-322.

Shlesinger, M. 1994. Intonation in the production and perception of simultaneous interpretation. In Lambert, S. & B. Moser-Mercer (eds.), *Bridging the Gap: Empirical Research in Simultaneous Interpretation*. Philadelphia, PA: John Benjamins Publishing Company.

Shreve, G. & B. Diamond. 1997. Cognitive processes in translation and interpreting: Critical issues. In J. Danks, G. Shreve, S. Fountain, & M. McBeath (eds.), *Cognitive Processes in Translation and Interpreting*. Thousand Oaks, CA: SAGE Publications, Inc.

Shuy, R. 1987. A sociolinguistic view of interpreter education. In M. McIntire (ed.), New Directions in Interpreter Education: Curriculum & Instruction: Proceedings of the Sixth National Convention of the Conference of Interpreter Trainers. Silver Spring, MD: RID Publications.

Sole, L. 1993. The use of pausing by sign language interpreters. *Sign Language Studies*, 79: 147-179.

Smith, T. 1994. Guidelines: Practical Tips for Working and Socializing with Deaf-Blind People. Burtonsville, MD: Linstok Press.

Smith, T. 1983. Response to B. Moser-Mercer - "Simultaneous Interpreting." *Proceedings of the 4th CIT Conventions.* Silver Spring, MD: RID Publications.

Solow, S. 1981. *Sign Language Interpreting: A Basic Resource Book.* Silver Spring, MD: National Association of the Deaf.

Solow, S. 1984. A method for teaching ASL interpreting. Conference of Interpreter Trainers Fifth National Convention: New Dimensions in Interpreter Education: Task Analysis - Theory and Application. Silver Spring, MD: RID Publications.

Stauffer, L. 1991. Enhancing visualization skills for interpretation between ASL and English. In J. Plant-Moeller (ed.), *Expanding Horizons: Proceedings of the Twelfth National Convention of the Registry of Interpreters for the Deaf.* Silver Spring, MD: RID Publications.

Sternberg, M., C. Tipton, & J. Schein. *Interpreter Training: A Curriculum Guide.* New York, NY: Deafness Research & Training Center, New York University School of Education.

Stewart, D., J. Schein, & B. Cartwright. 1998. *Sign Language Interpreting: Its Art and Science* Boston, MA: Allyn & Bacon.

Stokoe, W. 1960. Sign language structure: An outline of the visual communication systems of the American deaf. *Studies in Linguistics, Occasional Papers, 8.* (Revised 1992 Silver Spring, MD Linstok Press)

Stokoe, W., D. Casterline & C. Croneberg. 1965. *A Dictionary of American Sign Language or Linguistic Principles.* Washington, DC: Gallaudet College Press. 2nd Edition 1976 Silver Spring MD: Linstok Press)

Stokoe, W. 1969. Sign language diglossia. *Studies in Linguistics,* 21: 27-41.

Stokoe, W. 1991. Semantic Phonology. *Sign Language Studies,* 71: 107-114.

Stokoe, W. 2002. *Language in Hand: Why Sign Came Before Speech.* Washington, DC: Gallaude University Press.

Strong, M & S. Rudser. 1986. The subjective assessment of sign language interpreters. *Sig Language Studies,* 53: 299-314.

Stubbs, M. 1983. Discourse Analysis: The Sociolinguistic Analysis of Natural Language. Chicago IL: The University of Chicago Press.

Supalla, S. 1991. Manually Coded English: The Modality Question in Signed Languag Development. In P. Siple & S. Fischer (eds.), *Theoretical Issues in Sign Language Researc Vol. 2: Psychology.* University of Chicago Press.

Swabey, L. 1987. Cloze skills and comprehension. In M. McIntire (ed.), New Directions Interpreter Education: Curriculum & Instruction: Proceedings of the Sixth National Conventic of the Conference of Interpreter Trainers. Silver Spring, MD: RID Publications.

Tannen, D. 1984. *Conversational Style: Analyzing Talk Among Friends.* Norwood, NJ: Able Publishing Corp.

Tannen, D. 1986. That's Not What I Meant: How Conversational Style Makes or Breal Relationships. New York, NY: Ballentine Books

Tannen, D. 1990. You Just Don't Understand: Women and Men in Conversation. New York, N Ballentine Books

Tannen, D. 1994. Talking from 9 to 5: Women and Men in the Workplace: Language, Sex, a Power. New York, NY: William Morrow.

Taylor, M. 1993. *Interpretation Skills: English to American Sign Language.* Edmonton, Canad Interpreting Consolidated.

Tennant, R. & M. Brown. 1998. *The American Sign Language Handshape Dictionary.* Washingtc DC: Clerc Books (Gallaudet University Press).

Turner, G. 1995. Contact signing and language shift. In H. Bos & T. Schermer (eds.), Si Language Research 1994: Proceedings of the 4th European Congress on Sign Langua Research, Munich, September 1 - 3, 1994. Hamburg: Signum Press.

Valli, C. 1990. The nature of the line in ASL poetry. In W. Edmondson & F. Karlsson (eds.), S. '87: Papers from the fourth international symposium on sign language research. Hambu Signum Press.

Bibliography 277

Valli, C. & C. Lucas. 1992. *Linguistics of American Sign Language*. Washington, DC: Clerc Books.

Van Cleve, J. & B. Crouch. 1989. *A Place of Their Own: Creating the Deaf Community in America*. Washington, DC: Gallaudet University Press.

Van Dam, I. 1989. Strategies of simultaneous interpretation. In L. Gran & J. Dodds (eds.), *The Theoretical and Practical Aspects of Teaching Conference Interpretation*. Udine: Campanotto.

Vernon, M. & K. Miller. 2001. Interpreting in Mental Health Settings: Issues and Concerns. *American Annals of the Deaf,* 146: 429-433.

Vernon, M. & K. Miller. 2001. Linguistic incompetence to stand trial: A unique condition in some Deaf defendants. *Journal of Interpretation,* 99-120.

Viaggio, S. 1997. Kinesics and the simultaneous interpreter: The advantages of listening with one's eyes and speaking with one's body. In F. Poyatos (ed.), *Nonverbal Communication and Translation: New Perspectives and Challenges in Literature, Interpretation and the Media*. Philadelphia, PA: John Benjamins Publishing Co.

Wandel, Jean E. 1989. *Use of Internal Speech in Reading by Hearing and Hearing Impaired Students in Oral, Total Communication, and Cued Speech Programs*. Doctoral dissertation: Teacher's College, Columbia University, New York.

Washabaugh, W. 1981. Sign language in its social context. *Annual Review of Anthropology,* 10: 237-52.

Wathum-Ocama. 2002. Hmong immigrants' views on the education of their Deaf and hard of hearing children. *American Annals of the Deaf,* 147: 44-53.

Whynot, L. 1999. The mutual relvance of ethnography and American Sign Language / English interpreting. *RID 1999 National Convention Proceedings*. Silver Spring, MD: RID Publications.

Wilbur, R. 1990. Metaphors in American Sign Language and English. In W. Edmondson & F. Karlsson (eds.), *SLR '87: Papers From The Fourth International Symposium On Sign Language Research*. Hamburg: Signum Press.

Wilbur, R. 1995. Why so-called 'Rhetorical Questions' are neither rhetorical nor questions. In H. Bos & T. Schermer (eds.), *Sign Language Research 1994: Proceedings of the 4th European Congress on Sign Language Research, Munich, September 1 - 3, 1994*. Hamburg: Signum Press.

Wilbur, R. & L. Petitto. 1983. Discourse structure in American Sign Language conversations (or, how to know a conversation when you see one). *Discourse Processes,* 6:. 225-241.

Wilcox, Phillis. 1995. Dual interpretation and discourse effectiveness in legal settings. *Journal of Interpretation,* 89-98.

Wilcox, S. (Ed). 1992. *Academic Acceptance of American Sign Language*. Burtonsville, MD: Linstok Press.

Wilcox, S, (Ed). 1989. *American Deaf Culture: An anthology*. Burtonsville, MD: Linstok Press.

Wilcox, S & P. Wilcox. 1985. Schema theory and language interpretation: A study of sign language interpreters. *Journal of Interpretation,* 2: 84-93.

Willig, P. 1993. How to determine your mentorship needs. *RID Views,* 16:10.

Wilson, J. 1996. The tobacco story: Narrative structure in an American Sign Language story. In Ceil Lucas (ed.), *Multicultural Aspects of Sociolinguistics in Deaf Communities*. Washington, DC: Gallaudet University Press.

Winston, E. & C. Monikowski. 2000. Disourse mapping: Developing textual coherence skills in interpreters. In C. Roy (ed.), *Innovative Practices for Teaching Sign Language Interpreters*. Washington, DC: Gallaudet University Press.

Winston, E. 1989. Transliteration: What's the message? In C. Lucas (ed.), *The Sociolinguistics of the Deaf Community*. San Diego, CA: Academic Press.

Winston, E. 1990. Techniques for improving accent in sign language interpreters. In A. Willson (ed.), *Proceedings of the 31st Annual Conference of the American Translators Association*. Medford, NJ: Learned Information, Inc.

Winston, E. 1991. Space and involvement in an American Sign Language lecture. In J. Plant-Moeller (ed.), *Expanding Horizons: Proceedings of the Twelfth National Convention of the Registry of Interpreters for the Deaf.* Silver Spring, MD: RID Publications.

Winston, E. 1991. Spatial Referencing & Cohesion in an American Sign Language Text. *Sign Language Studies,* 73: 397-410.

Winston, E. 1993. Spatial Mapping in Comparative Discourse Frames in an American Sign Language Lecture. Doctoral Dissertation, Georgetown University, Washington, DC.

Witter-Merithew, A. 1986. Claiming our destiny. *RID Views,* 1986-October: 12.

Witter-Merithew, A. 1987. Text Analysis. In M. McIntire (ed.), New Directions in Interpreter Education: Curriculum & Instruction: Proceedings of the Sixth National Convention of the Conference of Interpreter Trainers. Silver Spring, MD: RID Publications.

Woll, B. 1988. Report on a survey of sign language interpreter training and provision within the member nations of the European Community. *Babel: International Journal of Translation,* 34 (4): 193-209.

Woodward, J. 1972. Implications for sociolinguistic research among the deaf. *Sign Language Studies,* 1: 1-7.

Woodward, J. 1973. Some characteristics of Pidgin Sign English. *Sign Language Studies,* 3: 39-46.

Yarger, C. 2001.Educational interpreting: Understanding the rural experience. *American Annals of the Deaf,* 146: 16-26.

Zimmer, J. 1989a. ASL/English interpreting in an interactive setting. In D. Hammond (ed.), *Proceedings of the 30th Annual Conference of the American Translators Association.* Medford, NJ: Learned Information, Inc.

Zimmer, J. 1989b. Toward a description of register variation in American Sign Language. In C Lucas (ed.), *The Sociolinguistics of the Deaf Community.* San Diego, CA: Academic Press.

Zimmer, J. 1990. From ASL to English in two versions: An analysis of differences in register. *Word,* 41:1, 19-34.

Zimmer, J. & C. Patschke. 1990. A class of determiners in ASL. In C. Lucas (ed.), *Sign Language Research: Theoretical Issues.* Washington, DC: Gallaudet University Press.

Zimmer, J. 1991. Appropriateness and naturalness in ASL/English interpreting. In J. Plant-Moeller (ed.), *Expanding Horizons: Proceedings of the Twelfth National Convention of the Registry of Interpreters for the Deaf.* Silver Spring, MD: RID Publications.

Appendix A - RID CERTIFICATION INFORMATION
(REGISTRY OF INTERPRETERS FOR THE DEAF)

Tips From The Raters

Many candidates have expressed concerns regarding what it is, exactly, that the certification raters are looking for. Quite simply the raters are looking at everything the candidate does to ensure that each candidate has the minimum skills necessary to professionally interpret. These minimal skill levels were determined by the members who attended the St. Paul national RID convention in 1987. Here are some suggestions from the Raters of both the CI and CT tests.

What is "Transliteration" As Required For Performance Testing?
Critical areas:

Message - make sure that your interpretations do not add information, delete information, or alter the essential meaning of the original message. Be confident in your work. Do not produce messages with uncertainty or doubt unless the original message was produced in this way.

Production - speak or sign clearly in grammatically correct constructions for the task you are performing. Do not produce distracting information (e.g. "um, er, you know" or back and forth weaving while signing).

Task - know which test you are taking. Do not perform "transliteration" when the test is for interpreting. Do not perform interpreting when the test is for "transliteration." The transliteration task for the test is not one of manual English coding. It is conceptually correct signing with English words mouthed on the lips.

Less critical areas:

You will be simulating platform interpreting. Make sure you are dressed appropriately for the task. Do not be noisy in your signing style. Be sure to speak with enough volume to be clearly recorded. In short, behave as you normally would for a real interpreting performance.

What Is "Transliteration" As Required For Performance Testing?

Many candidates for the Transliteration Performance Examination have requested guidance for understanding what the goal of the English-to-sign portion of the test is. The raters have reviewed the minimum standard and the performances of passing and failing candidates and have agreed upon the following definition of "Transliteration." Three categories of variables have been defined: Grammar and Vocabulary, Processing, and Mouth Movement Patterns.

Grammar and Vocabulary
Use of space for role taking (characterization)
Use of space for subject-object agreement and verb inflections
Conceptually correct sign choices (based on meaning rather than form)
Some amount of "initialization" but only to the extent that initialization is used by deaf adults not to the extent of Manual English Codes).

Processing
Lexical to phrasal levels of processing, e.g. word meaning for word meaning with some structuring or paraphrasing for clearer conveyance of meaning.
Some additions of ASL signs which enhance the clarity of the visual message (Modals such as CAN, classifier constructions, indexing, and listing structures)
Detailed English morphology (e.g. manual English coding of "ing," "ed," and the copula) is conveyed on the mouth but not with manual signs.

Mouth Movement Patterns

Cohesive English sentences are visibly presented on the lips, either as exact words from the original text or as English paraphrasing of the original text.

Overriding all of these details is the requirement that the target message resulting from the transliteration process remains true and accurate with regard to the source text. There should be no substitutions (missing a concept from the original and replacing it with a different concept) and no significant omissions (all of the main points and nearly all of the supporting details of the source text should be reflected in the target text).

Working into Spoken English

For the Transliteration Performance Exams, candidates should create a grammatically correct and coherent English text which remains true and accurate with regard to the source text. There should be no substitutions and very few (if any) omissions.

What is "Interpretation" As Required For Performance Testing?

Many candidates for the Interpretation Performance Examination have requested guidance for understanding what the target production of the English-to-sign portion of the test should look like. The raters have reviewed the minimum standard and the performances of passing and failing candidates and have agreed upon the following definition of "Interpretation" as applied to the RID Performance Examinations. Three categories of variables have been defined: ASL Grammar and Vocabulary, Processing, and Mouth Movement Patterns.

ASL Grammar and Vocabulary (English to ASL Interpreting)

Use of appropriate ASL grammar (use of space for characterization, subject-object agreement and verb inflections; facial grammatical forms for questions, topics, commands, etc.)

Semantically correct sign choices used appropriately for ASL syntax.

Limited amounts of "initialization" are acceptable.

Processing

The minimum acceptable level of processing is at the phrasal to sentential levels. Word for word processing will not pass the certification examination.

Some syntactic influences of the original text may appear in the interpretation, but only so long as the interpretation remains clear and makes "visual sense."

Mouth Movement Patterns

Mouth patterns should reflect appropriate adult ASL usage.

Mouth movements which only represent exact English word order will not pass the test.

Overriding all of these details is the requirement that the target message resulting from the interpretation process remains true and accurate with regard to the source text. There should be no substitutions (missing a concept from the original and replacing it with a different concept) and no significant omissions (all of the main points and nearly all of the supporting details of the source text should be reflected in the target text).

Working into Spoken English

For the Interpretation Performance Exams, candidates should create a grammatically correct and coherent English text which remains true and accurate with regard to the source text. There should be no substitutions. Extended periods of silence (processing time) are acceptable so long as there are no significant omissions.

Description of the RID CI and CT Rating Scales

RID's rating system for the Certificates of Interpretation and Transliteration is based on a set of 3 items, which we refer to as behaviorally anchored scales. These items represent key behaviors an interpreter must demonstrate in order to be awarded certification. The 13 behaviors are scored on a 1-5 Likert-type scale, with one being low and five being high. They are weighted according to criticality and importance to the task in order to correspond to the St. Paul standard voted on by the certified membership in 1987. There are seven scales/behaviors for the Voice-to-Sign (V-S) section, and six for the Sign-to-Voice (S-V) section. These 13 scales (items) are duplicated for the One-to-One section of the test as the candidate does both V-S and S-V. therefore a candidate for certification is rated on 26 scales. There are three categories of raters: Deaf consumers, hearing consumers, and certified interpreters. A candidate's tape of their performance is sent to a rater in each of the three categories.

This information co-exists with the raters description of "What is Interpretation?" and "What is Transliteration?" Although all RID tests continue to be non-diagnostic in nature, these documents will prove beneficial for those preparing for the performance exams.

A general description of the seven scales for the Voice-to-Sign segment are:
1) Sign Parameters - correct and consistent production of sign parameters (handshape, palm orientation, location and movement).
2) Flow - comfort level of sign flow; Example - smooth, comfortable for viewing, not choppy with few false starts and unnecessary pauses, not over smooth without appropriate pauses
3) Message Equivalence - message completion with regard to factual information, register and cultural/linguistic adjustments with few minor miscues (omissions/substitutions, additions, and intrusions)
4) Target Language - uses appropriate target language (e.g. signed English for the transliteration test and ASL for the interpretation test)
5) Affect - consistency of facial grammar and affect to source language
6) Vocabulary Choice - conceptually correct sign choices based on meaning rather than form
7) Sentence Boundaries - clear and consistent identification of sentence types and topic boundaries which match source language

A general description of the six scales for the Sign-to-Voice segment are:
8) Enunciation - clarity and consistency throughout task
9) Flow - comfort level for listening; example: few false starts, pauses, and non-linguistic behaviors (distracting mannerisms - uh, um, etc.), not over smooth without appropriate pauses
10) Message Equivalence - message completion with regard to factual information, register and cultural/linguistic adjustments with few minor miscues (omissions/substitutions, additions, and intrusions)
11) Inflection - consistency of inflection to source language
12) Vocabulary Choice - conceptually correct sign choices based on meaning rather than form
13) Sentence Boundaries - clear and consistent identification of sentence types and topic boundaries which match source language

Scales 1-13 are repeated for the One-to-One section of the exam.
© Copyright 1997 Registry of Interpreters for the Deaf   REV7/97

Appendix B - Ethical Guidelines For Transcommunicators

RID Code of Ethics (Registry of Interpreters for the Deaf)
(Adopted 1979)

1) Interpreter/Transliterator shall keep all assignment-related information strictly confidential.
2) Interpreter/Transliterator shall render the message faithfully, always conveying th content and spirit of the speaker, using language most readily understood by th person(s) whom they serve.
3) Interpreter/Transliterator shall not counsel, advise, or interject personal opinions.
4) Interpreter/Transliterator shall accept assignments using discretion with regard t skill, setting, and the consumers involved.
5) Interpreter/Transliterator shall request compensation for services in a profession and judicious manner.
6) Interpreter/Transliterator shall function in a manner appropriate to the situation.
7) Interpreter/Transliterator shall strive to further knowledge and skills throug participation in workshops, professional meetings, interaction with profession colleagues and reading of current literature in the field.
8) Interpreter/Transliterator, by virtue of membership in or certification by the R.I.D inc. shall strive to maintain high professional standards in compliance with the co of ethics.

RID Code of Ethics (Registry of Interpreters for the Deaf)
(Adopted 2005)

Interpreters have a professional responsibility to:

1) Adhere to standards of confidential communication.
2) Possess interpreting competence commensurate with the communication event.
3) Actively engage in ongoing professional development.
4) Demonstrate respect for all consumers and their diversity.
5) Demonstrate respect for the profession, other colleagues, and students of profession.
6) Render services linguistically accessible and appropriate for the situation.
7) Conduct themselves in a manner befitting the assigned setting.
8) Ensure that working conditions are conducive to excellence in service delivery.
9) Serve as a resource on interpreting and relevant services, as needed.
10) Maintain ethical business practices.

AVLIC Code of Ethics (Association of Visual Language Interpreters of Canada)

1) The visual language interpreter will keep all assignment-related information strictly confidential.
2) The visual language interpreter will render the message by faithfully conveying its intent and spirit.
3) The visual language interpreter will not counsel, advise, or interject personal opinions related to the interpreted assignment.
4) The visual language interpreter will use the preferred language of the person(s) for whom she/he is interpreting.
5) The visual language interpreter will accept assignments using discretion with regard to the interpreting skills required, the setting, and the person(s) involved.
6) The visual language interpreter will approach the matter of compensation in a fair and equitable manner.
7) The visual language interpreter will conduct herself/himself in all phases of the interpreting situation in a manner befitting the profession.
8) The visual language interpreter will strive to further individual knowledge and skill in order to maintain high professional standards.

AIIC Code of Professional Conduct (Association Internationale Des Interpretes de Conférence / International Association of Conference Interpreters)

I. Purpose and Scope
Article 1
a) This code of Professional Conduct and Practice (hereinafter called "the Code") lays down the conditions governing the practice of the profession by members of the Association.
b) Members are bound by the provisions of the Code. The Council, with the assistance of the Association's members, shall ensure compliance with the provisions of the Code.
c) Candidates for admission shall undertake to adhere strictly to the provisions of the Code and all other AIIC rules.
d) Penalties, as provided in the Statutes, may be imposed on any member who infringes the rules of the profession as laid down in the Code.

II. Code of Ethics
Article 2
a) Members of the Association shall be bound by the strictest secrecy, which must be observed towards all persons with regard to information gathered in the course of professional practice at non-public meetings.
b) Members shall not derive any personal gain from confidential information acquired them in the exercise of their duties as interpreters.
Article 3
Members of the Association shall not accept engagements for which they are no qualified. Their acceptance shall imply a moral undertaking on their part that they wi perform their services in a professional manner.*
Article 4
a) Members of the Association shall not accept any employment or situation which mig detract from the dignity of the profession or jeopardize the observation of secrecy.
b) They shall refrain from any conduct which might bring the profession into disreput and particularly from any form of personal publicity. They may, however, f professional reasons advertise the fact that they are conference interpreters ar members of the association.
Article 5
a) It shall be the duty of members of the Association to afford their colleagues mor assistance and solidarity.
b) Members shall refrain from statements or actions prejudicial to the interests of t Association or its members. any disagreement with the decisions of the Association any complaint about the conduct of another member shall be raised and settled with the Association itself.
c) Any professional problem which arises between two or more members of t Association may be referred to the Council for arbitration.
d) As regards candidates, however, infringements of the code or other rules of t Association shall be adjudicated by the Admissions and Language Classificati Committee.

Article 6

Members of the Association shall not accept, and still less offer, conditions of work which do not meet the standards laid down in the Code, either for themselves or for interpreters engaged through them.

* The moral undertaking given by AIIC members under article 3 of the Code of Professional Conduct shall apply equally to the performance of services by interpreters who are not members of AIIC but are engaged through a member.

The Cued Speech Transliterator Code of Conduct
©1989 Fleetwood, Metzger

A Cued Speech Transliterator shall:

1) Facilitate communication for hearing-impaired/deaf consumers of cued speech (clients)
Cued speech transliterators serve to remove expressive and receptive communication difficulties/ambiguities between hearing-impaired/deaf clients and hearing consumers. Facilitation of communication (spoken), however, should not exclude concurrent consideration for and conveyance of auditory environmental stimuli.

2) Provide sound-based environmental information to hearing-impaired/deaf consumers of cued speech (clients)
Cued speech transliterators should include appropriate representation of auditory environmental stimuli as it occurs, without the influence of personal judgment as to its value to the hearing-impaired/deaf client. This conveyance of auditory environmental stimuli should serve to facilitate a common mainstream experience. Inclusion of auditory Environmental Stimuli, however, should not exclude concurrent consideration for and facilitation of communication (spoken).

3) Provide appropriate client training to allow for proper transliterator utilization
Cued speech transliterators serve in an ongoing training capacity with regard to client transliterator utilization. The development of transliterator usage skills should always be facilitated with tact, reasonable judgment, and prudent regard for the rights of the hearing-impaired/deaf client.

4) Provide hearing consumers with appropriate demonstration/explanation of the transliterator role
It is reasonable to assume that hearing consumers are unfamiliar with or do not understand the aspects of a transliterating situation which are intended to preserve the equal access rights of the hearing-impaired/deaf client. Consequently, Cued Speech transliterators must secure the confidence and support of said consumers through role demonstration and/or explanation in order to appropriately implement methods used preserve these equal access rights.

5) Demonstrate and implement ongoing reverence for the preservation and promotion of complete and equal access for the hearing-impaired/deaf client
Cued speech transliterators should always maintain the skills and conduct necessary preserve the equal access rights of the hearing-impaired/deaf client. This includes appropriate remediation of the lack of logistical and/or ethical considerations on the part of others. Equal access rights include unconventional as well as conventional factors available to the mainstream population.

6)**Promote the progression of events as if circumstances do not necessitate transliterator presence**
Cued speech transliterators strive to maintain an atmosphere, environment, and consequent experience unaffected, even incidentally, by their necessary presence and function. Most individuals rarely come in contact with a working transliterator in a mainstream situation. consequently, the common mainstream experience is not influenced by the presence of a transliterator. Therefore to allow the hearing-impaired/ deaf client equal access to this common experience, transliterators must avoid influencing the atmosphere, environment, and resulting experience of the mainstream.

7)**Adhere to the ethical standards of transliterating for hearing-impaired/deaf clients**
Clients must have reason to trust that through Cued Speech transliterator utilization they are afforded the same conventional and unconventional rights, privileges, and opportunities as individuals who need not utilize such services. Ethical standards* have been adopted and must be practiced by transliterators to secure the trust of clients and offer them fair and equal access. (* the Code of Ethics of the Registry of Interpreters for the Deaf; ©1989 RID, Inc.)

)**Support the profession of cued speech transliteration by striving to improve related skills and knowledge and the application thereof**
The hearing-impaired/deaf client is entitled to receive the most effective service available in the field of cued speech transliteration. Therefore, it is the professional responsibility and ethical obligation of cued speech transliterators to adhere to and implement the currently acceptable philosophies and techniques in the field.

Appendix C – Practice Source Texts

The Constitution of the United States
*Sections that are underlined have been changed by various amendments

PREAMBLE
We the People of the United States, in Order to form a more perfect Union, establish Justice insure domestic Tranquility, provide for the common defense, promote the general Welfare, and secure the Blessings of Liberty to ourselves and our Posterity, do ordain and establish this Constitution for the United States of America.

Article. I.
Section. 1.
All legislative Powers herein granted shall be vested in a Congress of the United States, which shall consist of a Senate and House of Representatives.

Section. 2.
The House of Representatives shall be composed of Members chosen every second Year by the People of the several States, and the Electors in each State shall have the Qualifications requisite for Electors of the most numerous Branch of the State Legislature.

No Person shall be a Representative who shall not have attained to the Age of twenty five Years, and been seven Years a Citizen of the United States, and who shall not, when elected, be an Inhabitant of that State in which he shall be chosen.

Representatives and direct Taxes shall be apportioned among the several States which may be included within this Union, according to their respective Numbers, which shall be determined by adding to the whole Number of free Persons, including those bound to Service for a Term of Years and excluding Indians not taxed, three fifths of all other Persons. The actual Enumeration shall be made within three Years after the first Meeting of the Congress of the United States, and within every subsequent Term of ten Years, in such Manner as they shall by Law direct. The Number of Representatives shall not exceed one for every thirty Thousand, but each State shall have at Least one Representative; and until such enumeration shall be made, the State of New Hampshire shall be entitled to chuse three, Massachusetts eight, Rhode-Island and Providence Plantations one, Connecticut five, New-York six, New Jersey four, Pennsylvania eight, Delaware one, Maryland six, Virginia ten, North Carolina five, South Carolina five, and Georgia three.

When vacancies happen in the Representation from any State, the Executive Authority thereof shall issue Writs of Election to fill such Vacancies.

The House of Representatives shall chuse their Speaker and other Officers; and shall have the sole Power of Impeachment.

Section. 3.
The Senate of the United States shall be composed of two Senators from each State, chosen by the Legislature thereof for six Years; and each Senator shall have one Vote.

Immediately after they shall be assembled in Consequence of the first Election, they shall be divided as equally as may be into three Classes. The Seats of the Senators of the first Class shall be vacated at the Expiration of the second Year, of the second Class at the Expiration of the fourth Year, and of the third Class at the Expiration of the sixth Year, so that one third may be chosen every second Year; and if Vacancies happen by Resignation, or otherwise, during the Recess of the Legislature of any State, the Executive thereof may make temporary Appointments until the next Meeting of the Legislature, which shall then fill such Vacancies.

No Person shall be a Senator who shall not have attained to the Age of thirty Years, and been nine Years a Citizen of the United States, and who shall not, when elected, be an Inhabitant of that State for which he shall be chosen.

The Vice President of the United States shall be President of the Senate, but shall have no Vote, unless they be equally divided.

The Senate shall chuse their other Officers, and also a President pro tempore, in the Absence of the Vice President, or when he shall exercise the Office of President of the United States.

The Senate shall have the sole Power to try all Impeachments. When sitting for that Purpose, they shall be on Oath or Affirmation. When the President of the United States is tried, the Chief Justice shall preside: And no Person shall be convicted without the Concurrence of two thirds of the Members present.

Judgment in Cases of Impeachment shall not extend further than to removal from Office, and disqualification to hold and enjoy any Office of honor, Trust or Profit under the United States: but the Party convicted shall nevertheless be liable and subject to Indictment, Trial, Judgment and Punishment, according to Law.

Section. 4.

The Times, Places and Manner of holding Elections for Senators and Representatives, shall be prescribed in each State by the Legislature thereof; but the Congress may at any time by Law make or alter such Regulations, except as to the Places of chusing Senators.

The Congress shall assemble at least once in every Year, and such Meeting shall <u>be on the first Monday in December</u>, unless they shall by Law appoint a different Day.

Section. 5.

Each House shall be the Judge of the Elections, Returns and Qualifications of its own Members, and a Majority of each shall constitute a Quorum to do Business; but a smaller Number may adjourn from day to day, and may be authorized to compel the Attendance of absent Members, in such Manner, and under such Penalties as each House may provide.

Each House may determine the Rules of its Proceedings, punish its Members for disorderly Behaviour, and, with the Concurrence of two thirds, expel a Member.

Each House shall keep a Journal of its Proceedings, and from time to time publish the same, excepting such Parts as may in their Judgment require Secrecy; and the Yeas and Nays of the Members of either House on any question shall, at the Desire of one fifth of those Present, be entered on the Journal.

Neither House, during the Session of Congress, shall, without the Consent of the other, adjourn for more than three days, nor to any other Place than that in which the two Houses shall be sitting.

Section. 6.

The Senators and Representatives shall receive a Compensation for their Services, to be ascertained by Law, and paid out of the Treasury of the United States. They shall in all Cases, except Treason, Felony and Breach of the Peace, be privileged from Arrest during their Attendance at the Session of their respective Houses, and in going to and returning from the same; and for any Speech or Debate in either House, they shall not be questioned in any other Place.

No Senator or Representative shall, during the Time for which he was elected, be appointed to any civil Office under the Authority of the United States, which shall have been created, or the Emoluments whereof shall have been encreased during such time; and no Person holding any Office under the United States, shall be a Member of either House during his Continuance in Office.

Section. 7.

All Bills for raising Revenue shall originate in the House of Representatives; but the Senate may propose or concur with Amendments as on other Bills.

Every Bill which shall have passed the House of Representatives and the Senate, shall, before it become a Law, be presented to the President of the United States: If he approve he shall sign it, but if not he shall return it, with his Objections to that House in which it shall have originated, who shall enter the Objections at large on their Journal, and proceed to reconsider it.If after such Reconsideration two thirds of that House shall agree to pass the Bill, it shall be sent, together with the Objections, to the other House, by which it shall likewise be reconsidered, and if approved by two thirds of that House, it shall become a Law. But in all such Cases the Votes of both Houses shall be determined by yeas and Nays, and the Names of the Persons voting for and against the Bill shall be entered on the Journal of each House respectively. If any Bill shall not be returned by the President within ten Days (Sundays excepted) after it shall have been presented to him, the Same shall be a Law, in like Manner as if he had signed it, unless the Congress by their Adjournment prevent its Return, in which Case it shall not be a Law.

Every Order, Resolution, or Vote to which the Concurrence of the Senate and House of Representatives may be necessary (except on a question of Adjournment) shall be presented to the President of the United States; and before the Same shall take Effect, shall be approved by him, or being disapproved by him, shall be repassed by two thirds of the Senate and House of Representatives, according to the Rules and Limitations prescribed in the Case of a Bill.

Section. 8.

The Congress shall have Power To lay and collect Taxes, Duties, Imposts and Excises, to pay the Debts and provide for the common Defence and general Welfare of the United States; but all Duties, Imposts and Excises shall be uniform throughout the United States;

To borrow Money on the credit of the United States;

To regulate Commerce with foreign Nations, and among the several States, and with the Indian Tribes;

To establish an uniform Rule of Naturalization, and uniform Laws on the subject of Bankruptcies throughout the United States;

To coin Money, regulate the Value thereof, and of foreign Coin, and fix the Standard of Weights and Measures;

To provide for the Punishment of counterfeiting the Securities and current Coin of the United States;

To establish Post Offices and post Roads;

To promote the Progress of Science and useful Arts, by securing for limited Times to Authors and Inventors the exclusive Right to their respective Writings and Discoveries;

To constitute Tribunals inferior to the supreme Court;

To define and punish Piracies and Felonies committed on the high Seas, and Offences against the Law of Nations;

To declare War, grant Letters of Marque and Reprisal, and make Rules concerning Captures on Land and Water;

To raise and support Armies, but no Appropriation of Money to that Use shall be for a longer Term than two Years;

To provide and maintain a Navy;

To make Rules for the Government and Regulation of the land and naval Forces;

To provide for calling forth the Militia to execute the Laws of the Union, suppress Insurrections and repel Invasions;

To provide for organizing, arming, and disciplining, the Militia, and for governing such Part of them as may be employed in the Service of the United States, reserving to the States respectively, the Appointment of the Officers, and the Authority of training the Militia according to the discipline prescribed by Congress;

To exercise exclusive Legislation in all Cases whatsoever, over such District (not exceeding ten Miles square) as may, by Cession of particular States, and the Acceptance of Congress, become the Seat of the Government of the United States, and to exercise like Authority over all Places purchased by the Consent of the Legislature of the State in which the Same shall be, for the Erection of Forts, Magazines, Arsenals, dock-Yards, and other needful Buildings;--And

To make all Laws which shall be necessary and proper for carrying into Execution the foregoing Powers, and all other Powers vested by this Constitution in the Government of the United States, or in any Department or Officer thereof.

Section. 9.

The Migration or Importation of such Persons as any of the States now existing shall think proper to admit, shall not be prohibited by the Congress prior to the Year one thousand eight hundred and eight, but a Tax or duty may be imposed on such Importation, not exceeding ten dollars for each Person.

The Privilege of the Writ of Habeas Corpus shall not be suspended, unless when in Cases of Rebellion or Invasion the public Safety may require it.

No Bill of Attainder or ex post facto Law shall be passed.

No Capitation, or other direct, Tax shall be laid, <u>unless in Proportion to the Census or enumeration herein before directed to be taken</u>.

No Tax or Duty shall be laid on Articles exported from any State.

No Preference shall be given by any Regulation of Commerce or Revenue to the Ports of one State over those of another; nor shall Vessels bound to, or from, one State, be obliged to enter, clear, or pay Duties in another.

No Money shall be drawn from the Treasury, but in Consequence of Appropriations made by Law; and a regular Statement and Account of the Receipts and Expenditures of all public Money shall be published from time to time.

No Title of Nobility shall be granted by the United States: And no Person holding any Office of Profit or Trust under them, shall, without the Consent of the Congress, accept of any present, Emolument, Office, or Title, of any kind whatever, from any King, Prince, or foreign State.

Section. 10.

No State shall enter into any Treaty, Alliance, or Confederation; grant Letters of Marque and Reprisal; coin Money; emit Bills of Credit; make any Thing but gold and silver Coin a Tender in Payment of Debts; pass any Bill of Attainder, ex post facto Law, or Law impairing the Obligation of Contracts, or grant any Title of Nobility.

No State shall, without the Consent of the Congress, lay any Imposts or Duties on Imports or Exports, except what may be absolutely necessary for executing it's inspection Laws: and the net Produce of all Duties and Imposts, laid by any State on Imports or Exports, shall be for the Use of the Treasury of the United States; and all such Laws shall be subject to the Revision and Controul of the Congress.

No State shall, without the Consent of Congress, lay any Duty of Tonnage, keep Troops, or Ships of War in time of Peace, enter into any Agreement or Compact with another State, or with a foreign Power, or engage in War, unless actually invaded, or in such imminent Danger as will not admit of delay.

Article. II.
Section. 1.

The executive Power shall be vested in a President of the United States of America. He shall hold his Office during the Term of four Years, and, together with the Vice President, chosen for the same Term, be elected, as follows:

Each State shall appoint, in such Manner as the Legislature thereof may direct, a Number of Electors, equal to the whole Number of Senators and Representatives to which the State may be entitled in the Congress: but no Senator or Representative, or Person holding an Office of Trust or Profit under the United States, shall be appointed an Elector.

The Electors shall meet in their respective States, and vote by Ballot for two Persons, of whom one at least shall not be an Inhabitant of the same State with themselves. And they shall make a List of all the Persons voted for, and of the Number of Votes for each; which List they shall sign and certify, and transmit sealed to the Seat of the Government of the United States, directed to the President of the Senate. The President of the Senate shall, in the Presence of the Senate and House of Representatives, open all the Certificates, and the Votes shall then be counted. The Person having the greatest Number of Votes shall be the President, if such Number be a Majority of the whole Number of Electors appointed; and if there be more than one who have such Majority, and have an equal Number of Votes, then the House of Representatives shall immediately chuse by Ballot one of them for President; and if no Person have a Majority, then from the five highest on the List the said House shall in like Manner chuse the President. But in chusing the President, the Votes shall be taken by States, the Representation from each State having one Vote; A quorum for this purpose shall consist of a Member or Members from two thirds of the States, and a Majority of all the States shall be necessary to a Choice. In every Case, after the Choice of the President, the Person having the greatest Number of Votes of the Electors shall be the Vice President. But if there should remain two or more who have equal Votes, the Senate shall chuse from them by Ballot the Vice President.

The Congress may determine the Time of chusing the Electors, and the Day on which they shall give their Votes; which Day shall be the same throughout the United States.

No Person except a natural born Citizen, or a Citizen of the United States, at the time of the Adoption of this Constitution, shall be eligible to the Office of President; neither shall any Person be eligible to that Office who shall not have attained to the Age of thirty five Years, and been fourteen Years a Resident within the United States.

In Case of the Removal of the President from Office, or of his Death, Resignation, or Inability to discharge the Powers and Duties of the said Office, the Same shall devolve on the Vice President, and the Congress may by Law provide for the Case of Removal, Death, Resignation or Inability, both of the President and Vice President, declaring what Officer shall then act as President, and such Officer shall act accordingly, until the Disability be removed, or a President shall be elected.

The President shall, at stated Times, receive for his Services, a Compensation, which shall neither be increased nor diminished during the Period for which he shall have been elected, and he shall not receive within that Period any other Emolument from the United States, or any of them.

Before he enter on the Execution of his Office, he shall take the following Oath or Affirmation:--"I do solemnly swear (or affirm) that I will faithfully execute the Office of President of the United States, and will to the best of my Ability, preserve, protect and defend the Constitution of the United States."

Section. 2.

The President shall be Commander in Chief of the Army and Navy of the United States, and of the Militia of the several States, when called into the actual Service of the United States; he may require the Opinion, in writing, of the principal Officer in each of the executive Departments, upon any Subject relating to the Duties of their respective Offices, and he shall have Power to grant Reprieves and Pardons for Offences against the United States, except in Cases of Impeachment.

He shall have Power, by and with the Advice and Consent of the Senate, to make Treaties, provided two thirds of the Senators present concur; and he shall nominate, and by and with the Advice and Consent of the Senate, shall appoint Ambassadors, other public Ministers and Consuls, Judges of the supreme Court, and all other Officers of the United States, whose Appointments are not herein otherwise provided for, and which shall be established by Law: but the Congress may by

Law vest the Appointment of such inferior Officers, as they think proper, in the President alone, in the Courts of Law, or in the Heads of Departments.

The President shall have Power to fill up all Vacancies that may happen during the Recess of the Senate, by granting Commissions which shall expire at the End of their next Session.

Section. 3.
He shall from time to time give to the Congress Information of the State of the Union, and recommend to their Consideration such Measures as he shall judge necessary and expedient; he may, on extraordinary Occasions, convene both Houses, or either of them, and in Case of Disagreement between them, with Respect to the Time of Adjournment, he may adjourn them to such Time as he shall think proper; he shall receive Ambassadors and other public Ministers; he shall take Care that the Laws be faithfully executed, and shall Commission all the Officers of the United States.

Section. 4.
The President, Vice President and all civil Officers of the United States, shall be removed from Office on Impeachment for, and Conviction of, Treason, Bribery, or other high Crimes and Misdemeanors.

Article III.
Section. 1.
The judicial Power of the United States shall be vested in one supreme Court, and in such inferior Courts as the Congress may from time to time ordain and establish. The Judges, both of the supreme and inferior Courts, shall hold their Offices during good Behaviour, and shall, at stated Times, receive for their Services a Compensation, which shall not be diminished during their Continuance in Office.

Section. 2.
The judicial Power shall extend to all Cases, in Law and Equity, arising under this Constitution, the Laws of the United States, and Treaties made, or which shall be made, under their Authority;--to all Cases affecting Ambassadors, other public Ministers and Consuls;--to all Cases of admiralty and maritime Jurisdiction;--to Controversies to which the United States shall be a Party;--to Controversies between two or more States;-- between a State and Citizens of another State;--between Citizens of different States;--between Citizens of the same State claiming Lands under Grants of different States, and between a State, or the Citizens thereof, and foreign States, Citizens or Subjects.

In all Cases affecting Ambassadors, other public Ministers and Consuls, and those in which a State shall be Party, the supreme Court shall have original Jurisdiction. In all the other Cases before mentioned, the supreme Court shall have appellate Jurisdiction, both as to Law and Fact, with such Exceptions, and under such Regulations as the Congress shall make.

The Trial of all Crimes, except in Cases of Impeachment, shall be by Jury; and such Trial shall be held in the State where the said Crimes shall have been committed; but when not committed within any State, the Trial shall be at such Place or Places as the Congress may by Law have directed.

Section. 3.
Treason against the United States, shall consist only in levying War against them, or in adhering to their Enemies, giving them Aid and Comfort. No Person shall be convicted of Treason unless on the Testimony of two Witnesses to the same overt Act, or on Confession in open Court.

The Congress shall have Power to declare the Punishment of Treason, but no Attainder of Treason shall work Corruption of Blood, or Forfeiture except during the Life of the Person attainted.

Article. IV.
Section. 1.
Full Faith and Credit shall be given in each State to the public Acts, Records, and judicial Proceedings of every other State. And the Congress may by general Laws prescribe the Manner in which such Acts, Records and Proceedings shall be proved, and the Effect thereof.

Section. 2.
The Citizens of each State shall be entitled to all Privileges and Immunities of Citizens in the several States.

A Person charged in any State with Treason, Felony, or other Crime, who shall flee from Justice, and be found in another State, shall on Demand of the executive Authority of the State from which he fled, be delivered up, to be removed to the State having Jurisdiction of the Crime.

No Person held to Service or Labour in one State, under the Laws thereof, escaping into another, shall, in Consequence of any Law or Regulation therein, be discharged from such Service or Labour, but shall be delivered up on Claim of the Party to whom such Service or Labour may be due.

Section. 3.
New States may be admitted by the Congress into this Union; but no new State shall be formed or erected within the Jurisdiction of any other State; nor any State be formed by the Junction of two or more States, or Parts of States, without the Consent of the Legislatures of the States concerned as well as of the Congress.

The Congress shall have Power to dispose of and make all needful Rules and Regulations respecting the Territory or other Property belonging to the United States; and nothing in this Constitution shall be so construed as to Prejudice any Claims of the United States, or of any particular State.

Section. 4.
The United States shall guarantee to every State in this Union a Republican Form of Government, and shall protect each of them against Invasion; and on Application of the Legislature, or of the Executive (when the Legislature cannot be convened), against domestic Violence.

Article. V.
The Congress, whenever two thirds of both Houses shall deem it necessary, shall propose Amendments to this Constitution, or, on the Application of the Legislatures of two thirds of the several States, shall call a Convention for proposing Amendments, which, in either Case, shall be valid to all Intents and Purposes, as Part of this Constitution, when ratified by the Legislatures of three fourths of the several States, or by Conventions in three fourths thereof, as the one or the other Mode of Ratification may be proposed by the Congress; Provided that no Amendment which may be made prior to the Year One thousand eight hundred and eight shall in any Manner affect the first and fourth Clauses in the Ninth Section of the first Article; and that no State, without its Consent, shall be deprived of its equal Suffrage in the Senate.

Article. VI.
All Debts contracted and Engagements entered into, before the Adoption of this Constitution, shall be as valid against the United States under this Constitution, as under the Confederation.

This Constitution, and the Laws of the United States which shall be made in Pursuance thereof; and all Treaties made, or which shall be made, under the Authority of the United States, shall be the supreme Law of the Land; and the Judges in every State shall be bound thereby, any Thing in the Constitution or Laws of any State to the Contrary notwithstanding.

The Senators and Representatives before mentioned, and the Members of the several State Legislatures, and all executive and judicial Officers, both of the United States and of the several States, shall be bound by Oath or Affirmation, to support this Constitution; but no religious Test shall ever be required as a Qualification to any Office or public Trust under the United States.

Article. VII.

The Ratification of the Conventions of nine States, shall be sufficient for the Establishment of this Constitution between the States so ratifying the Same.

The Word, "the," being interlined between the seventh and eighth Lines of the first Page, the Word "Thirty" being partly written on an Erazure in the fifteenth Line of the first Page, The Words "is tried" being interlined between the thirty second and thirty third Lines of the first Page and the Word "the" being interlined between the forty third and forty fourth Lines of the second Page.

Attest William Jackson Secretary

Done in Convention by the Unanimous Consent of the States present the Seventeenth Day of September in the Year of our Lord one thousand seven hundred and Eighty seven and of the Independence of the United States of America the Twelfth In witness whereof We have hereunto subscribed our Names,

G°. Washington
Presidt and deputy from Virginia

Delaware
Geo: Read
Gunning Bedford jun
John Dickinson
Richard Bassett
Jaco: Broom

Maryland
James McHenry
Dan of St Thos. Jenifer
Danl. Carroll

Virginia
John Blair
James Madison Jr.

North Carolina
Wm. Blount
Richd. Dobbs Spaight
Hu Williamson

South Carolina
J. Rutledge
Charles Cotesworth Pinckney
Charles Pinckney
Pierce Butler

Georgia
William Few
Abr Baldwin

New Hampshire
John Langdon
Nicholas Gilman

Massachusetts
Nathaniel Gorham
Rufus King

Connecticut
Wm. Saml. Johnson
Roger Sherman

New York
Alexander Hamilton

New Jersey
Wil: Livingston
David Brearley
Wm. Paterson
Jona: Dayton

Pennsylvania
B Franklin
Thomas Mifflin
Robt. Morris
Geo. Clymer
Thos. FitzSimons
Jared Ingersoll
James Wilson
Gouv Morris

The Amendments to the Constitution of the United States

The Preamble to The Bill of Rights
Congress of the United States
begun and held at the City of New-York, on Wednesday the fourth of March, one thousand seven hundred and eighty nine.

THE Conventions of a number of the States, having at the time of their adopting the Constitution, expressed a desire, in order to prevent misconstruction or abuse of its powers, that further declaratory and restrictive clauses should be added: And as extending the ground of public confidence in the Government, will best ensure the beneficent ends of its institution.

RESOLVED by the Senate and House of Representatives of the United States of America, in Congress assembled, two thirds of both Houses concurring, that the following Articles be proposed to the Legislatures of the several States, as amendments to the Constitution of the United States, all, or any of which Articles, when ratified by three fourths of the said Legislatures, to be valid to all intents and purposes, as part of the said Constitution; viz.

ARTICLES in addition to, and Amendment of the Constitution of the United States of America, proposed by Congress, and ratified by the Legislatures of the several States, pursuant to the fifth Article of the original Constitution.

The Bill of Rights: The first ten amendments to the Constitution were ratified on December 15, 1791, and are known as the "Bill of Rights."

Amendment I
Congress shall make no law respecting an establishment of religion, or prohibiting the free exercise thereof; or abridging the freedom of speech, or of the press; or the right of the people peaceably to assemble, and to petition the Government for a redress of grievances.

Amendment II
A well regulated Militia, being necessary to the security of a free State, the right of the people to keep and bear Arms, shall not be infringed.

Amendment III
No Soldier shall, in time of peace be quartered in any house, without the consent of the Owner, nor in time of war, but in a manner to be prescribed by law.

Amendment IV
The right of the people to be secure in their persons, houses, papers, and effects, against unreasonable searches and seizures, shall not be violated, and no Warrants shall issue, but upon probable cause, supported by Oath or affirmation, and particularly describing the place to be searched, and the persons or things to be seized.

Amendment V

No person shall be held to answer for a capital, or otherwise infamous crime, unless on a resentment or indictment of a Grand Jury, except in cases arising in the land or naval forces, or in he Militia, when in actual service in time of War or public danger; nor shall any person be subject or the same offence to be twice put in jeopardy of life or limb; nor shall be compelled in any riminal case to be a witness against himself, nor be deprived of life, liberty, or property, without ue process of law; nor shall private property be taken for public use, without just compensation.

Amendment VI

In all criminal prosecutions, the accused shall enjoy the right to a speedy and public trial, by an npartial jury of the State and district wherein the crime shall have been committed, which district all have been previously ascertained by law, and to be informed of the nature and cause of the cusation; to be confronted with the witnesses against him; to have compulsory process for otaining witnesses in his favor, and to have the Assistance of Counsel for his defence.

Amendment VII

In Suits at common law, where the value in controversy shall exceed twenty dollars, the right of al by jury shall be preserved, and no fact tried by a jury, shall be otherwise re-examined in any ourt of the United States, than according to the rules of the common law.

Amendment VIII

Excessive bail shall not be required, nor excessive fines imposed, nor cruel and unusual nishments inflicted.

Amendment IX

The enumeration in the Constitution, of certain rights, shall not be construed to deny or sparage others retained by the people.

Amendment X

The powers not delegated to the United States by the Constitution, nor prohibited by it to the tes, are reserved to the States respectively, or to the people.

Amendment XI

Passed by Congress March 4, 1794. Ratified February 7, 1795.
Note: Article III, section 2, of the Constitution was modified by amendment 11.
The Judicial power of the United States shall not be construed to extend to any suit in law or uity, commenced or prosecuted against one of the United States by Citizens of another State, or Citizens or Subjects of any Foreign State.

Amendment XII

Passed by Congress December 9, 1803. Ratified June 15, 1804.

Note: A portion of Article II, section 1 of the Constitution was superseded by the 12th amendment.

The Electors shall meet in their respective states and vote by ballot for President and Vice President, one of whom, at least, shall not be an inhabitant of the same state with themselves; they shall name in their ballots the person voted for as President, and in distinct ballots the person voted for as Vice-President, and they shall make distinct lists of all persons voted for as President, and of all persons voted for as Vice-President, and of the number of votes for each, which lists they shall sign and certify, and transmit sealed to the seat of the government of the United States, directed to the President of the Senate; -- the President of the Senate shall, in the presence of the Senate and House of Representatives, open all the certificates and the votes shall then be counted; -- The person having the greatest number of votes for President, shall be the President, if such number be a majority of the whole number of Electors appointed; and if no person have such majority, then from the persons having the highest numbers not exceeding three on the list of those voted for as President, the House of Representatives shall choose immediately, by ballot, the President. But in choosing the President, the votes shall be taken by states, the representation from each state having one vote; a quorum for this purpose shall consist of a member or members from two-thirds of the states, and a majority of all the states shall be necessary to a choice. [And if the House of Representatives shall not choose a President whenever the right of choice shall devolve upon them, before the fourth day of March next following, then the Vice-President shall act as President, as in case of the death or other constitutional disability of the President. --]* The person having the greatest number of votes as Vice-President, shall be the Vice-President, if such number be majority of the whole number of Electors appointed, and if no person have a majority, then from the two highest numbers on the list, the Senate shall choose the Vice-President; a quorum for the purpose shall consist of two-thirds of the whole number of Senators, and a majority of the whole number shall be necessary to a choice. But no person constitutionally ineligible to the office President shall be eligible to that of Vice-President of the United States.

*Superseded by section 3 of the 20th amendment.

Amendment XIII

Passed by Congress January 31, 1865. Ratified December 6, 1865.

Note: A portion of Article IV, section 2, of the Constitution was superseded by the 13th amendment.

Section 1.

Neither slavery nor involuntary servitude, except as a punishment for crime whereof the party shall have been duly convicted, shall exist within the United States, or any place subject to their jurisdiction.

Section 2.

Congress shall have power to enforce this article by appropriate legislation.

Amendment XIV
Passed by Congress June 13, 1866. Ratified July 9, 1868.
Note: Article I, section 2, of the Constitution was modified by section 2 of the 14th
.mendment.
Section 1.
All persons born or naturalized in the United States, and subject to the jurisdiction thereof, are
itizens of the United States and of the State wherein they reside. No State shall make or enforce
ny law which shall abridge the privileges or immunities of citizens of the United States; nor shall
ny State deprive any person of life, liberty, or property, without due process of law; nor deny to
ny person within its jurisdiction the equal protection of the laws.
Section 2.
Representatives shall be apportioned among the several States according to their respective
umbers, counting the whole number of persons in each State, excluding Indians not taxed. But
hen the right to vote at any election for the choice of electors for President and Vice-President of
e United States, Representatives in Congress, the Executive and Judicial officers of a State, or the
embers of the Legislature thereof, is denied to any of the male inhabitants of such State, being
venty-one years of age,* and citizens of the United States, or in any way abridged, except for
rticipation in rebellion, or other crime, the basis of representation therein shall be reduced in the
oportion which the number of such male citizens shall bear to the whole number of male citizens
venty-one years of age in such State.
Section 3.
No person shall be a Senator or Representative in Congress, or elector of President and Vice-
resident, or hold any office, civil or military, under the United States, or under any State, who,
ving previously taken an oath, as a member of Congress, or as an officer of the United States, or
: a member of any State legislature, or as an executive or judicial officer of any State, to support
e Constitution of the United States, shall have engaged in insurrection or rebellion against the
me, or given aid or comfort to the enemies thereof. But Congress may by a vote of two-thirds of
.ch House, remove such disability.
Section 4.
The validity of the public debt of the United States, authorized by law, including debts incurred
r payment of pensions and bounties for services in suppressing insurrection or rebellion, shall not
questioned. But neither the United States nor any State shall assume or pay any debt or
ligation incurred in aid of insurrection or rebellion against the United States, or any claim for the
ss or emancipation of any slave; but all such debts, obligations and claims shall be held illegal
d void.
Section 5.
The Congress shall have the power to enforce, by appropriate legislation, the provisions of this
ticle.
Changed by section 1 of the 26th amendment.

Amendment XV
Passed by Congress February 26, 1869. Ratified February 3, 1870.
Section 1.
The right of citizens of the United States to vote shall not be denied or abridged by the United
ates or by any State on account of race, color, or previous condition of servitude--
Section 2.
The Congress shall have the power to enforce this article by appropriate legislation.

Amendment XVI

Passed by Congress July 2, 1909. Ratified February 3, 1913.

Note: Article I, section 9, of the Constitution was modified by amendment 16.

The Congress shall have power to lay and collect taxes on incomes, from whatever source derived, without apportionment among the several States, and without regard to any census o enumeration.

Amendment XVII

Passed by Congress May 13, 1912. Ratified April 8, 1913.

Note: Article I, section 3, of the Constitution was modified by the 17th amendment.

The Senate of the United States shall be composed of two Senators from each State, elected b the people thereof, for six years; and each Senator shall have one vote. The electors in each Stat shall have the qualifications requisite for electors of the most numerous branch of the Stat legislatures.

When vacancies happen in the representation of any State in the Senate, the executive authorit of such State shall issue writs of election to fill such vacancies: *Provided*, That the legislature c any State may empower the executive thereof to make temporary appointments until the people fi the vacancies by election as the legislature may direct.

This amendment shall not be so construed as to affect the election or term of any Senatc chosen before it becomes valid as part of the Constitution.

Amendment XVIII

Passed by Congress December 18, 1917. Ratified January 16, 1919. Repealed by amendmei 21.

Section 1.

After one year from the ratification of this article the manufacture, sale, or transportation c intoxicating liquors within, the importation thereof into, or the exportation thereof from the Unite States and all territory subject to the jurisdiction thereof for beverage purposes is hereby prohibitec

Section 2.

The Congress and the several States shall have concurrent power to enforce this article t appropriate legislation.

Section 3.

This article shall be inoperative unless it shall have been ratified as an amendment to tl Constitution by the legislatures of the several States, as provided in the Constitution, within sevt years from the date of the submission hereof to the States by the Congress.

Amendment XIX

Passed by Congress June 4, 1919. Ratified August 18, 1920.

The right of citizens of the United States to vote shall not be denied or abridged by the Unite States or by any State on account of sex.

Congress shall have power to enforce this article by appropriate legislation.

Amendment XX

Passed by Congress March 2, 1932. Ratified January 23, 1933.

Note: Article I, section 4, of the Constitution was modified by section 2 of this amendment. In addition, a portion of the 12th amendment was superseded by section 3.

Section 1.

The terms of the President and the Vice President shall end at noon on the 20th day of January, and the terms of Senators and Representatives at noon on the 3d day of January, of the years in which such terms would have ended if this article had not been ratified; and the terms of their successors shall then begin.

Section 2.

The Congress shall assemble at least once in every year, and such meeting shall begin at noon on the 3d day of January, unless they shall by law appoint a different day.

Section 3.

If, at the time fixed for the beginning of the term of the President, the President elect shall have died, the Vice President elect shall become President. If a President shall not have been chosen before the time fixed for the beginning of his term, or if the President elect shall have failed to qualify, then the Vice President elect shall act as President until a President shall have qualified; and the Congress may by law provide for the case wherein neither a President elect nor a Vice President shall have qualified, declaring who shall then act as President, or the manner in which one who is to act shall be selected, and such person shall act accordingly until a President or Vice President shall have qualified.

Section 4.

The Congress may by law provide for the case of the death of any of the persons from whom the House of Representatives may choose a President whenever the right of choice shall have devolved upon them, and for the case of the death of any of the persons from whom the Senate may choose a Vice President whenever the right of choice shall have devolved upon them.

Section 5.

Sections 1 and 2 shall take effect on the 15th day of October following the ratification of this article.

Section 6.

This article shall be inoperative unless it shall have been ratified as an amendment to the Constitution by the legislatures of three-fourths of the several States within seven years from the date of its submission.

Amendment XXI

Passed by Congress February 20, 1933. Ratified December 5, 1933.

Section 1.

The eighteenth article of amendment to the Constitution of the United States is hereby repealed.

Section 2.

The transportation or importation into any State, Territory, or Possession of the United States delivery or use therein of intoxicating liquors, in violation of the laws thereof, is hereby prohibited.

Section 3.

This article shall be inoperative unless it shall have been ratified as an amendment to the Constitution by conventions in the several States, as provided in the Constitution, within seven years from the date of the submission hereof to the States by the Congress.

Amendment XXII
Passed by Congress March 21, 1947. Ratified February 27, 1951.
Section 1.
No person shall be elected to the office of the President more than twice, and no person wh⸱ has held the office of President, or acted as President, for more than two years of a term to whic⸱ some other person was elected President shall be elected to the office of President more than onc⸱ But this Article shall not apply to any person holding the office of President when this Article wa⸱ proposed by Congress, and shall not prevent any person who may be holding the office ⸱ President, or acting as President, during the term within which this Article becomes operative fro⸱ holding the office of President or acting as President during the remainder of such term.
Section 2.
This article shall be inoperative unless it shall have been ratified as an amendment to th⸱ Constitution by the legislatures of three-fourths of the several States within seven years from th⸱ date of its submission to the States by the Congress.

Amendment XXIII
Passed by Congress June 16, 1960. Ratified March 29, 1961.
Section 1.
The District constituting the seat of Government of the United States shall appoint in suc⸱ manner as Congress may direct:
A number of electors of President and Vice President equal to the whole number of Senato⸱ and Representatives in Congress to which the District would be entitled if it were a State, but in ⸱ event more than the least populous State; they shall be in addition to those appointed by the State⸱ but they shall be considered, for the purposes of the election of President and Vice President, to ⸱ electors appointed by a State; and they shall meet in the District and perform such duties ⸱ provided by the twelfth article of amendment.
Section 2.
The Congress shall have power to enforce this article by appropriate legislation.

Amendment XXIV
Passed by Congress August 27, 1962. Ratified January 23, 1964.
Section 1.
The right of citizens of the United States to vote in any primary or other election for Presid⸱ or Vice President, for electors for President or Vice President, or for Senator or Representative ⸱ Congress, shall not be denied or abridged by the United States or any State by reason of failure ⸱ pay poll tax or other tax.
Section 2.
The Congress shall have power to enforce this article by appropriate legislation.

Amendment XXV
Passed by Congress July 6, 1965. Ratified February 10, 1967.
Note: Article II, section 1, of the Constitution was affected by the 25th amendment.
Section 1.
In case of the removal of the President from office or of his death or resignation, the Vice esident shall become President.
Section 2.
Whenever there is a vacancy in the office of the Vice President, the President shall nominate a ce President who shall take office upon confirmation by a majority vote of both Houses of ongress.
Section 3.
Whenever the President transmits to the President pro tempore of the Senate and the Speaker of ‹ House of Representatives his written declaration that he is unable to discharge the powers and ties of his office, and until he transmits to them a written declaration to the contrary, such powers d duties shall be discharged by the Vice President as Acting President.
Section 4.
Whenever the Vice President and a majority of either the principal officers of the executive partments or of such other body as Congress may by law provide, transmit to the President pro npore of the Senate and the Speaker of the House of Representatives their written declaration t the President is unable to discharge the powers and duties of his office, the Vice President shall mediately assume the powers and duties of the office as Acting President.

Thereafter, when the President transmits to the President pro tempore of the Senate and the aker of the House of Representatives his written declaration that no inability exists, he shall ame the powers and duties of his office unless the Vice President and a majority of either the icipal officers of the executive department or of such other body as Congress may by law vide, transmit within four days to the President pro tempore of the Senate and the Speaker of the use of Representatives their written declaration that the President is unable to discharge the vers and duties of his office. Thereupon Congress shall decide the issue, assembling within y-eight hours for that purpose if not in session. If the Congress, within twenty-one days after ipt of the latter written declaration, or, if Congress is not in session, within twenty-one days r Congress is required to assemble, determines by two-thirds vote of both Houses that the sident is unable to discharge the powers and duties of his office, the Vice President shall tinue to discharge the same as Acting President; otherwise, the President shall resume the vers and duties of his office.

Amendment XXVI
Passed by Congress March 23, 1971. Ratified July 1, 1971.
Note: Amendment 14, section 2, of the Constitution was modified by section 1 of the 26th ndment.
Section 1.
The right of citizens of the United States, who are eighteen years of age or older, to vote shall be denied or abridged by the United States or by any State on account of age.
Section 2.
The Congress shall have power to enforce this article by appropriate legislation.

Amendment XXVII
Originally proposed Sept. 25, 1789. Ratified May 7, 1992.
No law, varying the compensation for the services of the Senators and Representatives, shall ‹ effect, until an election of representatives shall have intervened.